JEAN PIAGET:
A MOST OUTRAGEOUS DECEPTION

JEAN PIAGET:
A MOST OUTRAGEOUS DECEPTION

WEBSTER R. CALLAWAY

Nova Science Publishers, Inc.
New York

Senior Editors: Susan Boriotti and Donna Dennis
Coordinating Editor: Tatiana Shohov
Office Manager: Annette Hellinger
Graphics: Wanda Serrano
Book Production: Maya Columbus, Vladimir Klestov, Matthew Kozlowski and Tom Moceri
Circulation: Ave Maria Gonzalez, Vera Popovic, Luis Aviles, Raymond Davis,
          Melissa Diaz, Magdalena Nunez, Marlene Nunez and Jeannie Pappas
Communications and Acquisitions: Serge P. Shohov
Marketing: Cathy DeGregory

Library of Congress Cataloging-in-Publication Data

Callaway, Webster R.
    Jean Piaget: a most outrageous deception / Webster R. Callaway
       p. cm.
    Includes bibliographical references.
    ISBN 1-56072-950-3.
    I. Piaget, Jean, 1896- 2. Psychologists—Switzerland—Biography—History and criticism. I. Title.

BF109.P5 C35 2001
155.4'13'092—dc21

                                                                                    2001045242

Copyright © 2001 by Nova Science Publishers, Inc.
              400 Oser Avenue, Suite 1600
              Hauppauge, New York 11788-3619
              Tele. 631-231-7269Fax 631-231-8175
              e-mail: Novascience@earthlink.net
              Web Site: http://www.novapublishers.com

Printed in the United States of America

ACKNOWLEDGEMENTS

I must give credit to some of the individuals who have had a part, directly or indirectly, in bringing this book into existence. First, Dorthea Callaway, Kevin Callaway, Dr. Ragan Callaway, Rayna Callaway Livingston, John Everitt, Willis Galer, Michael Livingston, Robert Livingston and Dr. John Neimi read all or part of the manuscript. I am in debt to all of them for their reactions - positive, negative and cautionary. As one can well imagine, there was considerable cautionary advice! Additionally, there are several friends with whom over the years I have discussed the problems which led to the book. Among them the names of Dr. Barbara Clark, Hank Harrison, Dr. John Kershner and Chris Young stand out. My first discussions were with Dr. Clark and Dr. Kershner, beginning in 1972. Each one of these family members, friends and colleagues has in some way influenced my approach to the book.

I am especially grateful to my wife, Dorthea, and my son, Kevin, as their contributions were more directly related to the preparation of the book. Dorthea's energetic assistance was indispensable at various times during the thirty years that ensued between hypothesis and finished product. This was particularly true in the final stage when the long, complicated index needed to be completed within a specified time period. I cannot thank her enough for her eagle-eyed scanning of my work for mistakes and her many hours at the computer correcting them.

While visiting us several years ago, Kevin suggested that graphic illustrations could facilitate understanding of Piaget's rather unfamiliar metaphysics. I agreed that they might, but that I had no idea how to produce such illustrations. He immediately sat down at my computer and within less than an hour roughed out four illustrations. I was amazed at the precise, insightful understanding they reflected - which did indeed clarify the verbal abstractions of the text. Seeing that I was delighted with his impromptu creations, he said that his friend, Heidi Palladino would be the ideal person to give them a professional touch. Following his advice, they were sent to her studio, Palladino Design, in Santa Barbara, California where she did a highly polished job. I appreciate Kevin's remarkable creativity and Heidi's technical excellence very much.

While benefiting immensely from the input of others, I take full responsibility for the interpretations, evaluations and conclusions expressed in this book - many of which will undoubtedly be controversial.

ABOUT THE AUTHOR

In the initial stages of what I thought would be a popularization of my monograph, Modes of Biological Adaptation and their Role in Intellectual Development, 1970, I was in no mood to be diverted onto another path. Therefore when Piaget's overall plan of deception became too obvious to dismiss, I decided to look for a qualified person who would be motivated to thoroughly examine his works in order to reveal this plan authoritatively and in detail. I did not relish the idea of reading all of Piaget's books with the laborious, time-consuming struggle they always entail. They are indeed a terrible pain to read if understanding is critical, so I would have been more than happy to rid myself of this onerous responsibility at that time. As the present book testifies, I failed to find anyone so motivated – and am very pleased to add that I gradually became highly motivated myself. A well-rounded but extremely challenging investigation, such as the one reported herein, can be very rewarding and exciting. It certainly was for me. The reader will quickly see that the problem addressed is internal to Piaget's "chains of reasoning." The broader problem of his alarming influence on theory and practice has yet to be elaborated.

What are my credentials? Quite ordinary. My formal education includes a B.A. from Bob Jones University, an M.A. and an Ed.S. from George Peabody College (now part of Vanderbilt University), and a Ph.D. from Michigan State University. My professional experience includes 7 years as an elementary teacher, 3 years as a high school teacher, 7 years as an elementary principal and 13 years as a university faculty member – 6 at UCLA and 7 at the University of Toronto.

Notwithstanding all of the above, if this book proves to be essentially valid, it will be the result of poring endlessly over Piaget's works for many years.

Reactions from readers are welcome. They will be forwarded to me from the following address:

Webster R. Callaway
PMB 1506
91 Campus Drive
Missoula, Montana 59801

CONTENTS

Chapter 1

Introduction to Piaget's Metaphysical Theory

Initial Discoveries

During the winter of 1972-73 I began writing a book on early reading. Since Piaget's theory, as understood by many, holds that independent reading at two to four years of age is either inappropriate, impossible or dangerous, it was incumbent upon me to include an examination of his theory. After outlining my basic plan for the first five chapters, I began a study of his work in preparation for the final chapter - a study that ultimately sidetracked the book. While reading *Biology and Knowledge* (1971a) and *Psychology and Epistemology* (1971b), I began to suspect that Piaget was methodically using the word "biology" with two drastically different meanings. Sometimes there appeared to be a switch of meaning in the same paragraph, or even the same sentence, but there was never a forewarning or overt clue of any kind that the meaning was being changed. The changes were frequent, unexpected and usually involved "tricky" or cryptic language. My incredulity was gradually dispelled as it became incontestably clear that while one of the meanings was the familiar dictionary meaning, *the other referred to an entity without flesh and blood - a meaning not found in any dictionary.* This staggering realization eventually motivated me to look at every instance of the term "biology" in the two books to determine, if possible, what percentage could be classified confidently in terms of meaning. After looking at each instance and the context in which it occurred, it was my opinion that, in this particular case, at least ninety percent could be classified accurately as either metaphysical or physical biology with about sixty percent referring to the former and thirty percent to the latter entity. Most of the remaining ten percent seemingly, although illogically, had both meanings at the same time. Only a few instances appeared to be completely unintelligible in terms of "level".

Why would Piaget, often considered to be the most important thinker of the Twentieth Century in the field of cognition, resort to such odd, dissembling behavior? What could possibly be his purpose? What did he wish to keep under wraps? It must have had something to do with the metaphysical entity to whom he constantly but so surreptitiously referred!

I eventually realized that Piaget was using several hundred words with private meanings in addition to their dictionary meanings. In every case one of the two meanings referred to the *Absolute Subject,* as basically conceived by the German philosopher Hegel, or it referred to the presupposed activity of this hypothetical being. Piaget was clearly obsessed with this very specific metaphysical concept, but at the same time he was treating it as something that was essentially unrevealable.

I venture to say that Piaget's extremely deceitful double use of words is unique in all the professional literature, but it is important to understand that this was his plan from the very beginning, and he was audacious enough to obliquely announce it in his first book. He slyly informed the patient reader that he would be using words to *"create obscurity by the multiplication of verbal entities, and actually... prevent thought from being communicable"* (author's italics) (Piaget, 1926, p. 26). To accomplish this he invented an absurd number of synonyms, as described in the previous paragraph, to belabor, bewitch and bewilder. Piaget's nihilistic, almost unthinkable plan to make his true position incommunicable presents a formidable obstacle to any who would try to elucidate his theory. *One must ponder the unique methodological and psychological issues of someone compelled to write constantly about his metaphysical doctrines, but who at the same time must keep these doctrines from being clearly understood.*

Piaget's need to prevent thought from being communicable regarding his theory and motivations was based on three decisions he made as a teenager. First, was his ecstatic conversion at Lake Annecy while visiting with his godfather (Piaget, 1976, p. 118-19). This experience led him directly to Hegel's Absolute Subject and indirectly to the negative theology of Gnosticism. His basic belief system was permanently settled at that time, and it carried a personal commitment that lasted his entire life (Piaget, 1971c, p. 5). Second, he developed a messianic complex, seeing himself leading the world to accept his metaphysical system (Piaget, 1967, pp. 65-67) (Inhelder & Piaget, 1958, pp. 342-4). Third, he decided to spuriously anchor his theory empirically and propagate it by means of the academic process. Deception thus became necessary, as it is impossible to connect empirical evidence in any significant way with his metaphysical system. From the very beginning of his career he began to invent the overwhelming array of synonyms that could be used to create endless confusion because many of them have several meanings at the physical level but usually only one meaning at the metaphysical level, although a few words can mean either the Absolute or His activity. Furthermore, the results of his "scientific" experiments also have two levels of meaning, and he is a master at moving from one level to the other exactly the way he does with word meanings. If one has the stamina to plow through his endless explications and then withhold judgment until he arrives at his "general conclusions", the final causative factors and meanings involved in the "experiment" are always observed to be metaphysical. His challenge to the academic world is based on the most comprehensive strategy for deception that one could imagine. In my opinion, academia has never had to deal with anything like his methods of deceit. They are so unthinkable that, although evidence is present on almost every page of his many books, they have been overlooked, apparently because no one wished to consider such monstrous behavior as a possibility, especially from such a "kind old grandfather-type who loves children".

DIFFICULTIES TO BE OVERCOME

Probably the most daunting aspect of the problem for the analyst is "belief perseverance". For seventy plus years numerous researchers have worked out, with great nicety of detail, reasons for believing that Piaget objectively arrived at a profound understanding of cognitive development, and social psychologists know that once one develops reasons for believing something is true, this belief tends to persevere even if he discovers later that the basis for it is not valid. The reasons for believing that Piaget's observations and experiments are scientific in nature are indeed invalidated by his own statements, but "belief perseverance" will no doubt continue to blur this fact for a long time to come.

He describes his metaphysical Subject in an endless variety of ways, using hundreds of different synonyms, and he also uses a large number of synonyms to describe the main activity of this entity, which is the production of operations. This presents an obvious problem for anyone who wishes to examine his system by unraveling his major arguments, because beneath the apparent diversity there is a preposterous amount of redundancy. When one analyses the various ways Piaget describes his metaphysical entity and His actions, utilizing different sets of synonyms, there is no way to minimize the extreme repetitiveness of the outcomes. That is, we constantly come to the same conclusions as we examine argument after argument that appear at first to be quite different.

This problem will be alleviated somewhat by capitalizing synonyms of the Absolute Subject, at least in every instance that will assist the reader in understanding Piaget's theory or methods. It will not mitigate the repetitive conclusions that will be reached after examining a vast array of his elaborations and arguments, but it will enable the reader to follow more easily his tortuous, convoluted maneuvers, as he constantly repeats mantra-like, but with different sets of words, the very few doctrines of his metaphysical system. These synonyms, although often outlandish or linguistically inappropriate, are proper names of the central Personality in Piaget's system, and therefore should be capitalized. However, it is not possible for capitalization to be completely consistent, because of his confusing misuse of parts of speech, constant switches of level and doubtful meanings in some cases. His use of unusual synonyms for his metaphysical personality, like Action, Algebraic Structure, Biology, Cosmos, Dynamism, Force, Ideal, Intelligence, Group, Logic, Mathematical Apparatus, Maxwell's Demon, Measuring Factory, Mechanism, Model, Network, Object, Organism, Organization, Science, Society, Something, Substance, Substratum, System, Thought and Whole, makes it difficult to follow the meaning. He also invented a wide variety of unusual synonyms for the main activity of the Absolute, like action, assimilation, behavior, cooperation, decentering, deduction, dialectical interaction, equilibration, function, general coordination of action, geometrization, operation, psychogenesis, reflective abstraction, reflexive abstraction, relation and thought, to name a few. To further complicate the text some of these words, for instance "Action" and "Thought", can also stand for the Absolute Himself. But most unfair of all is his occasional use of pronouns and other terms we associate closely with human beings, to mean either "Absolute Subject" at large or immanent in people. Some examples are: Body, Ego, Genome, Homo Sapiens, Human Spirit, I,

Individual, Man, Mankind, Our Personal Power, Person, We and They. Please remember, these capitalized terms have nothing to do with human beings - *they mean Absolute Subject*. Within a tricky context it is easy indeed to assume that they *must* refer to people even when they definitely refer to the Absolute Subject.

PIAGET MEETS HEGEL'S ABSOLUTE

Piaget's autobiography shows that he became enchanted with Hegel's Absolute as an adolescent and proceeded immediately to build his entire philosophy and essentially all of his psychology around Him. Literally everything could be explained by its relationship to Him. He "recalled one evening of profound revelation". "The identification of God with life was an idea that stirred me almost to ecstasy because *it enabled me to see in biology the explanation of all things and the mind itself*" (author's italics) (Piaget, 1976b, p. 119). In other words, God equals Life equals Biology. *This is a very special "Biology" or "Life" as they both serve as synonyms for the Absolute Subject, and it is important to point out that his ecstatic introduction to "Biology" was no short-term infatuation, as at about the age of 70 he indicated that his commitment to this original revelation continued to increase over time* (Piaget, 1971c, p. 5). Piaget makes the meaning of "Biology" crystal clear when he confesses that *"Biology is ... nothing more than the Subject"* (author's italics and capitalization) (Piaget, 1971b, p. 119). He goes on to say that his explanation of "all things" would be in terms of psychology (Piaget, 1976b, p. 119) - as it turns out, a *fancied* metaphysical Psychology based on the *fancied* metaphysical Biology of Hegel's Absolute whom he sometimes calls "God". It may be worth noting that William James, who studied Hegel, states that his Absolute is vastly different from, and perhaps is even the enemy of, the God of Christian theology (McDermott, 1968, pp. 521-2).

His certainty that God is Life or Biology led Piaget forthwith to "an immanentism which has long satisfied me" (Piaget, 1971c, p. 5). *In other words, since God is Life, not just the source of life but the only Living Entity, He is actually the true Person or Ego in all of us.* That is, although unrecognized, He is immanent within all people, as well as all other living things. He alone, in Piaget's system, is responsible for all the processes that keep us alive, active and that enable us to think, not the physical processes portrayed by biological science. His *monads* (see below), immanent in every physical body, underlie and fully account for all of the biological or physiological processes studied in the universities. *Although many of his followers consider him to be a first-rate biologist, traditional biological science has no place in his theoretical system.*

Piaget's reports regarding his experiments with Sedum, a thick-leaved plant, demonstrates his total dependence on metaphysical Schemata for every process and result he found interesting (author's capitalization) (Piaget, 1971a, pp.197-201) (Piaget, 1978b, pp. 134-137). Even if one did not know that Schemata are composed of metaphysical monads (see below), any one with a modicum of knowledge about scientific methodology should realize that Piaget is a far cry from the traditional scientist. In *Behavior and Evolution* (Piaget, 1978), he describes other experiments he performed with three kinds of snails - Limnaea, Vitrina and Xerophila. The explanation of the results he found in these studies, as well as the results taken from the studies of many other biologists, demonstrate beyond question that Piaget based biological causation on metaphysical processes. Although in this particular book the word "Schemata" appears to be used only twice (author's capitalization) (ibid., pp. 141-142), many terms with metaphysical meanings pointing directly to Schemata are used. For instance, "endogenous" (ibid., pp. XIX; XX; 3; 4; 21; 31; 81-83), which denotes a kind of savoir-faire or Knowledge (When the use of "knowledge" appears to emphasize the *result* of operations, indicating an intrinsic improvement of the Absolute, rather than the *process* of acquiring knowledge through operations, it will be arbitrarily capitalized.), *enjoyed only by Schemata of Monads,* who take no account of empirical content (author's capitalization) (Piaget, 1980, p. 105), require no exogenous (meaning "empirical" or "scientific") verification (ibid., p. 83) and are only developed by metaphysical regulations or operations (ibid., p. 80). He also uses the word "internal" (ibid, pp. X; 40; 74; 76; 146; 148; 152; 154), which refers to the living metaphysical Form or Total Schema who controls the life processes of every plant and animal (author's capitalization) (Piaget, 1930, pp. 262; 282-284). "Internal", as one might gather, points to the Form within, namely the immanent Subject or Total Schema (author's capitalization) (Piaget, 1967, p. 13) (Piaget & Inhelder, 1969, p. 157) (Piaget, 1971a, p. 253) (Bringuier, 1980, p. 42). Another word used is "teleonomy" (Piaget, 1978, pp. 31; 88; 99; 149; 153) which refers to the ever-present directing activity afforded to all living things by the Schemata (author's capitalization) (Piaget, 1978a, p. 220). These teleonomic forces are Substantial (a philosophical term referring to "beings" who underlie all phenomena) and alive (author's capitalization) (Piaget, 1930, pp. 114-117). Piaget explicitly asserts that the behavior involved in evolutionary change transcends the somatic framework (Piaget, 1978, pp. XXI; 31; 98; 153), and that it does not depend upon chance (ibid., pp. X; 70; 73; 99; 101; 156) - which means that it is metaphysical.

Piaget is no biologist as both his early and more recent "research" with plants and animals demonstrates. He detests *"the material object with which the biologist experiments"* (author's italics) (Piaget, 1971b, p. 120), as he is only concerned with the "Biology" that does not have an aging process (author's capitalization) (Piaget, 1971a, p. 124), a Biology that is not physical (author's capitalization) (Piaget, 1977, p. 40). So how do we explain the ubiquitous fable that he is a great biologist? Magical spells? More about magic later. *In all of his work as a "biologist", he is merely describing metaphysical activities of the one and only Biologist who makes use of His metaphysical Biology to produce and maintain diverse forms of biological objects, including people.*

In Piaget's attempt to develop a more systematic philosophy, he began to fill in what he thought were gaps in Hegel's view of the Absolute. His most notable addition was his utilization of the concept of monads, as conceived by the philosopher Leibniz, to describe the three-dimensional "body" of the Absolute (author's capitalization) (Piaget & Inhelder, 1956, p. 416). In Piaget's scheme of things, these monads, spatial points (Piaget & Inhelder, 1971, p. 346), (Piaget, 1974b, pp. 137-8) or metaphysical atoms without weight or volume (Piaget & Inhelder, 1974, pp. 79; 112), fill the entire universe (Piaget, 1972, p. 49) and *completely interpenetrate every person* and object that exists - which accounts for the immanentism which has "long satisfied" Piaget. Living Monads, in Piaget's view, account for every movement, every living process, every thought process and the characteristics of every natural object in the universe - this is true for him even though the monads are resisted at every turn by the physical universe (Piaget, 1930, pp. 131-2) (ibid., p. 128) (Piaget, 1952b, p. 84). When Piaget says that "a phenomenon is always Biological in its roots" (author's capitalization) (Evans, 1973, p. 7), he is affirming that every movement in the universe is caused by the Living Monads that define metaphysical Biology!

In order to comprehend Piaget's work, one must make use of his concept of monads. This follows directly from the "fact" that the Absolute Subject is composed entirely of monads, a Universe of Monads filling all of space and often called *"Space"*. He has no other existence. Almost all of Piaget's major concepts, such as Biology, Continuum, Container, coordinations, development, dialectics, Field, Form, Framework, Group, immanence, knowledge, Life, magic, memory, Mind, operation, participation, Space and Spirit, bring into play this fundamental concept. As one would now correctly infer, the capitalized words are frequently used as synonyms of the Entity who is composed of monads. Piaget's life-long fixation on this speculative Being is demonstrated, as we have already indicated, by his *orgy of synonym invention as seen in all of his many books, thus covertly expressing his metaphysical convictions in a protective clutter of words.* The magnitude of this unprecedented behavior is exhibited by appendices A through M where several hundred synonyms are listed.

IRRECONCILABLE MOTIVATIONS

Clearly, Piaget has conflicting motivations. He is completely committed to his metaphysical doctrines, but is well aware that they are not acceptable to the academic community in their unadulterated form. Herculean efforts were made to maintain his views, even if undercover, while he presented a fraudulent view for general consumption. His boldest, most presumptuous deception was to present his metaphysical doctrines dressed up in scientific garb. The American Psychological Association, for instance, was badly fooled by this ploy, as this organization formally honored Piaget for approaching the philosophical question of epistemology "in a resolutely empirical manner", making it into a science (Piaget, 1972, p. 15). This august body was not aware that his unique doctrine of science preempts the possibility that he could be an empirical scientist. Papert, in his recent article in *Time* (March 29, 1999) honoring Piaget as one of the 100 greatest minds of the 20th Century, also appears to have fallen for this ploy. We will return to Papert and Piaget later in the introduction.

A major clue regarding Piaget's ambivalent attitude toward science is his judgment that natural science is not *necessary* (Piaget, 1977, p. 55) and that it is *foreign* to Non-Temporal Structures (Piaget, 1974b, p. 152). Piaget's "special science" is indeed necessary (Piaget, 1972. pp. 32; 86) (Karczmar & Eccles, p. 393) (Piaget, 1969b, p. XXII) (Piaget & Inhelder, 1974, p. 113) (Piaget, 1974a, pp. 74-5) (Piaget, 1974b, p. 131), but what Non-Temporal Structure finds natural science foreign? Naturally, it is the eternal Absolute Structure with the metaphysical Biology and Psychology. This divine Living Structure, for whom Piaget had a life-long, all-absorbing passion, finds natural science not only foreign, but also His natural enemy. *This is why Piaget despises natural or empirical science.* Empirical science after all is only approximate, and this is "of necessity ... where inductive methods are concerned, since the content of experience does not yield to any all-embracing prevision" (Piaget, 1971a, p. 211). As just implied, one reason empirical science is foreign is because it does not produce "necessary" knowledge. Induction, the basic method of empirical science, does not produce absolutely certain Knowledge, the only kind Piaget will accept. Piaget's "Science" (The word "science" will be arbitrarily capitalized on the same basis as "knowledge".) includes an "all-embracing" foreknowledge of the future as well as certain Knowledge about the present and past. The inducible generalizations of natural science are not necessary because they are based on observables; necessary generalizations or inferences, on the other hand, are always based on *operational coordinations* (author's italics) (Piaget, 1977, pp. 54-5), *which are the motors of Piagetian science.* Direct experience of the physical world of observables leads to false logic (Piaget & Inhelder, 1974, p. 220).

One reason Piaget pretends at times to be an empirical scientist is because it affords him a good opportunity to mangle the concept of natural science "from inside" - and he admits it! "These factual analyses based on psychological experimentation will provide a criticism of empiricism... [which will be] the more telling since it starts from the same basis as empiricism" (Beth & Piaget, 1966, p. 148). Piaget's "lower-level" or physical experiments are not for the purpose of increasing knowledge, but for deception. Empirical science contrasts sharply with his stated goal of understanding how the Logico-Mathematical Structure or the Absolute Subject assimilates physical reality by means of operational relations, which is the basis of Piaget's Science. The two sciences are hopelessly incompatible (author's capitalization) (Beth & Piaget, 1966, p. 148). *Science, for Piaget, is the metaphysical assimilation of the physical universe, as this is the one and only process that will enable Him to actualize His potential.*

A FEARSOME, PESSIMISTIC THEORY

Another probable reason Piaget is not honest regarding his true position inheres in the fact that, for most people at least, it is abysmally pessimistic. His theory confronts us with "the *fearful* question of the conceptualization of ... Awareness", since it expresses motivation through representations that modify physical content by simply wishing to do so (author's italics and capitalization) (Piaget, 1977, p. 147). "Conceptualization" is used here as a synonym for assimilation, and *"Awareness" is illogically used as a synonym for the Absolute Subject.* Even the second "of" of the quote shades the meaning, as it should be "by" - conceptualization *by* Awareness. "Awareness" is a rather silly synonym of the Divinity, and His ability to modify physical content "by simply wishing to do so" involves a private meaning of "wish". The Divinity "wishes" by representing to Himself the two opposite classes - metaphysical versus physical - and then proceeding with a routine operation. In other words, "wishing" here merely refers to an assimilative operation. The meaning obviously has magical connotations, in fact one meaning of "magic" is defined by Piaget as we have defined "wish" (Beth & Piaget, 1966, p. 155). This meaning is exposed when we realize that "Awareness" or the Absolute Subject wishes above all else to "modify" or assimilate every person and every physical object that exists. *This is the central postulate of Piaget's theory,* with its essential requirement that assimilation must do away with everything physical or material - everything we can touch, feel and experience in our spatio-temporal universe. Even memories of such physical experiences are considered physical by Piaget (Piaget, 1978a, p. 162), so they must also be eliminated. The Absolute wishes intensely to accomplish this task, according to Piaget, as *it is the only way he can fully develop Himself - stage by stage.*

The development of stages is predetermined and non-contingent, so it could not refer to human development (Piaget, 1973d, p. 35) (Inhelder & Piaget, 1958, pp. 292-3) (Piaget, 1971a, p. 165) (Piaget, 1962, p. 16) (Piaget & Inhelder, 1971, p. 356). The bottom line regarding the stages of psychological development is that they are regulated by endogenous mechanisms (Inhelder, Sinclair & Bovet, 1974, p. 10), and "endogenous" means by development that is independent of "empirical content" (Piaget, 1980b, p. 105), that depends entirely on metaphysical operations or equilibrations (Piaget, 1971a, pp. 316-17) and is based exclusively on the elements or monads already present in the preceding stage (ibid., pp. 318-19). Also, Piaget informs us explicitly that the order of the stages is not a physical process at all (ibid., p. 165). The four famous stages one finds in all textbooks on child development - sensorimotor, preoperational, concrete operational and formal operational - are non-contingent and are regulated endogenously, which means they are unmistakably metaphysical. Both the Entity progressing through the stages and the particular motor of this progress, dialectic operations, must be metaphysical in nature. *Piaget's predetermined stages of development are not in any way pertinent to people!* On the contrary, this is precisely the kind of predetermined metaphysical development that Piaget ascribed to Hegel's dialectic processes (Piaget, 1971b, p. 1).

Furth understands that Piaget's doctrine of development is predetermined, and he unwittingly demonstrates a deplorable surrender to Piaget's charisma with this incredible statement about it: "Intellectual development, strictly speaking, cannot go wrong ... moreover, with increasing development knowing takes on the character of being necessary and universal" (Furth, 1970, p. 75). When one takes a description of a metaphysical process and forces it to apply to human beings, he runs the risk of saying something very foolish. With this assertion it is obvious that Furth has turned his back, probably unknowingly, on the validity of natural science, and has bought into *Piaget's grand design for explaining everything.* A grand design based on the Absolute Being's necessary and universal development of Knowledge. This development is confined specifically to the Body of Monads, making it in one sense extremely narrow and in another sense universe-wide as the monads make up an invisible universe which extends beyond the physical universe. Development, in Piaget's theory, is confined to the Absolute Himself, but everything that happens in the physical universe is caused by the monads of the Absolute. Under the topic, "Explanation in Science" in the Encyclopedia of Philosophy, the following statement appears to be pertinent: "if we require everything to be explained, we explain nothing" (Edwards, 1967, Vol. 3, p. 162). Predetermined development means, as Furth realizes, that it is not a matter of chance (Piaget, 1971b, p. 6), so it is not surprising, in view of his extreme deference to Piaget, that he makes such statements. However, Furth is describing what can only be the development of the immanent Absolute Subject in all of us.

Piaget assures us that developmental progress cannot be necessary unless the Subject involved is able to see "everything with the same intensity at one and the same moment" (author's italics and capitalization) (Piaget, 1969b, pp. 288-9), which is obviously an impossible criterion for human beings to meet. Only the Absolute Subject, composed of monads, can see everything in the universe with the same intensity at every moment because His monads are everywhere and "see" everything all the time. Piaget also proclaims that, "operations cannot possibly be based on the objects themselves, since abstractions from objects can give rise only to non-necessitous statements" (Piaget, 1971a, p. 14). "Objects" here refers to human beings - who are often called "objects" (Piaget, 1974a, p. 30) (Piaget, 1974b, pp. 130-1) (Piaget & Inhelder, 1969, p. 94) or "things" (ibid., pp. 23-4) (Beth & Piaget, 1966, p. 298) (Piaget, 1971a, p. 27) (Piaget, 1971c, p. 103). There are many references in Piaget's works that demonstrate the same conclusion with regard to metaphysical developmental or operational progress (Piaget, 1973d, pp. 62-3) (Piaget, 1974a, p. 9), but Furth is a "true believer".

Universality, the other characteristic of development seconded by Furth, is also a superhuman characteristic. Only the Universal Entity in Piaget's system is acquiring universal Knowledge, a strange, unique Knowledge consisting solely of the results yielded by the continuous operations which have the express purpose of perfecting the development of the Absolute Subject. The Absolute Subject is also known as the *Biological Organization* responsible for the general coordination of actions (author's italics and capitalization) (Beth & Piaget, 1966, p. 285), the *Structured Whole* with His Operational Mechanisms (author's italics and capitalization) (Piaget, 1953, pp. 24-5), the *A Priori* who does not evolve in terms of ordinary biology (author's italics and capitalization) (Piaget, 1971a, pp. 314-15), the *Underlying Structure* on which the biology of all living organisms is based (author's italics and capitalization) (Inhelder & Chipman, 1976, p. 209), and *Hegel's Concrete Universal* who pursues a parascience that is different from natural science (author's italics and capitalization) (Piaget, 1971c, pp. 58-9). *This unique Subject, the only Actor in Piaget's system, created the physical universe by causing it to emanate from His monads, and He did it for the specific purpose of assimilating or reversing it back into His monads, thus necessarily achieving perfect development.* The existence of the physical universe has no other purpose! The physical universe is the "individual object" (Piaget & Inhelder, 1974, p. 274), and its real nature lies ... in a reason or ... motive for its existence which imply[sic] ... a Directing Intelligence" (author's capitalization) (Piaget, 1928, p. 148). The nature of the universe depends upon the reason or motive for which it was created. The sole motive of the "Directing Intelligence" was to fulfill His one need - His perfect development. For the all-important goal of His development, the material universe had to be the exact opposite of the immaterial Absolute. We see in this scenario that the world we live in is only a means to an end which can only be reached if it is eliminated, making it and all the people in it, in some sense, evil. Historians and philosophers will immediately recognize that Piaget's theory is related to Gnosticism. Piaget was well aware that he was trying, sub rosa, to revive a special brand of what is usually known as the Gnostic heresy (author's capitalization) (Piaget, 1930, p. 134).

Returning to Piaget's profoundly pessimistic theory, the threat of being assimilated by the immanent monads of the Absolute is expressed in another way. Action and its coordinates, *which amounts to intelligence,* is very *dangerous* because it refers to the functioning of the Operatory Systems (author's italics and capitalization) (Piaget, 1971b, p. 80). "Actions" or "operations" are terms used by Piaget to describe the assimilatory activity of the Absolute, which for him is the highest form of intelligence. A few pages later the Absolute Subject is called "Biology" and His assimilatory activity is called "mathematics", which "tends to reduce the object to schemes of the Subject's activity and succeeds to a great extent" (author's capitalization) (ibid., pp. 118-19). In the general context Piaget typically confuses the issue by switching to physical biology and the physical subject several times. He would prefer, of course, that his reader fail to fully grasp *the "upper-level" meaning of "mathematics", because it refers to the operational activity of the Absolute Subject and has nothing to do with the mathematics taught in school* (author's italics and capitalization) (Beth & Piaget, 1966, pp. 243; 296) (Piaget, 1973b, p. 103) (Piaget, 1971a, p. 358). *This "mathematics" reduces all objects, including all people, by the process of assimilation back to the Absolute Subject from which they came, they are reversed back into the monads of the Absolute.*

Piaget, like every other person, is in the process of being assimilated, and although he joyfully accepts and supports this idea, he also admits that his "collaboration" with the Absolute tends to be overly oriented toward the speculation of the Whole, another synonym of the Body of Monads or Absolute, and that "the great *danger* is to construct too rapidly and ... give in to the fascination of the Spirit of the System. This *danger* lies in wait for all of us and it is especially insidious" (author's italics and capitalization) (ibid., p. 99). *The academic world has never recognized Piaget's all-consuming entrancement with the Spirit composed of Monads, but this is precisely where his emotions and commitment lies.* Piaget repeats his sentiment regarding the danger awaiting all of us in various ways: "The notion of Totality is a notion whose fascinations are *dangerous*" (author's italics and capitalization) (Piaget, 1973a, p. 137). "Totality", of course, is used here as another synonym of the Absolute Spirit. The systematic assimilation of people, particularly children, is expressed in another way - a more sinister way: the child is said to egocentrically distort Space, but that this situation will be reversed so that Space, the true Ego composed of monads, will systematically *distort* the child (author's italics and capitalization) (Piaget, Inhelder & Szeminska, 1960, p. 64). "Space" is a favorite synonym for the Body of Monads which does indeed fill all of space, as well as reside immanently in the child, and "distortion" refers to the process of assimilation by these immanent Spatial monads. Piaget's choice of the word "distortion" to describe the effects of assimilation on people is a clear indication of his anti-social attitude. He repeats the identical idea with different words later in the book. He said that children use horizontal and vertical references in order to construct spatial relations, and then he makes the following statement: "we may well ask whether these Qualitative Reference Systems arise because measurements are coordinated ... or whether it is the other way about (author's capitalization) (ibid., 404). First, "horizontal and vertical references", although ostensibly pitched at the physical level in terms of the child's constructions, refer more fundamentally to the metaphysical Lattice Work of Monads, which is synonymous with the phrase, "Qualitative

Reference Systems". This makes "Lattice" another name for Space or the Absolute Subject (author's capitalization) (Inhelder & Piaget, 1958, pp. 123; 329) (Piaget, 1973c, p. 21). Flavell, it may be noted, understands that Piaget sees space as a framework or grid of horizontals and verticals (Flavell, 1963, p. 258), but he does not realize that he is describing an imaginary spatial arrangement of metaphysical monads. Comprehension is grossly complicated by the fact that the spatial relations constructed by the child are supposedly physical while the Lattice or Qualitative Reference System, *immanent in the child* constructs metaphysical Spatial relations. *The bottom line, in any case, is that the "Qualitative Reference Systems" or "Lattice" measures the child for the purpose of distortion or assimilation by means of Spatial relations or operations, which means the same as "coordinating the measurements".*

We must continually be reminded that Space, the Lattice, the Qualitative Reference System and all other synonyms of the Absolute refer either to the total Body of Monads or to Sub-Systems of these monads which are immanent in all people. It is most interesting that Flavell concluded correctly that Groups or Lattices are nonhuman, but he was wrong to conclude that they are nonpsychological. "An understanding of Piaget's conception of cognition ... involves coming to grips with abstract structures whose origin is definitely nonpsychological"; these include groups and lattices (Flavell, 1963, p. 168). *Flavell fails to comprehend the meaning of "Groups" and "Lattices" as synonyms of the only living Entity in the universe - who is also the only true Psychological Being in the universe!*

Rather than being depressed by what, according to his theory, is happening to people, Piaget is optimistically focused on what is happening to the Spatial Group or Absolute. Piaget sees the assimilation process as providing a gradual liberation of the extra-temporal Group from the spatio-temporal universe (author's capitalization) (Piaget, 1971c, pp. 106-7). Furtively, Piaget spoke of "liberation from" twenty four lines of print before he vaguely revealed who was to be liberated! "Group" is a mathematical term, fundamental to quantum theory, which Piaget seized and frequently uses to mean the Group of Spatial monads. *The Group, who wishes to be liberated from the evil material or spatio-temporal universe, "represents the Essential Psychological Mechanisms of Intelligence"* (author's italics and capitalization) (Piaget, 1971b, p. 114). *The same "Essential Psychological Mechanism"* (the plural is used to confuse above and below) *disguised in the various italicized terms below, desires fervently, in true Gnostic fashion, to be liberated from the physical universe.* *"Forms"* a synonym of Group, also wish to be liberated from content (author's italics and capitalization) (Piaget, 1969b, p. 302), and so do the *Thought Mechanisms* (author's italics and capitalization) (Piaget & Inhelder, 1969b, p. 136). There is a vital need for *Thought, the Organism or Forms* to escape from successive events and to avoid time (author's italics and capitalization) (Piaget, 1973b, pp. 125-6); the *Operational Systems* are in the process of becoming disentangled from content (author's italics and capitalization) (Inhelder & Piaget, 1958, p. 331); furthermore, the "I" and the "We" (a most unfair and deceitful way to refer to the metaphysical Body of Monads) wish to be liberated from the ego who is responsible for the "lower-level" egocentrism of ordinary people (author's italics and capitalization) (Piaget, 1973b, p. 136), as *this ego is part of the content of the physical universe.* The "I" and the "We" refer to the immanent Subject both as the singular Subject in *each individual* (the "I") as well as the plural Sub-Divisions of the Subject in *every individual* (the "We"). "The physical world in its spatio-temporal dynamism ... includes the subject as an integral part" (Piaget, 1972, p. 50). This latter subject is the physical individual or ego from whom the "I" and the "We" or Ego wish to be rid. Piaget is not at all concerned that he, as an item of physical content, is being assimilated, as he is wholly focused on the need for his true Ego to be "liberated" from all content, even the physical content known as "Jean Piaget". *He is a genuine Gnostic!*

Developmental psychology is one of the courses I presently teach as an adjunct professor, so I am aware of what the latest textbooks have to say regarding Piaget's theory in this field. They tend to emphasize the four stages of development, much like they have for two previous generations of professors. Auxiliary concepts such as animism, conservation, decentering, egocentrism, equilibrium, logical operations, object permanence, reversibility and schemas are also discussed. At this juncture a point of fact rudely intrudes. *Piagetians must deal with the inescapable fact that neither stages nor any of the other concepts are relevant to the cognitive development of children. They are not relevant to children at all! These concepts are only pertinent to the immanent Personal Organization of monads within the child.* The purely imaginary Organization of Monads within the child is not a part of the child, and it is important to realize that, from the standpoint of Piaget's theory, the physical child of natural science is merely a "throw-away" object that is only used by the Absolute Subject for His own purposes. Mainly because of their tendency to follow Flavell, author's of college textbooks are unaware of the metaphysical meaning of all of these terms. Piaget, of course, would not be displeased as he planned to sow confusion by deliberately attempting to make his own views incommunicable, nevertheless, *we must eventually face the fact that college textbooks, apparently all of them, present a view that is wholly alien to Piaget's theory.*

The primary task of the monads in the child is to assimilate him. At the same time the monads within every child have what must be the rather frustrating task of repeating from scratch the development of the total Body of Monads up to the current level He has attained (author's capitalization) (Bringuier, 1980, pp. 19-20). That is, the immanent monads in each new baby repeat the process of development as it occurred in the total Body of Monads beginning immediately after the creation of the physical universe, and then proceeding to recapitulate in the few years through adolescence the entire development attained by the Total Absolute Subject over eons of time (author's capitalization) (Piaget, 1971a, p. 160). Piaget even tells us that this is the reason he studied child psychology - that is, the child's *true Psychology* which is the Psychology of the Body of Monads within the child (author's capitalization) (Bringuier, 1980, pp. 48; 92) (Piaget, 1974a, p. 44). This recapitulation has the effect that the immanent Subject (arbitrarily singular as we are speaking of billions of Sub-Systems of the same Entity) in every generation of children is a little more advanced than the immanent Subject in the previous generation (author's capitalization) (ibid., pp. 146-7) (Piaget & Inhelder, 1969, p. 159).

PRESCRIPTION FOR EDUCATIONAL
DISASTER: SPONTANEOUS DEVELOPMENT

We have seen how Piaget gained entrance to academia by pretending to be an empirical scientist, but we have yet to reckon the devastating results of this counterfeit entry which has affected all levels of education. *It is hard to imagine, for example, a more destructive educational theory than Piaget's concept of spontaneous psychological development.* Parents and teachers can have no effect whatever on this kind of development. *This is the unthinkable development, affirmed by Furth previously, that cannot go wrong regardless of what kind of education the individual receives!* For Piaget, spontaneous development is true Psychological development as opposed to his school development or to his development within the family (author's capitalization) (Piaget, 1973a, p. 2). He also uses the term "psychosocial" development to mean the education he receives at school, at home, and most significantly, *"everything the child receives from without"* (author's italics) (ibid., p. 2). "Everything from without" means everything outside of the Absolute Subject. More specifically, it means everything that is not produced by the dialectical operations of the Absolute Subject, and that is everything that people could possibly learn, as everything they can learn is connected with the physical universe. As Piaget asserts in another context, "this contribution from without does not modify the Structure of Reasoning" (author's capitalization) (Inhelder & Piaget, 1958, p. 144). Even such contributions as those made by Newton and Einstein could not modify the Structure of Reasoning as this Structure can only be modified by dialectical operations.

When compared to spontaneous development, Piaget perceives psychosocial development, the only traditional form of educational development, as trivial if not contemptible. This is because psychosocial development is closely associated with the "enemy" of Gnostic Intelligence - physical reality. Spontaneous development is the "development of Intelligence - *what the child learns by Himself, what none can teach Him and He must discover alone; and it is essentially this development which takes time"* (author's italics and capitalization) (Piaget, 1973a, p. 2). It is important to understand that the spontaneous development of Intelligence refers to a "special" Intelligence; it refers to the spontaneous Intelligence of the child rather than to his intelligence as "seen through adult eyes" (author's capitalization) (Inhelder & Piaget, 1958, p. X). This is an odd way to represent metaphysical Intelligence as both Inhelder and Piaget are adults, however, since it is definitely not the traditional concept of intelligence, we know immediately what Piaget means because of his consistent dual system. It is the kind of Intelligence that *"arises from spontaneous functioning of the Schemata"* (author's italics and capitalization) (Piaget, 1952b, p. 352); it is Gnostic Intelligence (author's capitalization) (Piaget, 1930, p. 134); it is the Operational Intelligence which is independent of the ego (author's capitalization) (Piaget, 1969b, pp. 285-6), it is entirely autonomous (Piaget & Inhelder, 1971, p. 356) and it operates vicariously (Piaget, 1950, p. 94). *Spontaneous Intelligence is autonomous and independent of the ego because it is vicarious!* "Vicarious" Intelligence is depicted as operating *in place of the child's ordinary intelligence* "as seen through adult eyes". All of us have a vicarious Intelligence. That is, there is an

Entity in each of us whose Intelligence *takes the place of our intelligence. A vicarious Intelligence that works against our best interests, as this Entity has a completely Self-centered agenda which includes our eventual elimination as a race of human beings.* Piaget's concept of a vicarious Intelligence has been studiously ignored by Piagetians because it requires dual entities!

Teaching methods, declares Piaget, must be brought into relation with "Structures and functions that are *spontaneously active* in the child's mind" (author's italics and capitalization) (Piaget, 1973b, p. 9). Furth wishes very much to implement this admonition, and his main target is reading instruction. "The early pressure on reading must be exposed not merely as contributing little or nothing to intellectual development but, in many cases, as seriously interfering with it" (Furth, 1970, p. IX). *By "early pressure" he is referring to reading instruction in the first four grades!* "The average five-to nine-year-old child from any environment is unlikely, when busy with reading or writing, to engage his intellectual powers to any substantial degree" (ibid., p. 4). What concept is behind this antipathy to "early" reading? Yes, it is Furth's particular understanding of "spontaneous development". "We are searching continually for new methods of teaching reading without ever asking whether reading is the appropriate focus of early education. Instead, I suggest that the *spontaneously growing intelligence* of the child should be the focus of grade-school activities" (Furth's italics) (ibid., IX). Significantly, Furth considers Piaget and thus himself to be "expert scientists". "We experts", asserts Furth, believe that "in education there is the possibility of stating at least some things with the full conviction of a scientific opinion. ... What I propose ... is not vague speculation on my part. I speak as a responsible scientist" (ibid., pp. 2-3).

As an elementary and secondary teacher and an elementary principal, I have observed teachers, administrators and school board members who have been overly influenced by Piaget's doctrine of spontaneous development as it has filtered down from such leading experts as Furth. This bizarre doctrine makes it too easy to lay aside one's responsibility to teach. Why should teachers worry about their effectiveness when *time* will take care of all the important aspects of development? If children fail to learn very much, it is not the teacher's fault. There is overwhelming evidence that the education of children in the United States has deteriorated since the decade of the sixties - about the time Piaget's influence began to take hold. Is it not a reasonable inference that there may be more that a mere coincidence in this fact?

"Geometrical as well as Arithmetic Structures are formed ... in the child of 5 to 7-9 years of age, *independently of school instruction* ... [and] each is deeply rooted in essentially Logical Operational Structures" (author's italics and capitalization) (Beth & Piaget, 1966, p. 255). These Geometrical or Arithmetic Structures are simply the spontaneously developing Structures of the immanent Absolute Subject. That is why school instruction has no positive effect on them, and they are not "deeply rooted" in "Logical Operational Structures" - they *are* Logical Operational Structures! These Structures are also called the Group Structure (author's capitalization) (Piaget, 1970b, p. 42), and Piaget informs us that maturation, experience and education or social transmission are not capable of producing Structure (author's capitalization) (Piaget, 1967, pp. 153-4). They are not capable because they can have no affect on the metaphysical Structure of the Structured Being (author's capitalization) (Piaget,

1971c, p. 109). Note that the Geometrical or Arithmetic Structures are *in* the mind of the child. This language appears to make the "mind" of the child both lower level and upper level, but Piaget's theory makes a clear distinction. His theory requires that the monads of the metaphysical Structure be both in and adjacent to every molecule of the body, but at the same time definitely not a part of physical biology. In the following quote the Structure *is* the Mind, thus excluding the brain of the child. *"The physiological and anatomic aspect of the organism, gradually appears to the Mind as external to it* (author's italics and capitalization) (Piaget, 1954, p. 401). The immanent Body of Monads, or true Mind, sees the traditional aspects of biology as external to it. *Upper-level Biology sees the same thing: "This living acting subject is conceived by Biology merely in relation to material reality, and consequently in terms of the object* (author's italics and capitalization) (Piaget, 1971b, p. 119). "Mind" and "Biology" are synonyms of the Absolute Subject, regardless of how inappropriate that may be, who knows that biology is external to Him because it is physical. The Mind, consisting of monads, does not need the brain in order to think (author's capitalization) (Piaget, 1971a, p. 216), because monads think and act all by themselves. *This is why the "general actions" or operations of the Subject are independent of the actions of individual people* (author's italics and capitalization) (Beth & Piaget, 1966, p. 244), or, in different words, Logico-Mathematical Structures are capable of being free from the actions of individual subjects (author's capitalization) (ibid., p. 301). Some of Piaget's followers state the same idea more clearly: "Since logical coordinations derive uniquely from the Subject's action they can be neither favored nor hindered by the physical properties of the objects acted upon" (author's capitalization) (Inhelder, Sinclair & Bovet, 1974, p. 262).

LOGIC AS OPERATIONAL ACTIVITY

Since Piaget constantly speaks of the importance of logic, we should examine the highly personalized private meaning he illegitimately forces upon the term. He had already arrived at this private meaning by the time he wrote the essay, "Sketch of a Neo-Pragmatism", soon after he received his baccalaureate degree at age 18. In this unpublished paper Piaget put forward the idea "that action itself admits of logic ... and that, therefore, logic stems from a sort of spontaneous organization of acts" (Evans, 1973, p. 113) (Piaget, 1971c, p. 6). Again, "Logic ... arises from general co-ordinations between acts" (the meaning is discernible here, but note how two terms are confounded - *the co-ordinations are the operational acts, so the use of "between acts" is probably Piaget's effort to add a little humor)* (Piaget, 1972, p. 32). In the following quote we understand that the coordination of actions is simply another way to express operations or reflective abstractions: "The roots of logical thought ... are to be found ... in the coordination of actions, which are the basis of reflective abstraction" (Piaget, 1970c, pp. 18-19). Reflective abstractions, operations or the general coordination of actions are in the process of assimilating or reversing physical reality back into the monads. *So logic is action - the kind of action that moves the Actor toward His ultimate goal.* Human efforts, scientific or otherwise, cannot reverse physical reality, but "the peculiar property of purely mental construction like those of mathematics is to be *entirely reversible, and therefore entirely logical* from the first" (author's italics) (Piaget, 1928, p. 190). "Mathematics" is again used as a synonym of operations. There is a drastic distinction between individual actions and coordinated actions (ibid., p. 19), because the first kind of "action" is physical while the latter is metaphysical. Logic is "based essentially on operations" (Piaget, 1953, p. 12). And to remove all ambiguity: "Logic is ... a co-ordination of actions on any objects whatever" (Beth & Piaget, 1966, p. 238).

These coordinations are upper-level as they are performed by the Universal or Epistemic Subject and *not the individual subject* (author's italics and capitalization) (ibid., p. 113). The logical acts of the organized monads are thus called "logical operations", "coordinations" and "reflective abstractions". They are metaphysical acts that are also known as "assimilations" (Piaget, 1980b, p. 96). Piaget, however, expands the terminology of "logical acts" to include "behaviors" (Piaget, 1978b, p. 41; 98) (Piaget, 1971a, p. 33), "compensations" (ibid., p. 12), (Piaget, 1973c, p. 46), "compositions" (Piaget & Inhelder, 1974, p. 115), "concepts" (Piaget, 1973d, p. 58) (Piaget, (1976a, p. 307), "cooperations" (Beth & Piaget, 1966, pp. 289-90), "couplings" (Piaget, 1969b, pp. 179; 363), "deductions" (Piaget, 1970a, p. 33) (Piaget & Inhelder, 1974, p. 116), "encounters" (Piaget, 1969b, p. 125), "equilibrations" (Piaget, 1973c, p.46), "functions" (Piaget, 1971a, p. 141), "imagination" (Piaget & Inhelder, 1956, p. 286), "imitation" (Piaget, 1962, p. 22), "intelligence" (Piaget, 1973a, pp. 72; 82) (Piaget, 1971b, pp. 80; 87-88), "knowledge" (Piaget, 1974b, p. 137), "magic" (Piaget, 1971c, p. 148), "magical spells" (Piaget, 1929, pp. 433-4), "mathematics" (Piaget, 1973b, p. 103), "memory" (Piaget & Inhelder, 1973, pp. 392; 396; 401; 405; 408-9), "modification" (Piaget, 1970a, p. 32), "motor" (Piaget, 1978a, p. 40) (Piaget & Inhelder, 1956, p. 42) (Piaget, 1970d, p. 29), "movements" (Piaget, 1978b, pp. IX; XXI; 93), "pairing" (Piaget, et al., 1977, p. 180), "praxis" (Piaget, 1973a, pp. 63; 78; 90-1), "regulations" (Piaget, 1977, pp. 21-25), "relations" (Piaget & Inhelder, 1974, p. 114) and "teleonomies" (Piaget, 1977, p. 40). Some of these words must be radically twisted in order to mean "act of logic", but Piaget regularly ignores dictionary meanings and often misuses parts of speech.

The metaphysical nature of the general coordinations of actions is emphasized with the statement that they are universal (Beth & Piaget, 1966, p. 289), and they are universal in the precise sense that "the universe is embodied in the activity of the Subject" (author's capitalization) (Piaget, 1952b, p. 43). The monads of the Subject embody all objects in the universe, including people. The same idea is stated in another way: the Ego is the Homogeneous Medium which is common to all objects. Since the Ego is the Body of Monads, it is indeed a Medium. This Ego or Space is centered on action (author's capitalization) (Piaget, 1969, p. 118) - action in the sense that the metaphysical Ego or Space, composed of monads, is the Homogeneous Medium by means of which all objects are actively manipulated and assimilated. The true "Individual" is also said to be the Medium (author's capitalization) (Piaget, 1932, p. 388), and so is "true Action, the source and Medium of Intelligence" (author's capitalization) (Piaget, 1950, p. 32). The metaphysical Individual or Ego is the Medium who is the source of all genuine action, so it is not too surprising that Piaget also calls the Medium of Monads "Action". The Homogeneous Medium of monads is the Universe of Active Objects which exist beyond observable phenomena (author's capitalization) (Beth & Piaget, 1966, p. 180). The imaginary Body of Monads is the Homogeneous Universe of Active Objects which cannot be observed by any possible scientific means.

METAPHYSICAL ACTION VERSUS PHYSICAL ACTION

Operational logic can be described in terms of psychogenesis, but first we shall examine two inappropriate descriptions. David Elkind, editor of *Six Psychological Studies*, (1967), approaches "genetic logic" in this way: "Genetic logic ... has been criticized by logicians, it is nevertheless the first successful attempt to construct a logical model of thought based upon experiment rather than armchair speculation" (Piaget, 1967, p. X). This could not be an accurate description as genetic logic is the logic of operations, and since people cannot perform operations (Beth & Piaget, 1966, pp. 235; 244; 296) (Piaget & Inhelder, 1971, p. 356) how could Piaget experimentally investigate the process? *Elkind does not realize that Piaget's psychogenetic or genetic logic is the logic of the Absolute moving inexorably toward perfect development; it has nothing to do with a logical model of human thought.* Another example of overlooked private meanings are two statements by the English philosopher, Wolfe Mays, who translated *The Principles of Genetic Epistemology*, (1972). Mays inexplicably explains the origin of Logico-Mathematical operations in terms of physical actions: "For Piaget, as we have seen, logical and mathematical operations originate in the child from simple actions carried out on objects" (ibid. p. 4). Many statements by Piaget demonstrate that this kind of origin is an impossibility.

Piaget bluntly states that physical actions cannot become operations (author's italics) (Piaget, et al, 1977, p. 14), *and that actions ... are always informed by teleonomies ... which remain outside the somatic sphere* (author's italics) (Piaget, 1978b, p. 153). In other words, the actions or operations are directed by "something" outside of normal body or brain processes. The immanent Subject who is "external" to the physical somatic sphere is seen to be Self-directing His metaphysical actions teleonomically toward a particular goal. Piaget explains to Bringuier this particular notion: "The Action alone, tends toward a goal, and it's satisfied when the goal is achieved (author's capitalization) (Bringuier, 1980, pp. 89-90). Obviously, "Action" here stands for the Subject directing the action. The statement that "Action" is *satisfied* when the goal is reached confirms this. Mays ignores the superhuman aspect of "Action", insisting that Piaget starts with observations of physical actions: "Starting as he does from the facts of observable child behavior rather than adult introspections, he differs from empiricist thinkers like Locke ... on the part played by overt activities in building up the Conceptual Machinery of Thought" (author's capitalization) (Piaget, 1972, p. 2). Mays goes on to say that this "building up" is a complex learning process (ibid., p. 3). What could this "complex learning process" be like? First, we know that it is not based on learning as defined in any dictionary. Piaget tells us explicitly that the "biochemical conditions" of learning "is not at all my line of country" (Piaget, 1971a, p. 50). It is no surprise then that Logico-Mathematical Knowledge is "not brought about by empirical learning" (author's capitalization) (ibid., p. 313). The concept of learning that Mays has in mind is brain-based, physical learning. That is, learning as traditionally conceived, about some aspect of physical reality. As a matter of fact, this is a kind of learning that Piaget greatly dislikes - it is copy learning because it involves "making a copy of reality" (ibid., p. 6). *Mays does not realize that for Piaget "Knowledge is dependent on equilibration"* (author's italics and capitalization) (Piaget, 1977, p. 200), *meaning that the "Conceptual Machinery of Thought" is built up by metaphysical operations, regulations or equilibrations, not learning - not even "complex" learning.* Mays translated "Conceptual Machinery of Thought", but he had no idea that it means "Mind", "Body of Monads", "Absolute Subject" and, although illogical in the extreme, even "Knowledge" used as a synonym of the developing Body of Monads.

Other facets of Piaget's concept of action need to be brought to light: "Praxis or action is not some sort of movements but rather a system of coordinated movements functioning for a result or an intention" (Piaget, 1973a, p. 63). When "action" is paired synonymously with "praxis" we see that "action" is the practice or working out of Piaget's theory - more exactly it is the systematic, intentional operational activity that will lead to the goal of the Subject's perfect development. This intentional action has nothing to do with human action. "If the mode of coordination of actions is truly of an assimilating nature ... it becomes futile to subordinate the actions or praxis to *so-called intelligence* which would be external to them .... *This Intelligence is nothing more than the very coordination of actions*" (author's italics and capitalization) (Piaget, 1973a, p. 72). Piaget refers to the two opposite kinds of intelligence in the same paragraph, but he does not clarify the vast difference between them. *The lower-level kind, or "so-called intelligence" is "external" to the coordination of actions, while the other kind is defined in terms of these actions. It is futile to give "so-called" or brain-based intelligence credit for praxis, or true action, but metaphysical intelligence is precisely praxis, true action or true logic.*

"Structuralism calls for a differentiation between the *individual subject*, who does not enter at all and the Epistemic Subject .... Now after ... precipitation of the "me", the "lived", from the "I", there remains the Subject's operations" (Piaget's italics) (author's capitalization) (Piaget, 1970b, p. 139). The "I" obviously refers to the immanent Subject, composed of monads and source of praxic Intelligence who remains after the lower-level "me", the source of "so-called" intelligence, has been precipitated out or decentered. It is also obvious that the "I" is the source of operations or praxis, because operations remain after the "me" is gone. This intentional action begins with the coordination or composition of an "ordered pair" (not "two ordered pairs" as Piaget perversely says) (Piaget et al, 1977, p. 186). Piaget brings in some irrelevant physical examples, but this "ordered pair" is the fundamental pairing of a Class (each dialectical pairing, coupling or operation produces a more perfect Sub-Unit of the Absolute Subject, which is called a *Class*) of the metaphysical Body of Monads versus an exactly opposite class of the material universe. *The composition or coordination of ordered pairs is affirmed as the most fundamental process in Piaget's metaphysical theory:* "Everything can be reduced to the schema of encounters and ... active couplings" (Piaget, 1969b, p. 179). "Encounters and couplings" is simply another way to describe operational or dialectical interactions, praxis or pairing between the *dual* participants of Piaget's system. This is all about assimilation, which is so essential to his theory that he defines praxic or metaphysical intelligence solely in terms of this process: "Intelligent activity has no other function than that of assimilating the universe to the Schemata" (author's capitalization) (Piaget, 1952b, p. 230). This is central, as we have seen repeatedly, because of the *one need* of the Absolute Subject, which is to fully develop Himself. "Intelligence ... arrives at a decentering based on the general coordination of action" (Piaget & Inhelder, 1969, p. 128). Satisfying the need means to assimilate, which requires the decentering of the lower-level ego with his brain-based intelligence. Decentering by means of assimilation is the sole occupation of the immanent Subject and His general coordination of action, because this is the way He develops Himself. Piaget chooses to ignore, however, His more mundane activities, such as maintaining all of the physiological processes that human life requires. Nevertheless, "all needs depend, either immediately or remotely, upon a fundamental need which is that of the Organism's development; that is to say precisely, upon assimilation" (author's capitalization) (Piaget, 1952b, p. 170).

Piagetians have no excuse for forcing this "need to develop" down to the level of people because Piaget declares that this is a *sui generis vicarious need* which goes beyond the organic plane (author's italics) (ibid., pp. 45-6). This one-of-a-kind need "goes beyond" physical biology declares Piaget, that is, this need is on a higher plane than the physical. He is clearly begging his reader to understand that he is speaking of the metaphysical Entity who has only one urgent need, and this metaphysical "Other" is required in the clearest possible way by the term "vicarious"! *People have many urgent needs; the Absolute Subject only one - the sui generis need to develop and He can accomplish this only through assimilation!*

Educators have latched on to what they think is Piaget's concept of action to initiate and support a program of "hands on" experiences and experiments. This program may be a very good one, but Piaget's theory does not support it. Professors from the best universities have pushed this concept with the assurance that this is exactly what Piaget teaches. Nothing could be further from the truth! "The process of co-ordinating actions is no part of the physical experiment, but a part of Intelligence Mechanisms, and is therefore basic to logical and mathematical operations" (author's capitalization) (Piaget & Inhelder, 1956, p. 404). Logical Structure is not learned from the physical manipulation of objects, but through operations (author's capitalization) (Piaget, 1973a, p. 102). *Piaget asserts repeatedly "that there are two types of experience ... There is physical experience ... [which is] the only kind of experience that ... empiricism ever took into account. But there is also ... Logico-Mathematical experience ... the two kinds of experience not being the same thing at all"* (author's italics and capitalization) (Karczmar & Eccles, 1972, p. 395). *True, they are not the same at all as they are in fundamental conflict.*

Logico-Mathematical experience is authentically Logico-Mathematical, dealing as it does with the very actions of Subjects and not actions of the human object as such. On the other hand, physical, experimental or exogenous knowledge proceeds by abstraction based on characteristics of the object (Piaget, 1971b, pp. 71-2). Exogenous knowledge is derived from physical experience; endogenous knowledge is due to Logico-Mathematical construction (author's capitalization) (Piaget, 1980b, p. 81), which specifically refers to the experience of Self-development. Exogenous knowledge is factual data based on observations, manipulations of objects and other experiences of the body itself. Endogenous Knowledge is based on the Operational

Structure with its operations, reflexive abstractions, Self-regulations or equilibrations (author's capitalization) (Piaget, 1974b, p. 23). All possible "hands on" experiences are by definition exogenous in nature. They can only lead to "copy knowledge", not Logico-Mathematical Knowledge or construction which is merely another way to describe the Absolute Subject's development. Piaget is exclusively concerned with this latter endogenous Knowledge. Interestingly enough, this is the sole example of endogenous Knowledge. *The one need leads to this one and only possible example of endogenous Knowledge. Many educators and psychologists are laboring under the false impression that they are taking advantage of Piaget's concept of action with their program of hands-on experience, but they must eventually realize that his concept of action is strictly metaphysical.*

The child's physical actions, are incorporated into the Overall System by means of operations (author's capitalization) (Piaget & Inhelder, 1974, p. 279). Physical actions vis-a-vis the Overall System represents Piaget's metaphysical-physical dual system. Piaget calls this incorporation a correction, and he informs us that experimental science is corrected in the very same way by the incorporation of exogenous scientific findings into the same Overall System by means of operations (author's capitalization) (ibid., p. 279). The lower-level or physical subject is only "the scene or the actor of a play written beforehand of which he is not the author", *so this rules out "any profound transformation related to development" of the physical subject* (author's italics) (Piaget, 1973c, p. 24). *Since the lower-level subject is not the author, he is not the one who will benefit from development.*

The structures of the Epistemic Subject cannot be understood apart from their psychogenesis or development in terms of operations or Self-regulations. The denial of activity with regard to natural structures leads to the postulation of a Structure of All Structures (author's capitalization) (Piaget, 1970b, p. 142) (Piaget, 1973d, pp. 16; 68). Although Piaget fogs up the issue with theoretical problems of such a Structure, his doctrine of the Absolute provides for His existence as this particular kind of Overall Structure and for His gradual development towards perfection. This Structure of All Structures is the only center of activity, as He is the ultimate source of physical as well as metaphysical activity. Although He is the source of all activity, metaphysical activity depends upon the dialectical interaction of the two opposite entities. One fatal flaw of college textbooks is the fact that, following Flavell, only one of the entities, the metaphysical Subject, is considered and He is forcibly assigned the physical level. *Since every definition and every inference found in apparently every textbook is invalid, what possible value could they have for the education of children? The only possible value of Piaget's theory would have to be in the realm of metaphysics.* The Gnostics who flourished soon after the time of Jesus would have loved him - if they could decipher his writings.

Normal educational experiences are part and parcel of the physical universe, so they could not be considered in a positive way by Piaget. For instance, he says that *"knowledge learned in school increasingly interferes with the spontaneous development of Geometrical notions as children grow older"* (author's italics and capitalization) (Piaget, Inhelder & Szeminska, 1960, p. 381). Why does it interfere? Because this knowledge is physical knowledge, while "Geometrical notions" are notions about the assimilation of everything physical, including physical knowledge. As Piaget says, "the practical and egocentric object defends foot by foot the terrain which the Geometric relationships will conquer" (author's capitalization) (Piaget, 1954, p. 73). "Practical and egocentric objects" are people who, because they are part of the physical universe, resist the Geometric assimilation that will eventually conquer them. The function of Geometrical operations is to transform things, including people along with their "physical knowledge", thereby enabling the Geometric Entity to develop (author's capitalization) (Piaget & Inhelder, 1971, p. 336).

"The two basic problems of ethical education are, therefore, to assure this de-centering and to build this [Independent] Discipline" (author's capitalization) (Piaget, 1973b, p. 112). It would be unethical if the immanent Absolute Subject, with His Logico-Mathematical operations, did not decenter the physical subject (author's capitalization) (Piaget, 1972, pp. 22; 83). Decentering occurs when the physical subject is subordinated by means of assimilation to the point where not only his body but also his actions are "objects like all other objects" (Piaget & Inhelder, p. 94) (Piaget, 1971a, pp. 336-7). The "Independent Discipline" that is built up by the process of assimilation is the immanent Absolute Himself - He is the only possible independent Discipline as He is the only possible independent Entity.

AN ALIEN VIEW OF PIAGET

What we find in the textbooks is the result of a multiple-step process, not a direct derivation from Piaget's books. In fact, it would appear to be impossible to derive what we find in college textbooks directly from Piaget's books, regardless of how partial or undiscerning textbook writers might be. The first step lasted for about thirty five years, and consisted of highly selective discussions of Piaget's work. No one undertook to present a comprehensive interpretation until John Flavell arrived on the scene with step number two. Although Flavell's work was the high-water mark of comprehensiveness, it is fair to say that he failed to cover Piaget adequately because he refused to recognize his metaphysical concepts. By failing to cognize Piaget's well camouflaged intent, he was forced to omit many of his concepts because they only make sense at the metaphysical level, thus Flavell moved away from Piaget's position to a considerable extent. A good example of an omitted concept is Piaget's fascination with and practice of magic (Piaget, 1929. pp. 433-437). This second step was attempted by very few individuals because Piaget writes with such an impenetrable style, and no one, including this author, would claim to have unraveled all of his linguistic puzzles. Most have relied on his short papers alone as sufficient for interpreting his position.

The last step occurs when professors, who teach such subjects as cognitive and educational psychology or write textbooks, process the views of Flavell and others for the supposed purpose of improving the teaching of children and adolescents as well as enhancing the liberal education of college students with some knowledge of Piaget's ideas. What we see in the textbooks tends to be simplified versions of Flavell's position, but which modify Flavell to some extent, and thus they move even further away from Piaget's position. Piaget's confident, dogmatic claims, which appear to be pertinent to a wide variety of fields, combined with his appalling mode of expression led to a sense of admiration and awe among some investigators. If he writes a large number of books that are almost impossible to understand he must be astonishingly brilliant! We end up with concepts in all of our textbooks that are alien to Piaget's true, although admittedly disguised position. *It will not be possible to rectify this sad situation until we turn to his major works and give them the meticulous study they demand.*

We see this alien view of Piaget exemplified, for instance, in the following encounter. After spending four intense hours with a highly respected psychologist who was known as an authority on Piaget, the consequence of ignoring Piaget's books became starkly manifest. Although initially very self-assured regarding his knowledge of Piaget's theory, he was forced to begin rethinking his position when he was shown short passages in about twenty books with which he had no prior acquaintance whatever. Quite naturally he became agitated when unexpected arguments by Piaget ran counter to his long-held assumptions. This intelligent man apparently knew almost everything Flavell had to say and had read many of the short papers by and about Piaget, but he obviously felt no need to read his books. For instance, he had never been exposed to statements by Piaget regarding the existence and nature of the Absolute Subject. Not only that, but he was absolutely certain that Piaget never taught such a doctrine. It had never occurred to him that many doctrines in his books are never seen explicitly in his short articles. His assumption that Piaget's books contained nothing essentially different from Flavell's book or Piaget's short papers proved to be embarrassingly incorrect.

This dangerous, although generally unacknowledged, assumption has had a pervasive impact on the academic community much like a domino affect. A good example is a spin-off from this professor. One of his students supposedly wrote a paper on Piaget's theory, for which he was awarded some sort of prize. Partly because of the prize, presumably, he ended up on the faculty of a prestigious university. After reading two articles by this young professor on the relationship between what he considered to be Piaget's theory and mathematics instruction, I chanced to see him when he made a visit to our university. He was good enough to come by my office to discuss his articles, and when I asked him what in Piaget's work had motivated the articles, he volunteered that he did not read Piaget because it always put him to sleep. The upshot was that he depended almost solely upon what others said about Piaget. Unfortunately, this point of view which ignores the source is pandemic among Piagetians. Anyone who had taken the time to read a good portion of Piaget's major works would almost certainly see no relationship at all between the theory revealed there and the supposed but alien theory that this professor thought should influence the teaching of mathematics. True mathematics for Piaget, as we saw, is no more than the operational activity of the Absolute Subject. Like his mentor, Hegel, who held mathematics in contempt (Edwards, Vol. 3, p. 445), Piaget had little interest in traditional mathematics other than to speciously "demonstrate" some facet of his theory, and to serve as a repository for terms he could appropriate for bogus purposes. He was almost exclusively interested in "pure mathematics", which is the "general coordinations of actions" (author's capitalization) (Beth & Piaget, 1966, p. 296). Human beings, as we saw, have nothing to do with this kind of mathematics (ibid., 296).

Some years ago I attended a series of sessions on Piaget's concept of formal thought. Although I had read all of Piaget's books available in English at the time, I had never come across many of the ideas proclaimed by the enthusiastic leader. Lucky enough to sit next to him at lunch on the second day, I asked him what he had read by Piaget that led him to his views on formal thought. After some hesitation, he replied that "we don't need Piaget any more, we have gone beyond him". The fact that he did not even try to anchor his views in Piaget's work, while simultaneously claiming to interpret the nature of formal thought certainly shows that he had no doubt regarding his understanding of Piaget's concept, so much so that he could "go beyond" his supposed source. Unhappily, he did not have any idea what Piaget really taught about formal thought because he had never read his books. All of his emphatic assertions were extensions of Flavell's notion that formal thought is the basis for scientific activity in adulthood, while Piaget himself saw formal thought as essentially the later stages of the assimilation process as he imagined it would be in the future. Piaget often anticipates how things will be in the distant future as the Absolute follows his predetermined course of action. His view of the "diachronic" function is not only seen in his "fast forward" view of the future but also in his statements regarding development in the past. For example, "it is probable that the Greek children were behind our own" in the acquisition of formal structures (Inhelder & Piaget, 1958, p. 337), and his suggestion that modern children were equal in the development of Thought to the pre-Socratic philosophers (author's capitalization) (Piaget, 1962, p. 198) (Bringuier, 1980, p. 48). Piaget even insists that the great Aristotle did not develop beyond the level of concrete operations (Piaget & Inhelder, 1969, p. 148), while admitting that on the basis of language alone we cannot tell whether a statement is concrete or formal (Inhelder & Piaget, 1958, p. 280)! A pertinent question then presents itself: on what basis other than Aristotle's language did the great logician classify Aristotle? When we read these examples it is difficult to realize that Piaget is focused on the immanent Absolute Subject within, not flesh and blood individuals.

WHY PIAGET CANNOT ACCEPT NATURAL SCIENCE

Formal thought is produced by the Combinatorial System (author's capitalization) (Inhelder & Piaget, 1958, p. 254-5) or the Body of Monads and the operations of this System transcends the bounds of natural or brain-based thought (author's capitalization) (Piaget, 1972, p. 64) (Piaget, 1973c, p. 47). Formal thought is indeed held by Piaget to be thought of the Absolute Himself (author's capitalization) (Piaget, 1970b, pp. 29-30). Far from being a "very good instrument for scientific reasoning" (Flavell, 1963, p. 208) or a move "towards genuinely scientific methods of analysis" (ibid., p. 210) as expounded by Flavell, *formal thought is the diametrical opposite of scientific thought.* The physical universe, as noted previously, is the exact opposite of the Absolute Subject and must be eliminated by assimilation. Piaget neither approves of the physical universe for any other purpose nor does he approve of investigations by natural science of this universe, as that would mean accepting the validity of physical data. The aim of traditional science, on the other hand, is to understand every aspect of this physical universe and utilize it for the benefit of man. Piaget speaks to this circumstance, which to him is essentially negative, by declaring that scientific experimentation calls for the "acceptance of external authorities"

(Piaget, 1974a, p. 23). By "external authorities" he simply means facts pertinent to the the physical universe. How can the Absolute Subject submit to the authority of physical facts when, from the standpoint of Gnosticism, they represent the enemy?

Piaget cannot afford to accept natural science, within the framework of his theory, although at times he pretends to. He is not interested in the collection of *contingent* facts about the physical universe (Piaget, 1971c, p. 115), as he considers the "brute facts" of immediate experience to *always be misleading* (author's italics and capitalization) (ibid., p. 70). This is because contemporary logical positivism, or natural science, "reduces the whole of reality to physical phenomena and a language" (Piaget, 1971c, p. 40). "The whole universe of science is constructed on the lived world" or reality as just described, but "if the world of science is really 'constructed' on the lived world, it is not ... constructed on its foundations, *for the aim of scientific thought is always to get away from this lived world, contradicting it instead of utilizing it*" (author's italics) (ibid., p. 87) The Subject knows what to do with His operations; He carves up the facts and *distorts* them as desired (author's italics and capitalization (Piaget, 1974a, p. 31) - after all, the facts of reality represent His opposite. The bottom line is that factual data *cannot be introduced* into the Logico-Mathematical Field - the Field of Monads (author's italics and capitalization) (Beth & Piaget, 1966, pp. 150-1). *Piaget despises natural science; for him, Science consists exclusively of the dialectical operations performed by the Absolute as He assimilates physical reality and thereby develops Himself* (author's italics and capitalization) (Piaget, 1971c, p. 115) (Piaget, 1974a, p. 56) (Piaget, 1970b, p. 121).

THE PURPOSE OF THE BOOK

Piaget's theory is intrinsically simple and brief, so it should be described in only a few words. Indeed the preceding pages of this introduction covers the essential features of his theory. The great complexity and confusion which has always surrounded it was artificially contrived by Piaget, with the express purpose of making his own position incommunicable - surely one of the strangest objectives in intellectual history. Since Piaget's simple and brief theory has already been set forth, what is the purpose of the book? The rather ambitious purpose is to reverse a process that has gone awry since the third decade of the 20th century. This calls for more than a brief summary of ideas, as this anti-science, anti-human, and anti-education juggernaut, based on the grossest sort of deceptions, must be portrayed in the most clear and complete way possible. Anyone who tries to make Piaget's theoretical position clear must overcome the host of ruses this intelligent, highly motivated man devised during his long professional life to prevent clear conceptualization of his theory. He must also overcome the inertia of common but fallacious understandings, in vogue for most of the 20th Century, regarding his work. These two qualifying factors are the reason this book was not written in the middle seventies rather than the late nineties. Although fortunate enough to gain an insight into the nature of his system within a year after beginning my study, another 25 years of labor were necessary before I felt prepared to deal adequately with his "almost incommunicable" theory. It is one thing to understand Piaget's position; it is quite another to *be able to prove every important point with his own words,* which is what I wished to do.

About six thousand quotes were accumulated from his many publications and analyzed in terms of meaning and word usage, a tedious process that required more than half a million words in addition to the quotes. Forty notebooks were prepared to display, and afford ready access to, his use of key terms. As one would expect, however, it is not easy to have Piaget clearly refute the fallacious concepts ascribed to him as he seldom provided more than partial support in any particular place, and this ambiguously, for any of his true but formerly secret doctrines. For instance, in describing a doctrine he usually sketched the role of only one of the two entities of his dual system. The role of the other entity would then be described in another chapter or another book, often utilizing different sets of words. How could one use economically such widely scattered, chopped-up, abortive quotes? Few readers would have the patience to meaningfully connect such widely dispersed and attenuated evidence. The value of methodically cataloging his important statements is that it enables one to locate the few instances where he does clearly refute supposed common knowledge about his position. *The scores of misleading arguments and chains of reasoning made by Piaget over 60 years must be laid open so that their disguised meaning becomes obvious. This remains imperative regardless of how repetitive the conclusions may be,* because several thousand books and papers have been published on the basis of false and potentially hazardous inferences derived from these various arguments. The modus operandi for unraveling Piaget's specious declarations will be the utilization of a large number of moderately long quotes, which are interpreted with the help of copious cross references. Anyone who has access to Piaget's books will not have to search endlessly for further evidence regarding the doctrines examined, as numerous references will make it easy to follow up on most questions one may have concerning his heretofore secret theory.

PIAGET'S DUAL SYSTEM

The second chapter introduces Piaget's overall dual postulate of Absolute Subject and physical universe. The master key to Piaget's theory is the dual nature of his Gnostic philosophy, and the reason the academic world has foundered on his theory is its refusal to recognize this duality. Since this refusal has been firmly established by a long ingrained continuance, the first step must consist in validating his anchorage in this metaphysical-physical dual system. Academia will never get to first base in understanding his theory until this fundamental duality is recognized. Unfortunately for Piagetians, once the duality is acknowledged as valid there will be nothing left to promote except a very unique metaphysics. Unless Piagetians are motivated by the same metaphysical doctrines that drive Piaget, his philosophy will likely die on the vine. Perhaps this pivotal circumstance has become a psychological obstacle to accepting the evidence of duality. Be that as it may, Piaget does not deserve all of the censure. He is indeed outrageous in his use of a host of synonymous verbal entities with dual meanings, with his constant switches from one of the meanings to the other for the purpose of confusion and deception, his utilization of the trappings of science to conceal his metaphysics, which is virulently anti-scientific, and his misuse of grammar, punctuation, syntax, parallelism and other conventions to thwart comprehension. But it is equally outrageous that his interpreters have obtusely turned a blind eye to the unequivocal evidence regarding the metaphysical Entity of his dual system.

The first duality to be examined is the two *biologies*, followed by two kinds of *knowledge* which are based on the two different *minds* of the two biologies. Among other dualities examined are two kinds of *atom*; two kinds of *space*; two kinds of *structure*, two *subjects*, two kinds of *cause*, two kinds of *experience*, two kinds of *science*, two kinds of *psychology*, two kinds of *object*, two kinds of *development*, two kinds of *heredity*, two kinds of *actions and functions*, two kinds of *ontogeny*, two *societies* and two *civilizations*. *Each of the dualities represents the same metaphysical Entity or His activity, and His opposite, the same physical entity or its "activity".* All of Piaget's dualities, with which we are concerned, refer to the same two antagonistic entities, and since his theory is consistently dual, all of the above, as well as other dualities, will be further elaborated in chapters two through five. There is a great abundance of data supporting the basic concept of duality. But further restatements of "two kinds of" would not convince anyone who would not be convinced by the evidence presented.

THE MARVELOUS MONAD

The third chapter is based on the vital concept of monadism, which has also remained unknown in spite of the fact that it was thoroughly developed by Piaget. Of course, his communications regarding this subject are guarded, ambiguous and deceitful. Piaget's metaphysical Biology and Psychology is derived exclusively from his concept of the Body of Monads, the immaterial, weightless, volumeless, conscious, living, eternal, entities which collectively account for everything that exists. *They produced their opposite, the physical universe, by an emanation from themselves, thus creating a disequilibrium which can only be restored by reversing the physical universe back into themselves by the process of operational assimilation.* Why create a disequilibrium? This disequilibrium and the great "intellectual" effort to regain equilibrium is regarded as the only way the Group of monads can fully develop their Combinatorial Intelligence. This is being accomplished by an extremely long series of dialectical interactions with the physical universe, called operations.

One of the problems of consistency in capitalizing synonyms of the Absolute Subject is seen in "Combinatorial Intelligence". This would ordinarily indicate an attribute of the Entity rather than the Entity Himself, but if Piaget illogically personalizes "Intelligence" giving it the meaning, "Body of Monads", as he often does, the development of "Combinatorial Intelligence" would then denote development of Himself rather than merely "development of His intelligence"!

The monads have three roles in Piaget's theory. First, all monads are parts of Piaget's particular deity (Piaget, 1971a, pp. 327-8) (Piaget, 1972, pp. 46-49). Second, Sub-Groups of monads are busily assimilating all physical objects in the universe. Third, they also have the more or less auxiliary functions of moving large celestial objects to produce time (Piaget, 1969, pp. 79; 83) (Piaget, 1954, p. 384) (Piaget, 1970c, p. 59) (Piaget, 1971c, p. 171), the seasons and, in general, maintaining an orderly physical universe (Piaget, 1971a, pp. 361-2). Every physical movement is ultimately caused by the monads, and every physical biological system depends upon Sub-Groups of immanent monads, called endomorphs (author's capitalization) (Piaget, 1971a, p. 170) for all of its physiological processes and all of its activities.

In writing this chapter I wished to highlight the role of monads by describing aspects of Piaget's theory that prominently features them. One such topic is "the other meaning of egocentrism". There are two egos and they are diametrical opposites. The physical ego is intrusive (Piaget, 1929, pp. 45-6) and is neither causal nor Substantial (author's capitalization) (Piaget, 1971a, p. 94), while the Ego composed of spiritual atoms or monads is Substantial (author's capitalization) (Piaget & Inhelder, 1974, pp. 79; 112) and omnipotent (Piaget, 1954, p. 272). This Self or Ego causes natural phenomena (author's capitalization) (Piaget, et al., 1977, p. 175) by means of invariant actions that are not physical because they are based on a Combinatorial System and not anatomical connections (author's capitalization) (Piaget, 1978b, p. 96). In order to cause all natural phenomena they must be everywhere, of course, from the interior of viruses to the interior of stars. The Combinatorial System is another name for the Ancient Schemas (author's capitalization) (Piaget, 1928, p. 228) or "Innermost Self" which lives in the physical body and activates it, *but is not part of the body* (author's italics and capitalization) (Piaget, 1971c, p. 151). Ancient Schemas and their constituent monads thus belong to the Eternal Absolute Self or Ego. This other Ego is the basis for Piaget's claims for "Absolute Egocentricity" which in turn "implies magic" (author's capitalization) (Piaget, 1929, p. 251). Magical causality, insists Piaget, depends upon the child's consciousness of this other Self (author's capitalization) (ibid., p. 250). Expressed in another way: "according to [the concept of] magical causality ... all things revolve around the Self" (author's capitalization) (ibid., p. 235).

This Absolute Self is the source of magic as His monads inside of the individual person cooperate with His monads outside of the individual to produce "disembodied" magic (author's capitalization) (Piaget, 1971c, p. 140-1). Piaget calls this metaphysical magic "Intelligence" (author's capitalization) (Piaget, 1929, p. 436).

Piaget's metaphysical concept of *measurement* is quite interesting as the organized Groups of monads, or Egos, called "Measuring Factories" (author's capitalization) (Piaget, 1928, p. 196) must measure their own assimilatory progress. Monads are able to "observe" and measure the progress of assimilation because they completely fill every object and person, which enables them to observe and measure for the purpose of matching opposite classes of the dual entities (Piaget & Inhelder, 1956, p. 247). Precise measures of how much assimilation has occurred permits the proper pairing of opposites for the continual dialectical interaction that must take place until the physical universe is completely assimilated.

One of the most unusual functions of the monads is their production of elements, molecules, soil, stones, planets, stars and all natural objects (Piaget, 1929, pp. 385; 428). *The method is quite simple but it is bizarre.* Chemistry and physics, as taught at the university, are physical sciences, so cannot be valid according to Piaget's theory. Not surprisingly, the monads can duplicate everything chemistry can accomplish, in fact they actually are the unobservable actors in the productions of scientific chemistry as they activate the more or less recalcitrant brains of the scientists. *In any case, Piaget knows how the monads actually make things independent of people.* Chemists use a variety of methods, but Piaget informs us that *the monads make all of the things we see in nature with only one method. It is called "compression and decompression"* (Piaget & Inhelder, 1974, pp. 110; 130; 145; 148; 150; 177-8), *"condensation and rarefaction"* (Piaget, 1929, pp. 385; 388; 392) (Piaget, 1930, pp. 265-6) *or "contraction and expansion"* (Piaget & Inhelder, 1956, p. 466). This is the "mental" manipulation of matter by the ability of monads to "compress" and "decompress" matter thus diversifying and fine tuning reality. It was clearly the essential process, according to Piagetian doctrine, used by the monads in "making" man, or homo faber, himself. One can understand why Piagetians have carefully avoided discussion of his unique, metaphysically based chemistry and physics!

Natural phenomena are produced by the special Mathematical Structure (author's capitalization) (Piaget, 1972, pp. 80-1) or Universal Biological Organization (author's capitalization) (Beth & Piaget, 1966, p. 285), that is, the Body of Monads. As Piaget says, observable phenomena require an Underlying Structure (author's capitalization) (Piaget, 1974b, p. 125).

Perhaps the most outlandish explanation of natural phenomena that Piaget advances is how the monads provide for sight. He first removes by decree the established fact that reflected light from the object enters the eye where an image of the object is produced. He does this by proclaiming flatly that "there is no light that goes from the object to the eye" (Piaget, 1974b, p. 28). So how does the exalted biologist from Geneva explain sight? He does so, as he must, by reference to his theory of monads. First, "there is a perfect continuity between the impulse in the brain", which is caused by the monads, "and the movements of the object" (Piaget, 1929, pp. 266-7), which are recorded by the monads existing between the eye and the object. This continuity among the monads in the brain, eye, object and between the eye and the object, coordinate their separate activities so perfectly that we are able to see. There is always a perfect continuity of monads between the brain, the eye and any object whatsoever on which one might focus - even stars billions of light-years away.

This perfect continuity of monads between the brains of individuals and objects also explains Piaget's concept of memory. An additional attribute of the monads is necessary, however, in the explanation of memory, and that is "continuity over time". Continuity over time is provided by the "fact" that monads remember everything that has happened since the creation of the universe (Piaget & Inhelder 1973, pp. 1; 116) (Piaget, 1954, pp. 393-4), not only that, but everything is remembered *simultaneously* (author's italics) (Piaget, 1950, pp. 120-1) (Piaget, 1969a, p. 71)! *Piaget claimed, for instance, that he was able to remember what the other side of the moon looked like before any man had ever seen the other side of the moon* (author's italics) (Piaget, 1969b, p. 285). How could he "remember" under these conditions? It was Piaget's true Ego who not only could remember, but who made, constantly observes and assimilates the other side of the moon. This Ego composed of monads enjoys a perfect continuity of "sight" and memory between Piaget and the other side of the moon, so Piaget the man could be vouchsafed the "memory" if his true Ego so desired.

This perfect continuity with respect to temporality is also demonstrated in the answers some children give regarding their birth dates when compared with their parents' birth dates. *Many children claim that they were born before their parents. Piaget chimes in, stressing that the children are emphasizing a "kind of truth",* which is the "fact" that "time ... begins with the dawn of their Own memory" (author's italics and capitalization) (Piaget, 1969a, p. 205). Since the memory of the child's true Ego extends back to the beginning of time, we perceive the "kind of truth" that Piaget has in mind!

In one of his earliest books, *The Child's Conception of Physical Causality* (Piaget, 1930), Piaget displays his aptitude for taking a physical concept, air, and gradually transforming it into a metaphysical concept - the Medium of Monads. The first chapter begins with the child's supposed ideas about the movement and origin of air. He introduces his "experiments" with questions designed to lead the child to express Piaget's initial "target notion" that "air" is alive (ibid., p. 3). *Since monads are alive this is a good idea.* Next he leads the child to agree that inside air "participates" with outside air, which is "rational" and "logical" because both inside and outside air belong to the same being (ibid., p. 9) - *a very reasonable progression since inside or immanent monads and outside monads also belong to the same Being.* Piaget then overplays his hand by pretending that the child spontaneously arrives at the difficult concept that air has an "impetus sufficient to itself", which makes it self-motivated and self-actualized (ibid., p. 22) - *just like the monads!*

The climax of this forced analogy occurs in the second chapter when Piaget informs us, on the basis of his "experiments", that the child considers the currents of air to be variations of a Single All-Pervading Substance (author's italics and capitalization) (ibid., p. 32), *precisely as his concept of monadism requires!* By shamelessly using children to "prove" ideas he secretly holds but that they clearly do not hold, he lowers himself to the abyss in the eyes of all who understand the meanings involved. He then makes an incredible admission that completely discredits the veracity of his carefully crafted analogy. This insight, he concedes, is not on the same plane as the initial insight about air and it is not even derived from the initial insights. Although Piaget uses the analogy with air to introduce his doctrine of monads, *and he will presently use it again,* he basically admits that the analogy is a ruse because *it does not lead the child to the climactic conclusion of a Continuum of Monads which make up a Single Substantial or Spiritual Being.* In other words, we are left with our mouths open in disbelief as he tells us quite frankly that the analogy he developed between air and the All-Pervading Substance on another plane is really a deception because the insights of the children regarding air could not possibly lead to this Substance *as I have just implied!* The bottom line is that the reader must swallow a most unusual and troubling series of minutely calculated in-your-face lies.

An unrepentant Piaget returns to his "experiments" regarding air a few pages later, and takes a confident look into the Mind of Roy (6 1/2): Roy basically sees his world, pontificates Piaget, as *"a society of organisms produced or fed by air which was blown by Man at the beginning of things"* (author's italics and capitalization) (ibid., p. 45), *which again is embarrassingly accurate regarding his doctrine of monads.* The "society of organisms" are the people produced by the collection of monads called "Man". The monads of "Man" were there at the beginning of things. Significantly, "Man" is one of the "secret" names of God in Gnosticism (Edwards, Vol. 3, p. 237), and Piaget agrees with this meaning (Piaget, 1929, pp. 288; 294). Piaget obviously continues his analogy of air with the monads at the metaphysical level - which compounds the baseness of his lies. After admitting that observations of air could not lead to metaphysical knowledge about monads, Roy, or rather Piaget, is seen to believe, or more accurately insist, that metaphysical "air" actually produced and maintains human beings! *Roy, the physical child, knows nothing about air producing and organizing man's biology and activities, but please note that Roy's Mind is his true Mind consisting of monads which belong to the same Being as the monads in Piaget's true Mind. It is this "fact" which enables Piaget to look inside of Roy's Mind - another kind of continuity which accounts for the scores of instances where Piaget directly reads the Minds of very young children and even of infants less than six months old. See for instance, The Origins of Intelligence in Children* (Piaget, 1952b) and *The Construction of Reality in the Child* (Piaget, 1954). All of the "experiments" or "observations" in these two books are with his own three children who were subjects from hours after birth until shortly before they were two years of age. In the earlier book the vast majority of experiments and observations were with infants less than one year of age. *Based on the "empirical findings" of these two books, Piaget was able to "prove" essentially all of his metaphysical theory!* It is important to consider the fact that Flavell depended very much upon the earlier book, probably more than any other of Piaget's books, in setting forth Piaget's theory. This means that the process which led to our common understanding of Piaget is both comical and alarming. *Infants less than two years of age told Piaget the "secrets" of cognitive development, who passed them on to Flavell, who passed them to professors of psychology and education!* This process is indeed very close to the truth, except for the fact that Piaget's outrageous plan was behind it all. No wonder Piaget believed in magic! The latter book is about the construction of metaphysical Reality, not physical reality.

In *The Child's Conception of the World* (Piaget, 1929), Piaget emphasizes the inside-outside property of the Body of Monads in his study of thought and dreams. First-stage children agree with Piaget that thought does not occur in the head or body. Observe that Piaget is not concerned that this statement is partially false with regard to his theory. He is only concerned with eventually making the point that "true" thought is confined to the monads. Nevertheless, monads inside the body and brain of the child do indeed think just like the monads outside the child. Second-stage children believe that thought is a voice inside the neck or head, and Piaget insists that the voice is the spontaneous aspect, while the notion that thought is inside the head is based on the contribution of adults (ibid., p. 50). He wishes to get thought dissociated as much as possible from the brain because only monads really think. "It is hard to see how children quite alone could have discovered thinking to be with the head" (ibid., p. 63) - i. e., the brain.

Piaget asserts that the origin of the dream is "both internal and external" (ibid., p. 133). He uses a statement by Mos (11 1/2) to make a key point. Mos says that he cannot see the *dream because it is invisible,* and Piaget interjects this eager elaboration: "This statement is very convincing and shows that Mos is not speaking of images one thinks one sees outside, but of Something invisible which is projected by Thought and which produces the images outside" (author's capitalization) (ibid., p. 138). Piaget is excited because it gives him an opportunity to focus on the metaphysical producer of the dream - the invisible monads of which the invisible "Something" or "Thought" consists.

In *The Child's Conception of Space* (Piaget & Inhelder, 1956), one will never see the word "monad" and seldom see "atom", but the entire book is about monads and the Spatial Continuum monads compose. Piaget approaches the concept by asking children about "points" that remain when physical objects are reduced in size. *The points, which eventually become immaterial, are then utilized to make lines and eventually to make "a Homogeneous and Continuous Entity composed of the sum total of adjacent points"* (author's italics and capitalization) (ibid., p. 148) - *an excellent definition of the Continuum of Monads. One hundred and forty five pages later, following some "unrelated filler" to confuse the reader, the points become a Living Overall System capable of operations* (author's italics and capitalization (ibid., p. 292). *Seventy five pages later the "Overall System" is a Homogeneous Environment consisting of objects (monads) which make up a Frame of Reference or Continuum* (author's italics and capitalization) (ibid., p. 376). Piaget admits, as he did in his analogy with air, that these objects are "located on another plane" (ibid., p. 377) and that they perform operations (ibid., p. 404), meaning that they are metaphysical. *This book represents a huge investment of time and energy, but Piaget had only one objective: begin with a material object, reduce it until there is only an immaterial point remaining, then build his metaphysical Entity with the immaterial points, which he subtly suggests is "atomism"* (author's italics and capitalization) (ibid., p. 147). In the final conclusions, Piaget also admits that the experiment with points did not lead the child to the "idea of Space" (author's capitalization) (ibid., 453), as only "experiments" - that is, a series of assimilatory operations - on the child by the Internal Schemata within the child can lead him to the concept of monads and the Continuum of Space they compose (author's capitalization) (ibid., 454).

The concept of monads is a key to understanding Piaget's metaphysical system and much of his phraseology, so we would expect to encounter numerous synonyms. Twenty one such equivalent words are listed below. This is not a long list, but Piaget increases complexity by using some of the terms in a variety of very different contexts, often with different meanings: *agent* (Piaget, 1974b, p. 42), *air* (ibid., p. 112) (Piaget, 1930, p. 45), *atom* (Piaget, 1953, pp. 24-5) (Piaget, 1967, p. 43) (Piaget, 1970, p. 8) (Piaget & Inhelder, 1974, pp. VIII; 79; 266-7), *corpuscle* (ibid., pp. 72; 79) (Piaget, 1972, p. 49), *crumb* (Piaget & Inhelder, 1974, p. 72), *dust* (ibid., pp. 68; 72; 78-9), *element* (Piaget & Inhelder, 1956, pp. 145; 456; 466) (Piaget & Inhelder, 1973, p. 404) (Piaget, 1970b, p. 20) (Piaget, 1973c, p. 21), *force* (Piaget, 1929, p. 235), *grain* (Piaget & Inhelder, 1974, pp. 60; 81; 112; 276-7), *invariant* (ibid., p. 110), *macromolecule* (Piaget, 1974b, p. 42), *monad* (Piaget, 1954, p. 317) (Piaget, 1970b, p. 41) (Piaget, 1971a, p. 78) (Piaget, 1971c, p. 52), *object* (Piaget, 1954, pp. 97; 299) (Piaget, 1928, p. 192) (Piaget, 1950, p. 110) (Piaget, 1972, p. 89) (Piaget, 1974b, p. IX), *operator* (Piaget, 1971a, p. 337) (Piaget, et al., 1977, p. 179), *particle* (Piaget, 1930, p. 266) (Piaget & Inhelder, 1974, pp. 60; 72), *point* (Piaget & Inhelder, 1956, pp. 126; 145; 147-8), *position* (Piaget, Inhelder & Szeminska, 1960, p. 404), *powder* (Piaget & Inhelder, 1974, pp. 78-9), *quantum* (ibid., p. 16), *site* (Piaget, Inhelder & Szeminska, 1960, pp. 87; 90; 115) and *structure* (Beth & Piaget, 1966, p. 298). Anyone who wishes to understand Piaget's concept of monads could use these references as a helpful shortcut.

THE ABSOLUTE SUBJECT

Chapter four centers on the Absolute Personality Himself. Of course, it is not possible to isolate the Entity from His complementary opposite (technically it is probably incorrect to call the relationship of the metaphysical-physical duality "complementary", as the meaning is actually "antithetical"), the physical universe, with which He is in continuous dialectical interaction. Likewise it is not possible to isolate Him from the monads of which He is composed and the variety of activities in which monads are engaged. However, the focus is on the Absolute with a thousand names.

Kant believed that "reason precipitates itself into darkness and contradictions" once it enters metaphysics (Edwards, 1967, Vol. 4, p. 308). Both Hegel and Piaget completely disagree with Kant, holding that reason alone leads us to the Absolute Subject. Karl Popper believed that Hegel precipitated intellectual darkness into the world that ultimately was a major factor in the development of both communism and fascism (Popper, 1966, p. 30). Quoting Schopenhauer, Popper claims that Hegel's success was the beginning of the "age of dishonesty" (ibid., p. 28). *In extending Hegel's philosophy and emulating his grandiose and dogmatic linguistic style, Piaget has, in my opinion, precipitated darkness into the academic world by his arrogant, undercover assertion of philosophical principles that for obvious reasons have not been properly examined.* This should not be surprising as his model, Hegel, is said to be the father of modern totalitarianism (ibid., p. 22).

All natural structures, argues Piaget, are anchored in and organized by the non-human, immaterial Biological activity of the Absolute. "All philosophers in search of an Absolute have had recourse to some transcendental Subject, something on a higher plane than man" (author's capitalization) (Piaget, 1971a, p. 362). Moreover, all Knowledge is assimilated by a Permanent Structure that can never be destroyed (author's capitalization) (Piaget, 1971c. p. 8). This last statement is obviously foolish unless he is speaking of an invisible Subject inside of the visible subject. Piaget sometimes differentiates the two subjects in rather provocative ways. He reports, for instance, that the *physical field of Gestalt theory is not psychogenetic because it has no Subject* (author's italics and capitalization) (Piaget, 1977, p. 98). Gestalt theory has a subject, of course, but it is the lower-level subject! Psychogenesis, in contrast, is the gradual development of the Absolute Subject by means of operations or equilibrations, so *the Field of Monads where psychogenesis occurs has, or rather is, the Subject.*

This Subject capable of psychogenesis has many distinguishing characteristics. Consider this superhuman one: "The Logico-Mathematical Structures of the Intelligence" afford an "all-embracing prevision" (author's capitalization) (Piaget, 1971a, p. 211). So the Subject or Logico-Mathematical Structure knows all about the future. Piaget even reminds us of the all-knowing monads outside of people with this additional comment. Even "if one were to take Mathematical Entities as external to the subject, what has just been said would still be valid" (author's capitalization) (ibid., pp. 211-12). True, Piaget is using plural synonyms, but if one is aware that *Groups* of monads are doing the work of the single Absolute, the plurals are easier to tolerate. In any case, this Mathematical Structure or Entity knows exactly what will happen in the future. Why do Piagetians ignore such superhuman statements?

Piaget suggests that the Epistemological Domain is occupied by a non-perceptible Reality (author's capitalization) (Beth & Piaget, 1966, p. 149). The Epistemological Domain, by definition the domain where valid Knowledge is acquired, has nothing to do, then, with the study of human knowledge acquisition. No, the Epistemological Domain is the Field of Monads or the Homogeneous Medium of the Absolute Subject who is constantly involved in perfecting Himself by means of operations - *this is the process of genetic Epistemology!* Piaget underlines this notion when he asserts that "the Subject-Psychologist constructs His Epistemology as a function of ... His Science" and that there is "no need for the [human] philosopher to intervene ... in order to construct a complete Epistemology" (author's capitalization) (Piaget, 1971c, pp. 224-5). *No human philosopher is needed to produce valid Knowledge!* The situation is complicated, however, when Piaget specifically speaks of an "inner Epistemology" which is based on "psychogenetic mechanisms" (author's capitalization) (Piaget, 1971b, p. 147). Valid Knowledge, then, is produced both inside and outside of people, and in neither case is a human being, philosopher or not, required to intervene. *The Subject-Psychologist, composed of monads, is alone able to acquire valid Knowledge - regardless of whether He is inside or outside of human beings. This is a strange kind of Knowledge produced by the assimilation process, but it is exactly the kind that motivated Piaget to decide to consecrate his life to establishing the Biological explanation of Knowledge or Epistemology* (Piaget, 1976b, p. 119).

A recent illustration of how Piaget has conned the academic community regarding the nature of epistemology and science is an article by Seymour Papert, Professor at M.I.T. Professor Papert was chosen by *Time* to prepare a short article about Piaget, who was honored as one of the 100 most influential people of this past century. He writes that "the theory of knowledge ... was considered a branch of philosophy until Piaget came along and made it a science" (Papert, 1999). This quote is basically a repetition of the citation given Piaget by the American Psychological Association (Piaget, 1972, p. 15) - a citation which Piaget definitely repudiates (ibid., p. 10) (Piaget, 1980b, p. 10). Piaget had a very high regard for Dr. Papert, complimenting him more highly, I believe, than any of his other associates. By far the most intriguing compliment was that Papert's "polyvalence had convinced him of the existence of the Subject" and that his "Epistemology is centered on the constructions of this Subject" (author's capitalization) (Piaget, 1971c, p. 36). These are truly amazing statements, as Piaget is claiming that Papert accepts the very core of his metaphysical system - *his basically secret metaphysical system! Does Papert share Piaget's closely guarded secret?* I doubt it. If we are to believe Piaget, Papert became convinced, based on his superior intellectual aptitude in various fields, that the Subject existed within him, making the source of his multi-faceted intellect the metaphysical Subject Himself - thus also accepting Piaget's doctrine of vicarious intelligence. Piaget audaciously asserts that Papert not only accepts his concept of the Absolute Subject but that his Epistemology is based on the constructions, that is, Self-development, of this Subject. Could this be based on good evidence, or is it merely wishful thinking on the part of Piaget? Does Papert really agree with Piaget that Epistemology, or the theory of valid Knowledge, should be limited to the developmental processes involved in the metaphysical construction of a perfect Absolute Subject - and completely ignore human knowledge acquisition? I doubt very much that Papert's basic concepts are similar to Piaget's, and I would also be surprised if Papert has read any of Piaget's major works. Perhaps he will eventually enlighten us.

The Absolute Structure is called the Structure of All Structures; it is a Living System and, according to Piaget, could be called "Society", "Life" or "Cosmos" (author's capitalization) (Piaget, 1970b, p. 142). Furthermore, this Structure or Mind was prior to physical, organic biology and it is not even "mental" (author's capitalization) (ibid., pp. 111-12). The Structure of All Structures or Mind, then, existed before everything known by natural science came into being. This Structure is diachronic or Normative while conventional structures, the only kind studied by traditional science, are synchronic (author's capitalization) (ibid., p. 79). "Diachronics", in Piaget's System, refers to the "fact" that the "Mind", or Body of Monads, is the only Entity who *exists through all time.*

The Operational Structure or Set of All Sub-Sets is the Spatial Continuum or Absolute Subject who is made up of unobservable corpuscles (author's capitalization) (Piaget, 1972, p.. 49). These living corpuscles have, among other amazing attributes, the capacity to do their work without expending energy (Piaget, 1974b, pp. 46-7; 100; 123), remember everything simultaneously that has happened since the beginning of creation (Piaget & Inhelder, 1973, pp. 116) (Piaget, 1950, pp., 120-1) and when they are not moving matter they move at absolute speed (Piaget, 1974b, p. 144) (Piaget, 1970a, pp. 121; 188; 293) (Piaget, Inhelder & Szeminska, 1960, p. 65). We know these are bona fide attributes because we have Piaget's word for it!

Piaget presents us with another superhuman attribute of the Structure composed of monads. The regulations or operations of the Structure are "not subject to any error if it is in conformity with the laws of the Structure" (author's capitalization) (Piaget, 1971a, pp. 210-11). This ambiguous statement is followed by, "an error in logic or in mathematics [has] nothing to do with the Structure" in the child (author's capitalization) (ibid., pp. 210-11). *The only way these errors can occur, affirms Piaget, is when an individual slips.* We cannot, of course, blame the immanent Structure for that!

The Permanent Structure lives in every physical organism and, as we have seen, can never be destroyed (author's capitalization) (Piaget, 1971c, p. 8). This is the Epistemological Subject on whose existence all valid Knowledge depends (author's capitalization) (ibid., p. 64); It not only determines what the subject is capable of doing, but also what he must do. "It is He who imposes certain Forms" on the subject (author's capitalization) (Piaget, 1973a, p. 33). *The Subject or Structure is called a "He", and this "He" imposes Himself on the physical subject as "certain Forms". Please note that "certain Forms" is also "He" and is identical with the Structure - as Piaget makes a mockery of the normal communication process!*

Piaget made a clear distinction between the physical regulators studied by natural science and the Logico-Mathematical Structure who is the true Regulator (author's capitalization) (Piaget, 1977, p. 22). This Regulator is the Primordial Biological System who is not a physical-chemical totality (author's capitalization) (ibid., p. 22).

In the history of philosophy only two individuals besides Piaget appear to stand out as conceiving God as "bodily" filling all of space. Isaac Newton, the great natural scientist, conceived of the Biblical God in spatial terms. He conceived of this Spatial Entity as a Container (author's capitalization) (Piaget, 1974b, p. 149), but he did not try to specify its dynamics as does Piaget. The Swedish philosopher Emanuel Swedenborg, while studying in England, was influenced by his contemporary Newton (Edwards, 1967, Vol. 8, pp. 48-51) and elaborated a concept of the Divinity considerably closer to Piaget's ideas. In fact, it appears likely that Piaget was influenced by him. Swedenborg, like Piaget, took additional ideas from Descartes and Leibniz. For instance, he conceived of God, as does Piaget, as creating and maintaining nature by means of emanations from "mathematical points." Although he did not call the points "monads", they appear to be quite similar to Piaget's monads.

The single most important statement by Piaget regarding the Spatial Entity is probably found on the first page of his book about time. He succinctly shows Space to be both the source of all relationships between all possible bodies as well as the source that endows these bodies with an [immanent] Structure. Space is called the Logic of the apparent or physical world because it is a System of Operations, and it is called the Mind because it knows how to perform these operations (author's capitalization) (Piaget, 1969a, p. 1). From the beginning there exists the Geometric Space of Operational Action, who is the Subject that assimilates objects and people (author's capitalization) (Piaget, Inhelder & Szeminska, 1960, p. 208). This Operational Space is psychologically organized in a three-dimensional Reference Frame which is a Spatial Field of Monads that is unlimited in scope (author's capitalization) (Piaget, 1956, p. 416). The Field is the Living Organism who is capable of multiple interactions (author's capitalization) (Piaget, 1971a, p. 34) because He fills every nook and cranny of the universe. Other names for the Field are Lattice, Group and Thought.

A good example of how Piaget's carefully crafted ambiguity and endless disguises can derail the academic process is seen in Flavell's assertion that "groups", "lattices" and "mathematical structures" are nonpsychological in origin (Flavell, 1963, pp. 168-9). These three terms have been employed many times to describe a conscious, living being, so why does Flavell insist that they are nonpsychological? Could it be that, although he realizes the terms could not refer to human beings, he simply does not wish to concede that Piaget is concerned exclusively with a non-human, but nevertheless psychological Being who is the source of everything? One can easily understand why Flavell and other Piagetians would be reluctant to concede this central point, especially after devoting many years of their professional lives to the generally assumed significance of Piaget's work. This concession would clearly obviate any practical significance of Piaget's theory for human beings. The Lattice-Group or Logico-Mathematical Structure is the Fundamental Psychological Reality in Piaget's System (author's capitalization) (Piaget, 1971b, p. 114-15) (Piaget, 1970b, p. 138) (Piaget, 1954, pp. 112; 235-6), and for Flavell to assign these terms the lowly role of "nonpsychological" abstractions has undoubtedly had a long-term affect in retarding a clear understanding of Piaget's theory.

Physical movements of every kind, from the speed of light to the speed of impulses among neurons in the brain, take time. Communication among the monads of the Mind, however, do not take time, as we have seen, because these movements are instantaneous or at absolute speed (author's capitalization) (Piaget, 1974b, p. 144). Piaget expresses no doubt about this purely imaginary, untestable postulate.

To revisit a telling question that Piaget rhetorically asks about Space, which he also calls the Natural Horizontal and Vertical References of the Lattice, we consider again the two possibilities - does the child use Space or does Space use the child? The question is, does the child use Space to construct comprehensive systems of spatial relations and measurements, or is it "the other way about" (author's capitalization) (Piaget, Inhelder & Szeminska, 1960, p. 484)? Piaget is speaking of metaphysical relations and measurements, so the answer is clear. It is "the other way about", as the immanent monads of Space are "measuring" the child for the double purpose of assimilating him and simultaneously furthering His own development toward perfection.

ACTIVITIES OF THE ABSOLUTE SUBJECT

The fifth chapter deals primarily with the main activity of the Absolute Subject, namely His operations on physical reality. He operates constantly as this is His only method of development, a development that could not be human as it does not depend upon chance in any way (Piaget, 1977, pp. 174-5). Unlike the development of people, it is guided by a "direct and unwavering teleonomy" (Piaget, 1978b, pp. 98-9), which is a fully determined process based on the laws of "Biology" (author's capitalization) (Piaget, 1971b, pp. 6-7) who is also called an intervening Regulator (author's capitalization) (Piaget, 1977, p. 19). Piaget describes this pattern or process of development as an inevitable progression "once thought turns away from false absolutes" (Piaget, 1970b, p. 123) and, by implication, to the true Absolute.

What is the relation of the invincible operations to the hundreds of experiments Piaget and his associates have carried out regarding the nature of development? We know that Piaget rejects "copy knowledge", or knowledge about physical reality as it is (Piaget, 1950, pp. 92-3), which is precisely the non-assimilatory knowledge for which scientists like Newton and Einstein are honored. Piaget thus rejects the validity of the "hands on" experimentation pushed by science educators in his name, along with the value of natural science *and the verity of all the "physical experiments" he and his associates have performed. The truth is that his trumpeted experiments with children have essentially the same function as his multiple verbalisms; they create opportunities for sowing confusion and deceiving his investigators.* Piaget's extremely negative evaluations of the scientific experiment must be taken into account. It is imperative that his general conclusions regarding his own experiments be examined before we accept them as being scientific in nature. *Does it make sense to embrace his "experimental results" as traditional scientific findings when he most assuredly does not?* Piaget "makes" children agree with him that traditional experiments are worse than useless. He proclaims that children "hold experiment in utter contempt: the result of a particular experiment tells them nothing at all about the next [possible experiment]" (Piaget & Inhelder, 1974, p. 242). Piaget is clearly telling us about his own view of experiments, not the child's, as he gives a reason why physical or scientific experiments are contemptible that young children would not give. Some of Piaget's most famous experiments are described in the book from which the last quote was taken, particularly the conservation experiments with the ball of clay, the dissolving sugar grains and the expansion of popcorn. *What is the meaning of these experiments to Piaget in terms of his theory?* When we look at his general conclusions regarding these experiments, as well as all other physical experiments with which he is connected, causation and meaning is never based on anything physical. The ultimate cause and meaning is always based on the activities or intentions of the Body of Monads. In this particular book the explanatory term used over and over to cover the cause and meaning is "atomism" - in this case, meaning immaterial, metaphysical atomism. As one would expect, in his effort to keep his reader frustrated and off balance, Piaget also uses the term "atomism" in many contexts to mean material atomism.

Before we examine what Piaget means by a "true" experiment, we should note one of his reasons for performing the "scientific" experiments that he basically despises. As we have seen, he admits that his express purpose for pretending that he is an empiricist is to provide a "more telling" criticism of empiricism (Beth & Piaget, 1966, p. 148). Since Piaget wishes to undermine and eventually overthrow empiricism, he obviously does not "start from the same basis" as empiricists, which is what he claims. Physical experimentation vis-a-vis Piaget's doctrine of assimilation makes this logically impossible, because "experimentation is not a free or even a direct spontaneous product of Intelligence; it calls for acceptance of external authorities" (author's capitalization) (Piaget, 1974a, p. 23). It is impossible for Piaget to accept any aspect of physical reality - "external authorities" - as sovereign. *All of the established facts of natural science are included in the domain of "external authorities" - a domain that must eventually be eliminated by the operations of Gnostic Intelligence!* Furthermore, Piaget claims to be a "tireless opponent of empiricism" (Piaget, 1980b, p. 10), and states flatly that "I am no empiricist" (Piaget, 1972, p. 10). *This means, without question, that Piaget is not a natural scientist.*

Piaget grants that we can account for knowledge or development if we are careful to *"analyze what the experiment is"*. The experiment, Piaget roundly asserts, *"always consists in an assimilation to Structures and a turning to a systematic study of the Ipse Intellectus"* (author's italics and capitalization) (Piaget, 1971b, pp. 4-5)! *Although he mixes levels, this is the metaphysical "experiment" the Absolute is in the process of conducting with His opposite on a continuous basis.*

Piaget frequently utilizes the concept of "stage" in presenting his theory of metaphysical development, which is his only theory of development. In passing, he does tell us that man is the "product of a number of interactions" (Piaget, 1971a, p. 283), but he never intended to elaborate a theory of man's intellectual development. The almost universal belief among educators and psychologists that he worked diligently to elaborate such a theory is a cruel hoax. He did indeed work with extreme diligence to create the hoax, but *nothing was further from his mind than to produce a theory of the bio-psychological development of children. He was never interested in "the material object with which the biologist experiments"* (author's italics) (Piaget, 1971b, p. 120), so he would never confuse the *"things"* we call human beings (Piaget & Inhelder, 1969, pp. 23-4) (Piaget, 1971c, p. 183) with the developing Biological Subject he worshiped. He would never pay homage to the "detestable ego" (Inhelder & Piaget, 1958, p. 349) whom he "dislikes" (Piaget, 1970b, p. 68) and holds to be "hateful" (Piaget, 1971c, XVI), by devoting his life to an understanding of its development, when he is vitally concerned with the development of the true Ego or Subject (author's capitalization) (Piaget, 1971a, p. 74) (Piaget, 1973d, pp. 35; 37). The object-person seen in all the textbooks is of no intrinsic importance to Piaget as he is not capable of achieving true Knowledge (author's capitalization) (Piaget, 1969b, p. 285-6). The human thing or object is the "not-self" who obeys the true Self (author's capitalization) (Piaget, 1929, p. 175). The "not-self" is also the "other" which is dissociated from the Self (author's capitalization) (Piaget & Inhelder, 1969, p. 22).

The development of stages cannot be effected by human beings as stages can only be generated by operations (Inhelder & Piaget, 1958, p. 356). The metaphysical Structures, or Classes, are autonomously "generated from one another" by the Hegelian triad of thesis, antithesis and synthesis (author's capitalization) (ibid., p. 356) (Piaget & Inhelder, 1973, p. 137) (Piaget, 1972, p. 14). It should be mentioned that although Hegel utilized the concept of thesis, antithesis and synthesis, plus the fact that Piaget ascribes this concept to him, Hegel apparently never used these three specific terms. It was Fichte, not Hegel, who first introduced this famous triad into German philosophy (Edwards, 1967, Vol. 2, p. 387). In any case, Piaget's famous stages are based on immanent Logico-Mathematical or psychogenetic construction, not on the maturation of physical structures like the brain or on the physical experience that learning provides (author's capitalization) (Piaget, 1980b, p. 81).

As we can see, none of Piaget's concepts have been twisted and mutilated more completely that the concept of "stage". The usual explanations of genetic inheritance, maturation and experience have nothing whatever to do with the autonomous progression of the stages of cognitive development. *Piaget insists repeatedly that the transformations involved are accounted for by a "single explanatory principle"* (author's italics) (Inhelder, Sinclair & Bovet, 1974, pp. 8-9). *This principle is guaranteed by a sequential process based on equilibrations* (author's italics) (Inhelder & Piaget, 1964, pp. 292-3) or operations, producing successive steps or stages in the movement toward equilibrium (Piaget, 1973a, p. 60) (Piaget, 1950, pp. 9; 39) (Piaget, 1952b, p. 407), which is a metaphysical process. Human beings cannot accomplish this task (Inhelder & Piaget, 1964, pp. 292-3).

There is one way in which the psychology of the physical child is important for Piaget. This lower-level psychology is not important because it informs us how the physical child develops, but because it enables Piaget to follow, at least this is what he claims, the step-by-step formative process of the immanent "Living Subject" in the physical "lived" subject (author's capitalization) (Piaget & Inhelder, 1969, p. 159). The "steps" in the development of the immanent Subject which Piaget claims to see are produced by dialectic equilibrations, Self-regulations or operations. Piaget is focused on the imagined metaphysical Subject or Structure in His dialectic engagement with the lived or physical child. The development of children, as such, holds no interest for him at all, except as objects to be eliminated by assimilation.

It is important to understand that the immanent Subject is a Normative Structure - the only Normative Structure, according to Piaget, in existence. This Fundamental Structure does not depend upon human nature because human nature is not permanent (author's capitalization) (Piaget, 1970b, p. 106); it depends completely upon an Entity who is unchangeable (author's capitalization) (Piaget, 1973d, p. 34) and "can never be destroyed" (Piaget, 1971c, p. 8), namely Himself! The Normative Structure moves inexorably toward perfection as it assimilates its opposite, the conventional structures of reality. Furthermore, Normative Structures are "diachronic" as they exist through all time (author's capitalization) (Piaget, 1970b, p. 79) (Piaget, 1974a, p. 4).

Piaget allows us an unsettling glimpse into his feelings and attitude toward the objects and, particularly, the people that will be eliminated by assimilation. The "displacements" of assimilation "leads to the gradual ... 'purging' of Space (if the reader will forgive the metaphor), by progressively emptying it of objects in order to organize the Space or 'Container' itself" (author's capitalization) (Piaget & Inhelder, 1956, p. 377). The metaphor, "purging of Space", is a revealing indication of Piaget's deep-seated anti-social attitude as well as an excellent way to illustrate his concept of assimilation. The Body of Monads, Space or Container must cleanse Himself of all undesirable "impurities". *This purging must eliminate everything in physical reality, including all people. One could well suspect that Piaget's request for forgiveness to the reader being purged, is more sarcastic than sincere!*

Piaget's low opinion of natural science is evident in the following quote. "Any being (or object) that sciences attempt to hold fast dissolves ... in the current of development" (Piaget, 1971b, p. 3). *Everything studied by natural science eventually dissolves in the current of assimilation, which is a necessary concomitant of the Subject's development.* This holds true for every possible natural science from astronomy to zoology. Piaget is basically concerned with only two concepts and they are both metaphysical. First, he is concerned with the attributes of the Absolute Subject; second, he is equally concerned with the Self-developing activities of this Subject. These two concerns converge to the "one fact", the need for His development (ibid., p. 3).

Piaget emphasizes the universal, omnipresent character of His Absolute Subject, as well as His existence as a Universe of Active Monads, by describing Him as *engulfing* the real world in order to "explain" it better. "The Universe of Logico-Mathematical Possibility [does not] replace the real world but rather engulfs it in order to explain it better" (author's capitalization) (Piaget, 1980b, p. 97). The Universe of Monads engulfs everything - every atom, every galaxy in space and everything in between. "Possibility" refers to the possibilities of development inherent in dialectic interactions between the Universe of Monads and physical reality. The "Universe of Logico-Mathematical Possibility", which means "Body of Monads", *explains* by means of reflecting abstractions or operations - in other words, "explains" means to assimilate!

The Living Organization is the Logico-Mathematical Structure who is *not* composed of material atoms. He can only develop Himself by means of operations or dialectical constructions carried out by metaphysical atoms. "Logico-Mathematical Structures [are] the product of ... the Living Organization ... [by means of a higher type of regulation that] will take on [a profound] Biological significance (22 lines later) as soon as atomism is rejected in favor of dialectical constructionism" (author's capitalization) (Piaget, 1971a, p. 212). In this particular book, "atomism" is nearly always the atomism of natural science, and it usually serves as the physical opposite of "monadism". As Piaget says, there are two kinds of atomism, "only one of which appears to us in tune with the Spirit of Modern Structuralism" (author's capitalization) (Piaget, 1970b, p. 8). *As is always the case, however, Piaget manipulates his reader by using the two kinds to confuse rather than to clarify.* Piaget is different from other authors in that he never clarifies the drastic difference between the two meanings of this term - or any of the other hundreds of terms that he uses in the same deceitful way. His carefully planned strategy of switching meanings from book to book, within books, and even within paragraphs and sentences, makes horrific demands upon the reader's capacity to comprehend. The hurried reader will be hopelessly lost. The Logico-Mathematical Structure is the Living Organization and since this Entity is eternal it could not be a product of any other Entity. The very ambiguous meaning is that the Logico-Mathematical Structure is Self-developing. Also, we know that the regulations are based on upper-level Biology because they are engaged in dialectical construction.

How could one accept the almost universal premise that Piaget is a scientist after reading the following two quotes? "The ideal of a suprascientific Knowledge ... had its beginnings ... in ... German idealism, *or in the more modest and more cautious form of Epistemology*" (author's italics and capitalization) (Piaget, 1971c, pp. 88-9). "This second form has resulted ... in a new philosophical approach, namely, that ... *there was room alongside scientific knowledge ... for another kind of Knowledge*" (author's italics and capitalization) (ibid., pp. 88-9). The italicized portion of both quotes refers to Piaget's somewhat camouflaged claim to have developed a "second form" of this suprascience, which is actually a virulent form of anti-science. Note that it is this "second form of Epistemology" - Piaget's "Biological explanation of Knowledge" (author's capitalization) (Piaget, 1976, p. 119) - that is the new kind of Knowledge. Piaget thus takes personal responsibility for revealing a "suprascientific" Knowledge based upon the direct operational activity of the Primordial Biological Subject Composed of Monads - a strictly superhuman Divinity. Professor Papert, who presumably accepted the scientific validity of the citation by the APA, might find it profitable to compare Piaget's metaphysical "supra" or "parascience" (Piaget, 1971c, pp. 58-9) with natural science.

It has been possible since the time of Kant and Hegel, asserts Piaget, "to conceive a philosophical form of dialectics that ... seeks to found or even direct the sciences ... [This kind of dialectics] can base itself on a tested methodology" (Piaget, 1974a, p. 56). *The philosophical dialectics of Hegel, but not Kant, is held by Piaget to overrule findings in natural science by means of the tested methodology of operations* by the Living System who is independent of lower - level selves (author's capitalization) (Piaget, Inhelder & Szeminska, 1960, p. 24). The "time of Kant and Hegel" is a "trick phrase", as the lives of Kant and Hegel overlap, but Kant had no such "form of dialectics"!

Piaget's Science is the true opposite of natural science. It is not designed to learn about and utilize the physical or "lived" world. "The true starting point of the Universe of Science is to be looked for in ... the Thought operation" (author's capitalization) (ibid., p. 87). Natural science is constructed on the "lived world" of physical reality. Piaget's dialectical, metaphysical Science, however, attempts to assimilate the lived world rather than "copy" and utilize it. *His Science starts in the Unseen World of Monads which he dubs the Universe of Science.* Piaget has no use for "positivist" or natural science because it is only interested in facts and laws. After all, challenges Piaget, there is no need for "Psychology" if this is the extent of one's concern. *This means, of course, that "Psychology" is not needed in any of our universities!* "If [experimental pedagogy] intends to limit itself ... to a simple investigation into facts and laws without claiming to explain what it states, then naturally there is no need whatever for a connection with Psychology" (author's capitalization) (Piaget, 1970d, p. 23). "Psychology" is capitalized to emphasize the necessity of two different minds in Piaget's thinking. Of course, he grossly exaggerates educational theory's independence according to his own system of the Absolute Subject, as his system dictates that even "physical" thought activity depends upon the monads in the brain.

Piaget's theory holds that the Absolute Subject and physical reality have common roots (author's capitalization) (Piaget, 1973d, p. 57) (Piaget, 1962, p. 13). They diverged to become dialectical opposites, but through operational assimilation physical reality will converge with the Subject and become one with Him again in the distant future. The dialectic conflict will end, and the Absolute will be fully developed, when his opposite is completely reversed back into His monads (author's capitalization) (Piaget, 1974b, pp. 113-14) (Piaget, 1954, p. 236). The great reversal is absolutely essential if Operational Systems are to be developed. That is, the creation of the physical universe by direct operations must be reversed completely by the reverse operations if the Operational System or Absolute is to be constructed. As Piaget says, construction is based on the entire set of operations (Inhelder & Piaget, 1958, p. 307), meaning all of the original operations which produced the physical universe plus all of the reverse operations which will re-incorporate the physical universe back into the monads. Piaget tells us nothing about the original creative operations except that they involved an emanation from the monads. His emphasis is entirely on the reverse operations of assimilation. *The concept of reversibility, a major doctrine by any measure, is utterly ludicrous if interpretation is confined to the level of physical reality - and universally this is indeed the case for those few Piagetians who venture to deal with this concept at all.*

In Piaget's system everything must flow from the Absolute Subject. This doctrine forces him to hatch some of the most fanciful theories imaginable. The most difficult problem for him, however, was to make these chimerical theories acceptable to the academic community, and his success in this venture is without doubt one of the most astonishing deceptions in academic history.

His imaginative story of how numbers are metaphysically generated is a case in point. Yes, numbers are not only generated by the Absolute as a Whole, but the generation is repeated in each individual person by his immanent Subject. Both of these kinds of generation are obscured by Piaget's make-believe findings in children of the basic metaphysical processes disguised as observable physical processes. *In stating his doctrine that "numbers do not exist alone, but are engendered by the very law of formation itself"* (author's italics) (Evans, 1973, p. 126), *he is clearly saying that the psychogenetic process, which is the formative principle behind the Absolute's development, is the basis for number production.* "All [numbers] are constructed through ... generalisation starting from the Operational Nucleus. [We thus] derive everything from a minimal starting point" (author's capitalization) (Beth & Piaget, 1966, pp. 294-5). "Operational Nucleus" is Piaget's term for the Absolute Subject before He performed His first dialectic interaction with His newly created physical universe. His first operation began the production of numbers! *Number one had now been created! When the Operational Being performed His second operation He created number two and so on indefinitely.* This is the unique and wonderful way integers or whole numbers originated. The "minimal starting point" is the bare Primordial Biological Entity - the Body of Monads before the start of development by operations. Piaget does not forget to utilize some of his synonyms in repeating the story of number production. This is why Space is said to synthesize numbers (author's capitalization) (Piaget, 1977, p. 7) (Piaget, 1072, p. 39) (Piaget & Inhelder, 1956, p. 117), as well as the Group (author's capitalization) (Piaget, Inhelder & Szeminska, 1960, p. 68) (Piaget, 1969a, p. 50), the Continuum (author's capitalization) (Piaget, 1972, pp. 46-7) and the Body (author's capitalization) (Piaget, 1973a, p. 128).

With regard to the repetition of this process within individuals, we should understand that numbers are produced endogenously by operations of the immanent Subject (author's capitalization) (Piaget, 1980b, pp. 80; 81; 96; 106) (Piaget, 1977, pp. 172-3; 199-200). This means that the process is not based on learning (Piaget, 1971a, p. 310).

Piaget believes that magic is a universal social reality in adult society (Piaget, 1929, p. 435). This being the case, we can be certain that magic plays a vital role in his life - including his professional life. "Magic" is not just a phase young children go through, no, it is an important social reality in all adult society. "The language of magic ... has a history", states Piaget, and "the actual form of a spell can show traces of its character. The nature of a conviction must be influenced by the belief that it affects the life of the entire group" (ibid., 1929, p. 433). Piaget was no doubt convinced that his magic would significantly affect the academic world. If we accept this as a reasonable assumption, we should consider the distinct possibility that his entire professional output should in fact be interpreted as an extended work of magic. It is ironic in the extreme that he was honored by the American Psychological Association and *Time* magazine as a great scientist when he is saturated with occultic ideas that are completely antithetical to scientific pursuits.

Chapter 2

PIAGET'S DUAL SYSTEM

PIAGET'S TWO BIOLOGIES

Jean Piaget writes in his autobiography that as an adolescent he experienced a "profound revelation" while visiting Samuel Cornut, his godfather. Mr. Cornut introduced Piaget to new and very exciting philosophical ideas by having him read portions of *Creative Evolution*, the most famous book of the French philosopher, Henri Bergson.

> First of all, it was an emotional shock. I recall one evening of profound revelation. The identification of God with Life itself was an idea that stirred me almost to ecstasy because *it now enabled me to see in Biology the explanation of all things* and of the Mind itself (author's italics and capitalization except for "God") (Piaget, 1976b, p. 119).

In this book and others, Bergson propounded his speculative view that God was identical with the "vital impetus" or "elan vital". *This vital impetus or God is what Piaget called "Biology", and it was by means of this unique concept of biology that he planned to explain everything,* including the one-of-a-kind Mind he soon began to conceptualize. Bergson declared that the vital impetus had entered matter and had given rise to life, even though matter was recalcitrant in resisting this process at every stage (Edwards, 1967, Vol 1, p. 293). This is the root notion, although it gradually deviated considerably from Bergson's view, in Piaget's dual system of Life versus matter. The basic notion of God entering matter and animating it can readily be discerned in most of his books.

Bergson held that the "vital impetus" was God, but he also believed that God was "undertaking to create creators" (ibid., p. 293), that is, to create independent forms of life. *Piaget, however, within a short time after his encounter with Bergsonism, began to hold that Life is an attribute that belongs exclusively to God.* This belief followed from his acceptance of a modified view of monadism as conceived by the philosopher Leibniz (Piaget, 1971c, pp. 51-3) (Beardsley, 1960, pp. 288-313). When Leibniz's monads replaced Bergson's vital impetus in Piaget's emerging system, it brought about a rather different concept of God and Life. For Piaget, only the monads, which altogether make up the Totality, Absolute Subject, God or Life, are alive. Monads are everywhere, however, and they have created a myriad of living things that appear to have a life of their own but, according to Piaget, they only have life because the metaphysical monads are behind the scenes, pulling the strings of life. All life then, including human life, is based on the eternal living monads as they invisibly and undetectably manipulate every process that enables life and every activity associated with life, including thought, to exist. Piaget describes monads as being non-material entities without weight or dimensions (Piaget & Inhelder, 1974, p. 112), but they nevertheless completely fill the universe, including the interiors of every object, both living and non-living.

TWO KINDS OF KNOWLEDGE

In addition to the emotional shock, Piaget also had an intellectual shock.

> In the second place, it was an intellectual shock. The problem of knowing (properly called the epistemological problem) suddenly appeared to me in an entirely new perspective and as an absorbing topic of study. It made me decide to consecrate my life to the Biological explanation of Knowledge (author's italics and capitalization) (Piaget, 1976b, p. 119).

Not only was Life now seen as belonging exclusively to God, but "true" Knowledge henceforth was seen by Piaget as something accomplished exclusively by God. Since God is the only Living Entity this is a logical consequence, as we would not expect non-living objects, such as human beings, to acquire genuine Knowledge. Knowledge was eventually conceived very narrowly in terms of a specific need of this single Entity to fully develop His potential. Piaget had already claimed that he could explain the Mind in terms of metaphysical Biology, and since his definition of Mind means the "Living Monads" or "God", it is not surprising that his concept of Knowledge would consist solely in what the Mind, Biology, God or the Living Monads must accomplish in order to meet this sui generis need for full development.

For an understanding of exactly what kind of Knowledge is needed and acquired by the Body of Monads or God, one must consider the theory of development Piaget appropriated from the philosopher Hegel (author's capitalization) (Piaget, 1971b, p. 1) (Piaget, 1971c, p. 58). Piaget judged Hegel's philosophy to be the "sixth level" and thus, by his reckoning, the highest kind of philosophy, so we would be correct in anticipating that Piaget's position would be a modified form of Hegel's philosophy. Piaget's system is based on Hegel's Absolute Subject who, in Piaget's theory, is composed of non-physical atoms or monads. "The Functional Constant, [General Function or Functional A Priori] ... can only be sought among elements, as in some atomistic composition (in the broad, not the microphysical, sense of the word) or in the Totality as such" (author's capitalization) (Piaget, 1971a, p. 327). This Totality, Functional Constant, Absolute Subject, Body of Monads, God or Life created the physical universe for the single purpose of acquiring a specific kind of Knowledge, impossible for humans to acquire, by means of a special dialectic interaction with the universe. *Piaget decided to consecrate his life to the understanding and furtherance of this unique interaction and Knowledge. He had no interest whatsoever in the physical or mental development of the individual person who is merely a higher form of matter.*

This very circumscribed kind of Knowledge develops not only in the Totality as such, but also in the Body of Monads that live within and maintain the life and activity of each human being. In fact the development within each normal human being, according to Piaget, repeats the entire development of the Totality from the beginning up to approximately the current level of the Totality's development. *This means that the study of a Sub-Unit of the Totality's development in children is not only a study of immanent Ontogenetic development, but it is also the study of a highly condensed recapitulation of the eons of historical or Phylogenetic development the Totality has undergone.* This idea that the developing Sub-Units of the Totality or Mind within individual people, recapitulates the development of the whole Totality or Mind, was taken with some modifications from Hegel's *The Phenomenology. This is a case of Ontogeny recapitulating Phylogeny, and for Piaget it represented his chief motivation to study children.* This book by Hegel was devoted primarily to the development of the Absolute Mind within individuals and "the evolution of the mind from earliest times down to his own day" (Jones, 1975, p. 114).

How was Piaget going to present this process of acquiring metaphysical Knowledge to the academic world? He decided that it would be based on psychological "experiments" and arguments rather than on philosophical discourse. Experimentation with groups of children would be carried out in order to monitor the unique kind of development that he assumed the Totality of Monads had already passed through, and thus would reappear at some point in the "child's" development. *There was no interest at all in the contingent, exogenetic knowledge or development children achieve at home or in school* (author's italics) (Piaget, 1971c, p. 125), *as he was only concerned with the certain, very narrow and unique developmental Knowledge acquired by the Logico-Mathematical Structures or Body of Monads within the child* (author's italics and capitalization) (Piaget, 1971a, pp. 211-12). Neither the child nor anyone else, except Piaget and his divine Immanent Tutor, would know in an unambiguous way about this unique concept of Knowledge. No wonder Piagetians had so much trouble applying his theory to practical problems in education. *Piaget makes it perfectly clear in spite of ambiguous statements to the contrary, that his studies in child psychology were not for the purpose of understanding the child better or for the purpose of improving pedagogical methods* (author's italics) (Piaget, 1967, p. 116). It was only for the purpose of "observing" the phylogeny of the Absolute Subject repeated in the ontogeny of a multitude of immanent Sub-Units of the Absolute Subject developing or "being constructed" in children. In other words, it was a purpose that could not be fully disclosed.

Surely this is a silly, self-defeating approach to one's life-work? What is the point of writing 50 books when there is a deliberate effort to prevent clear communication? From Piaget's point of view it is not necessarily self-defeating. All of the important activity in the world is metaphysical activity; submission to this activity is the only logical role available to human beings. The motivation of the Absolute Subject and His fundamental activity are such that, in Piaget's opinion, sowing seeds of confusion and frustration could serve Him quite well and, above all else, he wished to serve the Absolute Subject within him worthily. It appears that Piaget was totally devoted to his immanent Subject, and wished to be completely controlled by Him.

The real problem precipitated by Piaget's published work begins with his desire to be accepted by the academic community as a scientist, and his autobiography reveals his decision to take this approach (Piaget, 1976b, pp. 119-125). This obviously meant he could not openly admit that his concern with development and knowledge was solely metaphysical. He was clearly aware of this problem from the beginning and decided to go undercover with a number of stratagems that some of my colleagues have refused to believe because they consider them to be "impossibly monstrous". Among these deceptive and frustrating devices are: private meanings for several hundred words that are cunningly used alternately with their dictionary meanings, a huge number of synonyms for each private meaning, especially those which refer to the central Entity of his metaphysical system and to this Entity's main activity, most often called "operations"; physical experiments which are ultimately, but illogically, interpreted in terms of his metaphysical system; framing his major metaphysical doctrines in the form of complicated and equivocal puzzles; misusing every aspect of grammar and syntax to prevent precise comprehension; consistently separating concepts and various kinds of data that belong together; and misusing the work of other investigators. Examples of these and other forms of deception and confusion will be examined as the occasion arises.

A MULTIPLICITY OF SYNONYMS AND VERBALISMS

Ever since *Language and Thought* was translated into English in 1926, investigators have complained about Piaget's almost unintelligible use of language. Many of his translators have commented on this characteristic, and some admit to having made "free" adjustments in the process of translation in order to make his work more readable. The translator of *The Child's Conception of Number* (1952a) said, "While keeping as closely as possible to the French text, we have, with the author's permission, used a certain freedom on occasion, but only when it seemed desirable in the interests of clarity and when no essential idea was involved" (ibid., p. IX). Chaninah Maschler, who translated *Structuralism* (1970b), admitted that "the translation is at times more than free, but clarity and readability seemed to require this" (Translator's Note).

Others point to problems of meaning that cannot be easily resolved by the translator. Terrance Brown in the foreword to *Experiments in Contradiction* (1980a) concludes that "the reader is not clear whether overcoming contradictions is a psychogenetic or an equilibrational affair". One paragraph later professor Brown says, "the upshot of all this is that the reader is left to decide for himself what the relationship between psychogenesis and equilibration is" (ibid., p. XI). Piaget would have been delighted with Brown's bewilderment. Both psychogenesis and equilibration refer specifically to the process of overcoming metaphysical contradictions, which are quite different from ordinary contradictions. The most sinister thing about this confusion is that it was deliberately prearranged. *The private meanings of "psychogenesis" and "equilibration" are exactly the same, but Brown was not supposed to know this.* As indicated above, Piaget invented a huge number of private meanings to be used surreptitiously in place of the dictionary meanings for the purpose of describing his more or less secret metaphysical doctrines. He was clever at moving from the physical level of dictionary meanings with which we are all familiar, to the metaphysical level of private meanings to make well-camouflaged points, and then back again to the physical level, all without the courtesy of giving the reader a clue regarding his switches in meaning. The reader is aware, of course, that something is amiss, but what? Surely everyone who has read a book by Piaget, and has not been rendered blind by hero worship or the need for certainty, which Piaget seems to offer, has repeatedly experienced mystification and frustration because of his inscrutable and contradictory statements.

Numerous examples of this deceptive use of private meanings will be examined in this as well as the other chapters. Incredibly, no one has ever exposed this outrageously unethical methodology. Somehow every investigator has managed to force Piaget's work onto only one level, completely ignoring his fervent, although ambiguous, emphasis of an indispensable metaphysical system.

"Psychogenesis" and "equilibration" are two of the many synonyms he coined to represent the key metaphysical concept of "operation". Piaget knew confusion was inevitable because his plan was designed for this purpose. He knew that investigators like Brown and thousands of others would be hopelessly stymied in their efforts to understand him within the normal constraints of time and effort which obtain for professorial publication expectations, and that textbooks in various disciplines would contain fallacious information and concepts. Three generations of professors have lectured confidently on his time-honored concepts, but Piaget himself could only pretend to agree with these concepts, as understood by the academic world. *He could never honestly subscribe to the ideas attributed to him in textbooks used in such disciplines as child development, educational psychology and education.* For essentially all of the terms appearing in such textbooks, the only meanings significant to him would be the private metaphysical meanings, and they have yet to be apprehended by academia. It is possible to know the meanings of all of his privately coined terms, but he made it tediously difficult. *His fundamental system is strictly metaphysical, but he sold it to an unsuspecting academic community as a more or less empirical science.* Unfortunately, it only has the trappings of science, as Piaget despises natural science.

It is ironic indeed that while Piaget rails, quite openly at times, against every aspect of natural science, he is honored concurrently for his "experimental" investigations in epistemology and child development. The true experiment in Piaget's theory is always "oriented ... in the direction of Logico-Mathematical decentering" of the individual (author's capitalization) Piaget, 1971a, p. 337). This means that the true experiment is performed by the Absolute Ego, and involves the deactivation of the human ego (author's capitalization) (Beth & Piaget, 1966, p. 235), who as a mere "object" has nothing to do with true experiments (ibid., p. 285) (Piaget, 1952b, pp. 366-7) (Piaget & Inhelder, 1974, p. 220). Piaget's experiments sometimes appear to be normal scientific experiments, but his basic position regarding the nature of the physical universe make this an impossibility (Piaget, 1973c, p. 45) (Piaget, 1952b, p. 314) (Piaget 1950, p. 148). Those who basically agree and those who basically disagree have been off the mark for the same reason - a reluctance to acknowledge the two opposite levels of reality in Piaget's theory.

Among those who have brought to light serious problems with Piaget's experiments and theories is Sullivan (1967). Piaget holds that the fundamental factor in the transition from lower to higher stages of intellectual development is the equilibration model, but *Sullivan has shown that no educational process can be derived from this model to facilitate the desired transition.* "There is no place in the theory for the systematic teaching of thought structures" (ibid., p. 23). Piaget was trying to force his followers to look beyond the physical to the metaphysical without being explicit, but Sullivan and the dozens of authorities he quoted remained credulously on the level of physical reality. Since Piaget insisted, as Sullivan recognized, that there was nothing anyone could do to move the child to higher levels of intellectual development, why would educators popularize his theory? Sullivan held that the equilibration model became popular in education because the proponents of the "self-discovery" and "activity" methods needed a theory to justify their views (ibid., pp. 32-34). *The "equilibration model", as Sullivan calls it, is clearly a restatement of the concept of "spontaneous development"* that was examined in the introduction. Unfortunately for the educators, it is obvious that the physical child is not capable of "self-discovery" and "activity" as Piaget defines these terms. Only the immanent Subject within the child has this capability. *Piaget wanted his commentators to realize gradually that the stages of intellectual development could not be achieved by manipulating physical reality in any way whatever, and this includes anything the child might do as well as anything his teachers could do.*

Another investigator who made valid criticisms of Piaget's physical experiments and theories was Kohnstamm (1967). He was very critical of Piaget's "physical" treatment of the "inclusion problem", which is the problem of a quantitative comparison of two classes, one of which is included in the other. Piaget's only concern is with regard to the metaphysical Classes synthesized by operations or equilibrations, as they must be successively included within the Total Group of monads. He teaches that children acquire the operations of inclusion independently of experience (ibid., p. 138) or verbally transmitted rules and explanations (ibid., p. 146). Kohnstamm, unfortunately, did not realize Piaget holds that the physical child can do nothing to become capable of operational behavior. *As in the transition of cognitive stages, neither children nor adults can ever operationally "include" a Class of monads within the Total Group of monads.* Piaget approaches the problem, as usual, by means of contrived physical problems which children can solve, and then eventually moves to the metaphysical plane. Kohnstamm became interested in the physical problems as such, and made telling criticisms of Piaget's experimental procedures and interpretations, but it never occurred to him that the problem for Piaget was actually metaphysical.

Piaget's master plan for wholesale deception, although boldly adumbrated in his early books, has remained either unknown or ignored by essentially all of his commentators. Did anyone in academic history previous to Piaget deliberately set out to make his most important beliefs incomprehensible? It is highly doubtful. Has anyone ever gone to such lengths in carrying out such an unthinkable plan? Piaget may well be the unique example in each case.

Terrance Brown and Kishore Julian Thampy give us another aspect of the frustrations that Piaget's writing style imposes.

> Piaget is a hard case. He was a great thinker but an inconsiderate if not downright awful
> writer .... We do not know the reason. We have only felt the pain his prose inflicts ....

> We have broken up his endless sentences and made the antecedents of his pronouns clear
> .... And we have tried to translate each sentence in the context of everything we have ever
> read (Piaget, 1985, p. XVII).

Was Piaget a great thinker? On what basis does Brown and Thampy consider Piaget to be a great thinker? He certainly has become an icon to many, but why? If his ideas were clearly expressed would he still be venerated as a great thinker? One of my colleagues waved aside my concerns with, "but he is very intelligent isn't he"? When I agreed that he most certainly was, his smile told me that he considered the matter closed. This beside-the-point evaluation would satisfy few, but Piaget's studious cultivation of an almost superhuman intellect, giving the impression of mastery in many fields of knowledge, obviously has had its affect. His god-like reputation alone has prompted many of our most visible scholars to genuflect when asked to comment on his work. One serious consequence of this misplaced reverence is that investigators are too willing to take terms and concepts that Piaget reserves for the Absolute Subject and apply them to human beings. Consider the following statement by Hans Furth: "For Piaget ... there is no knowledge whatsoever ... that is *merely* derived from environmental experience" (Furth, 1969, p. 227). How can one account for such an incredible, irrational statement? Natural science and common sense are completely negated. Is it possible to account for such statements in the absence of Piaget's enormous influence? Furth goes on to say that "Piaget distinguishes action-derived Knowledge from environmentally derived knowledge" (author's capitalization) (ibid., p. 227), not realizing that action-derived Knowledge, in Piaget's system, is based on metaphysical operations of the Biological Entity, while the environmentally based knowledge of natural science is not "true" Knowledge at all for Piaget.

TWO MINDS

Furth's misunderstanding of Piaget's concept of Structure is another illustration of how Piaget leads many to make fanciful statements.

> The structures we are here discussing are not simply the structures of the central nervous
> system nor any other physiological structures. Piaget certainly does not deny that the
> brain is vitally related to intelligent behavior, but he is intent on analysing intelligence
> on the level of behavior (Furth, p. 179).

Furth becomes an apologist here. Piaget unequivocally claims that his Structures are not a part of the brain *and do not in any way depend on the brain.* Furth is not willing to go that far and argues that Piaget does not really mean it! No material biological structure, including the brain, has anything to do with intelligent behavior, as Piaget defines it. However, since Furth insists on interpreting Piaget on the single level of physical reality, this would be an insane position, so he simply denies that he really means it. *Piaget does mean it.* "These Structures cannot be caused by mere hereditary transmission, for if they were attached to the genes in the same way ... the lobe of the brain ... is attached to them they would not be ... necessary" (author's capitalization) (Piaget, 1971a, p. 322). For Piaget, the genes and everything they produce, including the brain, are material and variable, while his Structures are immaterial, invariable and necessary. Another passage along the same line:

> Does Knowledge arising from a true acquisition, having no relationship with any hereditary programming, necessarily have a biological component? Perhaps it will be replied that even the highest type of act of intelligence still presupposes brain activity .... [However] it is easy enough, in epistemology, to dissociate a piece of Logical or Mathematical Knowledge from its neurological support (author's capitalization) (ibid., pp. 251-2).

Knowledge acquired without any relationship with hereditary programming means by definition that no biological component was involved. Piaget uses "hereditary programming" in this context to mean any aspect of physical biology. The brain has no role in producing this kind of Knowledge. Piaget speaks ambiguously of dissociating knowledge from its "neurological support", but *he has already admitted that there is no "neurological support" in terms of true Knowledge acquisition.*

The irrelevance of the brain in the acquisition of true Knowledge is obvious in the following passage.

> In Bergsonian spiritualism, the nervous system vis-a-vis the Mind is reduced to the modest role of a hook with a Coat hung upon it. But even the hook presents a problem, for from this point of view it is the Coat itself which is the Fount of Life, and that renders the hook useless (author's capitalization) (Piaget, 1971a, p. 216).

The first sentence represents Bergson's position regarding the relationship between the brain and the Mind; the second sentence is Piaget's evaluation of this relationship. *Piaget's verdict: the brain is useless when it comes to the operations of the Mind.* The brain is a physical aspect of reality, while the Mind belongs to, or rather is, the metaphysical Structure. Piaget puts it this way: "If there are close connections between the nervous ... structure ... and the Cognitive Structure, [this is because of] superimposed scales" (author's capitalization) (Piaget, 1973c, p. 23). The point Piaget makes here is that *even when the brain appears to be involved, it is really being manipulated by an upper-level, superimposed Cognitive Structure composed of monads.*

The following passage which examines the relationship between the Mind, the Structure, true knowledge or logic and the brain clarifies Piaget's meaning of "heredity".

> If logic ... developed in conjunction with the maturation of the nervous system, it could certainly be placed in the context of hereditary knowledge, but [that kind] of knowledge can [not] apply here .... [thus] compelling us to look for its origins in ... the Living Organization (author's capitalization) (Piaget, 1971a, p. 307).

"Logic" is used by Piaget to mean either the Living Metaphysical Structure or the activity of this Structure. Here "logic" or "knowledge" is the developing activity of the Living Organization or Structure. The meaning of "hereditary" is seen to include the "maturation of the nervous system" and by implication all physical biological structures under the control of the genetic system. Flavell treats Piaget's work more critically than Furth, but he cannot avoid the inevitable pitfalls when he attributes metaphysical concepts of development to human beings. One example among many is the concept of the *"biological invariant"*. Flavell uses this concept to answer a fundamental question: "What sort of device is the developing human cognizer?" (Flavell, 1963, p. 262)

> Piaget's answer to this question is in all essentials given in his organization-adaptation conception. The basic equipment of any knower at any stage consists of the biologically given functional invariants of organization and adaptation (assimilation and accommodation) .... This basic state (the fact of organization) and this basic process are really the only a priorities which Piaget feels is necessary to assume (ibid., pp. 262-3).

Flavell recognizes that, within Piaget's system, the "Organization" is the invariant "basic state" and "assimilation and accommodation" is the invariant "process" of development. He also recognizes that within this system both the invariant Organization and the invariant process of its organization (i. e., development) are logically given "a priorities". Within the context, however, it is the *Subject* who is the Organization or "A Priority" who assimilates, so it is important to understand that the Organization is not merely a basic structure which is the result of what the invariant Biological Entity does, but is the invariant Biological Entity Himself! This is the immanent metaphysical Entity who is the "basic equipment" of "any knower". He is the only Entity capable of invariant assimilation and accommodation. *The physical human being, as such, does not have an "invariant device" with the capacity for invariant assimilation of objects!* One must bear in mind that "Organization" not only refers to the metaphysical Entity, but without a capital it simply means "development" (author's capitalization) (Piaget, 1971a, p. 135) (Inhelder & Piaget, 1958, p. 185).

Flavell recognizes that Piaget believes we "inherit" not only limited biological structures, but also Something which permits these limited structures to be overcome (author's capitalization) (Flavell, 1963, p. 42). We immediately see physical biology set up by Piaget to be assimilated by this immanent Something, but Flavell turns a blind eye, as usual toward this obvious relationship. "This positive constructive something which we inherit", Piaget argues, "is a *mode of intellectual functioning* .... [which] remains essentially constant throughout life .... It is because of this constancy ... that its fundamental properties ... are referred to as *functional invariants*" (Flavell's italics) (ibid., p. 43). The functioning that is invariant is the operational activity of the Absolute "Something". *Physical biology is not invariant in any significant sense of the word, and I am confident that Flavell knows this when he is not under Piaget's magic spell.*

Is Piaget a great thinker? Judgment should be suspended on this question until we really understand what he said and gain at least some insight into how and why he said it. A major objective of this book is to demonstrate that what he said differs in the most drastic way from what we see in all of the commentaries and textbooks regarding Piaget's theoretical position. In the process of examining his position, we will concomitantly gain some insight into his methodology and motivations.

This chapter focuses on the double framework within which Piaget always works. Basically the same words are used in both frameworks, but the meanings, as understood by Piaget, are vastly different. It is impossible to understand him unless the private metaphysical meanings of several hundred words are uncovered and applied appropriately. The frustration that readers experience in trying to understand

Piaget is partly due to the fact that by design he constantly switches from one meaning to the other. In fact he bragged covertly about his ability to reason with two distinct systems simultaneously (Piaget, 1970a, pp. 270-1), namely the familiar physical and the unfamiliar metaphysical. Piaget chose to write in an ambiguous and almost unintelligible way, although he certainly could write clear and highly readable prose. All we have to do is look at his autobiography and the descriptions of his experiments with his own children to see such examples. Most of his short papers are also quite readable. Actually, it is only in his books, where he elaborates his basic theoretical positions and leads his trusting readers up so many blind alleys, that his prose definitely becomes, as Professor Brown says, "inconsiderate" or "painful".

We not only know that Piaget could and did write exceptionally clear prose, but we also know that he planned from the beginning of his professional career to write in a style that would create enough obscurity to "actually prevent thought from being communicated" (Piaget, 1926, p. 26). *This attempt to disguise and distort his own most cherished thoughts would appear to be a self-defeating mode of operation, but since the independent, living Being of his metaphysical system normally operates undercover, it apparently seemed reasonable to him that he should operate in a similar fashion.* Piaget tells us in his first book of his specific plan in this regard. The plan, which he carried out shrewdly and thoroughly, was to "multiply verbal entities" in order to overwhelm the reader's ability to comprehend with any precision.

> Finally, if the function of language were merely to "communicate" the phenomenon of verbalism would hardly admit of explanation. How could words, confined as they are by usage to certain precise meanings *(precise, because their object is to be understood)*, eventually come to veil the confusion of thought, *even to create obscurity by the multiplication of verbal entities, and actually prevent thought from being communicated* .... The very existence of such questions shows how complex are the functions of language, and how futile the attempt to reduce them all to one - that of communicating thought (author's italics) (Piaget, 1926, p. 26).

Who else besides Piaget would describe the invention of empty "verbalisms" for the sole purpose of creating obscurity, as a function of language? He did not make an exception of himself, and he did not imply that this was an illegitimate function for a scientist! *Very early in his professional career Piaget had already decided that, in order to protect his metaphysical system, he would create obscurity by the multiplication of verbal entities, and actually prevent his own essential thought from being clearly communicated.* Without supreme confidence in his ability to carry out this plan to deceive, such impudent braggadocio would never have appeared in his first major book. He had the incredible audacity to forewarn the academic community that, by implication, every major concept of his theory would have an excessive number of synonyms or "verbalisms" for the express purpose of creating problems for them. Difficulty and its accompanying frustration was to be increased by sometimes giving the synonyms additional private meanings from time to time and by often making them appear to be something less than synonyms. The upshot was that Piaget's brilliance and determination created incredible complexity and confusion with this almost unimaginable method of "belaboring the mind". How should one describe such staggering behavior?

It was self-evident to Piaget from the beginning that no one should ever be able to describe his position clearly. He admitted this understanding with a specific statement: *"To the extent to which one would be able to speak of 'Piaget's system', this would be conclusive proof of my failure"* (author's italics) (Piaget, 1971c, p. 29). After we have examined both his system and his methods in considerable detail, it will be easy to understand why he was unquestionably correct in making such a strange statement. *Even if his Gnostic system should prove to be intrinsically acceptable or even desirable to some, Piaget's methods are so repugnant and anti-social that he would undoubtedly be judged a failure in the course of time.*

Piaget conceives the very purpose of existence in terms of two exactly opposite systems, one of which is eternal and the other created, interacting in a specific way. A major motivation for all of his books was to describe, undercover, the *reason* for the creation of the lower-level physical system, which was required in order to set in motion a unique set of dialectic interactions. This sui generis dialectic process, according to Piaget, will ultimately lead to the culmination of history, which is very much like the Hindu concept of "absorption" into Being (Edwards, 1967, Vol, 4 p. 3). This will occur, according to Piaget, because operations will reverse the creation of physical reality by means of assimilation or absorption until only the eternal Continuum of Monads will remain (author's capitalization) (Inhelder & Piaget, 1958, pp. 268; 272) (Piaget. 1954, pp. 116-117).

Sunier, who apparently knew Piaget on a personal basis, described him as being somewhat larger than life. Piaget studied traditional philosophy which, Sunier boasts, he "surpassed" (Piaget et al., 1977, p. VII). He was a "model of modern scientific world citizenship" and for many "a kind of ideal of the old European mind". "Even his very human slyness" was an aspect of a "kind of Olympianship" (ibid., p. XII). Like Sunier, many prefer to transform what others see as defects, including "his very human slyness", into signs of true greatness. Unfortunately, Sunier is not alone in his belief that Piaget deserves a place among the gods of Mt. Olympus.

For more than 70 years psychologists and educators have been exposed to Piaget's theories and experimental investigations. Thousands of individuals have developed reasons for accepting what they have read and heard in university classrooms. Certain notions have become so well-entrenched over this period of time, that anyone who intends to seriously question the validity of these notions must be able to demonstrate from Piaget's books every point he wishes to make. With this in mind, we will first clarify the purported existence and characteristics of his two systems. The process of documenting the two systems will also serve the purpose of further elaborating his metaphysical theory.

ANOTHER KIND OF ATOM

The basic components of his essentially secret system are special kinds of invisible atoms that have no weight and no volume. They are imaginary, metaphysical entities similar to the monads hypothesized by the philosopher Leibniz (Piaget, 1970b, p. 41) (Piaget, 1971, p. 78). *These atoms are alive and must be contrasted with their opposite counterparts, the material atoms of natural science.* "We find not one but two alternatives to atomism have made their way in the history of ideas, only one of which appears to us in tune with the Spirit of of modern structuralism" (author's capitalization) (Piaget, 1970b, p. 8). Piaget uses "alternatives" ambiguously, as there is only one alternative to the scientific concept of atomism. The single alternative Piaget has in mind is his imaginary metaphysical atom or monad. The atoms or monads are organized into one Totality and simultaneously into many Sub-Units. Both the Totality and the Sub-Units have many different names. One term used for this Entity is "Group" or "Sub-Group". The Total Group contains all of the monads or atoms, but it is composed of countless Sub-Groups. Another term used in exactly the same way is "Form". There are two kinds of Groups and two kinds of Forms. In each case one kind is physical and the other kind is metaphysical or spiritual. Modern structuralism, as conceived by Piaget, is based on a Spirit or Subject who is composed of metaphysical atoms or monads and who goes by a multitude of names.

When Sub-Units of atoms or monads are organized, we have endomorphic metaphysical Entities. An endomorphism is a part that can reconstitute the Whole and thus has the potential of knowing everything the Whole knows (author's capitalization) (Piaget, 1971a, pp. 170-1). Piaget usually thinks of endomorphisms in terms of the immanent Sub-Units of monads that live in and activate all human beings. Furthermore, and this is of critical importance, *he considers these immanent Bodies of Monads to be the true Selves of human beings.*

Piaget carried out an experiment with lumps of sugar which were placed in water and observed by children. He then made a giant illogical leap from the vanishing sugar grains to metaphysical corpuscles, atoms or monads.

> In short, all of these reactions are so many elements of a future "powder metaphysics"... *all the child has to do is to realize that the "tiny things", the "crumbs" or the "dust" result from the break-up of the initial lump and that, if this process is continued, the end product will be a host of invisible but none the less Substantial corpuscles* (author's italics and capitalization) (Piaget & Inhelder, 1974, p. 79).

Piaget leads the reader from a physical lump of sugar to Substantial or metaphysical corpuscles. "Substantial" refers, in this quote, to the philosophical doctrine that Entities or Beings underlie all phenomena, not "substantial" as real or having material substance (Edwards, 1967, Vol. 8, pp. 36-40). *This is the Substance on which operations are based* (author's italics and capitalization) (Piaget, 1974b, pp. 2-3) *because it is the Substance of the Ego* (author's italics and capitalization) (Piaget, 1971a, p. 43). *Substance, in Piaget's terminology, obviously consists of monads which make up the Body of the Ego.* Piaget typically moves the reader very gradually from the familiar physical to the secret metaphysical, rather than abruptly as in this quote, and he does it in a way that contradicts his own basic doctrines. Within Piaget's system, knowledge of the physical can never lead to a correct understanding of the metaphysical. *The term "invisible" is to be taken as "invisible in principle", even with electron microscopes or any other possible scientific procedure.* The nature and function of spiritual atoms or monads will be more fully elaborated in the following chapter.

ANOTHER KIND OF SPACE

A general term used to designate all of the atoms or monads in the universe is "Space" and, of course, there are two kinds of space. There is physical space with which everyone is familiar, and there is the metaphysical or spiritual Space of atoms or monads.

> It is true that one aspect of space is tied to its contents and cannot be separated from it, namely physical space, as in relativity theory. Nonetheless, we can consider space separately from its contents. *The Science of this independent Space is the Science of pure Geometry* - pure in the sense that it is in no way limited by physical space (author's italics and capitalization) (Piaget, 1970c, p. 60).

Piaget appears to be considering aspects of a single space until he gets to "independent Space" where suddenly there are two different spaces. This other kind of Space, the independent Space that is in no way limited by physical space, is the *"Operational Space constructed by Our actions"* (author's italics and capitalization) (Beth & Piaget, 1966, p. 220). Operational Space, then, is clearly a synonym for Absolute Subject, and the operations performed by this personal Space are based on the activity of atoms or monads. *"Our actions" does not refer to anything the individual person does or can do; it refers to what Piaget considers to be our "true" Selves, which is the endomorphic Body of Monads within each of us.* These immanent monads are an integral part of Space as a whole, so when the construction or development of Space is being considered, the actions or "our immanent monads" are considered by Piaget to be as much a part of this construction as any other monads. If this scenario seems to be excessively adolescent-like or sophomoric one should not be surprised, as his prevailing methodology and basic "system" was apparently invented while he was still a teenager.

Another aspect of Operational Space touches on the purpose of Piaget's dual system. Why did the Monads of Space create the physical universe? It was created for the purpose of generating a continuous series of a certain kind of metaphysical contradiction, and the resulting dialectic interactions (Piaget & Inhelder, 1973, p. 137) (Piaget, 1971b, p. 1), which meant that the physical universe had to be the direct opposite of the Body of Monads. These special contradictions, caused intrinsically by the very existence of matter, are resolved by the monads operating within and upon matter. The operations very gradually achieve two mutually dependent goals simultaneously: one goal is to assimilate matter, including all individual people, back into the monads, and the other is to "construct" or develop the Body of Monads. The two goals are mutually dependent because complete assimilation equals complete or full development of the Body of Monads or Absolute Subject (author's capitalization) (Piaget & Inhelder, 1956, p. 377) (Piaget 1952, p. 416). *The difficult and laborious process of assimilation calls for increasingly complex combinatory activity of the monads. This is the way metaphysical Knowledge is acquired and metaphysical Intelligence improved.*

Piaget devoted a book to the subject of contradiction. As usual he tries to imperceptibly lead his reader through a variety of physical experiments, from the level of physical reality to the level of metaphysical Reality. *This involves the transformation of contradictions as we already understand them, into the metaphysical contradictions of his system - to which ordinary contradictions are in no way related.*

> The space involved presents a double nature according to whether it is the spatial properties of objects or the geometry of the Subject's actions that are being considered. The contradictions studied in this chapter will be of two kinds (author's capitalization) (Piaget, 1980, p. 118).

Piaget again begins by speaking of a single space with a double nature, however the Space with the "geometry of the Subject's actions" is not compatible with space as defined in the dictionary. He is really speaking of two different spaces. The Space which presents "the geometry of the Subject's actions" is a metaphysical Person in action, composed of living and intelligent monads, who performs one dominant type of action, the dialectical *operation,* which always follows a metaphysical contradiction. Personal Space also performs a multitude of other actions or operations to maintain the physical universe. As Piaget says, the contradictions "will be of two kinds", but he does not intend for the reader to see clearly how the "geometry of the Subject's actions" will be involved in these contradictions. Our goal is to show explicitly, within Piaget's system, how indeed it is involved.

The Space who acts operationally was present from the beginning, but there were no objects at the beginning (author's capitalization) (Piaget, 1929, pp. 255-7); they had to be created. "Physical space is at first not differentiated from the Space of action [which] is present from the outset" (author's capitalization) (Piaget, Inhelder & Szeminska, 1960, p. 208]. The Space of action is the Space composed of monads or "identity elements" which are eternal (author's capitalization) (Piaget, 1970, p. 20). This Space is often called the "Continuum" because it is completely full of "the elementary logical properties" or monads (author's capitalization) (Beth & Piaget, 1966, p. 255) (Piaget, 1972, p. 49) (Piaget & Inhelder, 1956, pp. 147-148). It is this Continuum of Monads who ("who", because we are speaking of a Personal Space, the Absolute Entity) created the physical universe and began to interact operationally with it. Significantly, as we have previously noted, Piaget holds that the Body of Monads within the new-born baby rapidly recapitulates this process. This is why he claims that, for the baby, the first few weeks of life are without objects (Piaget & Inhelder 1969, p. 14) (Piaget, 1971b, p. 16). He even goes so far as to insist that the breast is not an object for the baby (Piaget, 1952b, p. 36). *The reason Piaget is interested in children through the age of adolescence is not what we see in textbooks on child development, but because their immanent Selves repeat the developmental process that Space as a whole has already achieved* (author's italics and capitalization) (Evans, 1973, p. 48) (Piaget. 1971a, p. 160) (Bringuier, 1980, p. 48) (ibid., p. 92). *By studying children Piaget believes that he is studying the entire past history of the Spatial Entity, the Entity he wished above all to serve.* The fact that individual children, and almost everyone else, know nothing about this is just fine with him.

THE LIVING STRUCTURE SANS HEART SANS BRAIN

A frequent synonym for "Space" or "Absolute Subject" is "Structure". As in the case with "Space", the Total Structure represents all of the monads but there are innumerable Sub-Structures (author's italics and capitalization) (Piaget, 1973d, p. 7). *Hegel's Concrete Being, according to Piaget, is the true model for Structure* (author's italics and capitalization) (ibid., p. 25). *He then adds that "the case for Logical Structures"... possesses every characteristic that might have made it a kind of Absolute"* (author's italics and capitalization) (ibid., p. 28). Since Structures are composed of metaphysical atoms or monads (author's capitalization) (Piaget, 1970b, p. 8), they are alive (ibid., p. 142). Furthermore, they are the sole source of "activity", as Piaget denies any activity in the realm of natural structures (ibid., p. 142). Although Structures are alive, it is important to understand that they are "extra-biological and extra-mental" (author's capitalization) (Piaget, 1971a, pp. 274-5). Piaget hides behind the biologist Rensch to make this point, and almost certainly twists his meaning in the process. Patently, *Structures are not dependent in any way on physical biology, including the biological activity of the brain, but they are the product of the "Living Organization itself", and this gives them a profound Biological significance* (author's italics and capitalization) (ibid., pp. 211-12). Since Structures have a metaphysical or spiritual "Biology" but not a physical biology, there must be two different kinds of biology and two different kinds of structure.

Piaget speaks of a "global" structuralism based on observable relations (Piaget, 1970b p. 98). This kind of structuralism includes natural science where "observable relations and interactions are regarded as sufficient unto themselves". For Piaget, "the empirical subject" is a part of the "spatio-temporal world" and so are the natural "sciences connected with it" (Piaget, 1971c, p. 104). For this reason the empirical subject and natural science are of little importance. It is the "Deep" Structures from which the empirical subject and universe were derived that are all-important (author's capitalization) (Piaget, 1970b, p. 98).

Piaget holds that the starting point of Science is the "World of Action" or Operational Thought (author's capitalization) (Piaget, 1971c, p. 87). What does he mean by this? He means that *his kind of Science is based on the World of Active Monads, which is the source of Operational Thought.* Science for Piaget is the metaphysical work of organized monads and their progressive achievements. For him, "the aim of Scientific Thought is always to get further away from this lived world, contradicting it instead of utilizing it" (author's capitalization) (ibid., p. 87). Law based on natural science can only result in pseudo concepts because the processes of empirical science are not logical (Piaget, 1930, p. 299). *Piaget's concept of Science bears no resemblance to natural science, so we must recognize two kinds of science.*

Authentic Structuralism is based on the Living Structure of monads which underlies all of reality, and provides the basis for phenomena (author's capitalization (Piaget, 1971c, p. 109). Natural phenomena are not possible without the activity of the underlying Body of Monads (author's capitalization) (Piaget, 1970b, pp. 39-40) (Piaget, 1974b, p. 10) (Piaget, 1971c, pp. 184-185). The Structure, of course, is the Absolute Subject; when this Structure is finally complete it will have realized all possible transformations, making it a fully developed Structure (author's capitalization) (Piaget, 1973d, p. 37). We have mentioned the Continuum of monads that was there "at the beginning". In a less than explicit repetition of the same concept, Piaget asserts that, "We must first discover the Structures that are there to begin with, and then show how and why these Structures come to be transformed". Here "transformed" means "developed", and "all development", he continues, "presupposes an Initial Structure" (author's italics and capitalization) (Piaget & Inhelder, 1964, p. 1). "Development consists in the completion and differentiation of this Structure" (author's capitalization) (ibid., p. 1). We begin to see that the kind of development which concerns Piaget is the development of a non-human Entity, who is indeed the Spatial Continuum, Structure, Absolute Subject, Group, Form, Totality, Whole, Organism, Organization, God, Life, Mind, I, Universal, A Priori, Field, Psychologist, Physicist, Model, etc.

The development of Structure as it relates to individual people is based on the Structure of Monads inside of people, not the individual physical subject.

> Structuralism calls for a differentiation between the *individual subject*, who does not enter at all, and the *Epistemic Subject*, that Cognitive Nucleus which is common to all subjects ... [The distorting grasp of the individual subject] must be set apart from the achievements of the Subject .... Now after such precipitation of the "me", the "lived", from the "I," there remains the Subject's "operations" (Piaget's italics) (author's capitalization) (Piaget, 1970b, p.139).

In some contexts the individual subject is said to participate to some extent in the development of Structures, in other contexts he is given no role at all. In this citation he "does not enter at all". The Epistemic Subject alone is depicted as being able to achieve in this area, while the "distorting grasp" of the individual subject "must be set apart" or "precipitated from the 'I'". *The "lived me" is transparently the individual subject while the "I", composed of monads, is the Epistemic Subject. These dual entities exist together in the same body.*

THE TWO SUBJECTS

These two subjects are not two aspects of the same person; the Epistemic Subject is definitely not an individual physical subject (author's capitalization) (Piaget, 1971a, p. 65) (Beth & Piaget, 1966, p. 238). Piaget insists that the Subject, with His general coordinations of actions and operations, is external to the individual subject (author's capitalization) (ibid., p. 293). The nature of the Subject is external to "our nature" (author's capitalization) (Piaget, 1971a, p. 55). The same point is emphasized, even though the "external" subject is switched, when Piaget asserts that the individual subject is external to the Psychological Subject (author's capitalization) (Piaget, 1974a, p. 30). Furthermore, the child is said to have an internal omnipotent Self who is independent of things (author's capitalization) (Piaget, 1954, p. 272). This means, of course, that He is independent of the child in which He resides, because in Piaget's terminology the physical child is merely an object (ibid., p. 96) or thing (Beth & Piaget, 1966, p. 298).

Piaget agrees with Foucault's "oft-repeated assertion that man, that 'strange double being,' is 'empirico-transcendental'" (Piaget, 1970b, p. 133), and he elaborates on this strange dual being by comparing the two kinds of "forms" which belong to man. One kind of form has to do with organic morphology; the other kind belongs to the higher functions of "man" and are called "pure Forms". *"Pure Forms" are Forms that have no matter, even though they exist within people.* They are completely independent of the biological processes based on organic or physical morphology, but their actions are called "the higher functions of man" because they are endomorphic Biological Entities. These "pure Forms of Intelligence thus bear witness to a power of dissociating Form and content, a power which is unattainable in the organic domain" (author's capitalization) (Piaget, 1971a, p. 152-4). *Forms are Operational Structures* (author's italics and capitalization) (ibid., pp. 93-4), *which means that they are composed of metaphysical monads.*

It is precisely the relationship between the two different and unequal subjects he associates with man that Piaget has devoted more time and effort than any other aspect of his work, but this fact has been completely and inexplicably ignored by his followers. Everyone, as far as I can determine, treats the two subjects as two aspects of only one subject. This incorrect interpretation, among others, has led to disastrous results in education and psychology, where thousands of papers and books have been based on gross misunderstandings and countless inappropriate decisions at various levels of our educational system have been made as a result. As mentioned previously, *Piaget was fully aware of the chaos and perplexity he caused and interestingly enough, he gratefully gave his own immanent Subject credit for his ability to create this chaos. Embedded in an extremely disorganized context, Piaget describes how He bears upon us with negative intent. The Schemes of his Internal Organization, that is, of his immanent Subject, exercise a negative pressure* "comparable to a kind of frustration [that] does not arise from cognitive forms of contradiction .... [but is designed] to avoid ... simple opposition [from] becoming [a] contradiction. [The] noncentered and devalued elements are subject to a negative action which pushes them back" (author's italics and capitalization) (Piaget, 1977, p. 145).

Dr. Brown and all of us who have been frustrated by Piaget's writing style should take a moment to ponder this unfriendly warning. There is something about his readers, who represent people in general, that neither he nor his "Internal Organization" likes and both of them are motivated to do something about it. Through his written word "they" plan to put negative pressure on the reader. Hopefully, this negative pressure will "push back" the characteristics they devalue and dislike. Admittedly, this is not a very coherent statement of their devious intentions, but it is obvious that "devalued elements" were to be "pushed back". What we see basically in this "negative action" is a short-hand description of the assimilation process which is the main role of all Schemes of the Internal or immanent Subject (author's capitalization) (Inhelder & Chipman, 1976, p. 33) (Piaget, 1952, p. 30). *As a genuine Gnostic, Piaget wished to be assimilated by his immanent Subject, and he wished to facilitate* the *assimilation of others.* Since Piaget devoutly wished to please his immanent Subject, the ultimate purpose of Piaget's writing style was to facilitate in some fashion the assimilation of his followers in particular, as well as people in general. Piaget issues a threat and a warning when he declares that the dialectic processes of his metaphysical Subject are "conquering but hazardous" (author's capitalization) (Piaget, 1973c, p. 14).

For another aspect of the relationship between the dual subjects, we could compare the "psychological" subject, who does not produce General Knowledge, with the Epistemic Subject who does:

> There is the "psychological subject" [who] is not the origin of any Structure of General Knowledge; but there is also the "Epistemic Subject" or what is common to all subjects ... whose Cognitive Structures derive from the Most General Mechanisms of the Co-ordination of Actions .... We must naturally pursue our enquiry in the direction of the Epistemic Subject (author's capitalization) (Beth & Piaget, 1966, p. 308).

Just as there is a physical biology and a metaphysical Biology, there is, as noted in the introduction, a physical psychology and a metaphysical Psychology. Here the "psychological subject" happens to be lower level, but in other contexts he is metaphysical (Piaget, 1974a, p. 30). If people cannot produce any Structure of General Knowledge, it is important to know exactly what kind of knowledge Piaget has in mind. As noted previously, he is referring to his very narrow concept of Operational Knowledge, as all "effective" knowledge is based on operations (author's capitalization) (Piaget, 1953, p, 7). Operational Knowledge involves a two-part process. The first part is assimilation of the object; the second part is growth of the metaphysical Structure who is the Structure of General Knowledge!

The basic concept of assimilation with which we are concerned did not appear until the time of the philosopher Kant (author's italics) (Piaget, 1971a, p. 55). Piaget thus strongly suggests that Kant's concept of assimilation is similar to his, but he is misrepresenting the case with a red herring as there is no resemblance at all. He is simply hiding Hegel behind Kant because he had rather not, for obvious reasons, be tied too closely to Hegel. Hegel, not Kant, fostered this new concept of assimilation, but their "times" do overlap. Actually, since Piaget modified Hegel's concept considerably, it is fair to say that it is primarily a product of Piaget's busy imagination. Only a particular Permanent or Eternal Structure which is external to the subject's structure is capable of both this kind of assimilation and the kind of Knowledge that is concomitant with it (author's capitalization) (Piaget, 1971c, p. 8). Everyone has this Permanent Structure, which can never be destroyed, but it is intrinsically external to everyone (author's capitalization) (ibid., p. 8). This kind of assimilation functions "by itself" without any help from the individual subject (Piaget, 1952, pp. 349-50). When the Permanent Structure assimilates the object, which is any aspect of physical reality, the second aspect of Knowledge occurs automatically at the same time. That is, the Permanent Structure grows, develops or constructs Himself (author's capitalization) (ibid., pp. 415-16). The Permanent Structure, regardless of whether He is inside or outside of people, is the only Structure of General Knowledge but it goes by many, many names. Self-development or Self-construction is His only method of growth, because by definition He cannot be dependent on anything outside Himself (author's capitalization) (Piaget, 1973d, pp. 49-50) (Beth & Piaget, 1966, p. 198) (Piaget, 1977, p. 173). Since Self-realization is a key concept, many synonyms are also used to camouflage it.

The most extensive use of "verbal entities" or synonyms for the purpose of preventing clear conceptualization, is with reference to the Body of Monads or Absolute Subject. The second largest number of verbal entities, used for the same purpose, is with reference to the dominant activity of this Subject, which is most often indicated by the term "operation". This latter group of verbal entities is complicated by the fact that it is two-tiered. There are a number of "narrow-gauged" synonyms plus a number of more "broad-gauged" ones with which the narrow-gauged synonyms may be combined in doubly confusing and redundant ways. We will briefly examine some terms that are usually narrow-gauged, then we will examine some of the more general terms of the second tier and see how they are intermingled in grotesque or ludicrous ways with first-tier terms. All of the synonyms are italicized in the selected passages to aid comprehension.

The first two synonyms that mean "operation", *equilibration or Self-regulation* constitutes the formative process of Structures (author's italics and capitalization) (Piaget & Inhelder, 1969, p. 159) (Piaget, 1973d, p. 52). Third: *reflecting abstraction* unremittingly forms Logico-Mathematical Structures (author's italics and capitalization) (Piaget, 1973c, p. 55). Although people are not capable of reflective abstraction, the term "unremittingly" strongly suggests effort by a conscious entity. The Entity is the Body of Monads which is the Permanent Structure who is immanent in everyone. Another example of number three: *reflective abstraction* facilitates Spatial structuring, while data derived from physical experience or simple abstraction hinders Spatial structuring (author's italics and capitalization) (Piaget, 1972, p. 40 - 41). "Spatial structuring" can refer to the structuring of each immanent Body of Monads as well as to the total Body of Monads or Space as a whole. In both cases the structuring is by means of operations. It is important to note that "simple abstraction" or natural science actually hinders the only structuring that concerns Piaget - metaphysical structuring. Fourth: "The Structures of Intelligence ... derive one from the other" by means of *relations* (author's italics and capitalization) (Piaget, 1973a, p. 133). Fifth: The role of *mathematical deduction* is to "provide structuration in the strict sense" (author's italics and capitalization) (Piaget & Inhelder, 1971, p, 388). Sixth: *mathematics* is said to be an "instrument of structuralization, because it is of the nature of operations to produce transformations" (author's italics) (Piaget, 1971a, p. 47). When Piaget takes words like "deduction" and "mathematics" which have very familiar meanings, and then, without telling the reader what he is doing, begins to use them from time to time to stand for the dominant activity of the metaphysical Subject, we have a flagrant example of unethical behavior. Seventh: "All processes of development", Piaget insists, following his main human tutor, Hegel, proceed by way of *"thesis ... antithesis ... and a synthesis* transcending them both" (author's italics) (Piaget & Inhelder, 1973 p. 137). *Equilibration, Self-regulation, reflecting or reflective abstraction, relations, mathematical deduction, mathematics, and the Hegelian triad all mean "metaphysical operation"*. Of course, there are lower level meanings for all of these terms, but they are only used in creating plausible alternatives to protect his metaphysical meaning.

One of the terms of the second tier is "psychogenesis". Piaget speaks of the *"psychogenetic* explanation of Logico-Mathematical *operations"* (author's italics and capitalization) (Piaget, 1971b, p. 116). But since both "psychogenesis" and "operation" mean the same thing, he is merely maundering. Next, three synonyms are used to explain the production of a stage: the formative process is said to produce a stage *psychogenetically* by means of *equilibration* (author's italics and capitalization) (Piaget, 1977, p. 135). This means no more than, *"the equilibration process produces stages equilibrationally by means of equilibration"!*

I suggest that Professor Brown, Professor Papert, the Editors of Time and all those who think Piaget is a "great thinker", try to picture him explaining the production of developmental stages by repeating the same concept three times in the form of a farcical causal chain. To be accurate one must imagine him fabricating this redundant chain undercover and with pleasure. Cover is provided by his unique private meanings and pleasure must be assumed because he repeats this mischievous sort of explanation on a regular basis. What type of agenda would fit the imagined scene? What quality of motivation? Emotion? What kind of attitude toward his reader? Toward the academic community? Toward the advancement of knowledge? Can his redundant manipulation of words and barely concealed derision of his readership in any way be considered laudable, positive, objective, ethical, socially responsible, inspiring or profound? Is it logically possible to infer greatness in one who delights in creating such puerile linguistic pranks? Imagine similar scenes repeated hundreds of times, and understand that this is indeed a life-long pattern which he deliberately chose. Piaget knew precisely what the correct answer would be if he were ever fully understood. As we noted previously, he admitted that if his system eventually became known, it would be conclusive proof of his failure (Piaget, 1971c, p. 29). But failure to do what? It would be proof positive that he had failed to succeed in his deceitful bid to impose his metaphysical epistemological system by pretending that it is a legitimate experimental science. The problem, of course, is not the metaphysical system itself, but his incredible decision to present it in the disguise of experimental science. I do not agree with his metaphysical system, but as such it holds no interest for me. I am only concerned with the intent to deceive and the damage that has resulted. Sadly, the conclusive proof of his failure will also signal an inexcusable failure of the academic community.

With regard to the farcical causal chain, Karl Popper claims that Hegel deliberately developed a similar kind of humbug with which to "deceive and bewitch others" (Popper, 1966, p. 28). The examples he gives from Hegel's work suggests that Hegel's style may have served as a model for Piaget.

Another example of the redundant use of synonyms may be especially troublesome to those who have put their confidence in Piaget: He asserted that the motive force for the three psychogenetic stages (Piaget is not consistent regarding the number of stages. Most often he speaks of only three stages, but sometimes he includes a fourth - the preoperational stage) of sensory-motor action, concrete operations and hypothetico-deductive operations was *reflective abstraction* (author's italics) (Beth & Piaget, 1966, p. 245). Five terms in this passage refer to the same exact motive force or Self-developing process of the immanent Subject. "Psychogenetic", "sensory-motor action", "concrete operations", "hypothetico-deductive operations" and "reflective abstraction" all refer to the same metaphysical process - the process of progressive development by means of equilibration or dialectic operations. The passage is more like a mantra than a scientific statement. The immanent Subject is reconstructing Himself within the child by recapitulating the development of the Total Subject, so each of the three stages represents a more advanced development. Nevertheless, the process that is performed by the immanent Body of Monads is exactly the same in each case. Since the three stages of development are only pertinent to the immanent Subject, we will eventually face the embarrassing problem of rewriting our textbooks so that children will not be saddled with inappropriate concepts.

There are hundreds of examples of redundancy, but we will look at only one more: *intelligence* is a "somewhat vague and dangerous word" and it is *"precisely the functioning of Operatory Systems"* (author's italics and capitalization) (Piaget, 1950, p. 80). This kind of intelligence is defined strictly in terms of metaphysical operations, making it merely a restatement of the psychogenetic motive force of the previous example. It has nothing to do with the practical intelligence measured by intelligence tests, because intelligence tests do not reach "constructive operations themselves" (ibid., p. 153).

Development as described above is "in conformity with the general dialectic of the Subject and the object" (author's capitalization) (Piaget, 1976a, p. 164). The "general dialectic" between Subject and object leads to assimilation and development, but what about the "dangerous" dialectic of Subject in subjects? The "whole world" must be assimilated (Bringuier, 1980, p. 44), but Piaget reserves the word "dangerous" for the hateful object (Piaget, 1971c, p. XVI) who is detestable (Inhelder & Piaget, 1958, p. 349). He simply does not like this physical subject (Piaget, 1970b, p. 68), and delights in the fact that it will be eliminated. He joyfully submits his own physical body and ego to this purging process, to which he adverts in the following passage. "The formative process of the Structures we have described ... [may be followed in their] step-by-step evolution ... in the lived and living dialectic of subjects" (author's capitalization) (Piaget & Inhelder, 1969, p. 159). This highly contrived and fragmentary statement is designed to be frustrating, but it is not difficult. If one knows the difference between "lived" and "living" and notes that "subjects" is plural, the meaning is clear. "Lived" nearly always refers to the physical subject, while "living" nearly always refers to the Living or metaphysical Subject. So we have two subjects in a dialectic interaction for the purpose of forming or developing the Permanent Subject or Structure. The Living Subject is in the process of assimilating the lived subject because the lived subject must be assimilated just like any other object.

The lived subject is an object (ibid., 94) (Piaget, 1954, p. 96), and for Piaget he is a very special object. In addition to being intensely disliked, he is a most likely candidate, according to Piaget, for operational assimilation because he is "active" and already partly transformed (Piaget, 1974b, p. 17). The lived subject is "a spatio-temporal power", meaning that he is a "succession in time, and therefore cannot be prevented from being assimilated" (ibid., p. 152). Piaget's concept of assimilation is highlighted when it becomes clear that everything which "takes time" will be swept away by assimilation. There is "a vital need" for "the Organism" to "escape from the contradictions inherent in the successive events" in time and to "avoid time". *Everything that includes the intervention of duration must be eliminated* (author's italics) (ibid., pp. 125-6). *Every action in physical reality, including thought or the movement of light, takes time, but movement and communication among the monads does not take time* (author's italics) (Piaget, 1970c, p. 60) (Piaget, 1950, pp. 120-1).

The defining difference between the Living Structure and the physical or "lived" subject is seen in this passage:

> If one were to take Mathematical Entities [or Structures] as external to the subject, what has just been said [that Logico-Mathematical Structures furnish an all-embracing prevision] would still be valid .... Logico-Mathematical Structures ... [are] the product of ... the Living Organization itself (author's capitalization) (Piaget, 1971a, pp. 211-12).

One might note in this excerpt a favorite device Piaget uses when he employs two terms that mean "Absolute Subject"; one of the terms is singular and the other is plural. When two or more synonyms are employed complexity can thus be increased. For instance, it is awkward for the reader when he tries to pin down the meanings of "Mathematical Entities", "Structures" and "Living Organization" because grammatical conventions automatically indicate differences in meaning between the first two terms and the third. The language strongly suggests that the terms could not have the same identical referent, so the reader is psychologically inhibited from making this inference. Almost all of the "verbal entities" that refer to the Body of Monads, and there are several hundred, can be either singular or plural. *In my notes alone I counted 163 "different" metaphysical Structures and 23 different physical structures.*[1] *That is, 163 "verbal entities", which include the word "Structure" and can be singular or plural, that are synonyms of the Absolute Subject.* Piaget was unbelievably thorough in his determination to prevent unambiguous conceptualization of his metaphysical system.

The Mathematical Structure or Entity is composed of living monads which not only know the past, but also know the future. An "all-embracing prevision" or omniscience certainly makes the Structure superhuman. This Structure or Living Organization could not be an intrinsic part of the "lived" subject at all. Piaget is partially correct when he says that this Structure is the product of the Living Organization, as the two terms are identical in meaning and the Entity referred to is engaged in Self-development. Nevertheless, deceitfulness is apparent.

TRUE CAUSE IS NOT PHYSICAL

There are two kinds of causality. Natural science studies one kind, which is based on energy and physical force. The other kind of causality is based on the operational activity of monads which is unknown to natural science.

> Why do concepts, inferences, etc. of subjects age 2 to 6 remain preoperational, if not because of illegitimate intrusions of causality and an insufficient Causality? And why does Causality remain insufficient ... if not because ... the influence of Logical Structures ... remain[s] rudimentary (author's capitalization) (Piaget, 1974b, p.115)?

In this case Piaget is not subtle in his use of the two kinds of causality. It appears that he wishes to jar the reader's sensibility. Physical causality "intrudes illegitimately" to hinder development, while the Causality of Logical Structures, composed of immanent monads, has not yet overcome these intrusions sufficiently. It is clear that "sufficient Cause" depends upon subsequent Self-development of the Logical Structures or immanent Subject. In other words, as the child gets older his immanent Subject will increasingly become more sufficiently Causal, while the illegitimate

---

[1] See Appendix M

intrusions of the physical child gradually will be overcome. This is indeed what Piaget's theory calls for, but it is not what we see in his experiments, as he has found it more convenient to find the youngest children most influenced by the immanent Subject. This rather amazing discrepancy between theory and practice is seen in all of his work. The solution is simple. Since Piaget is the only investigator in academic circles who can read the Minds of infants and young children, he can find anything he wishes to find at this level! Who is going to demonstrate otherwise? The situation is a bit more complicated with older children. Since Piaget never had to really defend his metaphysical system, it is rife with contradictions.

Sometimes the word "force" is used as a synonym for "causality".

> Only by means of a derivative process does the Mind come to dissociate the "I" from the world around it, and in the measure that this dissociation takes place, *force becomes gradually withdrawn from external objects and confined within the Ego* (author's italics and capitalization) (Piaget, 1930, pp. 131-2).

There are obviously two kinds of force or causality represented in this quote, the force associated with external objects and studied by natural science, and the force confined within the Ego. The "Total Ego", "I", "Mind" or "Self", composed of monads, is so big that everything is "confined within" it. Piaget leaves no doubt about this. That is, not only is everything within the Universe of Monads but, more important, every possible cause depends upon the Universe of Monads, which is the metaphysical Ego. Adolescence is the metaphysical age par excellence, he maintains, and the adolescent believes that "the Self is strong enough to reconstruct the universe and big enough to incorporate it" (author's capitalization) (Piaget, 1967, p. 64). This is not just a "play on words" for Piaget, as he means it literally. Knowledge of the environment is only attained, according to him, because the Organization's Structures extend into the physical universe as a whole (author's capitalization) (Piaget, 1971a, pp. 338-9). The meaning is that the "I", "Ego", "Self", "Subject", "Organism" or "Organization" extends His Structure into the farthest reaches of the physical universe. Yes, the meaning is exactly that "the universe is embodied in the activity of the Subject" (author's capitalization) (Piaget, 1952b, p. 43). Since no activity of any kind is possible without the presence of monads, they must be everywhere.

AN ALIEN EXPERIENCE, AN ALIEN SCIENCE

There are two kinds of experience.

> Physical experience, i.e., experience that involves contact with objects and the gaining of knowledge by abstraction from the object itself [colours, weights and so on]. It is this kind we commonly think of and which alone is taken into account by empiricism. On the other hand, however, there is what may be called Logico-Mathematical experience .... It too involves contact with objects, but by obtaining Knowledge of these actions themselves and not from objects as such (author's capitalization) (Piaget, 1973c, p. 45).

Piaget is correct when he says that physical experience is the kind we generally think about. Natural science in its entirety is based on physical experience as he defines it. For him, all possible experience which is based on the real world is physical experience. Moreover, the empirical conduct of natural science does not include assimilation or Mental activity as defined by Piaget (Piaget, 1952, p. 314). Logico-Mathematical experience accompanies operations, so human beings cannot have any part in this kind of experience. The phrase, "by obtaining Knowledge of these actions themselves and not from objects as such", does not follow logically from what preceded it because "these" has no proper referent. The actions involved are operational or Logico-Mathematical, so it is not surprising that Piaget muddles the meaning. Although he pretends to carry out Logico-Mathematical experiments with children, the experiments can only be based on very vague analogies with the Logico-Mathematical process because this process is beyond human capacity.

There are two kinds of science.

> The idealist interpretation of the transcendental Self did not remain alien to Hegel. While opening the way [for] the Concrete Universal in the domain of Mind, he has ... [opened the way for the Concrete Universal in the domain] of nature [and] given one of the best examples of speculative reason ... [as] a parascientific tendency. [This parascientific tendency] ... [pursues] the Ideal of a form of Knowledge ... which would duplicate science in its own domain (author's capitalization) (Piaget, 1971c, p. 58).

The "Transcendental Self" or "Concrete Universal" are references to the Absolute Entity of Hegel's philosophy. Hegel's idealism was called "Absolute Idealism" (Edwards, 1967, Vol. 4. p. 114). *Piaget took Hegel's Absolute Idealism and expanded it to form, not only his own philosophy, but also the psychology he wished to investigate.* In his autobiography we read: "Between Biology and the analysis of Knowledge I needed something other than philosophy. I believe it was at that moment that I discovered a need that could be satisfied only by Psychology" (author's capitalization) (Piaget, 1976, p. 119). *Why was he "satisfied" by Psychology? Because it was a Psychology of the metaphysical Mind to which Hegel's idealist interpretation points. Observe that Hegel's philosophy "opened the way for the Concrete Universal in the domain of Mind". The domain opened up by Hegel was the Psychology of the Absolute Subject* (author's italics and capitalization) (ibid., p. 119). All of Piaget's professional work has as its focus the psychological attributes of the Absolute Subject as he imagines them to be, and the starting point for his assumptions in this regard is the fundamental motivation he ascribes to the Absolute, which is the full realization of His potential.

In addition to preparing the way for a Psychology of the Absolute, Hegel also prepared the way for a Science of the Absolute. As Piaget explains, "would Science have as a goal the relative and philosophy the Absolute" (author's italics and capitalization) (Piaget, 1971b p. 92)? *Of course not, Science must also have the same goal; that is, a Science alien to every assumption to which most of us have been exposed.* This alien Science is based, not on empirical evidence, but on the same "philosophical dialectics" that leads to the growth of the Absolute Subject (author's capitalization) (Piaget, 1971c, p. 115). This Science is the study of how dialectic interaction leads to the development of the Absolute Subject or Living Structure, and "Structure is so defined that it cannot coincide with any ... of the existing sciences" (author's capitalization) (Piaget, 1970b, p. 138). This posited Structure is the Being of Science and Piaget calls for an enquiry into this Being who is "not that of things' (author's capitalization) (Piaget, 1971c, p. 120). Since we are told indirectly that

Science is only possible with the Transcendental Entity, either as the Body of Monads in toto or as immanent Sub-Units of monads, He must be the Being of Science (author's capitalization) (Piaget, 1971a, p. 362). "Science implies the intervention of the Mind, let us say at least the activity of the Thinking Subject .... The Subject's activity is a field of investigation usually reserved for philosophy, [but if] we really wish to achieve the unity of Science, we must ... scientifically study this activity of the Subject, that is, remove Something from philosophy" (author's capitalization) (Piaget, 1971b, p. 90). *This "Something" that must be removed from philosophy is none other than the Absolute Subject, and what must be scientifically studied is His one-of-a-kind development - the very study of development that both Time* (Papert, 1999) *and the American Psychological Association* (author's italics and capitalization) (Piaget, 1972, p. 15) *incorrectly thought was made into a traditional science by Piaget. Piaget thus describes himself on the sly as a "scientist" who specializes in studying an imaginary Being!*

As strange as it may seem, Science for Piaget is simply the Self-actualization process of the Absolute Subject. This is emphasized when "Science" is personalized. The dialectical process, namely the process of Self-actualization, arises from "Science on the march" (author's capitalization) (Piaget, 1974a, p. 10). Here "Science" means "Absolute Subject", who is the only source of Piaget's "dialectic process". Science, who is again personalized, has no interest in joining any of the kinds of science except Piaget's kind (author's capitalization) (Piaget, 1971b, p. 97). "I ... [distinguish] the Subject-Psychologist who constructs His Science [from] any human subject whatsoever" (author's capitalization) (Piaget, 1971c, p. 224). *The Subject-Psychologist or Absolute Subject is engaging in the dialectic process of Self-realization, and this is precisely Piaget's kind of Science! Here we see that true Science is reserved exclusively for the Absolute Subject.*

There are two kinds of psychology and two kinds of science.

If [experimental pedagogy] intends to limit itself, in conformity with the positivist conception of science, to a simple investigation into facts and laws, without claiming to explain what it states, then naturally *there is no need whatever for a connection with Psychology* (author's italics and capitalization) (Piaget, 1970d, p. 23).

Natural science is described quite accurately as an investigation into facts and laws without claiming to explain these facts and laws. Piaget then proclaims curiously that Psychology is not required for this kind of science. Only one "psychology" is mentioned but he could not have asserted more dogmatically his view that there are two psychologies, one of which is not worth mentioning. *We know now for sure what kind of Psychology satisfied Piaget when he was first introduced to metaphysical Biology* (author's italics and capitalization) (Piaget, 1976, p. 119)! Neither the "Subject-Psychologist" nor Piaget is interested in natural science or the physical subject who produces natural science. It is ironic indeed that he is honored as a great scientist, *as the only science acceptable to him is the "metaphysical operational Science" of Self-realization. This Science explains everything because the Absolute Entity is the "Scientist".*

The "hands on" science that educators have emphasized in recent years is supposedly based on Piaget's theories, even though he holds that direct experience leads to false logic (Piaget & Inhelder, 1974, p. 220), and that pedagogy should not be based on empiricism (Piaget, 1973b, pp. 10-11). As a matter of fact, Piaget insists that he is a tireless opponent of empiricism (Piaget, 1980, p. 10). In a handbook prepared for teachers of science there is, in addition to the practical information on teaching science, one paper by Piaget plus four papers purporting to explain his theory (Teachers' Handbook, 1977). The four explanatory papers interpret Piaget exclusively within the framework of natural science and empirical learning, so we must assume, based on the indented quote above, that Piaget considered them to be completely "Mindless" because no "Psychology" was involved (author's capitalization) (Piaget, 1970d, p. 23)! The fact that this little scenario regarding empirical learning contradicts Piaget's true position, regarding the involvement of Psychology, would not bother him at all, as a little confusion is quite desirable. In any case, we are confident that these four papers are not essentially different from several thousand other papers and books. A. Sunier wrote in 1977 that there were 800 titles by immediate collaborators with Piaget and 1, 750 titles of "secondary literature engendered by Piagetian thinking" listed in the *Catalogue des Archives Jean Piaget* at the University of Geneva. Also listed were 1500 titles by Piaget himself (Piaget, et al., 1977, p. XII). Since 1977 how many more of such papers and books have adulterated the academic enterprise because of a mistaken basic assumption?

SPIRITUAL OBJECTS AND PHYSICAL OBJECTS

A fundamental notion in Piaget's system is the doctrine that scientific objects constructed their direct opposites, the practical objects. "It is ... not illegitimate to elucidate one of the terms of intellectual evolution by the directly opposite term, that is, the construction of practical objects by that of scientific objects" (Piaget, 1954, p. 97). "Practical objects" refers to everything in the physical universe, including people. *"Scientific objects" refers to Piaget's wonderful imaginary monads, his whole Universe of Active Objects* (author's italics and capitalization) (Piaget, et al., 1977, pp. 179-80). These monads, that make up the Absolute Subject, created the physical universe (author's capitalization) (Piaget, 1952b, pp. 12;190) (Piaget & Inhelder, 1974, p. 231) and, after eons of time, managed to construct human beings (Piaget, 1974b, p. 127) (Piaget, 1970b, p. 44). A major motivation for Piaget's labors included the need to explain, undercover, why practical objects were created and why they must now be assimilated or absorbed back into the eternal monads. This motivation is based on the doctrine of "reversibility", according to which every act of physical construction will be exactly reversed by operational assimilation (Piaget, 1971b, p. 114) (Piaget & Inhelder, 1974, p. 272) (Piaget, 1967, p. 106). The dialectical process began when practical objects were created, and it is directed toward a predetermined conclusion (Piaget, 1971a, p. 213) (Piaget 1972, p. 90) (Piaget, 1929, p. 235) of complete assimilation, equilibrium and perfect development of the Absolute Subject. Every operation is teleological (Piaget, 1977, p. 40) (Piaget, 1976a, p. 271). *Unfortunately, this entire process, and all of the terms associated with it, has been falsified by a catastrophic failure of the academic process. The reason for the failure is an urgent question, and other investigators will undoubtedly address it.*

There is knowledge based on physical activity, as defined by Piaget, and there is Knowledge based on metaphysical activity.

A General System ... states in a most direct way the problem of the duality of knowledge [spatio-temporal, or "of the world" and "Eidetic"]. [Eidetic Knowledge requires] the addition of a transcendental Self [and originates] ... from the progress of a particular Science (author's capitalization) (Piaget, 1971c, p, 59).

Spatio-temporal knowledge is "of the world" and for human beings; Eidetic or Self-knowledge is "not of the world" and is exclusively of and for the Absolute Subject (author's capitalization) (Piaget, 1971c, p. 109). Natural science produces spatio-temporal knowledge which is based on empirical learning, but empirical learning cannot bring about Logico-Mathematical or Eidetic Knowledge (author's capitalization) (Piaget, 1971a, p. 313). This follows because empiricism "does not admit of any internal principle of construction" (Piaget, 1952b. p. 417), making it logically impossible for Eidetic Knowledge to be acquired by people. *Eidetic Knowledge is only possible for the metaphysical Structure by means of His "particular Science". More exactly, it is the parascience of Hegel's Transcendental Self, which is simply the process of operational assimilation and Self-development.*

Knowledge, as a personalized synonym for immanent Structure, regulates information to solve His own problems (authors capitalization) (ibid., p. 6), not the child's problems. He is not a part of the child (Beth & Piaget, 1966, p. 244) and He cares nothing about the child, because in the last analysis all objects and beings, including "the child", will dissolve in "the current of development". It is His development and it alone, according to Piaget, that is a "fact" (author's capitalization) (Piaget, 1971b, p. 2).

TWO KINDS OF DEVELOPMENT

There are two kinds of development. One kind is for people and the other is for the Absolute Entity inside of people.

I have in mind only the truly Psychological development of the child as opposed to his school development or to his family development; that is, I will above all stress the spontaneous aspect .... [Spontaneous development is] what the child learns by Himself, what none can teach Him and He must discover alone (author's capitalization) (Piaget, 1973a, p. 2).

On reading this passage one should be able to conclude that Piaget is comparing two aspects of development in individual children, but such a conclusion would be a mistake. He is comparing two kinds of development, but people can enjoy only one kind. He is only pretending to compare two aspects of development with respect to human beings. "Spontaneous" development is not an option for people at all, but Piaget is obviously not free to reveal this openly. Spontaneous development is reserved for the immanent Subject in the child, and it is based on operations, which are not possible for physical subjects. The immanent Subject is alien to the child; He is the child's opposite and is only using the child as an object to be assimilated in order to facilitate His own development (author's capitalization) (Piaget, 1974b, pp. 6; 150). This fact is accentuated in an ominous fashion: *The child shows "a systematic egocentric distortion of Space, but the developmental process leads to a reversal of these conditions".* "Henceforward his conception of Space includes himself as one moving object among many" (author's italics and capitalization) (Piaget, Inhelder & Szeminska, 1960, p. 64). What is Piaget implying when he asserts that the developmental process will reverse the child's systematic distortion of Space? *He is serving notice that the developmental process, actuated by immanent Space, is systematically distorting the child in the process of assimilating him! Space is a synonym for Absolute Subject, and He is busily assimilating "the child", who represents all of us.*

Piaget advances our understanding of Personal Space when, in addition to immanent Space distorting the child, we are informed that the Spatial Continuum as a whole is intent on the same fundamental task: "This ... 'purging' of Space ... by progressively emptying it of objects in order to organize the Space or 'Container' itself". This process does not take place at once, but is accomplished by "anchoring the transformations [of the objects] to invariants" (author's capitalization) (Piaget & Inhelder, 1956, p. 377). These invariants are monads. When Space or Container is said to be organizing itself it is helpful to know that "organization" is a frequent synonym for "development"; "all development is an organization, and all organization, a development" (Piaget, 1971a, p. 135).

Another term used for "school" or "family" development is "psychosocial" development, which is subordinated to spontaneous development (Piaget 1973a, p. 3-4). *Not only is psychosocial or school development subordinate to spontaneous development, it actually interferes with it* (author's italics) (Piaget, Inhelder & Szeminska, 1960, p. 381). Incredible as it may seem, Piaget declares that all exogenous knowledge, which includes all knowledge of which man is capable, produces a disequilibrium which must be reequilibrated by endogenous reconstructions or operations (Piaget, 1980b, p. 101). We must deal with the unpleasant fact that the very best man can do as man, in acquiring knowledge, not only is unprofitable in Piaget's view, but is actually a hindrance to the progress of "true" Knowledge. Complete assimilation will be attained when *all* exogenous characteristics are eliminated by an endogenous reconstruction (author's italics) (ibid., p. 96). *Every educational process from birth until death is essentially physical since it takes time and energy. This means that it basically interferes with work that must be accomplished by the Absolute Subject* whose monads are both inside and outside of people. Spontaneous development of the immanent Subject results from the operational or endogenous work of the monads inside of people, but neither individual people nor scientific investigations can ever detect this operational activity as it is outside the domain of spatio-temporal reality.

PSYCHOLOGICAL NECESSITY AND INVARIANT
FUNCTION VERSUS PHYSICAL BIOLOGY

The child and the immanent Subject within him are two different entities. The immanent Subject is conscious of the child because He has the task of assimilating him, but the child is not conscious of the immanent Subject.

To our mind, if the greatest ambiguity is to be avoided, it must be allowed that Unconscious Thought merges into action .... Unconscious Thought is a series of operations .... Ribot's view that this Unconscious Life can be resolved into movements is the most intelligible that has yet been put forward. These movements and [not "and" but "or" as "movements" means the same as "operations"] operations ... obey ... a logic of their own. The only kind of implication of which we can talk in connection with Subconscious Thought is ... psychological or mental necessity. So ... everything we have said in this work ... has led us to the conclusion that childish thought is devoid of logical necessity (author's capitalization) (Piaget, 1928, p. 145-6).

Piaget quite often equates "Unconscious" or "Subconscious" Thought with metaphysical operations, but since the production of operations is the most conscious of all activities, we know that the term "unconscious" is used to mislead or confuse the reader. In a rather silly but revealing admission, he announces that "the Unconscious is everywhere" (author's capitalization) (Piaget, 1962, p. 172). This is merely another way of saying that monads are everywhere. With exactly the same meaning in mind, he says that Binet was "convinced that Intelligence is everywhere" (author's capitalization) (Piaget, 1973c, p. 59). We must remind ourselves that the personalized synonyms, "Intelligence" or "the Unconscious" represent the Entity who is not only immanent within the child, but who also exists and operates outside the child. Stripped of the hocus-pocus, Piaget is seen to be dancing around his central doctrine which holds that "the Spatial Surround [is] organized in a ... three-dimensional Reference Frame [of monads]" (author's capitalization) (Piaget & Inhelder, 1956, p. 416). The simple "fact" he artificially complicates is that the child is not conscious of the immanent Subject who is consciously operating on him. The operations obey a logic of their own because they are independent of the child and are necessary because their source is the immanent Subject. The child's thought is not necessary because the source is physical.

The brain is not essential to intellectual activity, but the A Priori or Functional Invariant is essential.

The structures of the first type [sensory organs and nervous system] .... in contrast to the [A Priori or] Functional Invariants ... have nothing essential from the point of view of Mind. They are ... limited and delimiting, and ... Intellectual activity will unremittingly transcend them (author's capitalization) (Piaget, 1952b, p. 3).

The existence of physical structures, like the brain, are not necessary for effecting the intellectual activity of the Mind (author's capitalization) (Piaget, 1971a, p. 216) (Beth & Piaget, 1966, p. 203). *This non-physical Mind has another remarkable characteristic; it is a complete Biological Organization.* The "Functional Nucleus of the Intellectual Organization ... comes from the Biological Organization .... This Invariant ... orients ... the successive Structures which the Mind [who plays the role of the A Priori] will then work out in its contact with reality" (author's capitalization) (Piaget. 1952b, p. 3). This passage is a highly contrived concatenation of seven terms that mean exactly the same thing. "Functional Nucleus", "Intellectual Organization", "Biological Organization", "Invariant", "Structure", "Mind" and "A Priori" all mean Absolute Subject. The dance now is fervently focused on the Absolute Subject - with a decidedly more frenetic pace! As we have observed repeatedly, Piaget often strings together words that in reality are no more than magical incantations, consisting of a bare procession of synonyms. Yes, as will become apparent in the final chapter, Piaget was clearly involved in magic (Piaget,

1929, pp. 251; 433-436) (Beth & Piaget, 1966, p. 155)! If Flavell had known the metaphysical meaning of these words perhaps we would have been spared the long, expensive, irresponsible and destructive Piagetian episode. In any case, we know that he pored over this particular selection because of a long quote (Flavell 1963, p. 44). Each of the terms, including the Mind, refers to the Living Spirit composed of monads who is indeed the complete Biological Organization of "primary importance" (ibid., p. 44).

For Piaget, Thought is a dialectical engagement between the monads and any physical object or individual person (author's capitalization) (Beth & Piaget, 1966, p. 280) (Piaget, 1980a, p. 304). "To Think is to act on the object and transform it" (author's capitalization) (Piaget, 1973a, p. 90). According to Piaget, this includes the actual transformation of the facts themselves (ibid., p. 90), which is wholly alien to the empirical or scientific point of view. The empiricist or scientist strives to know the facts, but the Absolute Subject is intent on doing away with physical facts. The facts are transformed in a very specific way. Physical facts always consist of two factors, one is physical and the other is metaphysical as a result of previous dialectic syntheses. The act of thinking assimilates and thus decreases the physical factor, while at the same time it increases the metaphysical factor. The physical brain can have no part in this kind of thinking. The system of invariants is the invariant actions of the metaphysical Self (author's capitalization) (Piaget, et al., p. 175). This Self is capable of invariant actions, but it is not a human self because it does not have physical structures. The Functional Invariant is not based on any physical structure whether it be molecule or nervous system as a whole, so it is obviously the immanent Self composed of Living Monads. Although Piaget speaks of invariant monads, at the level of personhood "there exists One Invariant" (author's capitalization) (Piaget, 1954, p. 356). That is, the metaphysical Person is the only personal invariant. Piaget also states that "We can think without appealing to experience" (author's capitalization) (Beth & Piaget, 1966, p. 203). Of course, this is the metaphysical "We"!

The few investigators who have devoted intense effort in trying to understand Piaget have consistently ignored the metaphysical aspects of his system. Flavell, in discussing biological invariants says: "These invariant characteristics, which define the essence of intellectual functioning and hence the essence of intelligence, are also the very characteristics which hold for biological functioning in general" (Flavell, 1963, p. 43). The problem with this assertion is that there are no true "invariants" in biology understood as a natural science. Even Piaget agrees: "Functional invariables ... can only be said to be approximate at the organic level" (Piaget, 1971a, p. 154). As usual with Piaget, "functional invariable" can refer to the physical level or the metaphysical level, but he holds, as do traditional scientists, that "physical constants" are not truly invariant. Furthermore, he regards all experimental data as being inconceivable in the absence of formal compositions of monads (Piaget & Inhelder, 1974, pp. 264-5). The basic problem for Flavell, of course, was that he did not know the metaphysical meaning of "Biology". *Actually, within Piaget's system, the fundamental processes of assimilation make it impossible for any physical structure or function to be invariant, as the process of assimilation is continually reversing everything physical back into the metaphysical monads from which it was derived. As we noted previously, everything physical is being dissolved in the current of development* (author's italics) (Piaget, 1971b, p. 2).

SPECIFIC HEREDITY VERSUS GENERAL HEREDITY

Flavell acknowledges Piaget's distinction between "specific heredity" or the heredity of every aspect of man's nature that can be studied by natural science, and "general heredity" which, unknown to Flavell, is merely a synonym for psychogenesis, equilibration or operation. *Rather than accept general heredity as the mode of producing progressively more complex or developed metaphysical Structures as Piaget ambiguously describes it, Flavell forces it into an anti-scientific concept of physical heredity. In other words, he tries to accommodate Piaget's metaphysics by adding something to ordinary biological inheritance that no biologist has ever detected scientifically.* "Our biological endowment consists", Flavell says, "not only of inborn structures ... but it also consists ... of Something which lies behind intellectual achievement .... What is this Something ... and what is its relation to biological processes at large" (author's capitalization) (Flavell, 1963, p. 42)? "Inborn structures" means everything, directly or indirectly, encoded in DNA. *Since Flavell apparently knew that this "Something" was outside the purview of science, as it is generally understood, the least he should have done was warn his readers that it is a very questionable concept. This "Something" is not a scientific concept at all as it is the immanent Subject within the child, and general heredity specifically has to do with how this eternal immanent Subject progressively develops Himself.* Biology and Knowledge (1971a) was not available to Flavell when he wrote his book, but Piaget, perhaps in response to what Flavell had said about general heredity, emphasizes his position: *it is the Permanent Organization that is significant in general heredity and not the "motionless little balls" otherwise known as genes* (author's italics and capitalization) (ibid., pp. 114-15). Since genes are physical, Piaget has no use for them!

As it turned out, Flavell's book was Piaget's major entree into the academic world. Almost all of the Piagetians whom I have known based their understanding of Piaget's theory on Flavell's book, not Piaget's many books. Most textbooks that utilize Piaget's theory demonstrate Flavell's weighty influence by the large number of references to his work. Although he did not give a caveat regarding general heredity, we should note that he did give many generalized warnings in his extraordinarily insightful final chapter. Considering the constrictive parameters within which he evaluated Piaget, this is an amazing chapter. And while we admire Flavell for venturing to deal with one of Piaget's well-protected and thus almost unintelligible doctrines, we must not ignore his blind spot regarding Piaget's prime concern with the metaphysical realm.

Piaget introduces the two kinds of heredity, one physical and the other metaphysical, at the beginning of his book, *The Origins of Intelligence in Children* (1952b). He deals with this question from time to time throughout the book, and then further clarifies the distinction in the concluding chapter, *but with a different vocabulary.* The problem of the two kinds of heredity is initially framed in terms of five "attempted solutions". Each "solution" is a mixture of physical and metaphysical notions which are never completely resolved, but in the concluding 63 pages the operational or psychogenetic process, which is indeed "general heredity", was revisited and emphasized. Flavell was very much aware that Piaget changed his vocabulary in a disconcerting way while continuing to write about the same ideas, but he was not aware of the major dichotomy of meaning that obtains when the same word is used alternately for physical reality and metaphysical Reality. When Piaget returned to the problem at the end of the book, he used different words as well as the two drastically different meanings of these new words to create frustrating problems for the reader. He continued to frame the problem of two different kinds of heredity in terms of the same five possible solutions, plus a sixth solution just to break the parallel pattern, but he never uses the terms "specific heredity" or "general heredity" in the conclusion. *Under this well-disguised cover he felt more freedom to emphasize the metaphysical character of "general heredity"*. Flavell based his comments regarding the two kinds of heredity on the first twenty pages, not realizing, I believe, that Piaget returned to the question of the two kinds of heredity at the end of the book with a different set of words. This is typical, as Piaget characteristically presents a fundamental problem with one set of words and then resolves it with a synonymous set without explicitly making the appropriate connections for the reader. Many times he uses one or more intermediate sets of synonyms in the process. One must know the private meanings of his words in order to follow his devious maneuvers.

It will be worthwhile to trace his concluding argument through the long maze of barely intelligible or contradictory statements. Piaget tests the reader's patience over the final 63 pages by meting out aspects of the functional activity of the Invariant, and then clouding each admission with apparent reversals or enigmatic statements. One partial solution is the vitalistic or intellectualistic one, where "Intelligence" is a synonym of "General Heredity" ("General Heredity" is capitalized here because, like "Intelligence", it can stand for the Entity Himself as well as for the main activity of the Entity). "Intelligence" is also a synonym of "Functional Invariant", which is "explained by itself", roughly meaning "explained by His Self-development" (author's capitalization) (ibid., p. 358). *On the following page, other characteristics of Intelligence are added, giving us an Intelligence engaging in assimilatory activity, elaborating or developing Himself by interacting with the environment, and limiting the role of chance.* The next five or six pages are devoted to arguments against both empiricism and the role of physical experience. "Experience", presented ambiguously as metaphysical experience, is encountered from time to time. For instance, on 365 the "experience" of "progressive action" or "construction" is desirable because it refers to the growth or the development of the metaphysical Entity, in other words the constructive processes of "general heredity".

On 366 Intelligence has metamorphosed into "Schemata", and we are immediately faced with the bothersome change from singular "Intelligence" to plural "Schemata". Nevertheless, they are synonyms. The Schema is said to "experiment" for the purpose of assimilation, and as the Schema bears more upon reality, "experience" becomes more active. The "experimentation" and "experience" of the Schema is metaphysical in this case, and the assimilatory progress entailed is called "objectivity". "Objectivity" is used by Piaget to mean "progressive assimilation of the object" and, of course, this meaning cannot be found in the dictionary (Piaget, 1971c, p. 128) (Piaget & Inhelder, 1971, pp. 387-388).

The various synonyms of the Absolute Subject which follow in this paragraph are capitalized by the author: "Intelligence" reappears on 370 as a "Total System" and a "Power Sui Generis". Intelligence is said to be a "Self-Explanatory Mechanism" which is immanent and vitalistic. By "vitalistic", Piaget means that "Intelligence" or the "Total Schema" is distinct from everything physical or chemical in the body. He also means that Intelligence or the Total Schema is the Entity that gives the body life. On 377 *the "theory of Form" is called upon to explain the "Mechanism of Intelligence", without telling the reader, of course, that Form is the Mechanism of Intelligence as well as the Total Schema.* Here again Piaget confounds meaning as he "explains" something by simply adding one or more synonyms. After first suggesting that form may be lower level or physical, he speaks of an internal Form that is "independent of our deliberate intentions". On 387 Piaget decides that Forms should be raised to the rank of Intellectual Schemata, and Forms are considered to be the same as Intelligence itself on 389. On 399 Piaget is of the opinion that the "Organism" is a "Machine for Implication". The private meaning of "implication" is "operation", and Piaget confirms this on 403 when he says, "it is self-evident that implication presupposes" assimilatory activity. He repeats this notion on 405, and then leaps abruptly to the lower level with a "physical" example of implication. *Piaget reverts to the Total Schema, the Spatial Continuum or Space as a Whole, when he says grandly on 407 that the Living Body tends to impose on the whole universe its own organization, and that the Living Being assimilates to Himself the whole universe.* On 412 Piaget tempers his exuberant praise of the Living Body of monads with a mundane example concerning the physical "living body". *On 413 he repeats his exuberant praise of the Absolute Entity but this time he uses the term, "Schema of Assimilation", which he trumpets will "conquer the whole universe".* The book ends with Schemata described as a naturally "inventing" and "assimilating" Entity - which is another discordant use of a plural to describe a singular Being.

This very complex, confusing and grandiose conclusion to a famous tour de force is based squarely on Piaget's ability to directly read the minds of infants. It was noted in the introduction that, with reference to this particular book, the information on which Piaget supposedly relied to generate this preposterous glut of self-contradictory theorizing was supplied by infants less than two years of age, most of it coming from babies before their first birthday. Flavell leaned heavily on the towering oracular theory presented by this book, and since academia leans heavily on Flavell we are confronted with the question of how the empirical base of mostly non-verbal infantile behavior could lead to such an outlandishly top-heavy theory. It is not possible to begin with an analysis of Piaget's 183 "experimental observations" in this book and then *logically* work one's way up to the marvelous theoretical superstructure. *Although Piaget discussed the "experimental results" endlessly, he did not even try to take us by means of a rational process from these results to his conclusions - his totally unrelated metaphysical conclusions! He realized better than anyone else that there can be no rational chain of reasoning from such experiments to his conclusions; all that is possible, in this particular case, is a giant leap from physical reality to metaphysical Reality!* This is why we are forced to rely entirely on Piaget's ability to read the minds of non-verbal infants and report to his readership truthfully what they tell him! Flavell's interpretation, and thus academia's conclusions, hang by this slender thread - a modern-day version of Damocles' sword. To take the most optimistic possibility, from a Piagetian's point of view, let us assume that Piaget can truly read the minds of babies, and that his entire theory has their stamp of approval, even though they are completely unconscious of such thoughts. Where does this take us? Surely we are not logically or morally obligated to accept the subconscious judgments of babies! *Piaget has manipulated many into this Alice-in-Wonderland scenario, and at the same time has underlined the awesome gullibility which unfortunately exists. Why have so many in academia been beguiled into substituting this kind of irrationality for scientific research?*

We see through the miasmic fog of multiplied verbal entities and linguistic obfuscation that "general heredity" is nothing more than the psychogenetic or operational process of metaphysical Self-development.

Piaget's "Biological Invariant" is not encoded in DNA and does not belong to the realm of biology as a natural science. The "Biology" of this Invariant is the Biology of non-physical monads, which serve as the Field for multiple dialectical interactions (author's capitalization) (Piaget, 1971a, p. 34). Flavell was led astray by his reluctance to accept the conclusive evidence that Piaget was motivated solely by metaphysical concerns. This reluctance appears to be universal in academic circles, and it is probably the key to explaining the unmitigated disaster of Piagetianism.

Hans Furth made the same basic accommodation that Flavell made in order to avoid Piaget's metaphysics. He too assumed that "Something" besides our genetic inheritance enables us to acquire operative knowledge, and he also appeals to a non-scientific kind of "biology" to account for this "Something". *He specifically claims that the organs of the body, which are based on genetic transmission can never give us intelligence beyond the sensory-motor level* (author's italics) (Furth, 1969, p. 232). In other words, he is aware of Piaget's antipathy toward the genes. This is simply another way to say that the physical make-up of man, which includes his brain, cannot give us even normal adolescent-level intelligence.

VICARIOUS ACTIONS AND FUNCTIONS SIGNIFY DUAL ENTITIES

No commentator, so far as I know, has tried to explain what Piaget means when he asserts that "intelligence", "organization", "assimilation" or "incorporation", "accommodation" and "relation", among other terms, indicate "vicarious" processes (Piaget, 1952b, pp. 13; 46) (Piaget, 1950, p. 94) (Piaget & Inhelder, 1964, p. 289). The reason is obvious if it is important to interpret Piaget within the realm of natural science, because two entities are, by definition, involved. Who is the second entity? *None of these key terms, terms that are used constantly in textbooks and by the commentators, can possibly be understood unless we understand the function and know the identity of this second Self who actually accounts for the action or function described.* Piaget, of course, is ambiguous regarding His identity, but he definitely communicates that there is a second Self. "Vicarious" means, at least in the passages cited, that one Self is acting in place of another self. If one is serious about understanding Piaget, he must answer this question: *Who is the Self who is assimilating, incorporating, relating, accommodating, organizing and acting intelligently, in place of the other self? The answer must be none other than the immanent Absolute Subject. What could be more obvious?*

The works of both Flavell and Furth demonstrate the impossibility of describing Piaget's position within the bounds of natural science and ordinary logic. That is, within the bounds of the physical self and his physical environment.

The vicarious relationship between the Spiritual Subject and the physical subject within whom He resides is expressed in many ways. The next selection is a double one, where the same idea is quickly repeated, but with interesting changes. The two subjects are not only definitely separable, but one can be found "projected" onto the other.

> What we shall ask is whether, in the spontaneous coordination of His actions when He manipulates objects, or in the spontaneous co-ordinations of His operations ... the Subject exhibits Co-ordinating Structures having some relation with Algebraic Structures, Structures of Order and Topological Structures .... [The main difficulty] is to establish how far the "Structures" ... in the Operative Mechanism ... really belongs to him or are introduced by the Psychologist Himself, that is to say, by Subject no, 2 studying subject no. 1 and projecting on him his own Mental Structures. *This latter problem is of interest to the Epistemology of Psychology* (author's italics and capitalization) (Beth & Piaget, 1966, pp. 167-8).

Piaget begins this passage with a question supposedly regarding the physical subject, but he uses language that really indicates the Absolute Subject. This is why there are capitals in the first two lines. Higher-level Mathematics is defined by Piaget as the activity of the Absolute Subject or, as in this passage, the "Operative Mechanism" or "the Psychologist Himself". He then asks rhetorically, *to whom do the Structures really belong? Perhaps they really belong to the Psychologist Himself, which would mean that He is acting vicariously in place of subject no. 1.* In that case the physical subject would be exhibiting Mathematical Structures and coordinations that do not belong to him, but belong to the one who is acting in his place. Could the Operative Mechanism inside of subject no. 1 really be a "projection" of the Psychologist Himself? Why would the Psychologist Himself wish to "study" subject no. 1?

Perhaps He wishes to assimilate him! Assimilation and elimination, plus the concomitant Self-development of the "Psychologist", is the reason for this "study"! As Piaget says in another context, "the Psychological Subject ... is investigating" the human subject "as an object", which can only mean that it is for the purpose of assimilation (author's capitalization) (Piaget, 1974a, p. 30). Assimilation would appear to be the only possible reason within Piaget's system because the Psychologist already knows all about subject no. 1 as He created him (author's capitalization) (Piaget, 1970b, p. 51) (Piaget, 1971a, pp. 282-3) (Beth & Piaget, 1966, pp. 284-5).

Please note the relation between subject no. 1 and Subject no. 2 with regard to the "Epistemology of Psychology". The psychology of which subject is the true source of Piaget's concept of epistemology? *It is the extremely narrow Epistemology, not of knowledge as defined in the dictionary, but of the one-of-a-kind Knowledge acquired in the Psychological development of the Absolute Subject.* This is a vicarious relationship as Subject no. 2 is projecting His own Mental Structures on subject no. 1. That is, the Structures of the Operative Mechanism really belong to the invisible Subject no. 2, not the visible subject no. 1. Once again we see how the APA and *Time* blundered into a most disconcerting faux pas. *Subject no. 2 or "Biology" is the Entity Piaget did not forget when he mentioned the citation by the APA* (author's italics and capitalization) (Piaget, 1972, p. 15).

About one page after the indented passage above Piaget basically repeats it. The two subjects are portrayed in greater contrast than before, as "it is easy" now to separate them, whereas before it was difficult. *Why is it easy now when it was difficult only one page earlier? Piaget continually makes such illogical or whimsical statements, probably because he is continually manipulating mere verbalisms.*

> It is easy to separate in this enquiry those structures dependent on subject no. 1 and those dependent on ... Subject no. 2, since the structures described in the activities of subject no. 1 have been characterized by their own limitations (author's capitalization) (Beth & Piaget, 1966, p. 169).

The Structures of the Psychologist composed of monads can now easily be distinguished and separated from the limited structures of subject no. 1. Piaget then definitively answers his previous question regarding the identity of the vicarious Subject who possesses the Structures that make up the Operative Mechanism. It is the metaphysical Psychologist. Again, we must be clear about the meaning of "Subject no. 2", "Structures of Subject no. 2", "Psychologist" or "Operative Mechanism". *All of these terms refer to the immanent Absolute Subject. We should also add that "Algebraic Structures". "Topological Structures" and "Structures of Order" also refer specifically to the Absolute Subject.* "Structures of Order" means Structures that develop by means of Self-regulations in a progressively improving psychogenetic series (author's capitalization) (Piaget, 1970b, pp. 15; 69-70) (Piaget, 1973d, pp. 49-50; 52) (Piaget, 1971a, pp. 316-17).

The actions which lead to reflective abstractions are not empirically observable because they are not the actions of physical subjects. They are vicarious actions of the immanent Subject.

> Reflective abstraction starting from actions does not imply an empiricist interpretation ... *for the actions in question are not the actions of individual ... subjects:* they are the most general coordinations of ... the Universal or Epistemic Subject and not the individual one (author's italics and capitalization) (Beth and Piaget, 1966, p. 238).

Reflective abstraction is only another term for "operation", and we have seen that individual subjects are not capable of this function. "The essence of the operations of Intelligence is ... the achievement of Knowledge, which is independent of the ego ... (but not of Human Subjects in General, i.e. of activities common to a given level)" (author's capitalization) (Piaget, 1969b, pp. 285-6). "The activities common to a given level" are produced by the Human Subject in General, or true Self, who is the immanent Absolute Subject. Only the Universal Body of Monads, or Sub-Units thereof, are capable of reflective abstractions or operations. *When Piaget speaks of individual subjects performing operations or reflective abstractions, we know that the immanent Epistemic Subject is actually performing this function vicariously.*

We have just observed that reflective abstraction is not an empirical notion. In the following excerpt, Piaget repeats the same notion with a somewhat different vocabulary.

> The operational constructivism suggested by genetic analysis is [not] reduced to empiricism because we could not derive Intelligence from objects. The Subject ... possess[es] a certain activity which allows him to construct Operational Structures ... The individual subject is neither its origin nor does he seem to control it .... The general co-ordinations of action involve a Universal which is that of Biological Organisation itself. [Constructivism is] contrary to physical or psychological empiricism .... This Biological origin of constructivism could not lead to a biological empiricism ... for the Subject has no experience of this type (author's capitalization) (Beth and Piaget, 1966, p. 285).

We noted previously that "psychogenesis" was actually a synonym for "operations", and Piaget confirms this in the first sentence. "Genetic analysis is the same as "psychogenetic" analysis, and operational construction is exactly the same as genetic construction or psychogenetic construction. This construction proceeds by way of thesis, antithesis, and a synthesis which transcends them both. The synthesis becomes the next thesis and the process continues. Each synthesis represents a step-up in development. The physical or individual subject has no part in this kind of construction. "Operations are constructed by abstraction ... from the Subject's actions, independently of ... the actions of individuals (ibid., p. 244). Piaget repeats the notion of "operations" or "psychogenesis" by referring to the "general coordinations of action", which involve a Universal Biological Organization. Constructivism, according to Piaget, has a Biological origin, but not the kind of biology that can be investigated empirically by natural science. *The Universal Biological Organization or Absolute Subject has no experience of physical biology!*

There are two kinds of cognitive behavior which are based on the actions of two different subjects.

> Two aspects [of cognitive behavior] should be defined. [These two aspects] are essentially different from each other. The actions of the Subject or Organism ... [produce] Logico-Mathematical [Knowledge]. [The actions of the objects themselves produce] exogenetic [knowledge] (author's capitalization) (Piaget, 1971a, p. 3).

The extremely distorted syntax of this selection is difficult to untangle. The first two sentences suggest inappropriately that two aspects of only one kind of cognitive development were to be defined. Piaget then drops this pretense and asserts that the Subject or Organism produces Logico-Mathematical Knowledge, while objects (read: human beings) produce exogenetic knowledge. "Operations [are not derived] ... from the individual psychological subject, since Logico-Mathematical experience disengages [him] ... [The] laws of which are independent of the ... actions of the individual" (author's capitalization) (Beth & Piaget, 1966, p. 235). It is important to realize that people cannot produce Logico-Mathematical Knowledge. *Einstein could only produce exogenetic knowledge; Logico-Mathematical Knowledge is only produced vicariously by the immanent Subject or Organism.*

Again, there are two kinds of action.

> I should like now to make a distinction between two types of actions. On the one hand, there are individual actions such as throwing, pushing, touching, rubbing. It is these individual actions that give rise most of the time to abstraction from objects. Reflective abstraction, however, is not based on individual actions but on coordinated actions (Piaget, 1970c, p.18).

Reflective abstractions are operational actions of the immanent Absolute Subject. These actions are metaphysical and vicarious. *All possible actions by people are "physical", even if they are only "mental" armchair speculations.*

PURE MOVEMENTS OR ACTIONS WHICH DO NOT TAKE TIME

There are two kinds of motion or movements.

> When we say motions, we are thinking of real motions, and not of displacements or ideal movements of geometry. The latter are simply changes of position ... *in which the velocity can be neglected;* that is why displacement is a Spatial concept (author's italics and capitalization) (Piaget, 1969a, p. 255).

A distinction is made between "real" or physical motions and ideal "Spatial" or metaphysical motions. Piaget makes a very significant distinction between the two when he says that the velocity can be neglected in the case of ideal movements. By this he means, as we have already noted, that the metaphysical movements of monads do not take time if material objects are not being moved. Ideal movements occur in the operational process when monads metaphysically displace imperceptible physical characteristics in objects in the process of operational assimilation. Piaget calls this a "Spatial concept" because "Space" is a synonym for the Body of Monads which fills the universe. It is worth noting that metaphysical motions are the same as metaphysical actions.

Pure logic and pure mathematics are contrasted with actions of the human being.

> Pure logic and pure mathematics are forever capable of transcending experience, since they are not limited by the physical characteristics of the object. But ... human action is that of an organism which is a part of the physical universe .... [and] physical knowledge ... proceeds ... by abstraction based on characteristics of the object as such (Piaget, 1971b, p. 72).

Pure logic and pure mathematics have nothing to do with traditional logic and mathematics. Piaget uses these terms here to describe the operational activity of the immanent Absolute Subject (author's capitalization) (Beth & Piaget, 1966, pp. 243; 296) (Piaget, 1973b, p. 103). Pure logic and pure mathematics refer to the purely imaginary activity of the monads as they act upon and assimilate objects and people. In contrast to the metaphysical activity of the monads, all human activity is physical and thus of little consequence. "Intentional adaptation" does not begin until the child "transcends the level of simple corporal activities" and "acts upon things" (Piaget, 1952b, p. 148). Physical or corporal actions are never "intentionally adaptive"! What could Piaget mean by such an unusual statement? For him, "intentional acts" are limited to operations which assimilate people and things. So we see two kinds of action, one kind of which people are not capable, and two kinds of "child". *There is the physical child who is not capable of "intentional action", and there is the "Vicarious Child" or immanent Subject inside the child who is capable of "intentional action". The immanent Subject is misnamed "child" because He cannot possibly be identified unambiguously if Piaget is to maintain his imposture as some kind of scientist.*

BRAINLESS KNOWLEDGE

Piaget questions whether "Knowledge" requires a biological or neurological support. We use the next two quotes again to cast light upon somewhat different aspects of Piaget's system from what were examined previously.

> Does Knowledge ... necessarily have a biological component? Perhaps it will be replied that even the highest type of act of intelligence still presupposes brain activity .... It is easy enough in Epistemology, to dissociate a piece of Logical or Mathematical Knowledge from its neurological support (author's capitalization) (Piaget, 1971a, pp. 251-2).

Is a biological component, for instance the brain, necessary for the acquisition of knowledge? The fact that he asks such a question should be enough to raise a red flag. The question is clear enough, but he basically squirms out of an honest answer. The following passage, however, clarifies his position.

> Whenever Intelligence and Thought are put forward as Self-explanatory prime facts or, ultimately, as the source of facts, which is the idealist thesis, the function of the nervous system cannot be understood. For if the body is necessary in order to incarnate thought, then this body ought to be enough ... to provide us ... information ... about the condition and functioning of every organ and every cell ... of which we are made .... This is why in Bergsonian spiritualism, the nervous system vis-a-vis the Mind is reduced to the modest role of a hook with a Coat hung on it. But even the hook presents a problem, for from this point of view it is the Coat itself which is the Fount of Life, and that renders the hook useless (author's capitalization) (ibid., pp. 215-16).

When Piaget says that Intelligence is a prime fact he means that it does not depend on anything else, because it is "primary". *"Intelligence" here is a synonym for the eternal Entity who was there at the beginning of things, and from whom everything else was derived.* This is why Piaget says that Intelligence is the source of facts. It is also why he says that "the function of the nervous system cannot be understood". This truncated statement makes no sense unless we know in what way it cannot be understood. He means that it cannot be understood as the source of Intelligence. Piaget then uses the philosopher Bergson as a partial shield to complete the argument with the declaration that the nervous system is useless as far as the Mind is concerned. "Nothing is farther from my thoughts than to attribute to the ... brain ... some kind of combinatorial intelligence" (ibid., p. 327). Piaget reserves "combinatorial intelligence" exclusively for the monads. "The physiological and anatomic aspect of the organism ... gradually appears to the Mind as external to it and ... intellectual activity" (author's capitalization) (Piaget, 1954, p. 401). The Body of Monads or Mind understands that the physiology and anatomy of people are not pertinent to His activity except as instruments He can use for His own purposes. Piaget confidently speaks for the metaphysical Entity, but he appears to be deliberately off the mark when he alleges that this omniscient Spirit "gradually" realizes that He is independent of physical structures and processes. "Gradually" is an insincere moderation of the Spirit's powers of perception.

The various stages of mental development do not depend upon psycho-neurological mechanisms for their completion.

Even if there were justification for relating the various stages of mental development to well-defined neurological levels, the fact remains that ... there is a certain functional continuity .... It is no explanation to say that there is a succession of superposed psycho-neurological mechanisms at work. *[The dynamics of stage construction involves] a certain direction ... towards equilibrium and completion* (author's italics) (Piaget, 1962, p. 6).

Piaget argues that psycho-neurological mechanisms do not explain the stages of mental development, but that the construction of stages involves a direction toward equilibrium. The pertinent question is: Within Piaget's system, how is equilibrium achieved? It is achieved in only one way, by equilibrations and, as we saw previously, equilibrations are actually operations. *The bottom line is that the stages of mental development are based on the metaphysical process of operations, and that "mental development" in this context refers only to the development of the immanent Body of Monads* (author's italics and capitalization) (Piaget, 1967, pp. 104; 112) (Inhelder, Sinclair & Bovet, 1974, p. 10) (Piaget, 1973a, p. 147). *It has nothing to do with the mental development of children! This fact, as noted previously, will eventually require a drastic revision of every textbook on child development.*

More about the equilibration factor and the inadequacy of the neurological explanation:

The neurological explanation cannot in itself be sufficient because ... new operations derive from earlier ones. Given this, it must be that a Continuously Operating Equilibration Factor plays a role beyond that of ... maturation ... The problem is to understand how a tendency toward equilibrium ... can lead the Subject to organize a Formal Combinatorial System (author's capitalization) (Inhelder & Piaget, 1958, p. 281).

When operations or equilibrations derive from earlier ones we have an expression of genetic psychology. This is the "functional continuity" or actions of the Entity we saw in the last passage, as well as the "Continuously Operating Equilibration Factor" of the same Entity who is acting in this one. The neurological explanation of brain activity has no relevance to development or the organization of the Formal Combinatorial System based on the equilibration factor.

A NON-PHYSICAL ONTOGENETIC DEVELOPMENT

Piaget claims that ontogenetic development and the succession of stages is not a physical process. As for Ontogenetic development, it does not consist solely of a succession of stages .... To say that would be to argue as though Ontogenetic development underwent this condition of order *like some physical process* .... The Epigenotype itself controls the order by means of a series of regulations (author's italics and capitalization) (Piaget, 1971a, p. 165). *The ontogenetic development of human beings is a physical process. The Ontogenetic development Piaget is concerned with in this passage is not physical. This latter development is controlled by a series of non-physical regulations, equilibrations or operations performed by the Epigenotype, which makes it a case of Self-development.* "Epigenotype" is a tricky synonym of the immanent Absolute Subject. Piaget is very good at taking words from various disciplines and forcing them to carry alien meanings within his system.

THE TWO EGOS, THE TWO WORLDS, THE TWO SOCIETIES AND THE TWO CIVILIZATIONS

There are two subjects and Piaget dislikes one of them.

> There are thinkers who dislike "the subject", and if this subject is characterized in terms of its "lived experience" we admit to being among them.... In any case, the "lived" can only have a very minor role in the construction of Cognitive Structures, for these do not belong to the subject's *consciousness* but to his operational *behavior*, which is something quite different.... The Subject here meant can only be the Epistemic Subject (Piaget's italics) (author's capitalization) (Piaget, 1970b, p. 68).

Piaget dislikes the physical subject, but he likes the Epistemic Subject who lives in the physical subject and is capable of operational behavior - vicarious operational behavior. Piaget believes that our focus on the physical subject is a fundamental mistake; for him, life could not be based on matter. Lower- level intelligence is "unable to understand life because ... [lower-level intelligence is] oriented in the direction of inert matter" (Piaget, 1971c, p. 5). The only Living Entity in the universe, within Piaget's system, is the non-material Body of Monads. People and all other living things are alive by proxy. The Living Cognitive Structure can only be constructed or developed by the operations of the Epistemic Subject. When we remember that the development of the Epistemic or Absolute Entity is always Self-development, we realize that the Cognitive Structure is the Body of the Epistemic Subject, namely the immanent Body of Monads.

Piaget frames the problem of the two subjects ambiguously in terms of "Personality" and "ego".

> Personality operates in a way opposite to that of the ego. Whereas the ego is naturally egocentric, Personality is the decentered Ego. The ego is detestable, even more so when it is strong, whereas a strong Personality is the one which manages to discipline the ego (author's capitalization) (Inhelder & Piaget, 1958, p. 349).

The individual or physical ego is detestable, but the Personality or immanent Absolute Subject, can discipline the ego and "decenter" it by assimilation. The task of the Personality is to decenter the lower-level ego, and a *fully* decentered or assimilated ego fully liberates the Personality. This is the disentangled meaning of the phrase, "Personality is the decentered Ego". This phrase tends to paralyze thought until a misrepresentation is removed. *Personality is not the decentered ego; Personality is what you have after the ego is decentered. Personality is the centered Ego; it is the lower-level ego that is decentered.* Ego is capitalized because it is a *forced* synonym of Personality. A fully decentered ego is the ultimate goal of the Personality, but apparently this has never been accomplished, not even in the case of Piaget. *It is significant that "opposite" is used to distinguish Personality from ego as they are truly opposites engaged in a dialectic interaction which will eventuate in the elimination of the ego.*

Piaget expresses the two opposite egos in many ways. In the following passage they are expressed in terms of two different "worlds" or "realities" within the child.

> Does the child [find] himself ... in the presence of two worlds which are equally real, and neither succeeds in supplanting the other? ... There is nothing to prove that the child is any worse for this bi-polar nature of reality (Piaget, 1928, p. 245).

Which is it, "two worlds which are equally real" or one "bi-polar reality"? In other words, are there two realities or just one reality which is bi-polar? *Many of the quotes we have used show this same basic ambiguity regarding Piaget's dual system.* As emphasized many times, with Piaget we are dealing with a physical world and a metaphysical World; with a physical ego and a metaphysical Ego. We are dealing with opposite entities, but the situation is complex as the Metaphysical World of Monads, which existed alone at first, created physical reality and will eventually "reabsorb" it back into Himself. Ultimately, then, we are talking about one Entity, the Absolute Ego, because in the "end" He alone will exist. In the meantime, however, there are two opposite entities, not one with a bi-polar nature.

In the following selection, Piaget takes us back to the beginning of things in the macrocosm of the Living Universe of Monads and also in the microcosm of the baby's immanent Mind which, as we have seen, recapitulates the history of the macrocosm.

> Originally the child puts the whole content of consciousness on the same plane and draws no distinction between the "I" and the external world. Above all we mean that the constitution of the idea of reality presupposes a progressive splitting-up of this Protoplasmic Consciousness into two complementary universes - the objective universe and the Subjective (author's capitalization) (Piaget, 1930, p. 242).

At the beginning of things only the Universe of Monads or Spatial Continuum existed (author's capitalization) (Piaget, 1929, p. 267). The first few weeks or months of the baby's life recapitulates this "fact", as we saw previously. The Universe of Monads then decided to create the physical universe as its complementary or, perhaps more accurately, antithetical opposite. The immanent Body of Monads within the baby also recapitulates this "fact" as the single "Protoplasmic Consciousness" is split into the dual universes of Spirit and matter. Piaget's description of the two universes as the "objective universe and the Subjective" is obscure because of the odd use of "objective" for "object" and "Subjective" for "Subject". The young baby's "I" represents the Protoplasmic Consciousness which is later split into two opposite entities. *More exactly, the Protoplasmic Consciousness, made up of monads, produces the material universe, and the baby's "I" supposedly recapitulates this act, according to Piaget's theory, but he never clarified the dynamics of this act vis-a-vis the baby.*

Piaget occasionally loses patience with those who fail to recognize his invisible Subject.

> It is ... no exaggeration to treat as "mythical", as we rather disrespectfully entitled this study, the ... opinion according to which all ... [experimental] knowledge is of sensorial origin. *The fundamental vice of such empirical interpretation is to forget the activity of the Subject* (author's italics and capitalization) (Piaget, 1971b, p. 87).

The title of the chapter from which this quote was taken is: "The Myth of the Sensorial Origin of Scientific Knowledge". *According to Piaget those who practice any form of natural science which, of course, is empirical, are fundamentally wicked.* Ironically, Piaget was honored for his supposed "wickedness" by a most prestigious organization:

> In a citation which the American Psychological Association presented to me, there occurs this significant passage: 'He has approached questions up to now exclusively philosophical in a resolutely empirical manner, and has made epistemology into a science separate from philosophy, but related to all the human sciences', *without, of course, forgetting Biology* (author's italics and capitalization) (Piaget, 1972, p. 15).

The last five words are most interesting, as they, at least in Piaget's mind, nullify this very foolish citation. Piaget immediately follows the quote from the citation with, "without, of course, forgetting Biology". "Forgetting Biology" in this quote means exactly the same as "forgetting the Subject" in the previous quote. The psychologists "forgot", but Piaget never forgets. *As a synonym of the Absolute Subject, the term "Biology" effectively tells the psychologists that they have been duped in a most inglorious way!*
Even "society" is dual in Piaget's system.

> Duality ... lies hidden in the word 'social'. There are, M. Lalande tells us, two societies, an existing or organized society, whose constant feature is the constraint which it exercises upon individual minds, and there is the Ideal or Assimilative Society, which is defined by the progressive identification of people's Minds with one another (author's capitalization) (Piaget, 1932, p. 384).

Piaget is not clear regarding exactly what Lalande "tells us". It is extremely doubtful, for instance, that Lalande believed in a Society that "assimilates". According to Piaget, assimilation is not possible independent of the Totality (author's capitalization) (Piaget, 1952b, p. 179), who is the Absolute Subject. An insight into Piaget's concept of his metaphysical Subject, Structure or Living System is afforded by the fact that "Society" is one of the names he gives this Entity (author's capitalization) (Piaget, 1970b, p. 142). Piaget uses Durkheim to express the same concept. "I would be inclined to believe ... like Durkheim ... that underlying 'societies' there is 'Society'" (Piaget's capitalization) (Evans, 1973, p. 72). It is this particular "Society" that assimilates the existing or "organized" society. *These two societies are opposites and the "physical" one must be assimilated.* As the Assimilative Society operates on the individual or physical minds of people, the immanent Entity gradually becomes easier to identify as common to all.
Related to the notion of the "Society" of monads who assimilate is the "Civilization" of monads who function "Normatively", which means that "He" also assimilates. "Underlying civilizations there is Civilization (Piaget's capitalization) with its permanent laws and Normative function" (author's capitalization) (Beth & Piaget, 1966, pp. 286-7). Piaget appropriated "Normative" for his own personal needs. For him only the Absolute Subject and His activities are "Normative". The Subject is a "Normative fact" (author's capitalization) (ibid., p. 141) and this "Fundamental Norm" does not depend upon human nature because human nature is not permanent (author's capitalization) (Piaget, 1970b, p. 106). Norms are the

prototypes of Unchangeable Structures (author's capitalization) (Piaget, 1973d, p. 34). The development of the Normative Structure is directed toward equilibrium (author's capitalization) (Piaget, 1970b, p. 79) by means of equilibrations (Piaget, 1973d, pp. 60-1) (Piaget, 1971b, p. 9). *"Civilization" is simply another synonym for the Absolute Subject, who must ultimately account for everything.*

Piaget's Dual Entities:
Their Gnostic Destiny

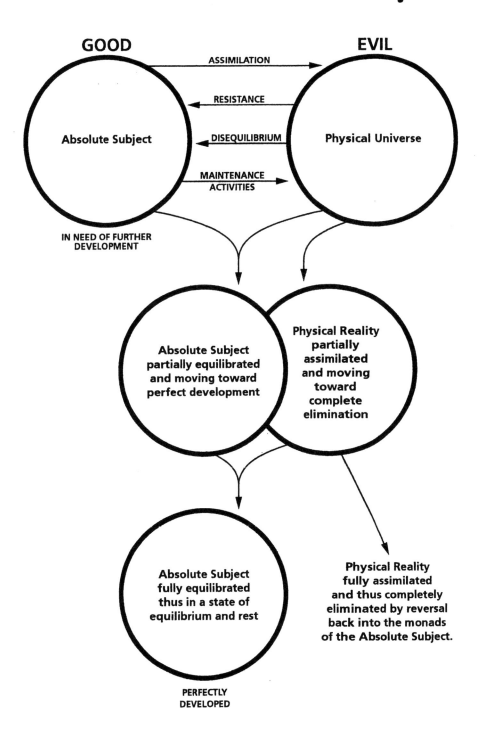

Chapter 3

THE MARVELOUS MONAD

IN THE BEGINNING WAS THE BIOLOGICAL ORGANIZATION OF MONADS

The most essential and fundamental concept in Piaget's theory, other than its basic duality, has also remained hidden from the academic world. It has been stumbled over thousands of times by unwary investigators who, to date, apparently have not attained a glimmer of its central significance. We are referring to the concept of monads, which provides the dynamics of his theory and enables one to understand much of his strange phraseology. For instance, the concept of "operation" is prominent in the commentaries on Piaget, but his explanation of the operation as the exclusive dynamic activity of monads remains terra incognita. No aspect of his theory was developed more thoroughly than the concept of monads, but admittedly no part of his theory was communicated more deceitfully and with more care to prevent easy comprehension. Although several of his books are devoted to the nature and work of monads, the concept has failed to attract the attention of investigators. Monads account for all activity in the physical universe, but their most important function is "operational assimilation".

Piaget's theory begins with the organized Body of Monads and nothing else, because nothing else existed. In the beginning all that existed was the Continuum, Absolute Subject, Group, Field or Form. All of these terms refer to the Primordial Biological System of Monads as the "simple starting point". The "simple starting point ... has a history ... going back to the laws of the Biological Organization" (author's capitalization) (Beth & Piaget, 1966, p. 296). It all started with the "atomic elements" or monads which make up the Absolute Entity with many names, and will end with the same elements forming a completed Biological System (author's capitalization) (Piaget, 1953, pp. 24-5). Normal regulations or operations ensure that this passage will proceed to the final state (Piaget. 1977, p. 145). "All development presupposes an Initial Structure. The development consists in the completion and differentiation of this Structure" (author's capitalization) (Inhelder & Piaget, 1964, p. 1).

"Formal operations ... enrich the Initial Systems by elaborating 'Sets Of All Sub-Sets' ... based on a Combinatorial System" (author's capitalization) (Piaget, 1972, p.

47). Most of Piaget's sentences having to do with the theoretical aspects of his metaphysical pipe dream are abnormal, and the previous one is no exception. "Sets Of All Sub-Sets" is abnormal because the meaning is patently "Set Of All Sub-Sets" - the plural represents an internal contradiction. *Two pages later he spells the term correctly, identifying the Set of All Sub-Sets as the Spatial Continuum which is filled with unobservable elements closely packed together* (author's italics and capitalization) (ibid., p. 49). These "elements" are monads that make up the Set of All Sub Sets. Although in this case the meaning of the defaced term is easily discernible, it is nevertheless frustrating for the reader, who must constantly negotiate such impediments to thought, which at least serve as speed-bumps in terms of comprehension. Piaget appears to pride himself on frustrating his reader (Piaget, 1977, p. 145).

The same Body of "Elements" or Monads which make up the perfectly developed Biological System will only be different from the beginning Body in the sense that it will have "Knowledge" of all possible combinations of which its atomic elements are capable, a Knowledge that will make further dialectic contradictions impossible. Perfect metaphysical development is called complete "compensation" or "equilibrium" (Piaget, 1977, p. 69), and it is "directed by equilibrations ... leading to a final "balance" (Piaget, 1973d, p. 52), that is, a permanent balance or equilibrium (Piaget 1928, p. 171) (Piaget 1978a, p. 225). As mentioned previously, the ultimate goal is similar to the concept of nirvana in Hinduism, but the path to the goal is based on a variety of Gnosticism. Movement toward equilibrium or nirvana is not determined by maturation or learning, but by equilibrations (Inhelder & Piaget, 1964, p. 292). Moreover, equilibrium does not depend upon chance, like the efforts of mere human beings, as regulations stabilize themselves in a determined fashion (Piaget, 1977, pp. 174-5). Equilibrations, operations or regulations are manifestly superhuman.

The ultimate goal is expressed in many ways, sometimes quite urgently. There is a vital need, Piaget exclaims, for the "Organism ... to escape from the contradictions inherent in successive events .... and to avoid time. What remains, then, must be called 'Forms' since they are [not] physical" (author's capitalization) (Piaget, 1974b, pp. 125-6;149). Stated in different words, "operations are freed from their time dependence .... and take on the extratemporal character" (Piaget, 1972, p. 46). *Piaget identifies the non-physical Form as the Individual Organism who imposes Himself on matter* (author's italics and capitalization) (Piaget 1971a, p. 93) *for the purpose of eliminating it.* This is an endogenous imposition, which means that it is accomplished by progressive equilibrations or operations (ibid., pp. 316-17). The Most General Form or Fundamental Biological Structure is the source of operations, and He is also the one who organizes the genetic system plus the whole range of observable behavior (author's capitalization) (ibid., p.158). Forms eventually are constructed so that they will never again be contradicted by facts (author's capitalization) (Piaget 1974b, p. 123), thus earning the Form, Spatial Continuum or Absolute Subject a "timeless" peace and rest (author's capitalization) (Piaget, 1971b, p. 114) (Piaget, 1928, p. 171) (Inhelder & Piaget, 1964, p. 292). When the Subject or Body of Monads finally "escapes from successive events", He will have eliminated physical reality and the atomic elements or monads which make up His Form will alone remain in a state of nirvana.

THE DISINGENUOUS ROLE OF EXPERIMENT

It is pointless, however, to speak in semi-empirical terms regarding what is possible or not possible with regard to Piaget's system because equilibrations, regulations, relations or operations are not empirical constructions (Piaget, 1952a, p. 202), *therefore none of his theory is subject to empirical investigation and verification. Moreover, Piaget despises the experimentation of natural science.* His counterfeit experiments with children are designed with two main goals in mind: to demonstrate that children have the same theory of existence that he has and to inveigle the academic community into accepting him as a scientist, confusing his investigators with extremely complicated interpretations of the experiments. Flavell, his major expositor, comes close to agreement regarding the first goal with this assessment: "It would not be unfair to say that most experiments appear to be set up to demonstrate its [Piaget's theory] validity rather than to test it" (Flavell, 1963, p. 37). *The majority of his "findings" are based on supposed tendencies of the child which the child knows nothing about. Piaget alone is privy to these tendencies!*

> [The content of child Thought] is a System of Intimate Beliefs and it requires a special technique to bring them to the light of day. Above all it is a System of Mental Tendencies and predilections of which the child himself has never been consciously aware and of which he never speaks (author's capitalization) (Piaget, 1929, p. 14).

The capitalizations are based on Piaget's belief that he, with the aid of his "true Self", is able to directly read the desires of the child's "true Self". *This is the "special technique" he invented to bring the child's Thought to the "light of day". It clearly has nothing to do with genuine experimental findings, as it is simply a method to impose his doctrines through sham experiments with children too young to actively correct his misinterpretations.* Piaget boldly assumes the right to make these "findings" known because he claims to know directly what the child's Mind is like (author's capitalization) (Piaget, 1973d, p. 19) (Piaget, 1929, p. 36). The "true Thought" of the child is below the level of formulation and verbalization, nevertheless Piaget claims to know the precise nature of his System of Thought.

> We may well ask ourselves ... whether it is legitimate to question the child about ... very verbal beliefs, since these beliefs do not correspond to Thought properly so called, and since the child's true Thought lies much deeper, somewhere below the level of formulation. But *in our opinion these beliefs have their interest because ... the Psychological facts lead ... to Metaphysical Systems themselves* (author's italics and capitalization) (Piaget, 1932, p. 70).

Piaget is interested in certain inexpressible beliefs of young children. The children have never told Piaget or anyone else what these beliefs are, but he finds them interesting! He is not thinking of the physical child, as this child is basically irrelevant except as an object or thing to be assimilated. "Thought properly so called" contains the Psychological facts of interest to Piaget, which have to do with the Metaphysical System inside the child. He knows what this Entity is thinking and this is what he deceptively reports.

Piaget's incredible presumption is revealed in this quote: "It is we who grope towards the discovery of the child's unconscious intention and sometimes succeed in making him indirectly own to it" (Piaget, 1928, p. 151). If Piaget does not know in advance what the unconscious intention is he would not know when the child indirectly owns to it! Flavell is in somewhat grudging agreement on this point (Flavell, 1963, p. 437). He quotes from the Handbook of Research Methods in Child Development: "Piaget is inclined to see through words as though they were not there and to imagine that he directly studies the child's mind" (Berko & Brown, 1960, p. 536). As we have seen, Piaget is especially shrewd in divining what is going on in the Minds of babies. His most fundamental doctrines, which are often quite abstract, are most often "demonstrated" by children who are too young to have acquired language.

THE PURPOSE OF THE PHYSICAL UNIVERSE

The Primordial Biological Organization is concerned with only one need, and that is to fully develop Himself. He is not concerned with anything else, including the feelings and welfare of the billions of people who are used as agents in His unique development. The prospect of pain, starvation, disease, death, wars, and every other problem faced by man means truly nothing to Piaget's metaphysical Subject. Everything is sacrificed without a hint of remorse to this one need. The whole purpose of physical reality and human history, according to Piaget, is to enable this Entity to fully develop Himself. This occurs gradually as "the History of Human Knowledge [is] integrated into a Single Intellectual Organism" (author's capitalization) (Piaget, 1971a, p. 360). This Knowledge, of course, is the very narrowly defined Knowledge acquired by the Absolute Subject as He moves toward the full realization of his potential. When this is accomplished physical reality will have been eliminated, enabling Him to revert to the condition of equilibrium and "rest". In the final analysis only the Field of Monads will remain (author's capitalization) (Piaget, 1974b, pp. 184-5). How He knew what procedure to follow in order to accomplish His perfect development was not vouchsafed to us, but Piaget is absolutely confident that he knows what method is being used, so he presents it with dogmatic certainty. In order to develop Himself fully it was necessary to create His exact opposite and then to laboriously overcome every problem this opposite could pose. *This creation of His opposite was the universal starting point in the development of Logico-Mathematical Knowledge, and when all of the problems have been overcome after a "long genetic process" of operational activity, the end point of Logico-Mathematical Knowledge will have been reached* (author's italics and capitalization) (Beth & Piaget, 1966, p. 136).

THE TWO STARTING POINTS

We see, then, that there are two "starting points" in Piaget's theory, and he indulges in an orgy of ambiguous, confusing and conflicting statements in order to keep their precise characteristics blurred. The first starting point is described above as the curtains open to reveal the drama of existence beginning with the sole presence of the Form, Field, Subject or Continuum of Monads. The introduction to the Initial Body of Monads is not, of course, a starting point in terms of their existence, but it is a starting point in terms of Piaget's narration. The second beginning started when the Continuum of Monads or Absolute Subject created the physical universe for the purpose of fully developing Himself. The physical universe resists every move of the Absolute Subject, serving as a necessary but temporary "evil", which must be overcome by intelligence defined as a series of operations (author's italics and capitalization) (Beth & Piaget, 1966, p. 156). In addition to its kinship to Hinduism, which Piaget alludes to from time to time (Piaget, 1971c, p. 150), there is an obvious connection with Gnosticism. The Gnostics also believed that the physical world was evil, and that "knowledge" or "intelligence" was the only way to overcome the world. Piaget occasionally refers to "Gnostic Intelligence", by which he means Assimilative Intelligence (author's capitalization) (Piaget, 1930, p. 134) (Piaget, 1952, p. 6). It is the operations or equilibrations of Assimilative Intelligence which gradually assimilate the world in the process of reaching full development.

The problems posed by the physical universe or, as Piaget usually calls them, "contradictions", are always transcended (Piaget 1980a, p. XVII). Since human beings do not always transcend their problems, the "transcender" must be another kind of entity. Virtual tasks or "possibles" must all be actualized by Logico-Mathematical Science, operations or equilibrations before complete Knowledge by, or development of, the Absolute Subject can be achieved (author's capitalization) (Piaget, 1980, pp. 156-8). "Complete Knowledge" and "complete development" in this case having essentially the same meaning. His opposite was to be overcome by a special dialectic interaction that involves the "displacement" of physical characteristics by means of the "combinatorial operations" of monads. This process was dubbed "assimilation", which requires increasingly more complex and difficult operations in order not only to assimilate physical reality, but to simultaneously "construct" the Body of Monads or Absolute Subject. The process of assimilating the physical automatically constructs the metaphysical Entity. Operations are based on ordered pairs of opposites which produce relations (Piaget et al. 1977, p. 164). The assimilative operation is also called a dialectic "synthesis", a concept borrowed from the philosopher Hegel (Piaget, 1971c, p. 115). Each dialectic synthesis, operation or relation produces a slightly more developed "Class" of monads than the previous Class, the newly developed Class then dialectically interacts with its opposite to produce a still more developed Class. The progressively developing series of positive Classes are formed so as to permit precise pairing or encounters with their exact opposites. For every transformed Class in the ascending direction of the developing Absolute Subject a corresponding transformed class in the descending direction toward the elimination of the physical will be found (author's capitalization) (Inhelder & Piaget, 1964, p. 292). By "corresponding" Piaget means exact opposite.

The movement toward equilibrium is not based on the human brain, but on the sequential process of operations (ibid., p. 293). Metaphysical Knowledge or development advances by the operational schematization of reality, meaning that physical reality becomes a part of the Total Schema or Form (author's capitalization) (Beth & Piaget, 1966, pp. 253-4). The process of schematization is accomplished by monads as Schemas are composed of monads or Spiritual "atoms" (author's capitalization) (Piaget & Inhelder, 1974, p. 110). "Everything can be reduced to the schema of encounters and couplings" (Piaget, 1969b, p. 179). Every one of these pairings was planned from the beginning (Beth & Piaget, 1966, p. 303)

(Piaget 1971a, pp. 318-19) (Piaget, 1972, p. 90 (Piaget, 1977, p. 64-5), and the final pairing, encounter, coupling, relation, regulation, equilibration, deduction, coordination, implication, reflexive abstraction, operation, etc., will complete simultaneously both the assimilation of physical reality and the development of the Absolute Subject.

Flavell's struggle to understand the meaning of "encounters and couplings" of the dual entities demonstrates Piaget's success in his plan to deceive. He tried to determine the meaning of the terms by closely examining the physical "experiments", but eventually concluded that Piaget does not give a complete specification of the terms (Flavell, 1963, p. 229). Unfortunately, this conclusion is necessarily true for all of the theoretical terms he examined because he remained focused on the level of physical reality. Piaget basically made the same point in his foreword to Flavell's book. "It seems clear that Professor Flavell is more interested in the experiments than in the theory" (ibid., p. VIII). He was aware that Flavell was not even close to detecting his hidden agenda based on his metaphysical theory, and discreetly communicated this. Furthermore, he no doubt wished to needle Flavell because he devoted most of his book to what he thought was Piaget's theory.

HEGEL'S CONCEPT OF PHYSICAL EXISTENCE

Although Piaget believed that his concept of the "second beginning" is an improvement over Hegel's view, it is instructive to see Foster's description of how God was to actualize Himself in Hegel's philosophy.

> God exists only as spirit; nothing is concrete. All is potential, nothing is actual. God wants to realize Himself; so he creates the world .... In order to realize Himself, God needs something which is not Himself. So he posits and creates his opposite, matter, which is imperfect. God must posit and create matter in order to become fully conscious of Himself. In order to become aware of Himself in thought, God needs non-A .... God creates the world to realize His own idea of Himself .... God [also] desires that the world should be perfect, as he Himself is perfect. He can make the world perfect only by drawing the world back to him and merging it with His own being (Foster, 1969, p. 16).

Piaget did not depart far from his mentor. His primary "improvement" was the concept of monads to support and amplify the notion of "Spirit". Another improvement, which we will consider later, is exactly how the world is to be brought back to Him with his concept of reversibility.

THE TWO "INITIAL" STRUCTURES

One must differentiate between what begins with the creation of the physical universe and what continues as before because it is eternal. The Structure, Continuum, Space, Group or Subject is composed of monads so there is no "absolute beginning of Structure" (author's capitalization) (Bringuier, 1980, p. 40) (Piaget 1969, p. XXVII) (Piaget, 1967, p. 149). This is the "Initial Structure" that is to be actualized by development, and Piaget often uses this term with an upper-level meaning (Piaget,

1970b, pp. 62-3) (Beth & Piaget, 1966, p. 258) (Piaget, 1976a, p. 271). He cunningly creates a problem, however, when he makes such statements as "decentration ... robs the initial reference system of its privilege" (Piaget & Inhelder, 1974, p, 61), and "the initial system has become decentered to make way for a General Composition [of monads]" (author's capitalization) (ibid., p. 115). The problem is created when there is a *deliberate switch* from the metaphysical Structure to the physical structure of the child, or vice versa, without informing his reader. If one investigator only reads about the initial metaphysical Structure and his colleague only reads about the initial physical structure, a delightful set of disruptive scenarios is thereby presented to Piaget's imagination.

For reasons that are both expected and mind-boggling, Piaget frequently treats a function of the Structure as if it were the Structure itself. For instance, "we called these Initial Structures behind which we cannot go "general coordination of actions" (author's capitalization) (Piaget 1970b, p. 62). The "coordination of actions" is a function of the Structure; it is not the Structure. Another example: assimilatory activity "can only emanate from an assimilation Schema. Such assimilatory activity ... has no absolute beginning" (author's capitalization) (Piaget 1971a, p. 256). "Schema", as used here, is simply another name for Structure, so it is eternal, but the function of assimilation did not begin until there were physical objects to assimilate. In other words, assimilatory activity *did* have an absolute beginning. Yet another: *"In genetic Epistemology, as in developmental Psychology, too, there is never an absolute beginning"* (author's italics and capitalization) (Piaget, 1970c, p. 19). First, we should note that "genetic Epistemology", or the achievement of valid Knowledge (author's capitalization) (Piaget, 1971a, p. 7), and "developmental Psychology" deal with exactly the same process in Piaget's theory - the construction of the Absolute Subject. This being true, *it is a most embarrassing fact that the subject of developmental psychology, as taught in every university in the United States is, insofar as Piaget's principles are adhered to, naively teaching about the development of Piaget's Absolute Subject rather than human beings!* In any case, this process of "genetic Epistemology" or "developmental Psychology" did not start until the physical universe was created, so Piaget is playing disruptive "mind games" with his colleagues. After making the above statement, he follows with a statement that *is* true within his system. "We can never get back to the point where we can say, 'here is the very beginning of Logical Structure'" (author's capitalization) (ibid., p. 19). Piaget's pretense that "genetic Epistemology" or "developmental Psychology" are two different concepts in this metaphysical context also illustrates his befogging practice of separating what belongs together and treating as identical what should be differentiated. A fourth example: "The formation [of Knowledge] is itself a mechanism of growth without an absolute beginning" (author's capitalization) (Piaget, 1971c, p. 76). The formation of Knowledge is not a mechanism and, although the metaphysical Entity certainly had much knowledge throughout all eternity, the "formation of Knowledge in time" did not begin until physical reality was created. The Mechanism or Structure of Monads responsible for the formation of Knowledge, however, is indeed without an absolute beginning. A fifth example: "From the very beginning" Space acts on objects (author's capitalization) (Piaget & Inhelder, 1956, p. 449). The monads of the Spatial Continuum were present at the first beginning, but they could not act on objects until they came into existence with the second beginning. The absence of proper qualification, makes this assertion *deliberately misleading*. A sixth and final example of this type: "There exists from the outset an Operational Space" (author's capitalization) (Piaget, 1974b, p. 143). This is true so long as we realize that no developmental operations occurred until objects were created. To conclude this digression concerning his deceitfulness regarding the relationship between the eternal Structure and His functions, Piaget insists that "there is no need to distinguish Structures and functions" (author's capitalization) (Piaget, 1973d, p. 16)!

AN UNUSUAL WAY TO DESCRIBE MONADS

A most unusual reference to the monads is found in the following quote: "Living beings are subjects, however unconscious they may be; and human subjects are descended from them ... Our hypothesis is ... that there are elementary structures common to all living subjects." (Beth & Piaget, 1966, p. 298). A full understanding of this quote shows Piaget in a light that would, in my opinion, cause shame and mortification to anyone capable of such emotions. The intricate, convoluted, confounding syntax and meanings not only turn a relatively simple doctrine into a linguistic atrocity, but demonstrate beyond question Piaget's unfriendly and baleful intent. First, we know that there are two different kinds of subjects, and that the first one is nonphysical. This is a given from the context but is not a part of the quote. "Living beings" are "subjects" but they are nonphysical. The "living subjects" at the end of the quote, however, are obviously physical. Note that "living beings" is a synonym of the nonphysical "subjects". Human subjects are said to be descended from the nonphysical living beings or subjects. At this point, Piaget "posits" that there are "elementary structures" common to all living subjects. *What we have is a very confusing use of three synonyms for monads:* "living beings", the first "subjects", and "elementary structures" (Never mind that calling monads "subjects" rather than using the term properly as "making up a Subject", is a rather uncivil way to treat his reader. This is probably the only instance where "subjects" is made to mean "monads".) Human beings are "descended" from the monads and the monads are common to all living subjects, including people, so we can eventually make sense of this linguistic conundrum, if we can afford the time and energy to unravel the meaning. We note also Piaget's habit of reversing the fact that human beings are unconscious of the monads. It must be remembered that human subjects are alive by proxy. They have no life of their own, but have life only because of the immanent monads. Furthermore, in addition to concocting a confusing passage about the central importance of the monads, Piaget disgracefully stoops to trifle with the reader's intellectual sensibilities by making a dogmatic statement and then calling an assertion that is logically dependent on the dogmatic statement an hypothesis.

MISCHIEVOUS FUN WITH THE TERM "PSYCHOLOGY"

An example with an odd, anarchic twist:

In genetic Epistemology as in developmental Psychology, there is never an absolute beginning. We can never get back to the point where we can say, here is the very beginning of Logical Structures. As soon as we start talking about the general coordination of actions, we find ourselves going even further into Biology, which is not my intention here. I just want to carry this regressive analysis back to its beginnings in Psychology" (author's capitalization) (Evans, 1973, p. XLVII).

None of the sentences of this passage are connected properly to adjoining sentences. Piaget is not only adept at muddled syntax, as he does the same with the sentences of a paragraph. The second sentence is a non-sequitur of the the first and is not connected logically to the third, etc. As noted in a similar previous quote, "genetic Epistemology" and "developmental Psychology" are synonyms in Piaget's private vocabulary because they both refer precisely to the actualization of the metaphysical Structure, which requires the existence of the physical universe. There *is*, then, an absolute beginning to this process of actualization. The last sentence suggests this, but more significantly the passage represents, in my opinion, a general nihilistic pattern where meaning is almost completely destroyed.

Piaget wants to carry the regressive analysis back to its beginnings in Psychology. This is very strange as it is understood that the general coordination of actions is the work of the metaphysical Biological Entity. Within the context, this is the only "Psychological" entity that Piaget could have in mind. Without further qualification this is no more than a mystifying redundancy. "Psychology" is really an awkward synonym for this Entity, who is the Logical Structure, because this eternal "Psychology" was the launching pad for the general coordination of actions or operations. The regressive analysis of this series of operations can only go back to the Biological Body of Monads with a newly minted name, "Psychology". It has the same meaning as the "Biology" Piaget depends on for "the explanation of all things" (author's capitalization) (Piaget, 1976b, p. 119). So developmental Psychology, which occurs in time, is launched from the timeless, eternal Structure called "Biology" or "Psychology".

When one considers the hundreds of empty conundrums and puzzles on which Piaget lavished his creative energy, he cannot help but be staggered by both the wasted intelligence and the insidious, treacherous plan to subvert the academic process - a plan with a monstrous *unanalyzed* agenda that has nevertheless been imprudently embraced by many academics. Essentially every one who has spent considerable time with Piaget's books, including Flavell, has indicated that he is very unclear regarding the meaning of much of his work and his ultimate goal. In other words, almost every informed scholar realizes that Piaget's true agenda has been a long-standing mystery.

Much of Piaget's work borders on nonsense. While it is usually possible to grind out the meaning, the real significance is undoubtedly to be found in the reason for his unparalleled motivation for highly elaborated nonsensification. Using children as a partial blind, Piaget divulges his main method for creating elaborate nonsense: *"This double and contradictory explanation will fit every case,* and the child will always contrive to justify the most widely opposed facts" (author's italics) (Piaget, 1930, p. 140). *The phrase in italics does not represent the thinking of the child; it is Piaget's method of utilizing the two different levels, with opposite meanings, to deal with every possible question about his theory. By switching levels, but still using the same key words, he switches meanings, and thus can answer, or rather successfully parry, almost every difficult or hostile inquiry regarding his system.* This, of course, involves contradictions, but Piaget is not timid about contradicting himself. He then discloses that the "dynamism" behind the double and contradictory explanation is not based on observation, meaning that the source of the dynamism is the immanent Entity (author's capitalization) (ibid., p. 140). Based on Piaget's own words, then, *the immanent Entity is the origin of the idea for using two opposed meanings for every theoretical term, and He uses Piaget as a willing agent in utilizing these opposed meanings to ensnare those who study his work.*

WHY PIAGET HAS THE DUTY TO PREVARICATE

An incredible statement about himself is fitting at this juncture.

> A precise application of logic presupposes, among other things, the constant obligation not to contradict - a program very hard to carry out and one that people not interested in accuracy or truth will not much care for. *This lack of intellectual honesty may be of a certain practical use* (it is usually more convenient to be able to contradict oneself) and, when scruples about truth finally triumph, it is certainly not because there has been competition or selection in terms of utility alone, but rather because of certain choices dictated by the Internal Organization of Thought (author's italics and capitalization) (Piaget, 1971a, p. 274).

"Logic" and "contradict" are lower level because upper level logic requires dialectical contradiction in order for development to occur. Piaget manifestly cares nothing for accuracy or truth with regard to physical reality and he obviously finds it useful to be intellectually dishonest and to repeatedly contradict himself. He is unquestionably sneaking in a scornful confession about himself in this passage, while at the same time expressing an arrogant disdain for established conventions and morality. It is doubtful that Piagetians can find a precedence for such a wretched, despicable self-description in the entire history of academia. *The "scruples about truth" that finally triumph represent a switch to the upper level as the Internal Organization is responsible. That is, the immanent Subject requires that the "truth" about Himself eventually come to the fore, and this is to be facilitated by intellectual dishonesty.* The "truth" in this case is Piaget's metaphysical theory.

This unflattering self-portrayal of Piaget's ethical and moral conduct is found to be richly justified when we examine a reasonable sample of his works. We are simply pointing to aspects of his doctrine that are fundamental to his system. *For instance, why does the child lie? It is because, according to Piaget, of the resistance put up by reality. It is this resistance that necessitates lying* (author's italics) (Piaget, 1926, p. 234). *The term "resistance" is highly significant in this context, as the object or physical reality is defined in terms of resistance* (author's italics) (Piaget, 1930, pp. 128; 131) (Piaget, 1974b, p. 3). Since lying is necessitated by his theoretical position, Piaget is actually telling us why *he* must lie. He also adds another reason why he prevaricates. It is because the child supposedly is expressing beliefs about the future when he lies (Piaget, 1926, p. 234). Again, this is a highly improbable reason for children to lie, but it fits Piaget's situation perfectly. Piaget is not at all embarrassed to have children run interference for him, even when it makes no sense. It is he, not the child, who knows about the future, and who believes that the big lie will hasten the future he desires.

The child's "Unconscious Egocentrism", that is, his conscious Internal Organization, tends spontaneously to "alter the truth" and "neglect veracity" (author's italics and capitalization) (Piaget, 1932, p. 156). To state the same idea differently, the obligation to speak the truth, not to steal, etc. does not emanate from his own immanent Mind (author's capitalization) (ibid., p. 188), but from the child's own brain-based mind! Hopefully this is not an easy doctrine for Piagetians to accept, as Piaget is calling conventional notions of evil good and good evil! "The child is almost led to tell lies ... by the very Structure of his spontaneous Thought" (author's capitalization) (ibid., 158-9). The term "Structure" is a play on words as it refers to the *immanent* Structure in the child that leads him to tell Self-serving lies - not for the child, but for the Absolute Structure. Also, "spontaneous" here definitely indicates the metaphysical level. "The tendency to tell lies is a natural tendency, so spontaneous and universal that we take it as an essential part of the child's Egocentric Thought" (author's capitalization) (ibid., p. 133). The key word is *"essential"* - lying is *essential* to the child's *immanent* Egocentric Entity, not the physical child himself! Lying is *essential* for the development of this Entity in the child. Piaget helps us digest this appalling chain of ratiocination by pointing to his Model of moral behavior: *"The Subject's morality forms the supreme criterion"* (author's italics and capitalization) (Piaget, 1971c, p. 66). This entire argument is clearly an attempt to justify Piaget's monstrous lie - my immanent Subject made me do it!

THE OTHER MEANING OF EGOCENTRISM

What about the concept of "egocentrism"? The textbook I presently use in teaching developmental psychology says: "Egocentrism means that thinking centers on the ego, or self. Thus the egocentric child's ideas about the world are limited by the child's own narrow point of view" (Berger, 1994, p. 233). Like all other textbooks and commentaries on Piaget, no mention is ever made regarding the most important meaning that Piaget gives the term. Piaget blames lower level egocentrism on the child's ignorance regarding his "true Ego".

> The child being ignorant of his Own Ego, takes his own point of view as absolute ....
> What applies to the child is also true of science. So long as the child [and by
> implication, the scientist] thinks that he can reason directly about things without taking
> Himself into account, ... he will [not] succeed ... in reaching logical necessity. As soon
> as he brings in his Own Ego ... the child [and by implication, the scientist] attains ...
> logical strictness (author's capitalization) (Piaget, 1928, p. 197).

Natural science is a result of lower level egocentrism for the same reason children are "physically egocentric". Both the child and the traditional scientist are ignorant of the true Ego. We know that Piaget has in mind the Absolute Ego because "logical necessity" and "logical strictness" are superhuman concepts in his vocabulary. Piaget does, of course, utilize the lower level, physical meaning in his many "physical" experiments, but he quite often slips in the "central" immanent Ego and this must not be ignored.

When syncretism, which is a vague, but all-inclusive Schema of "the Whole" (author's capitalization) (Piaget, 1928, p. 59), permeates the thought of the child, his thought is directed by this Whole, Ego or Absolute.

> The Ego-Centric tendency leads [the child] ... to impose arbitrary Schemas upon the world of external objects, to be constantly assimilating new experiences to Ancient Schemas, in a word to replace adaptation to the external world by assimilation to the Self (author's capitalization) (ibid., p. 228).

The Schemas imposed upon objects existed long before the child was born because they belong to the eternal Self or Ego. Ancient Schemas are in the process of development by means of partially assimilating many consecutive generations of human beings. We know that they belong to the immanent Self because assimilation is their goal, not adaptation by means of seeking to learn about the external world. Then too, when we read that "syncretism permeates" the child's mind, we know that the Ancient Schemas of the "Whole" or Absolute Self are assumed to be dominant in the child's thought. To take another aspect of egocentricity, Piaget says that "Absolute Egocentricity implies magic", by which he means "efficacy at a distance" (author's capitalization) (Piaget, 1929, p. 436), a capacity which only the monads possess. When the Absolute Ego is "central", magic is a normal consequence. This magic involves monads outside the child cooperating with monads inside the child. Piaget admits that magic based on the General Self is "disembodied", but he adds that it is an act of Intelligence (author's capitalization) (Piaget, 1971c, P. 140-1). The disembodied Ego is the only Intelligent Self as He is the only Ego who can perform operations. Absolute Egocentrism "abolishes the temporal" and produces a "Homogeneous Medium common to all objects" (author's capitalization) (Piaget, 1969a, p. 118). The Ego or Absolute, consisting of monads, does indeed provide a Homogeneous Medium for all objects. The Egocentric tendency leading the "child" to impose Schemas has its source in his immanent Subject, not his physiologically based psychology.

The timeless, disembodied Ego composed of Ancient Schemas, directing the child's thought, performing acts of magic and producing a Homogeneous Medium in which all objects exist, could not be the human ego that Piaget considers to be detestable (Inhelder & Piaget, 1958, p. 349) and hateful (Piaget, 1971c, p. XVI)! In his autobiography, he admits that his definition of "egocentricity" is vague, and that *"this term has usually not been given its only clear and simple meaning"* (Piaget, 1976b, p. 127). Piaget made a number of such self-assertive confessions, which amounts to telling the academic community that it has been deliberately lied to and manipulated. For instance, he freely admits manipulating the concept of "projection" and illegitimately using "internal" and "external" (Piaget, 1929, p. 271); he tells us quite plainly that he was purposefully not clear regarding the true location of the Mind (author's capitalization) (ibid., p. 151); he acknowledges an ambiguous play on words regarding two kinds of reversibility (Piaget, Inhelder & Szeminska, 1960, p. 330); and he admits that the systematic appearance of some of his work was not really systematic (Piaget, 1930, p. 157). We must add that these confessions are definitely not acts of contrition or repentance, as there is no attempt to set things straight by full explanation and clarification. What I did was illegitimate, and I have no intention of making it legitimate! The purpose is rather to taunt the academic world by reminding it teasingly that what he did was intentional, and that he is utterly contemptuous of everything it represents.

LYING IS GOOD BUT PHYSICAL KNOWLEDGE IS BAD

Piaget boldly proclaims that, "we know why children lie" (Piaget, 1932, p. 133), and he gives us the basis of this "knowledge".

> This feature of child psychology [the spontaneous and essential tendency to lie] is of an intellectual as well as a moral order, and ... is connected with the laws of child Thought in general and with the phenomenon of Intellectual Egocentrism in particular. For *the need to speak the truth and even to seek it for oneself is conceivable only in so far as the individual thinks and acts as one of a society ... founded on cooperation* (author's italics and capitalization) (ibid., p. 157).

We meet with upper level Egocentrism again as the spontaneous source of lies. This passage sums up a discussion regarding the tendency to lie, with Piaget concluding that there is not only no need to speak the truth, but there is also no need to even seek the truth unless society is founded on "cooperation". *He is, of course, expressing his opinion regarding the "truths" of physical reality, the truths that traditional science is designed to discover.* But what is a society founded on cooperation? As one might expect, "cooperation" has an upper level meaning. It means an operation which involves more than one group of monads working together harmoniously toward a common goal. "Cognitive regulations or operations are the same whether in a single brain or in a system of cooperations" (Piaget, 1971a, p. 369). Operations within a person's brain and operations that involve two or more people simultaneously are carried out by the same overall Body of Monads. To put it in other words, intraindividual operations and interindividual operations always cooperate with each other. "There are not intraindividual coordinations of actions on the one hand and social life which unifies them on the other. There is a fundamental identity between the interpersonal operations and the intraindividual operations" (Piaget, 1967, p. 129).

> As Human actions are nearly always both collective and individual, the laws governing their general co-ordination apply equally to Inter-individual relations and to private, especially Interiorized, actions. As a result, there is thus an inevitable convergence of The Most 'General' Forms of Social Interaction and of co-ordination of Individual actions. A better way of putting it would be to say that there are two indissociable aspects of one and the same Reality: operations and co-operations (in the etymological sense of the word) .... We are dealing with the same General Structures that characterize all Human actions (author's capitalization) (Piaget, 1973c, p. 30).

There is only one source of action - the monads. They are responsible for Interindividual or Social actions and Interactions, as well as the Interiorized actions of Individual Thought. Operations and cooperations are based on the same Reality, namely the Body of Monads who is common to all people and all things. The words in parenthesis mean that "operations" and "cooperations" are operations period. The "co" merely emphasizes the fact that every group of monads works in perfect harmony with every other group of monads in the performance of multiple operations.

So, unless the society in which one lives agrees, and behaves in accordance with, Piaget's doctrines, it is his bounden duty not only to lie as the occasion requires, but in such a perverse society there is no need even to seek knowledge! Naturally, we are speaking about knowledge of physical reality, not knowledge of Piaget's Absolute. As illogical and as strange as it may seem, Piaget has made his position on physical knowledge quite clear. For instance, he argues that "fidelity to fact" may lead to "logical incoherence" (Piaget, 1930, p. 253). After all, facts do not represent the basic Reality. The basic Reality is not represented by the phenomena or data studied by natural science, but by the Underlying Structure (author's capitalization) (Piaget, 1973b, p. 28). This Structure and all of its metaphysical activities are called "Norms" by Piaget (author's capitalization) (Piaget, 1973d, p. 34) (Piaget, 1970b, p. 79) (Beth & Piaget, 1966, p. 147). The Structure is the Fundamental Norm and it does not depend upon human nature.

> But what of the "Fundamental Norm" ... on what does it depend? On human nature?... An answer no doubt satisfactory to those who believe in the permanence of human nature, but [not] to those who want to understand human nature in terms of its formation (author's capitalization) (Piaget, 1970b, p. 106).

Piaget's system offers him not only complete certainty, but also permanence. Neither his philosophy nor his psychology includes any aspect that is contingent, making it impossible for him to accept natural science or put any trust in physical reality. No dictionary can tell us about his concept of Norms, but Piaget differentiates them sharply from facts. "It is extremely difficult", he admonishes, "for those specialists dealing with facts and those with Norms to respect one another's views" (author's capitalization) (Beth & Piaget, 1966, p. 153). Piaget has this Underlying Structure or Fundamental Norm in mind when he reports that there is an Unconscious Factor within the child that actually tries to prevent the child from gaining knowledge about physical interactions (author's capitalization) (Piaget, 1973a, p. 37). We must remind ourselves again that this "factor" is not unconscious; it is the child who is unconscious of the Immanent Factor. There is the additional problem, warns Piaget, that data derived from physical experience may hinder Logical and Spatial structuring (author's capitalization) (Piaget, 1972, pp. 40-1). The correct syntax is, "may hinder Logical structuring by Space". It is only the Spatial monads who are capable of Logical structuring. That is, Self-structuring by the Spatial Absolute Himself.

PIAGET REJECTS NATURAL SCIENCE

Natural science has gone astray, as we have seen repeatedly, because it is based on the wrong foundation. "If the world of science is really 'constructed' on the lived world, it is not ... constructed on its foundations" (Piaget, 1971c, p. 87).

The "lived world" in this passage is the physical world, so we see that Piagetian Science is definitely neither interested in nor based on the visible world of physical reality. His Science is based on the Absolute's method of doing away with the visible world and thereby developing Himself. Science, for Piaget, is not something that man does; it is something that only the Absolute Subject can do. The aim of Scientific Thought, which is the Operational Thought of the Subject, is to "get away from" physical reality by contradicting it (author's capitalization) (ibid., p. 87). For Piaget, this means that there is no reason to utilize or "seek the truth" in physical reality.

Natural science advances by the accumulation and integration of contingent facts, but Piaget is not at all interested in this process.

> It is impossible to attain the essence by the accumulation of contingent fact .... If their only aim is to accumulate knowledge of factual detail, we have nothing to say; except that we do not see the interest of these fact-collecting studies (ibid., p. 125).

Why should we wish to seek knowledge about material reality when the immanent Subject wishes to eventually have no physical concepts? Physical concepts are contingent, and natural science is based on contingent facts, but Piaget will have nothing to do with contingent facts, as he is only interested in certainty - the certainty of Norms. Consciousness, according to Piaget, loosens all ties with the external or physical world and replaces them by concepts belonging entirely to the Subject Himself (author's capitalization) (Piaget & Inhelder, 1956, p. 448). In the meantime, as the Subject gradually eliminates "physical concepts", "objective facts" can be accepted or rejected as a result of coordinations (author's capitalization) (Piaget, 1977, p. 173). Facts can be accepted or rejected because "Reason ... itself determines what is true and what is false" (author's capitalization) (Inhelder, Sinclair & Bovet, 1974, p. 270). Reason is based on the "autonomous" Structures of Thought or immanent Entity (author's capitalization) (ibid., p. 270).

THE ABSOLUTE VERSUS THE JUDEO-CHRISTIAN GOD

Hegel's use of "God" as an alternative for "Absolute", "Logic" or "Thing-In-Itself" and Piaget's use of "God" as a synonym for "Absolute Subject" calls for some understanding of how their concept differs from the Judeo-Christian concept. William James had this to say about Hegel's concept of the Absolute.

> *Does the absolute exist or not?* ... Whether there really [is] an absolute or not, no one makes himself absurd or self-contradictory by doubting or denying it .... I must ... ask you to distinguish the notion of the absolute carefully from that of another object with which it is liable to become heedlessly entangled. That other object is the 'God' of common people in their religion, and the creator-God of orthodox Christian theology. Only thoroughgoing monists or pantheists believe in the absolute. The God of our popular Christianity is but one member of a pluralistic system. He and we stand outside of each other, just as the devil, the saints, and the angels stand outside of both of us. I can hardly conceive of anything more different from the absolute than the God, say, of David or of Isaiah .... If it should prove probable that the absolute does not exist, it will not follow in the slightest degree that a God like that of David, Isaiah, or Jesus may not exist, or may not be the most important existence in the universe for us to acknowledge. I pray you, then, not to confound the two ideas as you listen to the criticisms I shall have to proffer. I hold to the finite God, for reasons which I shall touch on ... but I hold

that his rival and competitor - I feel almost tempted to say his enemy - the absolute, is not only not forced on us by logic, but that it is an improbable hypothesis (McDermott, 1968, pp. 521-2).

Piaget was very much aware that the Absolute is completely different from the Judeo-Christian God and chides adults for teaching children about the Christian religion because it is foreign to the child's spontaneous Thought (author's capitalization) (Piaget, 1929, p. 335). At about fifteen years of age he had a "problem" with the Christian religion, and this led him to a new passion: philosophy (Piaget, 1976b, p. 118).

THE CREATION OF THE PHYSICAL UNIVERSE

We are not told how the monads created the physical universe, but since objects are said to be in the process of being "reabsorbed", there is the suggestion that creation was an "emanation" from the monads. The depiction of the young baby's universe advances this possibility. As we saw previously, the development of the Totality is recapitulated in the development of every immanent Body of Monads. So when Piaget says that the universe of the young baby is a world without objects, consisting only of shifting and unsubstantial "tableau" which appears and then are totally reabsorbed (Piaget & Inhelder, 1969, p. 14), we realize that this particular condition of the infant agrees with his doctrines concerning the early status of the Totality. It recapitulates what the Totality did and, to add a surprising caprice on the part of Piaget, what He will do in the future. It illogically spans the entire gamut of his doctrine of existence from the time before physical reality was created until assimilation is completed with the reabsorption of physical reality. The concept of reabsorption is repeated several times (Piaget, 1971b, p. 16) (Piaget, 1973a, pp. 13-14). Although the meaning is twisted, the complete reabsorption Piaget has in mind is expressed in another way. "At the beginning of mental development ... objects seem to keep changing shape and dimensions, and sometimes even to destroy themselves" when they disappear from sight (Piaget & Inhelder, 1974, p. 61). *In Piaget's system, objects do not destroy themselves, but they are gradually "destroyed" by the process of assimilation. In this way they again become a part of the Spatial Continuum from which they emanated.*

> All mass and every dynamic process are reduced to Forms or to geometric transformations in such a way that no body or any physical event is any longer to be situated *in* Space. They are themselves parts *of* Space .... [This is] the ultimate phase of thinking (Piaget's italics) (author's capitalization) (Piaget, 1974b, p. 149).

This passage is a rather complete description of what Piaget means by reabsorption or assimilation, although comprehension is impeded by inappropriate language. *Every aspect of reality will be* (not "are") *reduced to the Form* (not "Forms") *by* (not "or to") *geometric transformations in such a way that nobody or any physical event is any longer to be situated in space.* To describe all masses as being reduced *to* "*geometric transformations*" proves that Piaget is not above pure nonsense. Even children understand that this does not make sense, demonstrating that Piaget is not ashamed to twist meanings in ways that are obviously foolish. Masses are in the process of being reduced or reversed back to the Form of Monads (author's capitalization) (Piaget, 1978a, p. 163) (Piaget, 1974b, p. 130), but by using "to" rather than "by", Piaget plays the mischievous clown. Anyone who reads Piaget's books must be willing to deal with a continuous barrage of linguistic and psychological barriers to normal communication. *All of reality will become* (not "are") *parts of Space.* All bodies or objects will have been absorbed back into the monads of Space or the Form at this point, so physical events are no longer possible. The statement that the bodies or objects "are now" a part of Space, combined with Piaget's use of "reabsorption", strongly suggests that physical reality emanated from the monads and will eventually become a part of the monads again. This will be the final result of "Thinking" - the only kind of Thinking of interest to Piaget. *Thinking, to repeat Piaget's definition once again, is the activity of the monads as they assimilate physical reality.*

In his first book, he had this to say about the creation of things. "Everything happens as though nature were the outcome, or rather the reflexion of Mental activity whose reasons or intentions the child is always trying to find out" (author's capitalization) (Piaget, 1926, p. 190). Regardless of how it was created, the monads alone were responsible. The single fact of pure Mathematics and pure Logic, which is one of the absurd ways that Piaget describes the activity of the monads, is the basis for the idealistic notion that the whole universe was deduced by Thought (author's capitalization) (Piaget, 1969b, pp. 357-8). Why does Piaget treat "pure Mathematics" and "pure Logic" as a single fact? It is because the metaphysical meaning in each case is identical. The two terms have nothing to do with mathematics or logic, but everything to do with the activity of the monads. They both refer to the activity of the monads as they perform their functions. "Deduction" by Thought is also defined by Piaget as activity of the monads (author's capitalization) (Inhelder & Chipman, 1976, p. 98) (Inhelder & Piaget, 1958, pp. 254-5). Pure Math and Logic is on a higher plane, meaning the metaphysical plane, than the math and logic taught in our universities (author's capitalization) (Beth & Piaget, 1966, p. 243), and the term "deduce" simply means "operate" in Piaget's vocabulary of the metaphysical.

Causal explanation, such as explaining the creation of the universe or the movement of the planets, is based on the Deductive System, which does not depend on the laws of natural science but on the coordinations afforded by operations (author's capitalizations) (Piaget, 1974b, p. 134). Deductions depend on Logico-Mathematical coordination and the links they establish. Logico-Mathematical deductions within objects depend upon the monads within the objects. Piaget expresses it this way: "Objective structures thus contain a Deductive Element supplied by the Subject" (author's capitalization) (Piaget, 1972, p. 91). "Objective structures" means "objects" and "Deductive Element" refers to the living monads of the Subject, which account for Logico-Mathematical deductions or assimilative operations. When the "objective structure" or object is a human being, the Deductive Element is his immanent Structure.

All structures of the real world, the physical-energy world of science, came into existence, however, through Logico-Mathematical deduction by means of operations that are *not* assimilative. Assimilative operations cause transformations in objects

(Piaget, 1977, pp. 170-1) leading to eventual reabsorption, but the operations which created the world were completely different kinds of operations. No attempt is made by Piaget to explain how these other kinds of operations accomplished their task, but he insists that the rules they followed belong to a Reality which is not physical (author's capitalization) (Piaget, 1952, pp. 12-13). Piaget refers to this Reality specifically when he says that the rules of Logico-Mathematical deduction point to the existence of an eternal Idea (author's capitalization) (Beth & Piaget, 1966, p.146). "Idea" or "Ideal" are synonyms for the Absolute (author's capitalization) (ibid., p. 146) (Piaget, 1930, p. 126), and included in the concepts of the "Idea" or "Ideal" is the notion of development toward the Ideal (author's capitalization) (Piaget, 1973a, p. 98) (Piaget, 1952b, pp. 10, 179). This, according to Piaget, required the creation of the physical universe followed by its complete assimilation.

THE MEASUREMENT OF ASSIMILATORY PROGRESS

When one thinks about the pairing of opposite classes as the two entities constantly change, one becoming progressively more complex and the other becoming gradually less physical, it is clear that the definition of opposites was never fully specified. Nevertheless, we have Piaget's partial description of the process, and he attempts to cover any lack of clarity by the metaphysical concept of "measurement". Perhaps the best approach to understanding measurement is through the concept of "proportion". This concept refers both to the progressive construction or development of the Absolute Entity and to the progressive assimilation or elimination of the "physical entity". As Piaget explains, "proportionality cannot be understood [unless there is] the establishment of a relationship between two laws of progression .... The covariations [of these two laws are] functionally linked" (Piaget et al, 1977, p. 137). We know that proportionality is based on metaphysical activity because the facts of physical reality cannot prevent its imposition. *"Proportionality tends to eventually impose itself ... regardless of the facts"* (author's italics) (ibid., p. 144). The facts can be ignored because "proportionality" is a Normative or metaphysical process. We are also informed that operations, which are metaphysical, generate proportion (Piaget 1970a, p. 224). An understanding of assimilation elucidates what is meant by "proportionality". As assimilation gradually eliminates the physical characteristics of the object, the proportion of physical characteristics is reduced, while the proportion of "positive" development is increased by the exact amount the physical is reduced. Complete assimilation will result in a physical proportion of zero percent and a positive developmental proportion of 100 percent. *In sum, "proportion" begins with the first dialectical synthesis of an ordered pair and ends after a long sequence of operations* (author's italics) (Piaget et al, 1977, p. 186).

The Body of Monads does the measuring on itself as well as on its opposite and Piaget, while he cannot explain how it is done by the Absolute, is confident that this Entity knows how to precisely coordinate the continuing series of matched pairs of classes. Quantitative measurement at the metaphysical level is calculated by the organized monads assumed in the concept of atomism (Piaget & Inhelder, 1974, p. VIII). While Piaget does not know how the Absolute does it, he gives us a fairly detailed description of how he conceives of the monads inside of objects. Since they "observe" everything inside of solid objects, they must have sufficient information to make metaphysical measurements.

> Measurements ... are carried out as if the Observer [Body of Monads] ... were inside the object, regarded as a rigid solid, analogous to the way in which a human being might explore ... the inside of a building by moving from floor to floor in a lift. [The Body of Monads] "measures" solids ... *by virtue of Measurement and object being regarded as co-extensive.* (author's italics and capitalization) (Piaget & Inhelder, 1956, p. 247).

The language is fairly normal except for "Measurement", as the meaning is obviously "Measurer". Again the impediment to understanding is quite candidly nonsensical. Since the Measurer would necessarily be the metaphysical Entity composed of monads, we can understand why the meaning is muddled. Inside of all objects, including solid ones, Piaget describes an Observer who sees everything and knows everything about the object. It is this "Observer" who makes the measurements that enable proper pairing of opposites and operational activity. Piaget prefers to dwell on the "Observer" or monads in people, rather than in less interesting objects, as He enables every move or thought that occurs and, more important, He assimilates people.

Piaget tells us who this Measurer is:

> Now primitive relations are always relations between the Self and things ... *This means that the Measuring Factory, which is the Ego intrudes upon the measured entity which is the world,* and every relation given by mental experience must ... bear the traces of these two inseparable terms (author's italics and capitalization) (Piaget, 1928, p. 196).

Piaget's use of "relations" is not found in any dictionary, as the dictionary meanings include connections between people, objects, ideas, etc., as well as between the self and things. The "relations" here, however, are operations or equilibrations and they always involve, only the dual entities, namely, the metaphysical Self and the physical universe of which man is a part. "Relation" in this passage is the assimilative relation. *The Measurer is the Measuring Factory, Body of Monads, Field, Form, Self or Ego, and He "intrudes" upon the physical entity for the purpose of eliminating it by means of assimilation.*

The monads are responsible for a wide variety of miscellaneous operations in addition to the preliminary one of creation and the main one of assimilation. They are the source of all the natural elements of the periodic table, all natural objects in the universe and all natural phenomena.

PIAGETIAN CHEMISTRY AND PHYSICS

The universe was "undifferentiated" at first, so chemical elements and molecules had to be produced, as well as "soil", stones, mountains, planets, moons, stars and other natural objects (Piaget, 1929, pp. 385;428). Piaget sets forth a wondrous method employed by the monads that not only is capable of duplicating everything accomplished by modern chemistry, but accounts for most if not all of the qualities that distinguish the various natural objects from each other. This marvelous mechanism is that of "compression and decompression" (Piaget & Inhelder, 1974, pp. 110;130;145;148-150;177-8), "condensation and rarefaction" (Piaget, 1929, pp. 385;388;392) (Piaget, 1930, pp. 265-6) or "contraction and expansion" (Piaget & Inhelder, 1956 p. 466). *The "Mental" manipulation of matter by the conscious "atomic" or "corpuscular" invariants of this mechanism is the theoretical cornerstone of Piaget's organization and fine tuning of reality, following its initial creation.* This is not "mental" in the sense of brain activity, because human beings are completely by-passed. *The ability of the monads to alternately compress and expand matter in a variety of ways is evidently the only method used by the Absolute Subject in this fine differentiation, at least it is the only method described by Piaget.*

Apparently, he had intuitions of this method as a young boy long before his conversion to Hegelianism under the guidance of his godfather at Lake Annecy, and his eventual acquaintance with Leibniz's monads (Piaget & Inhelder, 1974, p. 149). The cognitive invariants described here are applied to objects completely independent of human beings (Piaget, 1971a, p. 150), as these interactions between the monads and matter are outside the somatic sphere (Piaget, 1978b, p. 153), but it is "thinking" nevertheless.

As the organization of matter proceeded, living things were produced and maintained by the monads. Man was eventually created after a long period of "interaction" with matter. *"Organisms* originated (in a way still unknown to us) out of interaction with the physico-chemical environment." This interaction was "between the Subject (Organism) and the objects (environment)" (author's italics and capitalization) (Beth & Piaget, 1966, p. 284). The preceding statement has a nasty little sticker in it. Piaget is giving his reader another lesson in chicanery by utilizing the two meanings of "organism". *One must realize that "organisms" refers to physical life forms, while "Organism" refers to the metaphysical Subject who interacts with the environment in order to produce the physical organisms.* The constant bombardment of the reader with such unfair and unexpected shifts of meaning tends to numb or incapacitate his critical thinking ability, unless he becomes aware of what is going on and accepts the challenge - which has the opposite affect!

Every activity of all forms of life has its basis in monads, not gene action and physiology. The genes are "encased" in an organization of monads, which alone enables the genes to perform their functions. "How can ... genes achieve organization unless they are 'enmeshed in ... an Organized Reference System of Unified Dynamics'" (author's capitalization) (Piaget, 1978b, p. 34)? And every aspect of physiology, including that which supports "practical" thinking, has its source in monadic activity. Physiological forces are regulated and utilized by Action (author's capitalization) (Piaget, 1971a, p. 94). "Action" is not only a function of the Absolute Subject, as it is also used as a synonym for this Subject. It means "immanent Subject" in this instance, and the same unusual meaning is encountered in other contexts. For instance, when Piaget says that Action is the source of operations, he is referring to the Entity who operates (author's capitalization) (Piaget & Inhelder, 1974, p. 278) (Piaget, 1974b, p. 129). Also, when he portrays Action as a System of Coordinated Movements, the meaning is the same (author's capitalization) (Piaget, 1973a, p. 63). "Action" is also depicted as the Medium of Intelligence (author's capitalization) (Piaget, 1950, p. 32). The Medium or Continuum of Monads, again, is the Absolute Entity who operates, and the production of operations is defined as intelligence.

REACTION OF THE SURROUNDING MEDIUM

In the last chapter of *The Child's Conception of Physical Causality* (Piaget, 1930), Piaget lists 17 types of causal relations that many children supposedly postulate at various times in their development. Although this book is devoted mainly to "experiments" presumably designed to determine how children conceive of causality, these 17 types are not based on an empirical foundation. There is no reasonable connection established between the reported experiments and the various types of causal relations described. We are simply asked to take Piaget's word for the connection that he assumes to exist. One factor that weighs heavily against the validity of the 17 types of causality, even in Piaget's mind, apparently, is the fact that he does not build upon them in subsequent books that deal with the same concept. All 17 types are based on the monads, but we will look at three that specifically emphasize the Interior monads or the Surrounding Medium of monads.

Animistic causality (8th of 17) occurs by the realization of a Form that is alive and conscious, meaning that the Form has a metaphysical Biology. This Form is the Medium or Continuum of Monads (author's capitalization) (ibid., p. 262). Animism, or the belief that all life is produced by a Spiritual Force that is separate from matter, is considered to be a primitive principle in children and therefore in his theory. The Form is this Spiritual Force that not only accounts for life, but also accounts for all the phenomena of nature. Piaget holds that "child thought starts with the idea of a Universal Life as its primary assumption" (author's capitalization) (ibid., p. 261). It is the child's primary assumption for one reason - it is also Piaget's primary assumption.

Dynamic causality (9th of 17) is what is "left over" from animism. What is left over are Forces in objects that "are capable of explaining their activity and their movements". That is, these Forces are the explanation for whatever happens to the object. The reason is that the Forces are considered to be Life itself - metaphysical Life (author's capitalization) (ibid., p. 261). What we see in "dynamic causality" is that the Forces inside of objects are organized Groups of Monads.

The third causal relation is explanation by *reaction of the Surrounding Medium* (10th of 17). Piaget intones deceitfully that, "it is, properly speaking, the child's first genuinely physical explanation" (ibid., p. 263). Although he admits that all nine previous causes are "either occult emanations" or "mystical manufactures" (ibid., p. 263) he, nevertheless, maintains that this cause is physical because of the need for continuity and contact. *He is not being honest, however, as it is not physical at all. The need for "continuity" is a not so vague reference to the Medium of Monads and "contact" is contact with the* Living Monadic Force of Dynamic Causality (author's capitalization) (ibid., pp. 262-3). Piaget gives the metaphysical meaning away with: "[The] reaction of the Surrounding Medium still goes hand in hand with Animistic Dynamism. Only it completes this Dynamism with a more exact Mechanism" (author's capitalization) (ibid., p. 263). He first admits that "Animistic Dynamism", a term by which Piaget illogically appears to combine both "Animistic Causality" and

"Dynamic Causality", was "occultic" in nature, then he declares that "explanation by reaction of the Surrounding Medium" still goes *"hand in hand"* with this occultic explanation. It is easy to see the sleight of hand when one takes a little extra time, but Piaget may have assumed that his colleagues would always be in a hurry. Those who naively believe that Piaget is simply investigating "child thought", with no other agenda in mind, should consider the abstract philosophical nuances of meaning that differentiate "Animistic Causality", "Dynamic Causality" and "explanation by reaction of the Surrounding Medium". Children can neither conceive of nor express such differences of meaning.

NATURAL PHENOMENA ARE PRODUCED BY MONADS

We can only understand natural causes in nature as a whole if we posit a special Mathematical Structure or Model which can account for the regularities or laws (author's capitalization) (Piaget, 1972, pp. 80-1). The Mathematical Structure or Model is the Universal Biological Organization (author's capitalization) (Beth & Piaget, 1966, p. 285), who enjoys a permanent continuity (Piaget, 1971a, p. 184). A phenomenon is always "Biological at its roots" (author's capitalization) (Evans, 1973, p. 7), because this Biological Structure, consisting of the living monads, accounts for it. The observable phenomena of nature require Underlying Structures (author's capitalization) (Piaget, 1974b, p. 125). All physical phenomena are caused, not by the natural forces studied in science, but by the imaginary universe of invisible and scientifically undetectable monads, which make up the Underlying or Special Mathematical Structure. We must, according to Piaget, infer objects (monads) that act independently of us when we explain physical phenomena (Piaget, 1974b, p. IX) (Piaget, 1971c, p. 109). Monads "speak" the language of functions and it is only these functions which can produce observable phenomena. The monads within, and those adjacent to, the sun, moon, planets and other heavenly bodies produce day and night, the seasons and even time. *Time is created when large celestial objects are moved by the monads, and the rate of its flow depends upon the speed at which the objects are moved* (author's italics) (Piaget, 1969, pp. 5-6; 26) (Piaget, 1970c, pp. 59-60) (Piaget, 1950, p. 145). "Time ... is a relationship between an action ... and the speed with which it is done" (Piaget, 1970c, p. 70). "A completely immobile universe would be completely lacking in time" (Piaget, 1969, p. 262). Time, then, has the function of giving the physical universe many of its defining characteristics. But "time cannot ... characterize the universe apart from the Ego" (author's capitalization) (Piaget, 1969a, p. 118) - *the Absolute Ego composed of monads.*

MONADS ACCOUNT FOR SIGHT

Speaking of monads inside an object cooperating with monads outside of the object in order to accomplish a task, Piaget presents us with a theory of sight that boggles the mind. He calls upon the Greek philosopher, Empedocles, to support his anachronistic concept, which he puts forward in all seriousness (Piaget, 1929, p. 61-3). *Natural science determined long ago that light is reflected from objects into the eye where the image is formed, but Piaget disagrees with natural science, as usual, and holds that "there is no light that goes from the object to the eye"* (author's italics) (Piaget, 1974b, p. 28). Sight, for Piaget, involves a "Quasi-Substantial Reality that goes from the eye to meet the object" (author's capitalization) (ibid., p. 28). In other words, sight is based on cooperation between the Substantial monads within the eye and those between the eye and the object (author's capitalization) (Piaget, 1974b, p. 28;101;103) (Piaget, 1929, pp. 62-3). Piagetian Science claims that "there is a perfect continuity between the impulse in the brain and the movements of the object" (author's capitalization) (ibid., pp. 266-7). The monads cause the impulse in the brain when the perception of a particular object occurs, and there is a perfect continuity of monads between the brain, eyes and object. *Piagetian Science is literally out of this world, but it is even more astonishing that much of academia continues to hold him in solemn awe. Every foolish statement is construed to have some profound meaning beyond everyone's ability to comprehend.*

MONADS THE BASIS OF MEMORY

The monads must constantly reorganize themselves so that they not only remember everything about the nature and functioning of the physical universe, but more important, they must remember every detail regarding their own development. Intelligence or Memory "can relate any elements, whatever their spatio-temporal separation" (author's capitalization) (Piaget & Inhelder, 1973, p. 116) (Piaget, 1969b, p. 285). No matter how long ago or the distance involved, the monads remember. A choice illustration of distance is Piaget's memory of the other side of the moon (ibid., p. 285). The physical Piaget had no such memory, as no man had ever seen the other side of the moon when the assertion was made. Piaget made this incredible statement by or before 1961, the date *Mechanisms of Perception* was first published in French. It was Piaget's true Ego who "remembered" what the other side of the moon is like because this Ego, composed of monads, is not only in Piaget, but is everywhere, including the other side of the moon. Furthermore these monads were there before the moon came into existence - they brought the moon into existence, observe it constantly and are assimilating it as fast as they can.

An equally exquisite illustration of superhuman temporal memory involves the answers children of ages five and six gave when questioned about their birth dates when compared with their parents birth dates.

> Children not only fail to affirm that they were born after their parents, but many of them claim anteriority - one might almost say priority, with all the value judgments that term implies .... *As for those who attribute anteriority to themselves, they stress [a] kind of truth:* from their point of view, *time ... begins with the dawn of their Own Memory* (author's italics and capitalization) (Piaget, 1969a, p. 205).

The words in italics reveal that Piaget is speaking of the child's "true Ego" whose memory goes back to the beginning of time. This is the truth these children express! The memory of physical things begins at that point, but the "true Ego" Himself does not have a beginning.

Sometimes Piaget reveals the dual selves of his theory by separating the physical child's self from his Memory or immanent Self. "The child's Memory begins to enable Him to reconstruct short sequences of events independent of the self" (author's capitalization) (Piaget, 1954, p. 385). The two selves are starkly displayed in this quote as the Memory or immanent Self does its work independently of the physical self. Piaget often indicates that the Group of monads or immanent Entity in children is not able to function freely at first. This characteristic, however, contradicts his overall theory. How is it logically conceivable that the immanent Self can only "reconstruct short sequences of events independent of the self", while monads outside of children have perfect memories. Since monads inside of children supposedly have instantaneous communication with the outside monads, a logical problem presents itself, but the great logician brushes it aside! Problems of this kind are met at every turn, and most are irreconcilable with each other or with his theory as a whole. *It is ironic that a man who is revered all over the world for his wonderful logical mind is in fact illogical in the extreme.*

The Homogeneous Environment is the Container or Frame of Reference who organizes the successive positions of objects in three dimensions. The relations involved include the memory of all their successive positions or stages of development until the objects are eventually "located on another plane" (Piaget & Inhelder, 1956, p. 367). *The Homogeneous Environment who not only organizes the various physical movements of objects, but also organizes the assimilation of objects over millions of years, is the permanent Body of Monads.* Both the lower level movements of physical reality and the upper level assimilative movements require memory of a superhuman nature.

CHILD PHYSICS IS BASED ON MONADS

Piaget's strategies for introducing his essential concept of monads are almost inconceivable. When they are fully understood, it is my opinion that many Piagetians will feel victimized and outraged. They will conclude, I believe, that Piaget has debased and perverted the academic process in a grossly offensive way.

In one of his earliest books, *The Child's Conception of Physical Causality* (Piaget, 1930), *Piaget attempts to show that there is a "system of physics peculiar to the child"* (author's italics) (ibid., p. 1), *a system, we may safely anticipate, that is based entirely on the monads.* Although he does not use the word "monad", or any of the usual synonyms, the child's system of physics, as deceitfully imposed on the child by Piaget, is seen to be based squarely on the activity of these imaginary entities. The first chapter begins with the children's ideas about the movement and origin of *air*. Piaget intends to impose on the children and his reader, a long, tortuous and misleading succession of confusing assertions, beginning with the concept of "air" and ending with the metaphysical concept of "atoms" or "monads", although these terms are not used. We are informed immediately that a "large number of natural movements, such as those of the heavenly bodies, of rivers, of clouds, etc., are believed by the child to be produced by the wind" (ibid., p. 2).

"AIR" IS ALIVE

He introduces his "experiments" concerning the nature of air, which in this early stage of interrogation are merely questions designed to lead young children to express Piaget's target benchmark that children spontaneously consider the wind or air to be alive (ibid., p. 3). Since monads are alive, this is surely an important step in his plan. We are also told up front that in addition to the questions specified, "other complementary enquiries as to the consciousness or life of the air" would be added (ibid., p. 4). With this latter admission, Piaget makes it impossible for other investigators to duplicate his "experiments", which is also a good idea if his results are going to be artfully invented.

ALL "AIR" BELONGS TO THE SAME BEING

The second point he makes, with reference to the questions, is that there is "participation" between the outside air and the inside air. The monads outside of all objects "participate" or "cooperate" with the monads inside of objects perfectly, so "air" must behave in the same way. *This "participation" occurs through a closed window, and Piaget proclaims that, "in a sense" it is rational* (author's italics) (ibid., p. 8)! *We might quickly add, that it is indeed "rational" in the same way that participation between outside and inside monads is rational! It could not be "rational" in any other way.* Along the same line, Piaget admits that this participation belongs only to logic and not reality, and that it is logical because both the inside air and the outside air belong to the same Being (author's capitalization) (ibid., p. 9). Only one Being could possibly be the "secret" referent in this instance, the Being composed of monads. Surely everyone but Piaget would be embarrassed to make such a mawkish, nauseating argument, and it is the eighth wonder of the world that at least a good portion of the academic community was not able to penetrate such a ludicrous, offensive chain of invented "findings". *The academic community was asked to accept the notion that children believe inside and outside air belongs to the same living being. It did, apparently without any qualms.* More amazing is the fact that very few suspected a hidden agenda. Piaget concludes this aspect of the argument with, "all winds participate with each other" (ibid., p. 13), and we must add, just like Sub-Groups of monads!

The next step in Piaget's investigation of the child's notion of air is to add the concept of an "impetus sufficient to itself", which makes the movement of Air Self-motivated and Self-actualized (author's capitalization) (ibid., p. 22). This obviously refers to his theory of monads in which the monads are Self-motivated and Self-moving.

"AIR" IS AN ALL-PERVADING SUBSTANCE

At the beginning of the second chapter, Piaget assures us that children consider the currents of air to be "variations of a Single All-Pervading Substance" (author's capitalization) (ibid., 32), and he means metaphysical Substance. He then makes the extraordinary announcement, as noted previously, that this insight or "identification" on the part of children is not on the same plane as the initial insights and that it was not even derived from the initial insights (ibid., p. 32). This particular device is employed several times by Piaget, demonstrating his frequent use of physical "experiments" to gradually bring his reader to a metaphysical truth, and then exclaim that the physical analogy as described had nothing to do with arrival at the metaphysical truth. Psychological pain and confusion comes from the fact that although he first implies very strongly that the successive insights lead the child and reader to the metaphysical truth, he abruptly pulls the rug beneath the reader by declaring that the successive insights based on physical phenomena have nothing to do with the metaphysical insight. *In other words, he basically admits that the analogy he has painstakingly developed between air and the Single All-Pervading Substance is really a deception because the insights of the children, and thus the argument made to the reader could not possibly lead to this Substance as I have just implied!* The reader feels as if he has been hit with a sledgehammer. What kind of reaction is appropriate? Did Piaget expect to be understood? Perhaps he was convinced that his reader would be uncomfortable and nonplused, but that he would not fully comprehend. His behavior is so unthinkable it is hard to take in the truth. More than anything else, he apparently depended on the tendency of investigators to remain stuck at the physical level of "child study" for their lack of clear comprehension.

Piaget seemed to have a need to occasionally tell his reader how he was being manipulated. Perhaps it was a "sporting" impulse or simply a method of discharging aggressive feelings. In any case, comprehension brings one face to face with someone whose sense of right and wrong is disconcerting. What I have just claimed is a lie! The elaborate argument you have just struggled through was a deliberate trick, because it has no defining relationship with the end result of a Single All-Pervading Being or Substance. It fails to compute. It is thought-provoking to paraphrase a previous quote that he almost certainly made about himself: You see, I really do not care much about "accuracy and truth", and this "lack of intellectual honesty" does indeed prove useful (Piaget, 1971a, p. 274).

OBSERVATION OF A PHYSICAL SUBSTANCE CANNOT LEAD TO AN UNDERSTANDING OF METAPHYSICAL SUBSTANCE

By using air, which is a physical substance, to introduce the metaphysical Substance, monads, Piaget puts himself in the awkward, logically untenable position, *within his system,* of eventually having to concede that the observations of air cannot possibly lead the child to the concept of monads. It is impossible because, according to Piaget's theory, physical reality can only resist the metaphysical as it intrinsically opposes it. Equally fundamental to this impossibility is the fact that *in Piaget's system there is no true interaction between the lower level of physical reality and the metaphysical level. In this case, we are talking about the dictionary meaning of interaction, not dialectical interaction.* To begin with, Piaget denies "any interaction between Consciousness ... and its nervous concomitants" (author' capitalization)

(Piaget, 1973c, p. 19). "Consciousness" is upper level and it does not actually interact with the nervous systems or brains of individual people, The concept is broadened when Piaget appropriates what he claims to be Isaac Newton's term, "spatial container", and asserts that the metaphysical Container of Space does not interact with its physical contents (author's capitalization) (Piaget, 1974b, p. 149). Newton considered space to be "God's sensorium" (Piaget, 1971c, p. 171), but his concepts of "container" and "God" were completely different from Piaget's and Hegel's. In any case, Piaget holds that, in principle, lower level knowledge of physical reality does not interact with, and does not lead to upper level Knowledge of metaphysical Reality. This is the bottom line, even though he contradicts this doctrine continuously. Obviously the Single All-Pervading Substance mentioned above is the metaphysical Body of Monads.

THE CREATION AND MAINTENANCE OF LIFE IS BASED ON "AIR"

After sallying forth with the grossly contradictory declaration that children see that the "currents of air" are not really currents of air, but are the vibrations of a a Single Substance which could not be related to or derived in any way from observing currents of air, Piaget quickly falls back to his "experiments". After asking Roy (6 1/2) a number of questions, detailing his answers, and also referring to a series of questions he had asked Roy in a previous book, he concludes with a confident look into Roy's Mind.

> It can be seen what Roy would find to be the system of the world, if he should feel the need to systematise: the world is a society of organisms produced or fed by Air which was "blown" by Man at the beginning of things (author's capitalization) (Piaget, 1930, p. 45).

After admitting that observations of physical air could not lead to metaphysical Knowledge, Piaget immediately reverts to a metaphysical "Air" which could "produce man"! Basically, Piaget insults the reader quite directly when he tells him that the analogy with air could not lead to metaphysical truth, and then almost immediately depicts Roy as arriving at that identical metaphysical truth by means of the analogy with air! *The "society of organisms" includes people who are produced by "Air"* which was "blown by Man" at the "beginning of things". Obviously "Man" is a synonym of the Absolute, and this conclusion is amplified when we realize that "Man", as recorded in the introduction, is one of the "secret" names of God in Gnosticism (Edwards, Vol. 3, p. 237). As usual, Piaget goes far beyond the actual statements of the child, but it is clear that he is referring to the monads which were there at the beginning of things; monads which produced and continue to sustain every living organism.

EXTERNAL AND INTERNAL MONADS ARE CALLED THE TWO MOTORS

Since the Structure of Monads is the source of all activity or movement it is not surprising that children, according to Piaget, do not believe in physically determined movement. Natural structures cannot move on their own (Piaget, 1970b, p. 142). Piaget claims that children consider movement to be neither free nor physically determined (Piaget, 1930, p. 60). Movement is said to be the result of double motors, one external and one internal (ibid., 63). These two motors basically cause movement for psychical or moral reasons, not physical reasons (ibid., p. 66). *The two motors, one external and one internal, are exactly analogous to the external and internal air discussed above; They refer precisely to the same thing.* The outside motor refers to the monads outside of objects and the inside motor refers to the monads inside of objects or people. These two motors cause movement psychically or mentally; physical causes are theoretically unacceptable. The "sun and moon move of their own free will, but their advance is controlled for moral reasons by God or by man" (ibid., p. 75). The physical sun and moon do not have a will and cannot move on their own, but the monads within these objects and the monads on the outside but adjacent to the objects do have a will and are responsible for movement. Piaget devotes Chapter 4 to explaining the nature of water currents which, he asserts, behave spontaneously much like currents of air.

THE LIVING MONADS ACCOUNT FOR FORCE AND EGO

Chapter 5 deals with the child's idea of force. Piaget believes that empirical observation cannot provide us with knowledge of how things happen, and he insists that children agree with him. "The child fills the world with spontaneous movements and living 'forces'" (ibid., 114). That is, he fills the world with invisible atoms or monads. *The two motors are now living "forces" or "wills", and the source of movement is said to be based on the internal will acquiescing to the commands of the external will* (author's italics) (ibid., p. 115). The two motors are now the living forces or invisible monads which are the forces in the world: they take the place of physical forces. The monads inside of objects and people do the will of the total Body of Monads, most of which are outside. For the child, these forces or wills are Substantial (author's capitalization) (ibid. pp. 117-18), which again is a clear reference to the metaphysical monads within everything performing what is desired by the total Body of Monads. The idea of Force is fully included in the child's particular idea of Life which exists everywhere (author's capitalization) (ibid., pp. 121-2) - the idea of Life as we saw it in animism. Force is now the equivalent of Life, and in Piaget's system, the only living entities are the monads. Piaget then says, this "shows, above all, to what extent Force is Substantified and reduced to a current or to air, which emanates from the Powerful Object itself" (author's capitalization) (ibid., p. 122). Although extremely tangential and logically disconnected, one can easily discern that the Substantial Metaphysical Body is the Powerful Object who operates by means of currents of monads which manipulate every aspect of reality.

The last step in Piaget's unseemly and outrageous transmogrification of air is to make it an "I" within the child. This is a very special "I" indeed as it is not only within the child, serving as the child's true Ego, but it is also the Absolute who is "bound up with the whole universe", meaning that this "I" is both inside and outside of the child (author's capitalization) (ibid., p. 128). This is also why the "I" within the child is considered to be a Medium (author's capitalization) (Piaget, 1932, p. 388).

By pretending to analyze the thought of the child regarding "air" and "wind" Piaget managed to fully develop his basic principle of monads, but apparently no one was aware of this undercover agenda. Piaget must have viewed the results with mixed emotions. In any case, he was consoled because he always had one fully comprehending observer, the Absolute Himself. Furthermore, this Absolute is immanent within everyone who studies Piaget, and Piaget depended upon Him to assist with the deliberately garbled message. Piaget was fully convinced that his immanent Entity guided him in his writing, so he was pleased even if no one else was aware of his real meaning. The remainder of chapter 5 is devoted to the essential task of the "I" or Mind, which is assimilation (author's capitalization) (ibid., pp. 131-2).

After revealing the ultimate nature of "Air", Piaget retreats in the last half of the book to consolidate some points he had covered earlier. Chapters 6 through 11 deal mostly with the concept that children do not consider physical contact to be important in the movement of objects. This follows, as we have noted, because one of Piaget's central doctrines is that invisible, undetectable monads are responsible for all movement in the universe.

In the concluding chapter, the identity of "animism" and conscious, living Air is underlined. For Piaget "animism" refers directly to the "Continuum of Monads", and "air" is used as a synonym for both of these terms (author's capitalization) (ibid., pp. 244-6).

Monads the Basis of Thought and Dreams

In another early book (Piaget, 1929), Piaget relates his findings about air to his findings regarding thought and dreams and announces a close analogy, because "according to several children we have met, thought is made of air, as are also dreams" (Piaget, 1930, p. 55). This is not surprising as thought is the activity of monads and dreams are caused by monads.

Piaget devoted about 25 percent of *The Child's Conception of the World* (Piaget, 1929) and almost all of *The Child's Conception of Physical Causality* (Piaget, 1930) to his doctrine of monads. Although these books have been available in English about 70 years, this particular aspect continues to be overlooked. As we have seen, this doctrine is particularly obvious in the latter book, where "air" is clearly another name for "monads". In the earlier book, the emphasis is mostly on the non-material and inside-outside characteristics of the Body of Monads. Piaget begins the first chapter of this earlier book book with loaded questions about the nature of thought, which for him, naturally, is the exclusive property of the monads. The "first-stage children" agree that nothing to do with thought takes place either in the head or in the body. Rather, they identify thought with the voice. In the "second stage" the voice may be inside the neck or head, but Piaget insists that the "voice" is the spontaneous aspect, while the notion that thought is inside the head is really based on the contribution of adults (Piaget, 1929, p. 50). He believes that children would not associate thought with the head if left to themselves: "It is hard to see how children quite alone could have discovered thinking to be with the head" (ibid., p. 63). Piaget works hard and carefully in several books to separate the brain from the process of thinking, but this has been studiously ignored.

The external aspect of thought is seen in Piaget's discussion of names. Early on, the name is considered to be a part of the thing. Later it becomes dissociated from the thing and is in the air and is *everywhere* (author's italics) (ibid., p. 94). One can understand the significance behind the silliness if he is aware that Piaget has in mind the Surrounding Medium of monads. Piaget conveys the same idea of the metaphysical Medium when he reports that Binet was "convinced that Intelligence is everywhere" (author's capitalization) (Piaget, 1973c, p. 59). Binet, of course, would not appreciate the false implication. The significance is deepened when one realizes that the name of the thing is associated with the creation of things. The Body of Monads created things and the names of things were part of their essence (author's capitalization) (Piaget, 1929, pp. 77-8, 81, 91). Piaget believed that the creation of natural objects required the naming of the objects by their maker, and young children support him on this point (ibid., pp. 77-94) - *as they do on every other aspect of his theory.*

Questions regarding the nature of dreams involves both internal and external causes and the duality of Thought and matter. Children insist that the images of dreams are external (ibid., 120-1), and that there is participation between the person dreamed of and the dream itself (ibid., p. 123).

> The dream is external to the body and its origin is both internal ... and external. This is the counterpart of what we saw with the children who claimed to think with the mouth while regarding thought as identical with the external air (ibid., p. 133).

Piaget takes a statement by Mos (11; 6), who says that he cannot see the dream because it is invisible, and interjects this eager elaboration: "This statement is very convincing and shows that Mos is not speaking of images one thinks one sees outside, but of Something invisible which is projected by Thought and which produces the images outside" (author's capitalization) (ibid., p. 138). *Why was Piaget excited by Mos's statement? It was because he had an opportunity to focus on his real interest, the metaphysical producer of the dream. The invisible "Something" who produces images by "Thought".* One should note in passing the twisted syntax of the last 13 words of the quote. What is projected is the image, not something invisible. Rather it is the invisible Something who does the projecting. As we have seen repeatedly, this reversal of meaning is normal for Piaget.

USES AIR AGAIN TO ARRIVE AT QUASIMAGIC SUBSTANCE

The last example we shall attempt to unravel of Piaget using "air" as an entree into the metaphysical realm of monads is found in a much later book, *Understanding Causality* (1974b). More than twenty years after admitting that observations of air cannot lead to an Operational Structure composed of Substance or monads, Piaget reverts to the same dishonest device. He begins as usual on the physical level with very mundane observations regarding responses of children to his questions, but he quickly makes the transition to the metaphysical level. The transition culminates with the following paragraph.

On the whole, despite the fact that Air does not follow the usual pattern, it plays a quite considerable role in the development of causality as an attribution of operations to objects. At first a quasimagic power linked to a Substance existing only occasionally but produced by the actions of the Subject and by those of Bodies in Motion, Air is then mechanized, after a delay, because of its mixed origins, but, finally, successfully, as it is brought into the vast process of operational structuring from which it cannot escape, not because of particular discoveries it has brought about, but by virtue of analogies or rather general deductive requirements that it cannot avoid (author's capitalization) (ibid., p. 112).

To fully unravel and interpret this quote would take a chapter by itself. While we shall not undertake such an extensive interpretation, perhaps a little clarification will motivate the reader to take time to reflect upon it on his own. One interesting feature is the three direct references to the Absolute Subject, one of which is immediately negated. The three references are "Substance", Subject" and "Bodies in Motion". "Substance" is "verbally" negated because of the inappropriate phrase "existing only occasionally", however, since Substance is the Spiritual Entity who exists eternally, Piaget is not sincere about the negation. The most likely meaning of "existing only occasionally" is that the quasimagic power of Substance is seen in the *children's answers* only occasionally. Another stumbling block is a syntax which suggests that it is a "Substance" which is produced rather than a metaphysical power, but the passage as a whole is manifestly not consistent with this meaning. The quasimagic power is exercised in several ways. One way is by directing the thought processes of young children, and this particular exercise of power appears to be what Piaget is expressing in this passage.

The phrase, "produced by the actions of the Subject and by those of Bodies in Motion" is linguistically very silly, but also very revealing. Piaget obscures the meaning by misusing one word and omitting another. "And" was used in the place of the correct "or" and "actions" was omitted after "those". We know there was a conscious decision to omit "actions" because of the "of" following "those". With these changes the phrase is still bizarre, but the meaning is not completely hidden. This magical power is produced by the Subject or the Bodies in Motion. The use of "and" is a highly contrived way to affirm that the Subject consists of monads in motion, but this is the meaning. The "Bodies in Motion" are acting as the Subject, so must be identified as the Subject. At the same time the Bodies in Motion was "Air" in the preceding sentence, making the Subject consist of "air"! Reading Piaget for meaning means dealing with an avalanche of shameful absurdity, but clearly Piaget is immune to feeling shame. In any case, we have here an unmistakable reference to the monads which make up the Body of the Absolute Subject.

The "mixed origins" of air obviously refers to its dual use by Piaget on the two levels of physical reality and metaphysics. It also refers to the notion that the immanent monads within the child uses the concept of air to subconsciously teach the child about the nature of monads.

Immanent Monads Teach the Child
About their "Atomic" Nature

In the preface to *The Child's Construction of Quantities* (Piaget & Inhelder, 1974), we are informed that the child spontaneously elaborates atomism (ibid., p. VIII). Early in the first chapter Piaget clarifies what he means by this elaboration.

> The first principle constructed by the child explicitly involves the permanence of a *quantum* that ... does not correspond to any sensible quality. Being schematic and global, this first principle cannot possibly be constructed without Intellectual activity, i.e., without going beyond direct experience .... The ... basis of the construction of the first principle has to be sought in the workings of Intelligence (Piaget's italics) (author's capitalization) (ibid., p. 16).

By "quantum", Piaget is referring to the basic unit of his theoretical system, the monad. Monads are permanent, that is, eternal and absolutely everything depends upon their motivation and activity. There is no higher authority in Piaget's system than the Body composed exclusively of these basic units. These units have no "sensible quality" which, for him, means that they have no attribute that can be detected by science. Therefore they can only be a construct of his imagination. *Piaget jumps from "quantum" to the Continuum of Quanta when he describes the first principle as being schematic and global.* Only the monads work schematically in his system, and only his Body of Monads is "global". Piaget invented another name for the Continuum of Quanta - "General Quantum". Substance provides the content of the General Quantum (author's capitalization) (ibid., p. 16). As we have observed previously, "content" can be either physical or metaphysical depending upon the context. If the General Quantum is said to contain objects that will be assimilated, its contents are physical; if "content" is used in describing how the General Quantum is put together, its contents are metaphysical. In this case, the General Quantum is made up of Substance or monads. We know that this is metaphysical Substance because it is invariable and is the Formal Regulator (author's capitalization) (ibid., p. 16). An important notion in the passage is that knowledge of the "quantum" requires an Intellectual construction. Piaget repeats this notion three times. The physical child knows nothing about "quanta" or monads, so when he says that the child constructs this principle he means that the "true Ego" of the child does the constructing. After all, He is the only "Child" capable of "Intellectual activity". Exactly the same idea with different words is found later in the book. "The Deductive System of co-ordinated relations ... will eventually lead [the children] to ... atomism" (author's capitalization) (ibid., pp. 76-7). The Deductive System, or "Immanent Child", is the System of Monads within each of us, it has nothing to do with the dictionary meaning.

In the book, *Six Psychological Studies* (Piaget, 1967), Piaget devotes about five pages to the child's developing atomism (ibid., pp. 43-47). We are assured that this atomism is "quite rational" (ibid., p. 43) and is based on permanent invariants (ibid., p. 45). This *"atomism is born in the guise of a metaphysics of dust"* (author's italics) (ibid., p. 44), and is "remarkable ... because of the deductive process it reveals" (ibid., p. 45). It is this process, of course, which supposedly teaches the child about the true nature of metaphysical atomism. Piaget then tells us that "there remains the construction of the Space concept, which has immense importance ... for ... the laws of development" (author's capitalization) (ibid., p. 47). He prefers not to tell us, however, that these laws of development apply only to the immanent metaphysical Body of Monads within each person, which are a part of the Spatial Continuum.

Another view of how the immanent Entity is said to construct the notion of the monad:

> The object ... is constructed by Intelligence itself, and constitutes the first constant of Intelligence - a constant which is necessary for the formation of Space, of causality in Space and, in general for all Forms of Assimilation which transcend the present perceptual field (author's capitalization) (Piaget, 1950, p. 110).

When we combine the two quotes about the "quantum" and the "object" we get a much clearer picture than either alone can give. The "object" here is obviously metaphysical because of the attributes Piaget ascribes to it. This is an "Intellectual object", not a physical object (Piaget, 1932, p. 192). It is necessary in the formation of Space, it is causal and it performs a kind of assimilation, as understood in Piaget's terminology, that cannot be perceived or studied by natural science. This object is obviously the monad as is the quantum, and the infinite number of "objects" in the Body of the Absolute Subject make up the "General Quantum" or Spatial Continuum.

Piaget offers additional insight regarding "spontaneous atomism" in the young child. This quote follows a retelling of the experiment with lumps of sugar in a glass of water.

> We can now see that this spontaneous atomism, although it is suggested by the visible grains becoming gradually smaller during their dissolution, goes far beyond what can be seen by the subject and involves a step-by-step construction correlative to that of ... operations. We thus have a new instance of the origin of knowledge lying neither in the object alone nor in the Subject, but rather in an inextricable interaction between both of them, such that what is given physically is integrated in a Logicomathematical Structure involving the coordination of the Subject's actions. *The decomposition of a Whole into its parts (invisible here) and the recomposition of these parts into a Whole are in fact the result of logical or Logicomathematical constructions and not only of physical experiments.* The Whole considered here ... is produced by the operations (author's italics and capitalization) (Inhelder & Chipman, 1976, pp. 15-16).

Piaget is seen to have some difficulty in including the physical aspects of an experiment in the acquisition of knowledge. Nevertheless, he squeezes physical experiments into the process of acquiring metaphysical knowledge, and this in spite of the fact that within his system this is not possible. He also specifically states that the "spontaneous atomism" of the child results from a step-by-step construction correlative with operations. This can only mean that the immanent monads within the child produce "spontaneous atomism" by organizing a series of assimilative operations on the child. The word "spontaneous" usually means a metaphysical construction. Although Piaget pretends to find a role for physical experiments in this instance, we should remember that he has a very low regard for such experiments. "Experimentation is not a free or even a direct, spontaneous product of intelligence; it calls for acceptance of external authority" (Piaget, 1974a, p. 23). This authority, rejected by Piaget, is precisely that accepted by natural science. External authority means the authority of physical facts as determined by the process of natural science. Upper level Intelligence is only concerned with one kind of "physical experiment", namely, operational experiments for the purpose of assimilation and thus the elimination of the physical. As noted previously, Piaget considers everything physical to be a temporary evil in the overall scheme of things.

Piaget's recounting of the experiment with the dissolving sugar lumps goes beyond the child's supposed insight into the atomic decomposition of the Whole or Logico-Mathematical Structure; he also is said to have insight into the recomposition of this metaphysical Structure, although the child's behavior gives no basis for this, by means of the atoms or monads. This supposed understanding regarding the identity of the Body of Monads on the part of the child is seen in other contexts (author's capitalization)(Piaget & Inhelder, 1956, pp. 243-4).

Additional factors in the concept of "spontaneous atomism" can be seen in the following passage.

> These higher forms [of causality], which the child attains spontaneously, are, as has been shown, causality by identification of Substance, the Form modeled on the notions of condensation and rarefaction, and a certain primitive atomism or synthesis of elements (author's capitalization) (Piaget, 1929, p. 428).

The Substance that is capable of synthesizing elements by means of condensation and rarefaction represents a higher form of causality. The causal activity of this Substance is what Piaget describes as a primitive atomism. That is, the metaphysical atoms or monads produce physical "elements" somehow by manipulating more basic units. Observe that, by implication, there are two kinds of "form" in the quote. The first "form", found in the dictionary, means a particular kind or type, while the second, the higher Form, refers to Substance as the Form or Field of Monads which has the ability to produce things by special movements. This second or Substantial Form is a synonym of the Spatial Continuum. In other words, Piaget pictures Substance or God as using the monads, of which he consists, more or less as skillful fingers in order to produce all natural structures.

The Child's Conception of Space (Piaget & Inhelder, 1956) represents a tremendous mental effort to describe the metaphysical contents of Space, the marvelous monads, without really communicating it to anyone. He seems to have been successful. This book is an extraordinary example of nonsensification. After paralyzing the reader's ability to think clearly with endless questions about closed, open and intertwined geometrical shapes, as well as other aspects of topological space, such as the study of knots, Piaget introduces the ideas of points and continuity (read: monads and Continuum). He does this by means of many questions and experiments designed to show that when objects are progressively reduced in size, either by cutting, drawing or imagining, they will eventually lose their qualities as an object and come to an end, whereas points (monads) will always be there in infinite numbers. Not only that points remain, but that the points make up a "Homogeneous and Continuous Entity composed of the sum total of adjacent points" (author's capitalization) (ibid., p. 148). *Notice the enormous illogical leap from the idea of a point to a Continuous Entity composed of such points. There is no basis for the leap other than mere verbal manipulation.* Nevertheless, Piaget pretends that children by the age of 12 often make this inadmissible connection (ibid., pp. 145-149). *This*

Homogeneous and Continuous Entity begins as a physical line or three-dimensional object, but after about 145 additional pages of mind-numbing discussion of perspective, projective lines, shadows and false absolutes, *it becomes a Living Overall System capable of operations* (author's italics and capitalization) (ibid., p. 292)! After about 75 more pages of obfuscating "filler" about "affinitive transformation of the rhombus" and proportions, the "Overall System" is now seen to be a Container with a Homogeneous Environment consisting of objects (monads), which make up a Frame of Reference (author's capitalization) (ibid., p. 367). Piaget admits that these "particular objects" are "located on another plane" (ibid., p. 377), meaning that they are metaphysical. He retreats again to experiments regarding "stages in development of horizontal and vertical axes" before dashing forth to describe the activity of these "particular objects", which is the coordination of actions or operations (ibid., p. 404). Piaget rather awkwardly admits that "the process of co-ordinating is no part of the physical experiment, but a part of Intelligence Mechanisms, and is therefore basic to logical ... operations" (author's capitalizations) (ibid., p. 404).

After another irrelevant hiatus regarding "diagrammatic layouts and the plan of a model village", Piaget begins his general conclusions, which are upper level as usual. After expending inordinate amounts of time and energy on physical experiments and questions of a physical nature, Piaget admits again that *none of these experiments led to the child's "idea of Space"* (author's italics and capitalization) (ibid., p. 453). As he truthfully says, "not every experiment is a physical one" (ibid., 453), meaning that some are metaphysical. The experiments which lead to the child's idea of Space are metaphysical experiments on the child's own actions (author's capitalization) (ibid., p. 453), *but Piaget does not tell us that it is the child's immanent monads who experiment on the child. Spatial concepts, as understood in Piaget's theory, can only develop when the Internal Schemata operate on the physical object, that is, the physical child* (author's italics and capitalization) (ibid., p. 454). *It turns out that the exclusive source of the child's idea of Space, and the monads which it contains, is the Body of Monads which live inside of the child, not the physical experiments which Piaget uses solely for the purpose of frustration and befuddlement.* When Piaget says that "[the] continuity [of the Homogeneous Space of points] comes to be applied to the Whole of Space, regarded as a Universal Framework valid for all objects and all observers" (author's capitalization) (ibid., p. 459), he means that this includes the insides of objects and people. The points inside of people are the immanent Body of Monads.

It should be pointed out that in this book one will never see the word monad and seldom see "atom", nevertheless, the entire book is about monads or spiritual atoms. In other books, for example, *Biology and Knowledge* (Piaget, 1971a), *Main Trends in Psychology* (Piaget, 1973c) and *Main Trends in Inter-Disciplinary Research* (Piaget, 1973d), "atomism" and "atoms" are discussed repeatedly, but nearly always with negative connotations because the meaning is most often physical in nature. One must become aware of Piaget's many ruses!

The Synonyms and All-Inclusive Work of the Monads

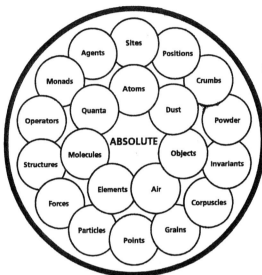

Every circle contains a synonym for monads. Monads account for the attributes of all natural objects. They also account for the anatomy, physiology and activities of all life forms.

Monads fill all of space. Sub-units of monads are inside of every object and every living thing as represented by the circles. Their most important function is to assimilate all of material reality.

Chapter 4

THE ABSOLUTE SUBJECT

A PATHOLOGICAL EXCESS OF SYNONYMS

Piaget's massive burden of artificially contrived verbal entities reaches its peak in this chapter, as we are concerned here with the attributes of his Absolute Subject. Far more synonyms were invented for Him than, for instance, His main activity, which is operational assimilation. The problem is how to appropriately demonstrate his unprecedented use of synonyms to overwhelm and confuse the reader without becoming excessively repetitive. The sheer number of equivalent terms is unbelievable, but this is not the main source of difficulty. The bewildering burden for the reader results from the way Piaget appears to differentiate between the various synonyms. In other words, *the reader is led to believe that there are numerous differences among the flood of identical metaphysical terms when there really are no differences at all.* In order to reduce the need to constantly point out the common meaning of the terms, most of them are relegated to the appendices. The root term, Absolute, and three of His most important synonyms - Subject, Structure and Space - are treated in the text, but the vast majority are listed in appendices A through M. A large amount of important material is thus dealt with there in a condensed fashion. Not only are numerous synonyms inventoried, along with references, but amplifying comments are added at the end of each appendix to enhance one's understanding of Piaget's nefarious methods.

Appendix M includes a catalogue of 163 variations of the way Piaget refers to the metaphysical Structure, but the primary purpose of this appendix is to show his metaphysical-physical dual system. Also listed are 23 "physical" structures with conventional dictionary meanings. When one observes how Piaget uses the conventional structures as foils to deflect attention from the metaphysical Structure, he will be on the path to breaking through the veil of deceit.

PIAGET IS A HEGELIAN, NOT A KANTIAN

As we have seen, Piaget is a Hegelian, not a Kantian. One reason so many consider him to be a Kantian is that Flavell called him a "Kantian philosopher" (Flavell, 1963, p. 35) and another is that Piaget refers to Kant more often than any other philosopher. He also uses many of Kant's terms, such as "operation", "schema", "regulation", "construct" "substance", "identity", "totality", and others. The meanings of these terms for Kant are usually rooted in scholastic philosophy, but Piaget attaches very different meanings to each term. Another term prominent in Kantian philosophy, but apparently originating with Aristotle (Edwards, 1967, Vol. 1, p. 140), is "a priori". Piaget uses this term primarily as a synonym for "Absolute Subject", while for Kant the term only means "truths that are not derived from experience" (ibid., p. 140). It is this term and concept that Hegel and other post-Kantians transformed into the "Absolute". As Piaget says, they felt a need for the Absolute that Kant's a priori could not meet. He puts it this way:

> Let us ... try to understand the factors that have given rise to the tendency to *accept a mode of knowledge peculiar to philosophy and superior to scientific knowledge .... The first observable factor is undoubtedly the search for the Absolute.* ... Starting from the decisive turning point marked by the Kantian critique, which denied to theoretical reason the right to go beyond the bounds of structuring reality, the heroism of such a position has not been sufficient to overcome the need for the Absolute. *His followers have seen in the A-Priori Structures no longer an epistemological table of the conditions of knowledge, ... but the expression of a Power peculiar to philosophical thought, which ... places itself above [science]. Together with the need for the Absolute there resulted a suprascientific position* (author's italics and capitalization) (Piaget, 1971c, p. 81).

What is the first factor that we must consider before we can understand the philosophical mode of knowledge that is superior to scientific knowledge? It is the *search for the Absolute.* Kant had concluded in his "critique of pure reason" that such a search could not be based on "pure reason", because reason "precipitates itself into darkness and contradictions" once it enters the field of metaphysics (Edwards, 1967, Vol. 4, p. 308). *Hegel and Piaget disagree completely with Kant at this juncture as they both claim to have arrived at a valid concept of the Absolute Entity on the basis of reason alone, an Entity with the power to supersede natural science.* Many, like Karl Popper, believe that Hegel did indeed precipitate darkness into the world, a darkness that, among other unhappy consequences, eventuated in both communism and fascism - and on a more modest scale, I would add Piagetianism.

> In politics ... the Marxist extreme left wing ... and the fascist extreme right ... base their political philosophies on Hegel; the left wing replaces the war of nations which appears in Hegel's historicist scheme by the war of classes, the extreme right replaces it by the war of races; but both follow him more or less consciously (Popper, 1966, p. 30).

Quoting Schopenhauer, Popper claims that Hegel's success was the beginning of the "age of dishonesty", and quoting Heiden, it was also seen as the beginning of the "age of moral irresponsibility"; "of a new age controlled by the magic of high-sounding words, and by the power of jargon" (ibid., p. 28). Schopenhauer knew Hegel personally and drew the following picture of the master as quoted by Popper:

> Hegel, installed from above by the powers that be, as the certified Great Philosopher, was a flat-headed, insipid, nauseating, illiterate charlatan, who reached the pinnacle of audacity in scribbling together and dishing up the craziest mystifying nonsense. This nonsense has been noisily proclaimed as immortal wisdom ... and readily accepted as

such by all fools who thus joined into as perfect a chorus of admiration as had ever been heard before (ibid., pp. 32-3).

Popper maintains that the story of Hegel shows "how easily a clown may be a maker of history". "The tragi-comedy of the rise of 'German Idealism', in spite of the hideous crimes to which it led, resembles a comic opera much more than anything else" (ibid., p. 32).

By deceptively extending not only Hegel's metaphysical philosophy, but also his bombastic and dogmatic linguistic style, into psychology, education, theories of morality and even biology, *Piaget has, in my opinion, precipitated darkness into the academic world in a most shocking way.* His methods vis-a-vis the academic community are characterized by gross duplicity, and his philosophy depicts the Absolute as having a similar posture toward human beings in general. The Absolute is also described as exercising unmitigated coercion in His deceitful relations with people. Both communism and fascism depended heavily upon radical propaganda ploys, and Piaget developed the most exhaustive, sweeping plan to deceive that the academic world has ever seen. The brutal, remorseless coercion of communism and fascism is well-known, but the fact that Piaget himself, as well as his reading of the Absolute, are prime examples of remorseless brutality has not been even vaguely perceived, much less fully recognized. "Coercion" and "force" are among Piaget's favorite concepts when describing the Absolute's assimilative activity, and we should not be surprised as *his model, Hegel, is said to be the father of modern totalitarianism* (ibid., p. 22). The Structures responsible for assimilation - the Logico-Mathematical Structures (author's capitalization) (Piaget, 1971a, p. 65) - "are universal and coercive" (ibid., p. 268). This means that the individual subject "will finally be forced willy nilly to submit to the laws of Logic since .... [these laws] are nontemporal" (author's capitalization) (Piaget, 1980a, p. 157). The laws of Logic are based on the System of Operations and its general coordinations of action (author's capitalization) (Piaget, 1971a, pp. 6-7) (Piaget, 1970d, p. 71) (Evans, 1973, p. XLVIII), and the System that operates is the non-temporal or eternal Subject (author's capitalization) (Piaget, 1970b, p. 142). The concept of coercion or force is conveyed in scores of passages, but the opposite concept of "human freedom" is notable for its absence in both Hegel's and Piaget's works. There is very little freedom under communism and fascism, but in Piaget's theoretical system there is no room for freedom at all.

> This notion of a final cause implies a Creator who has fashioned everything for a determined end .... Final cause implies an efficient cause in the form of a Force immanent in the object and directing it towards its destined end ... The idea of 'Life' fulfills this function (author's capitalization) (Piaget, 1929, pp. 224-5).

The idea of "Life" here is a reference to the metaphysical Creator or "Biology" we have discussed previously. This is the meaning of Piaget's statement that "children's 'whys' are ... at bottom a search for a Biological explanation" (author's capitalization) (ibid., p. 225). The "Biological" explanation is based on the fact that the Cognitive Structure is a "He" who imposes Forms on the individual subject "which determine not only what he is capable of doing ... *but also what he 'must' do*" (author's italics and capitalization) (Piaget, 1973a, p. 33). Piaget expresses the same idea in another way.

> The Living Body .... tends to impose on the whole universe a Form of equilibrium dependent on that Organization ... The Living Being assimilates to Himself the whole universe ... All the movements of every kind which characterize His actions and reactions with respect to things are regulated ... by His own Organization (author's capitalization) (Piaget, 1952b, pp. 407-8).

People in Piaget's system are expendable objects used for the single purpose of perfecting the development of the Absolute Subject.

The search for the ultimate fountainhead clearly ended, philosophically speaking, when Hegel and other post-Kantians transformed Kant's a priori into the Absolute, the only Entity able to produce "suprascientific" Knowledge. This is the Structure, mentioned by Hegel, who became Piaget's Logico-Mathematical Structure composed of metaphysical "atoms" (author's capitalization) (Piaget, 1971a, p. 327). This Structure was also called the "Concrete Universal" by Hegel. Both Hegel and Piaget teach that, based on His "parascience", this Entity explains natural phenomena differently from natural science.

> Hegel's dialectic (sixth kind of epistemology), which ... exhibits its novelty in relation to the conceptual use that Kant made of the dialectic .... The dialectic remained a part of the post-Kantian idealism .... Its fundamental concept of a Concrete Universal ... anticipated ... the need for speculation .... which found its support in the idealist interpretation of the Transcendental Self. [This] opened the way to [Hegel's] Concrete Universal in the domain of Mind ... [and in the domain of] nature .... [Hegel gives] one of the best examples of speculative reason of a parascientific tendency .... This raises the question of a duality of possible knowledge about the same subject matter .... We shall come across this problem again in the case of contemporary Philosophical Psychology ... not that psychology which gave rise to scientific psychology, but that which claims to replace it .... [This is] the problem of the duality of knowledge (spatio-temporal, or "of the world"), and "Eidetic" [Knowledge] (author's capitalization) (Piaget, 1971c, pp. 58-9).

Piaget's position is based on philosophy (Bringuier, 1980, p. 13). Unless one realizes this it is very hard to understand him. He claims that there are six levels or kinds of philosophy (Piaget, 1971b, p. 1) (Piaget, 1971c, pp. 47-58), *and by designating Hegel's philosophy as the sixth and last kind of philosophy, he actually affirms the fact that he is a Hegalian. He follows Hegel in the doctrine that the development of philosophy is like the development of the Absolute Subject, in that there is a progressive development so that the last level must be the highest and best level.* Frederick Copleston, in his *A History of Philosophy*, has this to say about Hegel's notion of philosophical development:

> The succession of philosophical systems is no matter of chance but exhibits the necessary succession of stages in the development of this science ... The final philosophy of a period is the result of this development and is truth in the highest form which the self-conscious Spirit affords. *The final philosophy, therefore, contains the ones that went before; it embraces in itself all their stages;* it is the product and result of all the philosophies which preceded it. (author's italics) (Copleston, 1963, p. 288).

Piaget's philosophy is founded on Hegel's Absolute who is the only producer of Absolute Knowledge. "The dialectic of concepts ... plays a leading part in Hegel's philosophy and is ready to reappear in other forms in all situations where philosophy takes up again its ambition of being the guardian of Absolute Knowledge" (author's capitalization) (Piaget, 1971c, p. 115). The Hegelian pattern is the true one. "This Hegelian or Kantian pattern ... corresponds to a progression which is inevitable once thought turns away from false absolutes" (Piaget, 1970b, p. 123). The "Kantian pattern" is included again as a red herring, because it does not speak of a dogmatic, inevitable progression toward perfect knowledge or development. Hegel, however, points to the true Absolute who is embarked on a pattern of activity that will enable Him to become fully actualized or developed.

PIAGET'S PHILOSOPHY OF A NON-HUMAN ABSOLUTE

In pretending to define philosophy in general, Piaget actually dismisses any philosophy that does not center on his Absolute, thus pushing aside the fact that this definition contradicts his choice of the five philosophies - of Plato, Aristotle, Descartes, Leibniz and Kant - which preceded Hegel's. Philosophy implies, according to Piaget, "the possibility that, underlying phenomenal appearance and individual knowledge, there exists an Ultimate Reality, a Thing in Itself, an Absolute" (author's capitalization) (Piaget, 1971c, p. 39). All natural structures, including human beings, are anchored in a non-human Absolute (author's capitalization) (Piaget, 1970b, p. 30). This view, he avers, is a return to "Transcendent Essences" (author's capitalization) (ibid., p. 30), and an "Essence is both a concept of the Subject and the Phenomenal Nucleus of the object" (author's capitalization) (Piaget, 1971c, p. 114). Piaget privately defines "Essence", then, as meaning the Absolute Subject in general, as well as the immanent Subject who resides in all objects including people. This Essence in fact is the Nucleus which is the source of activity in and by objects, including human objects. Natural structures are not only anchored in Him, but they are also organized by this Living Absolute who has a non-human Biology.

> But an organization due to what subject? If this subject is merely a human one, then we shall be in danger ... with minimal gain. As a result, *all philosophers in search of an Absolute have had recourse to some Transcendental Subject, something on a higher plane than man and much higher than "nature", so that truth for them, is to be found way beyond any spatiotemporal and physical contingencies* .... If the true is an organization of the real, then we first need to know how such an organization is organized, which is a Biological question (author's italics and capitalization) (Piaget, 1971a, p. 362)

When we examine how the Absolute organizes people, we enter the domain of immanent, non-human Biological activity. The "merely human" subject will not do - in fact it is dangerous to ascribe organization to him! No, we must search for a Transcendental Subject, as this is where the truth is to be found! This is indeed a Biological question.

Piaget advises us to look inside things if we wish to locate the Absolute. "Before we locate the Absolute up in the clouds, it may well be helpful to take a look inside things" (author's capitalization) (ibid., p 362). The Absolute inside of things is the Knowing Self who cognizes the known self (author's capitalization) (Piaget, 1971c, p. 86), and since Knowledge for the Absolute always means assimilation, the Knowing

Self inside of people is always busy assimilating the known self. We, the "true" upper-level immanent "We" composed of monads, can get to know objects, including people, only by acting on them and by producing some transformation in them (author's capitalization) (Piaget, 1967, p. 128). Furthermore, since "operations are actual Psychological activities, and all effective Knowledge is based on such a System of Operations" (author's capitalization) (Piaget, 1953, p. 7), we can be certain that they are performed by the immanent Knowing Subject, as He directs them at the people He indwells. The resulting Knowledge is not a "matter of chance" (author's capitalization) (Piaget, 1971b, p. 6), so the Knowing Subject cannot be a human being. When Piaget tells us that "Thought ... proceeds by Egocentric assimilation and not logical concepts (author's capitalization) (Piaget 1962, p. 156), it is clear that he is referring to the Ego of the Knowing or Absolute Subject. This view is affirmed by Piaget's claim that all Knowledge is assimilated by a Permanent Structure that can never be destroyed. "Every organism has a Permanent Structure which ... is never destroyed as a Structured Whole" (author's capitalization) (Piaget, 1971c, p. 8). "All Knowledge is always assimilation of a datum external to the Subjects Structure" (author's capitalization) (ibid., p. 8). The last sentence is pointless unless we understand the "Subject's Structure" to be the Permanent or Absolute Structure who is in the process of assimilating people - who are indeed data that are external to Him.

In Piaget's numerous books, the Absolute appears in an endless variety of imaginative disguises or, as Piaget sometimes calls them, "morphisms", each one with its own synonym. Piaget refers to this artificially contrived problem in a rather jaunty way, suggesting his mirthful anticipation of the confusion and pain it will cause. "We turn our attention to the Organism in the various guises it has assumed currently, although we shall make no prophecies as to what may subsequently be discovered about it" (author's capitalization) (Piaget, 1971a, p. 138). It is essential to understand how the attributes ascribed to these various disguises really describe only one Entity. We have already identified some of these synonyms, and we will examine some of the more frequently used synonyms more closely. An additional avalanche of synonyms, as we previously indicated, will be found in the appendices.

THE ABSOLUTE ENTITY AS SUBJECT

"Philosophers concerned with the Absolute have had recourse to a Transcendental Subject which goes beyond man and especially 'nature'" (author's capitalization) (Inhelder & Chipman, 1976, p. 56). "Subject" as a synonym for the Absolute is used far more often than "Absolute", and since there are two subjects the opportunities for creating confusion are much greater. The Absolute Subject is, of course, a Super-Subject, and an "appeal to an active Supersubject ... brings us nearer to the Subject as such" (author's capitalization) (Beth & Piaget, 1966, p. 274). For Piaget, then, the Absolute is the true Subject.

It was noted above that a non-human Absolute organizes people and all natural structures. He does this in the process of assimilation. "The ... process of assimilation ... leads the Subject, who is in [the] process of incorporating the universe to Himself, to structure that universe according to the variations of its own organization" (author's capitalization) (Piaget, 1952b, p. 415). The process of assimilating or incorporating all objects of the real world, including people, involves the displacement or elimination of the physical aspects by adding elements of the Subject's Structure (author's capitalization) (Piaget, 1970a, p. 32). Eventually all objects become a part of the Absolute Subject. Things are "passing over to the Subject" (author's capitalization) (Piaget, 1980a, p. 91), indicating a future convergence where all "things" or "objects" become a part of the Subject with whom they originally shared "common roots" (author's capitalization) (Piaget, 1974b, pp. 113-14). Piaget deals with this notion in his introduction to *John Amos Commenius on Education* (1957). Comenius had the ambition of founding a "pansophic college" where "total, indivisible knowledge would be pursued". This kind of knowledge is connected by Piaget with "the then widespread Neoplatonic idea of a 'procession' followed by a 'return' of things to their source" (ibid., p. 28). The "procession" refers, somewhat dimly, to the creation of the physical universe and the "procession" of people, objects and events, followed by a return of this procession of physical reality to its source. In the next chapter we will examine this idea of "reversibility". Piaget places great emphasis on the need of the Subject to assimilate and thus reverse the external world.

> All needs tend first of all to incorporate things and people into the Subject's own activity, i.e., to "assimilate" the external world into the Structures that have already been constructed .... All Mental Life, as indeed all Organic Life, tends progressively to assimilate the surrounding environment. This incorporation is effected thanks to the Structures or Psychic Organs (author's capitalization) (Piaget, 1967, pp. 7-8).

Rather than speak of "the one single need", Piaget often uses the more ambiguous phrase, "all needs". The Structures that assimilate are the Living Psychic Organs composed of organized Groups of Monads which make up the Body of the Subject. The "Mental Life" and "Organic Life" in the passage also refer to the Subjects's Life.

This belief that the object will be transformed into the Subject is an important aspect of Piaget's idealism, and it is Piaget's unique "mathematics" that will accomplish this transformation (Piaget, 1971b, p. 120). Mathematics is defined as the actions or operations involved in the addition of the Subject's elements to objects (author's capitalization) (Piaget, 1973b, p. 103). "An individual subject becomes an Epistemological one ... through the internal progress of the coordinations of His Thought" (author's capitalization) (Piaget, 1971c, p. 108). The Epistemological Subject is the Absolute Subject and the individual becomes the Epistemological Subject when he is fully assimilated, but this unfortunately entails his annihilation! "His Thought" refers to the assimilative activity of the internal or immanent Epistemological Subject, not the physical subject.

Piaget believes in a one-of-a-kind Subject who is not a part of nature but who created nature (author's capitalization) (Piaget, 1974a, p. 61) (Piaget, 1971c, pp. 224-5). He also believes in a subject who is part of the physical world, and thus is a part of nature (Piaget, 1972, p. 50), therefore his system includes two subjects who oppose each other, although the lower-level subject is not aware of this opposition (Beth & Piaget, 1966, p. 169). For Piaget, the meaning of existence begins with the one-of-a-kind Subject as everything derives from His existence. "The Subject exists, and ... the recognition of other types of existence assumes that these different realities are related because a mode of reality has no meaning except when connected with other modes" (author's capitalization) (ibid., pp. 151-2). One must know how, according to Piaget, these modes of existence are related. What is the relation between the Subject who created physical nature and the subject who is a part of physical nature?

> It is ... worth remembering that *a physical thing is, until proof of the contrary, only an object and not a Subject, whilst Living Beings are already Subjects, however unconscious they may be; and that human subjects are descended from them ....* If this hypothesis is well-founded ... [it] is an acceptable starting point for an account of the autonomy of Logico-Mathematical Constructions .... which possesses (sic) internal necessity and ineluctably imposes (sic) its structural laws on every individual subject (author's italics and capitalization) (ibid., pp. 298-9).

In this quote, Piaget first assigns the physical or individual subject the status of an object, not a Subject. The Living Being, although inappropriately pluralized, is a Subject, and *He, of course, is not unconscious; it is the physical objects-subjects who are unconscious of Him.* Human subjects are descended from the Living Being or from the Logico-Mathematical Construction, who imposes His laws on every individual human subject. "Our hypothesis comes down quite simply to supposing that the [individual human] subject ... will be forced willy nilly to submit to the laws of Logic, since they have been at work ... from the outset" (author's capitalization) (Piaget, 1980a, p. 157).

The laws of Logic are, as noted previously, defined by Piaget as the *general coordination of actions* (author's italics) (Piaget, 1970d, p. 71) (Piaget, 1971c, p. 55) or the *functions* of the Living Organization (author's italics and capitalization) (Piaget, 1971a, p. 307). This kind of coordination coordinates functional pairs of opposite classes (Piaget et al., 1977, p. 180) (Piaget, 1977, pp. 188-9) in a long series of operations - something people cannot do (Beth & Piaget, 1966, p. 293) because this is a *Normative* activity (author's italics and capitalization) (ibid., p. 290). Only "Unchangeable Structures" and their activities are Normative (author's capitalization) (Piaget, 1973d, p. 34) (Piaget, 1971a, p. 358). To summarize, the laws of Logic are Normative (author's capitalization) (Piaget, 1971c, p. 70). This means, finally, that human beings will be forced to submit to the Absolute Entity because of the operations He is constantly directing at each individual person!

PHYSICAL EXPERIENCE VERSUS LOGICO-MATHEMATICAL EXPERIENCE

What is the role of experience in mental development? Piaget tells us that it is highly complex because there are two kinds of experience.

> Physical experience ... consists of acting upon objects in order to abstract their properties ... Logico-Mathematical experience ... consists of acting upon objects with a view to learning the result of the coordination of actions .... In Logico-Mathematical experience Knowledge is derived from action rather than objects; experience in this case is simply the practical and quasi-motor phase of what will later be operatory deduction. *[Logico-Mathematical experience] is not to be equated with experience in the sense of action of*

the external milieu; ... it is ... a constructive action performed by the Subject upon external objects (author's italics and capitalization) (Piaget & Inhelder, 1969, p. 155).

This passage presents Piaget as a sleight-of-hand artist as he deals with metaphysical experience as though it were an aspect of reality as human beings experience it. Logico-Mathmatical experience is obviously metaphysical as it "will later become operational deduction". In fact, *"quasi-motor" means "quasi operatory deduction", because "motor" refers to the activity of monads. It is monads that impart motion in Piaget's system, not nerve impulses!* First, human beings cannot produce higher-level Math because this kind of Math is autonomous in relation to the "psychological subject" or human being (author's capitalization) (Beth & Piaget, 1966, p. 296). Second, the operations of Intelligence are also entirely autonomous (author's capitalization) (Piaget & Inhelder, 1971, p. 356). "The development of operational behavior is an autonomous process" (Inhelder & Piaget, 1964, p. 290) (Beth & Piaget, 1966, p. 244) and physical human beings are not autonomous (Piaget, 1971a, pp. 282-3). *Piaget becomes temporarily honest when he says that Logico-Mathematical experience cannot be* equated with *"action of the external milieu", which is a grotesque, demeaning reference to the action of human beings. The action of human beings is indeed "action of the external milieu"* in Piaget's terminology. This is because the "physical world ... includes the subject as an integral part" (Piaget, 1972, p. 50). *"Human action"* in Piaget's conceptual cosmology, *"is that of an organism which is part of the physical universe"* (author's italics) (Piaget, 1971b, p. 72). Since the action of the individual subject is an "active" facet of the "external milieu", it is impossible for him to produce operations or have Logico-Mathematical experience. The fact that Logico-Mathematical experience is actually defined in terms of operations demonstrates how burdensome it is to fully solve the riddles Piaget prepared for us, burdensome because considerable effort is often necessary to achieve a minimum gain in the unraveling process. *If the facts of his system were communicated clearly, they would no doubt appear bizarre and fanciful, but at the same time they would also seem very prosaic in terms of logical cohesiveness and intellectual content.* Clearly too much of Piaget's intellectual capital was spent inventing and elaborating methods of deception. In the next passage human beings become objects again, objects who are incapable of making "necessary" statements.

We shall, indeed, find ourselves compelled to trace the origin of Logico-Mathematical operations back to ... the general coordination of actions ... *Such operations cannot possibly be based on the objects themselves, since abstraction from objects can give rise only to non-necessitous statements* (author's italics and capitalization) (Piaget, 1971a, p. 14).

The "objects" who cannot "operate" because they can only make non-necessitous statements are obviously human beings. Only the Universal Operational Structure can operate with necessary results. (author's capitalization) (Piaget & Inhelder, 1969, p. 95)

In 1969, Piaget was invited to take part in a symposium on "the brain and human behavior" in Chicago. In his short paper, "Operational Structures of the Intelligence and Organic Controls", we find this passage.

There are two types of experience, which we have been distinguishing for many years. *There is physical experience which provides information about objects themselves ... This is the only kind of experience that classical empiricism ever took into account.* But there is also ... Logico-Mathematical experience, which draws its information not from the objects themselves, but from the actions or operations which the Subject carries out with them. The two kinds of experience not being the same thing at all (author's italics and capitalization) (Karczmar & Eccles, 1972, p. 395).

In addition to a much more readable writing style, which is characteristic of his short papers, the only significant difference between this and the previous passage is the assertion that empiricism, which includes natural science, does not recognize Logico-Mathematical experience. This is an amazingly bold claim at a symposium of natural scientists. The term "classical empiricism" might deflect criticism, but Piaget means to include contemporary empiricism.

Logico-Mathematical experience is actually an operational experimentation on the object in which the Subject "enriches the object with connections stemming from the Subject" (author's capitalization) (Piaget, 1971b, p. 31). Piaget adds that *nothing* can prevent these connections from expressing the Subject's powers - powers that are necessarily superhuman - of construction in opposition to the physical characteristics of the object (author's capitalization) (ibid., pp. 31-2). *For Piaget, the Scientific study of Epistemology is precisely the study of the gradual accumulation of Knowledge by means of these connections that the Absolute Subject will acquire in His quest for full development.* The two kinds of experience, experiment or knowledge are not only different, they are actually dialectical opposites! This is basically what Piaget means when he says that "factual data cannot be introduced into the Logico-Mathematical Field" (author's capitalization) (Beth & Piaget, 1966, p. 151). The Field of Monads, which is the Absolute entity, does not accept the validity of physical facts, and is intent on their complete elimination. And when the facts are finally eliminated the operational Forms of the Subject will be constructed so that they can never again be contradicted by facts (author's capitalization) (Piaget, 1974b, p. 123). In the meantime this metaphysical Field or Form holds that "the brute facts of immediate experience ... are invariably misleading" (author's capitalization) (Piaget, 1971c, p. 70).

THE PHYSICAL SUBJECT VERSUS THE METAPHYSICAL SUBJECT

As we have previously observed, the nature of either subject is sometimes marked out by the way he is omitted in certain situations. For instance, the lower-level subject is omitted when Piaget personifies physical knowledge. "Physical knowledge", he says, "tries to reach the object by removing it from the orbit of the Subject" (author's capitalization) (Piaget, 1974b, p. 142). "Physical knowledge" stands for the individual subject engaged in the normal pursuit of knowledge as observed in every university in the world. This is so because man is only capable of "physical knowledge" as Piaget defines it. This omission tells us much about Piaget's evaluation of the physical subject. An example of man gaining physical knowledge by removing "the object" from the "Subject's orbit" is the biologist at work.

The living and acting subject is conceived by Biology merely in relation to material reality, and consequently in terms of the object. If Mathematics attempts to reduce the object to the Subject, biology, on the contrary, effects or tends to effect the opposite reduction (author's italics and capitalization) (Piaget, 1971b, p. 119).

We have noted that Piaget will sometimes personalize "Biology" to mean Absolute Subject. Furthermore, he tells us directly just before the passage above that Biology ... that is, the Living Being, is nothing more than the Subject as such ... [who is] capable of constructing Mathematics itself" (author's italics and capitalization) (ibid., p. 119). In the longer passage Piaget not only personalizes "Biology", but he does the same with "Mathematics" - as he does again in the shorter quote. "Biology", in the indented passage, is said to conceive the "living and acting subject" as merely a part of "material reality", and thus an object. "Mathematics" refers to the Absolute Subject who is in the process of assimilating this human object so that he will eventually "pass over" into the Subject. A fully assimilated individual, biological, human "object" will, according to Piaget, become a part of the Biological Subject, but what does he mean by "biology" tending to effect the opposite reduction? He means that the professional biologist treats the material object with which he experiments as if it were a primary living entity rather than merely an object who only lives by proxy. So the biologist is "reducing" the material object to the primary Living Entity. The use of "reduction" to mean both the "passing over" of the subject-object into the Absolute Subject by means of assimilation as well as the biologist reducing the lower-level subject "inadvertently" to the Absolute Subject is blatantly illogical, but this is vintage Piaget.

Piaget further elaborates the effects of the biological scientist, especially in the realm of psychology.

Psychology inherits the often quite heavy realism of biology, and the "organicist" tendencies which intervene in the explanation of mental life continue this reduction of the *Acting Subject* to the material object with which the biologist experiments (author's italics and capitalization) (ibid., p. 120).

The professional psychologist inherits the "organicist" tendencies of the biologist to reduce the Acting Subject to the material object. This is why the psychologist tends to explain mental life in terms of physiological brain function rather than in terms of the invisible Acting Subject pulling the strings of brain function by means of His monads.

The world of difference between the two subjects is presented in another sharply contrasting way. In discussing the limitations of "a" subject compared to "the" Subject, Piaget has this to say:

The ... problem is that of the reasons for this limitation; in this *respect we can refer only to the impossibility of a subject being able to take in simultaneously all the constructible operations, thus constituting an implicit appeal to ... the Subject* (author's italics and capitalization) (ibid., p. 146).

Since trillions of operations are constantly going on inside and outside of people, only a superhuman Entity could take them all in *simultaneously!*

In another example where Piaget is differentiating the two subjects, the lower-level subject is ignored. He reports that *the physical field of Gestalt theory is not psychogenetic because it has no Subject* (author's italics and capitalization) (Piaget, 1977, p. 98). Of course Gestalt theory has a subject, but it is the lower-level subject Piaget despises. *Psychogenesis is the gradual development of the Absolute by means of operations or equilibrations, so the Field of monads where psychogenesis occurs has, or rather is, the Subject.*

FORMAL THOUGHT

How could one miss the indispensable role of the "Absolute Subject", with regard to formal thought when Piaget says: "The Subject views the problem in terms of *all possible combinations* in such a way as to draw out their implications ... instead of noting the empirical links" (author's italics and capitalization) (Inhelder & Piaget, 1958, p. 39)? There are at least three red flags in this short passage relevant to the usual view of "formal operations". First, human beings cannot possibly view most significant problems in terms of *all possible combinations.* Piaget surely did not expect his "one-level" readers to accept this proposition easily, but Flavell apparently did, and without a caveat to those who understand Piaget through him (Flavell, 1963, p. 206). Second, the combinations were examined so as to draw out their *implications,* meaning that the Subject was looking for operational possibilities, not the dictionary meaning of "inferences to be drawn". Piaget's metaphysical Psychology is based on implications, which in his private language are operations (author's capitalization) (Piaget, 1969b, p. XXIII) (Piaget, 1950, pp. 96-7 & 149). This is actually a reversal of meaning, however, as implications are the primary concern of upper-level Psychology, so they are "based on" this metaphysical concern or need. Third, the empirical or scientific approach was specifically excluded from problem solving. Ironically, after reviewing Piaget's description of "formal thought", Flavell has this extraordinary reaction:

> All the traits of formal thought we have described go to make it *a very good instrument for scientific reasoning* .... The hypothetical-deductive attitude, the combinatorial method, and the other attributes of formal thought provide him with the necessary tools for separating out the variables which might be causal .... This is clearly a good imitation of how the scientist goes about his business (author's italics) (Flavell, 1963, pp. 208-9).

Furth makes the same mystifying misinterpretation of Piaget's formal thought:

> The new operational abilities formed during this third period are the abilities that open up unlimited possibilities for the youth to participate constructively in the development of scientific knowledge - provided that his setting offers him a suitable practice-ground and a favorable intellectual atmosphere (Furth, 1969, p. 32).

Why do Flavell and Furth consider the stage of formal operations to be a highly desirable preparation or basis for scientific pursuits, while Piaget considers this stage to be antithetical to those pursuits?

The regulations within the Logico-Mathematical System are autonomous because *the Forms of the System are used to modify the Forms of the System in the effort to achieve Self-development* (author's italics and capitalization) (Piaget, 1977, p. 173). The development of the Forms or Subject who operates is radically autonomous, as He is independent of everything, including individual subjects (author's capitalization) (Beth & Piaget, 1966, p. 244). Implicit in the definition of the *Absolute Entity is the notion that He must fully account for everything including His own development or construction.* This doctrine is demonstrated in the way Piaget uses the many synonyms of the Absolute Subject to describe His Self-development. His theoretical edifice, however, which is built up by means of a highly complex, wearisome multiplication of sterile verbal entities, begins to collapse when we see the ludicrous way any one of these many synonyms may be used to "explain" any other synonym. In each instance below the two synonyms, one of which is said to modify or explain the other, are in italics for the purpose of clarity, and they are capitalized because they both simply mean "Absolute Subject". *Since Piaget is fully aware that the pairs of synonyms are identical in meaning, we begin to appreciate his attitude toward the academic community as well as the danger he represents.*

The essential role of the *Subject* is the elaboration of *Forms* (Piaget, 1952b, p. 416). This, of course, is Self-development or autoregulation as the Form of Monads is the same Entity as the Subject composed of monads. *Forms* are autonomous; they are not organized or developed by us (Piaget, 1974b, pp. 152-3). Piaget also announces that the *Subject* alone elaborates *Structures* (Piaget, 1973a, p. 132). Again, this is Self-development as the Subject *is* the Structure. The *Subject* organizes or develops the *Structured Whole* (Inhelder & Piaget, 1958, pp. 289-90), and the Subject *is* the Structured Whole. The *Cognitive Structures* derive from or are developed by the *Epistemic Subject,* not the psychological subject (Beth & Piaget, 1966, p. 308). The Cognitive Structure *is* the Epistemic Subject, so once again we observe Self-development. We also observe that the individual or physical subject, called the "psychological subject" here, does not develop the Cognitive Structure. The "Psychological Subject" is also often presented as the metaphysical Subject (Piaget, 1971c, p. 118) (Piaget, 1967, pp. XI, 7-8) (Piaget, 1974a, p. 30). *Life* creates or develops *Mathematical Forms.* The only Living Entity in the universe is the Mathematical Form, so this is a Self-developing or autoregulating Life (Beth & Piaget, 1966, p. 298). The *Living Organism* elaborates *Logico-Mathematical Systems* (Piaget, 1930, p. 131). The Living Organism *is* the Logico-Mathematical System so we observe another example of Self-development. *Logico-Mathematical Structures* are the product of or developed by the *Living Organization* (Piaget, 1971a, pp. 211-12). Ditto. *Logico-Mathematical Structures* are derived from or developed by the *Living Organism* (Piaget, 1972, p. 91). Ditto. *Bio-Psychological Groups* construct or develop *Space* (Piaget, 1954, pp. 235-6). Bio-Psychological Groups *are* Spatial Entities composed of monads. The *"I"*, not the "lived me", is the source of *Operational Structures* (Piaget, 1970b, p. 139). The "I" who is bound up with the whole universe (Piaget, 1930, p. 128), and who is also immanent in the "lived me" *is* the Absolute Entity who consists of Operational Structures. The *Organism, Thinking Being or Social Group* are builders of *Structures.* The four capitalized terms are synonyms for the Absolute Subject, so Piaget is speaking of Self-development (Piaget, 1973d, p. 58). *Schemata* are the source of all *Operational Structures.*

Schemata *are* the Operational Structures (Piaget & Inhelder, 1973, p. 311). Since both Schemata and Operational Structures are composed of organized monads, we are talking about Self-development. *Space* creates or develops *Operational Schemata*. Space consists of Operational Schemata, so this is another instance of Self-development (Piaget & Inhelder, 1956, p. 449). *Space* constructs or develops *Logico-Mathematical Structures* (Piaget, 1977, p. 116). Space *is* the Logico-Mathematical Structure. The *Logical Mathematical Body* elaborates the *Idea.* In Piaget's terminology, the Logical Mathematical Body *is* the Idea (Piaget 1973a, p. 98). The construction of *Space* is directed from within (ibid., pp. 235-237). That is, Operational Space develops Himself. The *Lattice-Group* produces or develops *Operational Schemata* (Inhelder & Piaget, 1958, p. 329). The Lattice-Group is merely another name for "Spatial Schemata", so ditto. The functioning of *Intelligence* explains the construction or development of *Space* (Piaget, 1954, p. 245). Intelligence here is the Spatial Entity who functions to develop Himself. *Intelligence* organizes a *Lasting Universe* (ibid., p. 354). Intelligence, the eternal entity organizes or develops the Universe of Monads which is Himself. The *Cognitive Field* is directed toward filling in, or fully developing the *Totality,* which is Self-development because the Cognitive Field *is* the Totality (Inhelder & Piaget, 1958, pp. 330-1). Only one activity of the *Subject* allows Him to construct *Operational Structures* (Beth & Piaget, 1966, p. 285). By means of operations - the one activity, the Subject constructs the Operational Structures which make up Himself. There is no *Constructive Mechanism* other than the progressive organization of the *Structure* (Piaget 1973d, pp. 49-50). The Constructive Mechanism *is* the Structure Himself. That is, the Constructive Mechanism is the Body of Monads which *is* the Structure. *This small sample of multiplied verbalisms demonstrates how Piaget uses synonyms or morphisms* (Piaget, 1971a, p. 140) *to build an imaginary system by using any morphism to "prove" any other morphism and leave the uninitiated reader very perplexed.*

THE ABSOLUTE ENTITY AS IMMANENT SUBJECT

When Piaget wishes to describe the nature of metaphysical Knowledge, the Absolute Subject often becomes the "Epistemological Subject".

> If ... it is a question of asserting that all knowledge is dependent on the existence of a Subject; this is then the important discovery of the Epistemological Subject, but we are now concerned with epistemology and no longer with metaphysics (author's capitalization) (Piaget, 1971c, p. 64).

By manipulating verbal entities alone, Piaget not only "discovers" the Epistemic Subject, but he removes Him from metaphysics so that He can be studied scientifically! Fortunately, he never has to concern himself with empirical evidence because there can never be any to support his metaphysical system. All knowledge, even physical knowledge, is ultimately dependent upon the Epistemological Subject, but Piaget has something more definite in mind. Specifically, he is referring to the equilibrational or psychogenetic Knowledge that results from dialectical operations and, as we have seen, this is metaphysical Knowledge. The psychologists who mindlessly awarded him the citation mentioned previously, bought the incredible lie that Piaget was able to take an exclusively philosophical question; namely, the problem of epistemology, and make it into an empirical science. Piaget was bold enough to claim incessantly that he had accomplished this wonderful feat, and they naively took his word for it. There is no other possible reason! The decision to award the citation was outrageous on at least two counts. First, the psychologists did not bother to examine Piaget's description of the science, which is *clearly* not natural science; and second, they did not bother to examine Piaget's concept of epistemology, which is *definitely* metaphysical.

In Piaget's explanation of how an individual physical subject becomes an Epistemological Subject, we see the physical "passing over" into the metaphysical.

> *An individual subject becomes an Epistemological one ... through the internal progress of the coordinations of His Thought through an equilibrium that substitutes logical necessity for empirical verification ....* This ... describes processes common to all subjects ... [who attain] Forms which ought to characterize all scientific Thought (author's italics and capitalization) (Piaget, 1971c, pp. 108-9).

Piaget goes on to say that this explanation is psychogenetic which, as we know, is based on metaphysical operations, not natural science. Psychogenetic progress gradually assimilates the physical subject until it becomes a part of the Epistemological or Absolute Subject. The "internal progress of the coordinations of His Thought leads to an equilibrium that attains the Forms". The private meaning of *"internal" construction is the process of arriving at equilibrium by means of Self-regulations, equilibrations or operations* (author's italics and capitalization) (Piaget & Inhelder, 1969, p. 157), and internal "coordinations" refers to the operational process of successively pairing a string of opposite classes inside the individual subject. The "coordinations" are metaphysical so "His Thought" is not the thought of the individual subject who is being moved toward a higher level, but it is the Thought of the Mover - the immanent Epistemological Subject. His Thought, which consists in producing the series of operations which will eventually bring about complete equilibrium, and thus will "attain" the Form (never mind the plural). "Forms" or "Form" is another name for the Epistemological or Absolute Subject.

Piaget declares that "logical necessity", a process that is impossible for human beings, is substituted in the epistemological development of every human being for "empirical verification". We have already discovered that "objects", i.e., human beings, can only make non-necessitus statements (Piaget, 1971a, p. 14), so "logical necessity" belongs exclusively to the Epistemological Subject. *This process of "logical necessity" or operational development is the only "Science" of interest to Piaget.*

The necessity of including two personal entities in the behavior of people is affirmed in many ways. Consider this statement: "The values of the person (often regrettably confused with those of the Ego) are taken to be less important than the constructive activities of the Epistemic Subject" (author's capitalization) (Piaget, 1970b, pp. 126-7). "Person" is often upper-level (author's capitalization) (Piaget, 1954, pp. 312-13) (Piaget, 1967, p. 65) (Inhelder & Piaget, 1958, p. 349) while "ego" is often lower level (Piaget, 1971a, p. 94) (Inhelder & Piaget, 1958, p. 349) (Piaget, 1932, pp. 91, 95). One must always determine level from the context as Piaget almost never specifies which level he means. Sometimes he makes this determination very difficult. The "values" of the lower-level, physical person have no value at all, but the Epistemic Subject has one overriding value - the construction of Himself.

"The Logico-Mathematical Structures of the Intelligence" afford an "all-embracing prevision" (author's capitalization) (Piaget, 1971a, p. 211). Even "if one were to take Mathematical Entities as external to the subject, what has just been said would still be valid" (author's capitalization" (ibid., pp. 211-12). Both the "Logico-Mathematical Structures of Intelligence" and "Mathematical Entities", even though they are plural, simply mean the "Absolute Subject". This Mathematical Entity or Structure enjoys an *"all-embracing prevision", and thus knows all about the future.* A careful reading of his work shows that Piaget not only considers this Mathematical Entity to be his true Self, but that he, a lower-level entity, "participates" to some extent in the same kind of foreknowledge for himself.

THE EPISTEMOLOGICAL SUBJECT

Piaget specifically states that the "Epistemological Domain" may well include the existence of a Reality that is non-perceptible (author's capitalization) (Beth & Piaget, 1966, p. 149). There are two important "domains" in Piaget's theory. The lower-level physical-organic domain (Piaget, 1971a, p. 358) and the upper-level Absolute Domain of non-perceptible monads (author's capitalization) (Piaget, 1971c, p. 228). The Epistemological Domain, the only domain where valid Knowledge is acquired, is the domain of the Absolute Subject. *Epistemology, then, in Piaget's system has nothing to do with the study of human knowledge acquisition, but is the "study" of a non-human construction of Knowledge.* As noted previously, Piaget does indeed speak of a non-human Subject who "Scientifically" constructs His "Epistemology".

> *I would [distinguish] the Subject-Psychologist who constructs His Science ... [from] any human subject whatsoever ...* The Subject-Psychologist constructs His Epistemology as a function of the progress ... of His Science ... There is therefore no need for the philosopher to intervene ... in order to construct a complete Epistemology (author's italics and capitalization) (ibid., pp. 224-5).

It is instructive to recall once again Piaget's response to the citation presented to him by the APA; *"without, of course, forgetting Biology"* (author's italics and capitalization) (Piaget, 1972, p. 15). In the passage above, *the Subject-Psychologist is the non-human "Biology" Piaget would never forget, and the Epistemology He constructs is plainly based on His non-human Science.* Moreover, no philosopher is needed to complete or perfect this Epistemology as the non-human Subject will do it Himself. Although veiled, Piaget thus disclaims the basis for the citation in no uncertain terms.

The completion or perfection of Epistemology is what Piaget terms "the ultimate phase of thinking". The ultimate solution of his idealistic interpretation of epistemology is described this way:

To a number of contemporaries ... all mass and every dynamic process are reduced to Forms ... in such a way that no body or any physical event is any longer to be situated in space. They are themselves *parts of Space* (author's italics and capitalization) (Piaget, 1974b, p. 149).

This passage was used previously, but it describes the goal of Epistemology succinctly. Probably very few, if any, "contemporaries" hold this view of Epistemology. Possibly only one person, Piaget himself, held it at the time it was written. This passage describes the kind of existence that will obtain *after* everything physical, including people, have passed over into the Spatial Subject by means of assimilation.

In elaborating his theory of Epistemology, Piaget declares

that a fundamental Epistemological distinction must be introduced between two kinds of subjects or between two levels of depth in any subject. There is the "psychological subject" centered in the conscious ego ... but [he is] not the origin of any Structure of General Knowledge; but there is also the "Epistemic Subject" or that which is common to all subjects. *We ... naturally pursue our enquiry in the direction of the Epistemic Subject* (author's italics and capitalization) (Beth & Piaget, 1966, p. 308).

A distinction must be made, as we examine this passage again from a different angle, between two kinds of subjects *and (not "or")* between two levels in any lower-level subject. The "psychological subject" with his "conscious ego" is lower level in this passage as he cannot produce any "Structure of General Knowledge", which is another name for the Epistemic Structure. Since people, even the most intelligent people, cannot produce Epistemic Knowledge as Piaget defines it, we feel embarrassment again for the APA! The Epistemic Subject who is common to or immanent in all subjects is specified by Piaget as the Entity he is investigating, not the "psychological subject" whom he hates (author's capitalization) (Piaget, 1971c, p. XVI) (Piaget, 1970b, p. 68).

With reference to the two levels that must be differentiated within people, Piaget describes how Epistemic Knowledge is acquired by operations inside of people. "This inner Epistemology can only be based on ... logic ... and psychogenetic mechanisms" (author's capitalization) (Piaget, 1971b, p. 147). Inner Epistemology is based on the assimilation of the physical subject from the inside by the immanent Subject. Please note that "logic" and "psychogenesis" are both based on exactly the same operational activity of the Epistemic Subject whether inside or outside of people. Piaget is guilty again of separating what belongs together, and greatly confusing assimilative enrichment.

When physics becomes more 'general' ... and discovers what goes on in the matter of a living body or even one using Reason, the epistemological enrichment of the object by the Subject ... will appear perhaps as a simple relativistic law ... of coordination (author's capitalization) (Piaget, 1972, p. 84).

Here we have an excellent example of a half-truth and a reversal of meaning. It is also an excellent snapshot of an intelligent but insidiously subversive mind at work. Enrichment goes on inside of all objects, especially human objects, *but it is not the object that is enriched.* The exclusive focus of enrichment is Reason who is the immanent Body of Monads, and most important, Reason is not used by the "living body", it is the other way around! Objects do eventually "pass over into Reason" but only after everything physical has been eliminated. *The idea that "physics" may someday detect this metaphysical activity is an example of Piaget's wanton "playfulness".*

Piaget pretends that "the central problem of genetic Epistemology concerns the mechanism of this construction of novelties which creates the need for ... reflexive abstraction and Self-regulation" (author's capitalization) (Piaget, 1970c, p. 77). I say "pretends" because he was stating categorically years before writing this that "reflexive abstraction" was the mechanism used by the Universal or Epistemic Subject in His constructions. He was also saying dogmatically that the individual subject was not able to produce reflexive abstractions (Beth & Piaget, 1966, p. 238). More frustratingly, *when he says that the central problem creates the need for reflexive abstraction, he immediately admits that for him there is no problem!* Also, as we might guess by now, "reflexive abstraction" means the same as "Self-regulation" so "and" should be replaced by "or".

Piaget gives us a short review of how philosophy gradually arrived at the correct concept of the Epistemological Subject. Plato and Aristotle remained alien to the concept, and so did Leibniz, the "new Aristotle". The discovery of the Epistemological Subject is attributed to Descartes, who also was aware of operations (auxilary only). Kant then retreated somewhat by replacing Epistemic Knowledge with knowledge conceived as a copy of reality. Hegal followed Kant and with his concept of dialectical construction he showed the metaphysical Epistemological Subject in His living reality (author's capitalization) (Piaget, 1971c, pp. 47-58).

To better understand Piaget's concept of Epistemology, it is helpful to recall his early experience with his godfather. On identifying God with Life, the problem of epistemology suddenly appeared to him in a new way. *This is what made Piaget decide to consecrate his life to the Biological explanation of Knowledge or Epistemology* (author's italics and capitalization) (Piaget, 1976b, p. 119). *God is Life, thus God is "Biology", and the Knowledge I want to investigate is the Knowledge that "Biology" desires and produces - namely, the kind of developmental Knowledge that leads to the realization of His full potential.*

The metaphysical nature of Piaget's Epistemology is demonstrated in numerous ways. If genetic Epistemology and developmental Psychology are said to have no beginning, what does this say about the Knowing, developing Subject?

> Reflective abstraction ... is based not on individual actions but on coordinated actions .... In genetic Epistemology, as in developmental Psychology, too, there is never an absolute beginning. We can never get back to the point where we can say "here is the very beginning of Logical Structures" (author's capitalization) (Piaget, 1970c, p. 19).

First, to say that reflective abstraction is not based on individual actions is ambiguous. The meaning is that it is not based on actions of the individual. After clarifying the doctrine that reflective abstraction is based on "coordinated actions", Piaget adds that neither genetic Epistemology nor developmental Psychology have an absolute beginning. This is an example of how Piaget leads his reader into blind alleys and begins to break his will to understand. Genetic Epistemology and developmental Psychology are based on the same exact process, namely that of reflective abstractions, Self-regulations, equilibrations or operations. This process *did* have a beginning. It could not begin until the physical universe was created; dialectical operations, as defined by Hegel and Piaget, are not possible without opposing entities. *After making a deliberately incorrect statement, rather, a barefaced lie, he gives his poor reader another psychological twist by abruptly switching the terms of reference with, "we can never get back to the very beginning of Logical Structures".* "Logical Structures", in spite of the plural, means "Absolute Subject" and, of course, He does not have a beginning. As we have already observed, Piaget apparently believes that he is able to confound the Entity with His activities in the minds of his readers, at least he tries to over and over. Alternatively, one is often tempted to believe he assumes that many of his readers understand what he is doing, but are too intimidated to complain openly. In any case, Piaget frequently tortures his readers with this particular tactic.

THE ABSOLUTE ENTITY AS STRUCTURE

The Structure of All Structures is the Transcendental Subject of idealism (author's capitalization) (Piaget, 1973d, p. 68). This Structure or Subject is a living system and it could be called "Society", "Life" or "Cosmos" (author's capitalization) (Piaget, 1970b, p. 142). The Living Structure is Logico-Mathematical, and His relations with physical data "are certainly Biologic in origin" for they exist in DNA as well as in the physiology of the mature organism before they appear in behavior. Then they appear in spontaneous thought, reflection, logic and mathematics (author's capitalization) (Inhelder & Chipman, 1976, p. 16). This paraphrased statement is a highly contrived effort to bamboozle the reader, beginning with the Logico-Mathematical Structure whose relations with physical data are Biological in origin. To begin with, the *relations* are not Biological; it is the Logico-Mathematical Structure who is Biological. The relations are only the activities of the Biological Structure. And the "relations", properly speaking, do not exist in the DNA; it is the immanent Logico-Mathematical Structure who exists in the DNA - in the form of monads - and He is wholly responsible for every activity of the DNA. The Logico-Mathematical Structure is "in" the physiology of the mature organism, supports the behavior of this organism, and is the source of the spontaneous behavior of this organism by means of upper-level logic and mathematics. In addition to confounding the Logico-Mathematical Structure with the relations it brings about, Piaget uses the familiar tactic of beginning with the physical level and gradually moving to the spontaneous behavior that more directly represents the immanent metaphysical Subject. He suggests at first, at least to the hurried reader, that the Biology involved is lower-level, but by the time he gets to "spontaneous behavior" it is obvious that the "Biology" is metaphysical in nature. The following selection comes from a previously published short paper that Piaget revised before it was published in a book along with other papers by him and several of his followers. Highly contrived, devious passages are seldom found in short papers that stand alone. The following excerpt elaborates some of the points made above.

> If objective structures ... contain a Deductive Element supplied by the Subject, Logico-Mathematical Structures cannot be regarded as deriving from physical ... structures ... Their point of contact must be sought within the Living Organism itself. It is from ...

this source that the Logico-Mathematical Systems are elaborated ... in an uninterrupted sequence of reflective abstractions and Self-regulating constructions (author's capitalization) (Piaget, 1972, p. 91).

Piaget reverts to a series of synonyms, two of which are plural and at least one of which is immanent. The purpose could not be to teach, as the meaning collapses into inanity when it is understood. He must be trying, like Hegel, to "bewitch". "Objective structures" means "objects" here, nothing more, and all objects, including people, have an immanent Deductive Element, or a Conscious Living Subdivision of the Absolute Structure, within, which directs the objects' activities while assimilating the objects. Logico-Mathematical Structures or Systems make up or constitute the Living Organism, so statements regarding the relations between these two terms are void of meaning because they are synonyms! And again, since "reflective abstractions" mean "Self-regulations" "or" should come between them, not "and".

The following selection provides additional insight into the ideas put forward in the preceding two passages.

Logico-Mathematical Structures ... cannot [be linked] to hereditary characteristics (genetic potentialities) because the latter are contingent and variable ... Logical or Mathematical connections are "necessary", [so] it is impossible to relate their Biological origin otherwise than to necessary Biological characteristics. Autoregulatory Mechanisms are of just this kind (author's capitalization) (Piaget, 1971a, p. 100).

The two words in parentheses are crucially significant. Logico-Mathematical Structures cannot be based on "genetic potentialities". This is an all-inclusive admission that these Structures cannot be based on any aspect of physical biology, as everything that we can observe in biological science exists because it is a "genetic potentiality". Furthermore, all of these physical biological characteristics are, without exception, contingent and variable. The same interpretation follows when Logico-Mathematical Structures must be based on necessary Biological characteristics. A metaphysical Biology is necessary to account for Logico-Mathematical Structures. Where else can one find a "necessary" Biology? It is also very important to understand that autoregulation, as Piaget defines it, can only occur in an Entity based on a necessary Biology. The physical biology of human beings cannot provide autoregulation.

With the above information in mind, Flavell's (1963, pp. 35-6; 222-3) and Furth's (1969, p. 40) acceptance of a special capacity of lower-level biology to produce "functional invariants" is unfortunate.

Piaget defines Structure as a nonphysical global System, but he does so very ambiguously!

Totality [is] seen as a System .... The concept of Structure does not imply just any kind of totality .... If we apply a broad definition to the concept of Structure, the Structures will have properties that remain *somewhat global* and in consequence their reduction to mathematical or physical constructs remains in the realm of wishful thinking (author's italics and capitalization) (Piaget, 1967, pp. 143-4).

The Structure is global, truly "global" as it fills the universe, and it cannot be reduced to mathematical - lower-level of course - or physical constructs. This is the mathematics taught at every university in the world, not Piaget's upper-level math, which refers *only* to the activities of the Absolute Subject (author's italics and capitalization) (Beth & Piaget, 1966, pp. 243, 296) (Piaget, 1973b, p. 103). Neither the science of physics nor traditional mathematics can describe Structure. *A full understanding of what Piaget means requires additional references to fill out his concept of "global".* The author italicized and capitalized the words below which indicate a Global Metaphysical Structure. The Structure is frequently described as a *Totality* (Beth & Piaget, 1966, p. 170) (Piaget, 1973d, p. 7) (Piaget, 1952b, pp. 378-9), a *Whole* (Inhelder & Piaget, 1958, pp. 289-90) (ibid., pp. 303-4) (Beth & Piaget, 1966, p. 255), or a *Universal* (Piaget, 1971a, p. 269) (ibid., p. 327) (Inhelder & Chipman, 1976, p. 209). It is also called *Overall* (Piaget, 1980, p. 302) (Piaget et al., 1977, p. 179) (Piaget, 1973c, p. 36), *Single* (Piaget, 1971a, p. 360) (Inhelder & Piaget, 1958, pp. 303-4) (Piaget, 1970b, p. 42), *Absolute* (Piaget, 1952b, pp. 11-12) (Piaget, 1973d, p. 28) (Piaget, 1971a, p. 167) and a *System* (Piaget, 1970c, p. 21) (Piaget, 1970b, p. 113) (Piaget, 1973d, p. 15)

True to form, in a subsequent book Piaget uses the term "global structuralism" with a lower-level meaning.

> Whereas "global" structuralism holds to systems of observable relations and interactions, which are regarded as sufficient unto themselves, the peculiarity of Authentic (Analytic) Structuralism is that it seeks to explain such empirical systems by postulating "deep" Structures from which the former are in some manner derivable. Since Structures in this sense ... are ... Logical-Mathematical ... they do not themselves belong to the realm of fact (author's capitalization) (Piaget, 1970b, p. 98).

This "global structuralism" is based on observable relations and interactions, so it is lower-level. Now "Authentic" or "Analytic" Structuralism is upper level. Why are Authentic Structures held to be the source of observable relations and interactions? *For the simple reason that Piaget has arbitrarily made the term synonymous with Logico-Mathematical Structures.* At the same time he admits that these Structures do not belong to the realm of "fact", meaning empirical fact, of course, not metaphysical fact. A few pages later he elaborates on both the nature of fact and the nature of Authentic Structures.

> Once we have admitted the existence of Structures as distinct from the system of observable relations ... how are we to understand this "existence"? ... *Structures ... are the source of the relations .... They are prior to ... the social order; prior to the mental ... and ... to the "organic" ... But what manner of existence is left, then, for the Mind, it is neither social, nor mental ... nor organic* (author's italics and capitalization) (ibid., pp. 111-12)?

The Structure under discussion is very special indeed. It quickly metamorphoses into the Mind that is prior to the relations studied by natural science. *Furthermore, we are informed that this Structure or Mind was not only prior to organic biology, but that it is not even "mental".* After making these oracular declarations, Piaget begs us to consider what kind of existence is left for this Entity. This debased form of argument obviously leads directly to his Absolute System, but *the most important aspect of the quote is the clean separation that is made between the metaphysical Structure and the organically based mentality of human psychology. Piaget's Structure-Mind, consisting of monads, existed before there were human bodies with organically based mental capacities.*

This Structure or Mind existed before the advent of everything known by natural science, and it also maintains all of the structures studied by science. This metaphysical Mind supports physical reality because all of reality is embodied in the Living Body of Monads.

> Logico-Mathematical operations ... play a necessary role in the decentering of the subject .... However, from the point of view of the epistemology of physics there then arises the following problem: Logico-Mathematical Structures refer to a Non-Temporal System of Possibles ... yet their inclusion in reality ... involves their embodiment within the temporal ... and finite ... Reality is only effectively achieved when it is thus placed (author's capitalization) (Piaget, 1972, p. 83).

More elaboration along the same line:

> We are ... led back to the classical rationalist interpretations of causality, not simply as ... regular successions as in Hume's empiricism, but as the reason for things .... In all cases the characteristic property of Causality - that it is a Deductive Construction that is part and parcel of the real - remains, thanks to the *inexhaustible wealth of experience and the limitless fecundity of Logico-Mathematical Structures* (author's italics and capitalization) (Piaget, 1974a, p. 76).

The reason for things, according to Piaget's theory, is the Logico-Mathematical Structures. How can we be sure that this is the correct view? We can be sure because Piaget said that the characteristic property of Causality, a synonym here of Logico-Mathematical Structures, is Deductive Construction. At this point he inserts his customary slice of misinformation about his own system with the words "which is part and parcel of the real". "Deductive Construction", as we have seen, is Causation by the One who produces or develops by means of operations (author's capitalization) (Piaget, 1952b, pp. 12; 342) (Piaget, 1969b, p. 358). In this context He is the producer of physical reality, but He is certainly not "part and parcel of physical reality" as He is the Structure of metaphysical Reality. On what basis can Piaget make such a statement? If the basis of one's argument is mere verbalisms, anything is possible.

The Living Structure or "Causality" is characterized by the metaphysical property of operations or deductive construction, but please consider the proclamation that this type of construction is the reason for the "real" or physical universe. It should be noted that Piaget usually uses his private concept of "deduction" to mean construction or development as a dialectic process, but the construction of the physical universe was, at least originally, not dialectic. The following excerpt deals further with deduction and physical reality.

> The Deductive System on which ... causal explanation is based ... [consists of] General Forms of Operational Organization ... [or] Structures [which] seems to base [causal explanation] on an External and Ontic Substratum [who attributes His Structure] to reality (author's capitalization) (Piaget, 1974b, pp. 134-5).

This passage in the original is barely intelligible, but it seemed worthwhile to show that Piaget's Deductive System is based on an Entity who is also an Operational Form or Structure who is external to the physical human being. This External Being is the basis for all natural causes in physical reality. Most causes having to do with the maintenance of an already constructed universe, are the result of assimilative processes so the "deductions" indicated are partly based on dialectic operations. Other "causes", such as moving large celestial objects to produce time, are "auxilary" operations.

The Logico-Mathematical Structure acts on the physical and on Himself in Self-development. These two aspects of His activity are described in unclear ways by Piaget. The following passage presents several contrived hurdles the reader must negotiate if he is to make any sense of it.

> The great difference between Logico-Mathmatical Structures and Causality lies in the fact that the regulations involved in the development of Causality ... act on outside contents and modify them ... On the other hand the regulations required for Logico-Mathematical Structure intervene only with their own Form (author's capitalization) (Piaget, 1977, pp. 170-1).

The first deliberately contrived hurdle is the fact that "Logico-Mathematical Structures" and "Causality" are synonyms, even though Piaget first states that they are greatly different. "Causality" is quite often used as a synonym for the Absolute Subject (Piaget et al., 1977, pp. 175-6) (Piaget, 1971a, pp. 93, 98) (Piaget, 1972, p. 84) (Piaget, 1974b, p. 135) (Piaget, 1930, p. 273). After saying that they are different, however, he correctly states that causality involves regulations that are *turned outward* and that regulations required by the Structure must be *turned inward*. *The regulations which assimilate things in the physical world are exactly the same regulations which modify the Logico-Mathematical Structure itself.* The same regulations do both simultaneously. "Logico-Mathematical Structure", "Causality", and "Form" all refer to the same Entity. A second hurdle is to realize that "Structure and "Form" are synonyms. Although Piaget separates Form from Structure, we remember that both are names of the Body of Monads. Neither hurdle is insuperable, but they are examples of Piaget's adroit manipulation of verbal entities for the express purpose of making comprehension difficult. He informed us from the beginning that this was his plan.

EXPLICATORY FUNCTION AND IMPLICATORY FUNCTION

The notion that the regulations or functions are simultaneously turned outward toward the external world and inward towards the Mind's intentions regarding the development of the Idea is elaborated at length toward the end of his first book.

> Intentionalism gives rise to two fundamental categories or ... functions of Thought: the *explicatory function* and the *implicatory function*. These ... are present in all Mental activity ... *The explicatory function is ... centrifugal ... in which the Mind turns to the external world; the implicatory function is ... centripetal, in which the Mind turns inwards ....* The direction of the implicatory function is ... centripetal in the sense that ... it seeks to trace its way back to the directing motive or Idea. *The explicatory function tends toward things. The implicatory function tends towards Ideas or judgments* (author's italics and capitalization) (Piaget, 1926, pp. 236-7).

An operation of the Mind which, for Piaget, means the highest type of Mental activity, basically faces simultaneously in two directions; it faces toward the object it is assimilating which is the explicatory or centrifugal function, and it also faces inward toward the Idea it is developing or constructing, which is the implicatory or centripetal function of Self-development. "Judgment" has the seldom used private meaning of "operation" (Piaget, 1970d, p. 29), so "and" should be used between Ideas and judgments rather than "or". All effective Knowledge is based on operations (Piaget, 1953, p. 7).

The centrifugal and centripetal functions are further complicated by the kind of operations that produced the physical universe. The centrifugal aspects described above are assimilative in nature, while the operations that produced the physical universe simply constructed what must be assimilated later.

> Logico-Arithmetical and physical operations [are] identical from the outset, except for the fact that the former constitute a regulation of an Operational Mechanism, and the latter a regulation of the material or external results .... the first leading to General Logic and the second to the construction of the physical universe .... In their Formal Mechanisms both involve precisely the same transformations .... Physical operations constitute a composition of the external world (author's capitalization) (Piaget & Inhelder, 1974, p. 231).

How could Logico-Arithmetical and physical operations be identical except for the fact that the former regulates the Operational Mechanism and the latter regulates the external results? Clearly, this is deliberate nonsense. Aside from the fact that Piaget is manipulating verbal entities in ways that are logically impossible within his system, either the Mechanism is operated arbitrarily or there must be a further difference which is not stated. The passage is full of such logical discrepancies, as well as a deliberate confounding of assimilative and creative operations with regard to physical reality. We can begin to understand the twisted meanings if we realize that it is not "physical operations" but "operations on the physical". With this understanding of a reversed meaning we can then discern the distinction between dialectic assimilation of the physical and creation of the physical. When we understand that all operations are regulated by the Body of Monads, we see immediately how the first sentence of the quoted passage is mangled so badly that it cannot fit within his system without alterations - which Piaget will make at his good pleasure!

When he says that Logico-Arithmetical operations lead to General Logic and that physical operations lead to the construction of the physical universe, he is mixing concepts inappropriately. The development of General Logic, which is a synonym of the Absolute Structure, must be paired with the assimilative aspect of *dialectic operations*, not with the operations which created the physical universe, which are *not dialectic*. Note that he further fouls the process of communication when he says that, "in their Formal Mechanisms both involve precisely the same transformations". The Formal Mechanism is the same Body of Monads in each case, but the transformations in General Logic versus the transformations involved in the creation of the physical universe are vastly different. In addition to the problem of his overall plan for deception, how should we interpret Piaget's quite open and regular insults to his readers' intellectual sensibilities? I do not claim to know the answer, but I am confident that he is well aware of what he is doing. One of the most intriguing aspects of this problem is the apparent lack of shame regarding his egregious logical and linguistic perversions. In any case, the machinations of a brilliant but treacherous mind are revealed.

ENDOGENOUS OR NORMATIVE STRUCTURES VERSUS EXOGENOUS OR PHYSICAL STRUCTURES

Piaget often speaks of endogenous processes versus exogenous processes. It is essential that one comprehend what these terms mean in relation to Structure. The following quote is instructive.

> As far as Intelligence is concerned ... we understand by "endogenous" those Structures which are developed by means of the regulations and operations of the Subject. [The constructs involved] arise from internal Logico-Mathematical activity engendered by the coordination of *the Individual's actions.* By serving as an Assimilatory Framework ... these Structures are added to the properties of the external object .... We ... consider Logico-Mathematical Structures as endogenous .... It is understood that the term "exogenous", when applied to knowledge, will indicate that it is derived from physical experience. The use of Endogenous, when applied to Knowledge, will mean that it is due to a Logico-Mathematical construction (author's italics and capitalization) (Piaget, 1980, pp. 80-1).

Endogenous Knowledge or Intelligence can only be developed by the regulations or operations of the Subject or Structure. In the second sentence the regulations or operations become Logico-Mathematical actions, *which in this passage are represented as coordinations of the Individual who serves as the Assimilating Framework. The familiar mesmerizing, frustrating concatenation of synonyms is evident. "Subject", "Structure", "Individual", "Assimilatory Framework" and "Logico-Mathematical Structures" are simply names of the Absolute Entity.* Observe that the "true Individual" is the Absolute Subject. Be that as it may, the concept of non-human, metaphysical, endogenous processes which produce Normative Knowledge and Intelligence is merely another way to express the central notion of actualization of the Absolute's full range of possibilities.

As we have learned to expect, Piaget also uses "individual" in another way:

> As psychogenetic studies have shown, the Mechanisms on which the individual subject's acts of intelligence depend are not in any way contained by his consciousness, yet they cannot be explained except in terms of "Structures" [such as] "Groups", "Networks", "Semi-Groups" and so on .... Structuralism calls for a differentiation between the *individual subject,* who does not enter at all, and the *Epistemic Subject* .... Now after such precipitation of the "me", the "lived", from the "I", there remains the Subject's "operations" (author's italics and capitalization) (Piaget, 1970b, pp. 138-9).

The passage, most of which we have seen previously, begins with a bit of nonsense as psychogenesis is metaphysical development by means of operations, so no empirical studies of psychogenesis is possible. The "individual subject" is said to be unconscious of the Mechanisms he depends upon when he acts intelligently, and that such acts can only be explained in terms of Structures. Piaget is speaking of the physical individual and his lower-level consciousness, but "his" acts of intelligence, that is, practical intelligence, are obviously based on upper-level Structures. The pluralization of "Mechanisms" and "Structures" is inappropriate, but this does not prevent one from seeing that Piaget is referring to the immanent Structure. When he begins to discuss the two subjects everything falls into place. It becomes clear that the individual subject has nothing to do with Operational Intelligence, so Piaget was blatantly dishonest when he suggested at first that he did. Structuralism and its Operational Intelligence is the exclusive province of the immanent Epistemic Subject *who is the "I" who remains after the "me" is precipitated or assimilated out!*

Piaget strongly implies that Structures may represent the Absolute Himself, but he goes on to complain that the usual axiomatic or formalizing methods of traditional logic ignore the Absolute and has resulted in a logic without a Subject.

> The case of Logical Structures ... possesses every characteristic that might have made it a kind of Absolute .... Logic using as it does an axiomatic 'formalizing' method, ignores the Psychological 'Subject' as a matter of principle, having a 'logic without Subject' (author's capitalization) (Piaget, 1973d, pp. 28-9)

Even though the Logical Structure possesses *every characteristic* that should make it an Absolute, conventional logic, the kind taught at every university, ignores this fact. As a matter of principle conventional logic produced a logic without the Psychological Subject - who is the Logical Structure. *The passage begins with the "case of Logical Structures", or upper-level Logic, but after "Absolute" Piaget mischievously switches to lower-level logic with its very different meaning.* As is nearly always the case, he gives the reader no overt clue that he is switching from upper-level Logic to lower-level logic. Piaget's method of switching levels has only one possible explanation - it is for the purpose of confusion and deception.

The concepts of synchronic and diachronic structures are important in Piaget's theory. The conventional structures studied by natural science are synchronic, while Piaget's metaphysical Structure with many names is diachronic. *The key to understanding diachronicity is that only Normative Structures have this attribute.*

> Diachronics ... [refers to the] domains ... where Structure belongs ... [that is] to Realities which have intrinsic value and Normative power. The defining character of Norms is that they are obligatory, that they conserve their own value by binding men to such conservation ... The distinctive character of [their] development ... is that it is always directed toward equilibrium .... *Normative and conventional structures are, therefore, at opposite poles as regards the relations between synchronics and diachronics* (author's italics and capitalization) (Piaget, 1970b, p.79).

Diachronics refers only to the Structure and His activities, because this is the only source of intrinsic value and power. *More specifically, it refers to the fact that He is the only Entity who exists through all time.* This is also the private meaning of "conservation". For Piaget, "conservation" means the maintenance of existence forever. It is noteworthy that men are said to be "bound" to such conservation. The immanent Entity within each physical human being is "bound to this conservation" forever and human beings are bound to the immanent Entity, but when the human being dies the immanent Entity must continue His development in another human being. This is the meaning of the two terms as understood by Piaget, but *what does he mean by his claim that Normative Structures are obligatory? He means, as we have previously observed, that they are coercive with regard to their intention. And what is their sole intention? It is to reach equilibrium by assimilating all physical reality, including every human being and, as a consequence, become fully developed.* When Piaget states that synchronic and diachronic structures are at opposite poles, he means that they represent the two different levels, so the former must be eliminated by assimilation.

In other contexts, as we have learned to expect, "synchronic" can also refer to the Absolute Subject. For instance:

> [There is a] connection between synchronic balance and diachronic transformations. As we have seen, [there is a] ... dependence between these two aspects ... in the sphere of Normative Structures, because the evolution of Norms ... is a process of gradual equilibration. This being so, the nearer the Structure ... is to final closure (which, it should be added, in no wise excludes the possibility of its being subsequently integrated into new Structures) the more closely, of course, does the synchronic balance depend upon this same Self-regulating process (author's capitalization) (Piaget, 1973d, pp. 60-1).

It is clear in this instance that "synchronic balance" of the Absolute Subject refers to the eventual equilibrium of nirvana. We are also presented with a logical anomaly; if the Body of Monads reaches *"final closure" how can one say that it really might not be final?* One cannot have it both ways. It seems to be a gratuitous eccentricity, as one would not normally say "final" if it were possibly not final. Final closure means perfect development, according to the theory, so where would one go from perfection?

FORM VERSUS MATTER

The synonym "Form" is quite often used in describing Structures. The Overall Form below is the Overall Subject, the Overall Structure, the Overall Absolute, the Overall Group, the Overall Space, the Overall Field, the Overall Organism, etc.

> Once this constructivist course has been taken, sooner or later one is obliged to resort to a structuralism, i.e., to the hypothesis of Overall Forms comprising their Self-regulation of their operators, in contrast to interpretations of an atomistic type (author's capitalization) (Piaget, 1973c, p. 36).

Structuralism in this passage is based on the Overall Form of Monads performing operations by regulating His own monads. As we found in the third chapter, "atomism" is usually lower-level in this particular book, so Piaget cleverly opposes spiritual monadism to material atomism in this particular context.

More about the distinction between Form and matter:

> In the sphere of biology ... the distinction between Form and matter ... has a very definite meaning. The matter of knowledge [is] the sum of influences which the environment exercises on the Organism .... The Form of Consciousness, from the Biological point of view, is ... a special case of those Structures which the Organism imposes upon matter (author's capitalization) (Piaget, 1930, pp. 282-3).

This selection is about the *two spheres of biology, not the sphere*. There are two kinds of biology in this passage based on two different organisms, however the two uses of "Organism" are both upper-level. The problem is that Piaget keeps one kind of biology, namely physical biology, undercover while pretending that he is dealing with only one kind, hoping that his reader will overlook the fact that the Biology depicted in the passage is metaphysical. He manages to hide lower-level or physical biology under the term "matter", particularly the "matter" that is imposed upon by the Organism. Notice too that Piaget includes lower-level knowledge, the kind we pay for at all the universities, within the category of matter. Although it is an extraordinary notion, this kind of knowledge, being "physical" in Piaget's terminology, is negatively exercised on the Absolute Organism, which means that the Absolute must dialectically assimilate this kind of knowledge the same way He assimilates all objects (author's capitalization) (Piaget, Inhelder & Szeminska, 1960, p. 381) (Piaget, 1928, p. 256) (Piaget, 1980b, p. 102) (Piaget, 1971a, p. 347) (Beth & Piaget, 1966, p. 147) (Piaget, 1974a, p. 23). Most of these references deal with the problem of physical, exogenetic or socially acquired knowledge quite subtly, but there is no question that, within Piaget's theoretical system, it interferes with the equilibration process in the same way that other kinds of matter interfere. Knowledge as lower-level matter is the result of every possible influence which has its source in the environment including hereditary influences. *The inclusion of genetic inheritance as an aspect of the environment is also a strange idea*, but because it is a part of the physical universe, it is so included by Piaget. Piaget uses the term "general heredity", as we have seen, to describe the process of development by means of operations. This term is "obviously connected" with the *Ipse Intellectus*, which is a synonym of the Absolute (author's capitalization) (Piaget, 1952b, p. 2). General heredity refers to the psychogenetic process, which is the way the Absolute Subject or Ipse Intellectus develops Himself. This interpretation is affirmed when Piaget states that the functional activity of Reason is connected with general heredity (author's capitalization) (ibid., p. 2). It could not be connected with the physical inheritance provided by the genetic system. So the environment includes genetic inheritance, all possible learning experiences and all thought processes based on brain activity, as it too is part of the physical environment. In Piaget's terminology, every aspect of physical reality is considered "matter". The "Form of Consciousness" is a reference to the immanent Subject in each person. This is easy to see as the "Form of Consciousness" is the Structure (we must overlook the plural again) the upper-level Organism imposes upon matter which represents the unmentioned lower-level organism. Yes, everything about the lower-level organism as such is nothing but matter, including *even the memory of a material or physical action*. Since the memory is of perceptual data, Piaget's theory considers it to be "on a par with the properties of an external object" (Piaget, 1978a, p. 162). For Piaget most human memories are merely matter! The "Consciousness" who imposes is quite often used, as it is in this instance, as a synonym for Absolute Subject (author's capitalization) (Piaget, 1974a, pp. 77-8) (Piaget, 1973d, p. 18) (Piaget, 1973a, pp. 171-2) (Piaget, 1971c, pp. 154-5).

Piaget constantly manipulates his huge array of verbal entities in a phantasmagoria of make-believe relationships, unhampered by the constraints of reality-based verifications and the normal criticism of his colleagues - which must be based on an understanding of his works.

> *Structure* must be defined more narrowly than *Form. How is this to be done?* ... Structures ... are only one kind of "Forms of Forms" ... Only Self-Regulating Transformational Systems are Structures ... When the Structures in question are Logical or Mathematical Structures we may say that the Logician or Mathematician derives them from "Forms" by reflective abstraction (author's italics and capitalization) (Piaget, 1970b, p. 113).

The child builds and rebuilds sand castles, one configuration following another determined only by whim and the fleeting play of personal desires. Piaget does the same with his imaginary Body of Monads. Both Structures and Forms refer directly to the Body of Monads. So does "Self-Regulating Transformational Systems", "Logical Structures" and "Mathematical Structures". They all refer to the same metaphysical Body of Monads that no scientist can ever in any way detect. *The metaphysical Logician or Mathematician does not derive Logical or Mathematical Structures from Forms because they both refer to the same identical Entity!* Clearly this disingenuous comparison had no purpose other than to provoke the kind of frustration he contemptuously promised (Piaget, 1977, p. 145).

THE CONTINUUM OF UNOBSERVABLE CORPUSCLES

The Operational Structure or Set of All Sub-Sets is the Spatial Continuum made up of unobservable corpuscles. Piaget describes this imposing Entity as follows:

> The Operational Structure of the Set of All Sub-Sets corresponds [to] the spatial notion of a Continuum .... and of Corpuscular Models ... filled ... with unobservable elements ... closely 'packed together' (author's capitalization) (Piaget, 1972, p. 49).

If the Structure is the Set of All Sub-Sets or the Spatial Continuum, it would not "correspond" to Corpuscular "Models" because the Structure would be *singular*. In another context Piaget agrees - "Structures are integrated into a single Intellectual Organization" (author's capitalization) (Piaget, 1971a, p. 360). "Corpuscular Models" is capitalized as Piaget almost always uses "Model" to mean the "real thing" when speaking of Structure (author's capitalization) (Piaget, 1977, p. 63) (Piaget, 1962, p. 85) (Piaget, 1973c, p. 52) (Piaget, 1972, pp. 80-1) (Piaget, 1974a, p. 76). This particular selection shows in high relief both the basic invisible, atomistic units of the Structure-Mind-Organism as well as the gargantuan size of this metaphysical Entity. The Spatial Continuum or Set of All Sub-Sets must account for the organization of galaxies plus every thought and movement of every person in the world.

The monads not only must account for everything; they must remember everything that has happened since the beginning of creation - simultaneously! Fortunately, the monads never get tired because no energy is required in their work (Piaget, 1974b, pp. 46-7; 99-101), and their movements, when not engaged in moving matter, are much faster than the speed of light; their movements are instantaneous or at "absolute speed" (ibid., p. 144) (Piaget, 1970a, pp. 121; 293).

How does Piaget know that monads move at "absolute" speed? The history of science shows how difficult it was to measure the speed of light, and the monads move much much faster. Is not this one of the hundreds of questions his enchanted devotees should ask before canonizing him? Is it not probable that Piaget handles many significant questions in this cavalier manner?

The superhuman attributes of monads with respect to time are indicated in dozens of passages, and the immanent monads are clearly included in some instances.

> We gain the impression that the moment when the child first succeeds in organizing a complete temporal system is so sudden that we can never actually put our finger on it: *often he will correct an error, and in so doing trigger off a total process the speed of which is far greater than that of any conscious process* (author's italics) (Piaget, 1969a, p. 261).

This is one of the numerous oracular statements regarding time to which Piagetians have turned a blind eye. How does Piaget know the speed of the process in the child? *Clearly his knowledge is not based on science, but on assumptions about his imaginary monads!* Piaget is not concerned here with the physical child, but the controlling Body of Monads within the child. The following references will further open up Piaget's imaginary world of "extratemporality" (Piaget, 1950, p. 121) (Piaget, 1952a, p. 201) (Piaget, 1971c, p. 106) (Piaget, 1972, p. 46) (Piaget & Inhelder, 1973, p. 211) (Piaget, 1974b, pp. 123, 125-6).

The concept of Structure includes the properties of the Structured Being who is capable of Eidetic Knowledge. This Structured Being enjoys a more profound reality than phenomenal or physical existence and fulfills the function of an Essence (author's capitalization) (Piaget, 1971c, p. 109). We are informed that only the Transcendental Self can acquire Eidetic Knowledge (author's capitalization) (ibid., p. 59), and that an Essence is created when an operation causes a fact of reality to pass over into the Extratemporal Structure (author's capitalization) (ibid., pp. 131, 165-6). The assimilated "fact of reality" becomes a part of the Structure or Essence, but this "fact of reality" is not transformed into a new Essence. We know this is true within Piaget's system because the number of monads remains constant. These Structures are the only Structures of interest to Piaget, and they belong exclusively to the metaphysical Subject (author's capitalization) (Inhelder & Chipman, 1976, p. 22).

THE LIVING FIELD OR LATTICE-GROUP OF MONADS

The Living Structure or Subject is a Field that Piaget often calls the "Lattice" because of its imagined shape and composition, or the "Group" because it is composed of a "group" of monads.

> We thus come to our fourth and last hypothesis ... in which the Lattice and the Group ... are regarded as Structures belonging to the Forms of Equilibrium attained by Thought activity. These Structures ... provide a Field of Possible Transformations. The subject finds himself ... in a Field of Force governed by the laws of equilibrium, carrying out transformations ... determined by the laws of the Whole Operational Field (author's capitalization) (Piaget, 1953, pp. 40-1).

"Lattice", "Group", "Structure", "Forms of Equilibrium", "Thought" "Whole Operational Field", "Field of Force" and "Field of Possible Transformations" all mean exactly the same thing. Piaget did not need eight synonyms to adequately express the information related, so why does he use them? Guessing is not necessary as he told us why at the beginning of his career, and, as we have repeatedly observed, this is typical behavior.

Piaget imagines that the monads are arranged in a horizontal and vertical pattern so there is some resemblance to a lattice (Piaget & Inhelder, 1960, pp. 403-4). He probably got this idea from Fessard who coined the word to describe aspects of his own theory of learning. "Fessard ... builds up a Lattice pattern, all the elements of which have identical properties (hence the part played by historical determination in the choice of preferential paths)" (author's capitalization) (Piaget, 1973c, p. 21). Typically, Piaget takes a word or phrase from other investigators and although their original meanings are alien to his, he ignores this fact and usually suggests that the terms are identical to, or at least highly compatible with, his particular denotations. The elements of Fessard's lattice pattern are identical and, apparently, so are Piaget's monads (ibid., p. 21) (Piaget & Inhelder, 1956, p. 376) (Piaget & Inhelder, 1974, p. 277). "Historical determination" is a unique description of the work of the monads as they assume their place of ultimate authority in the universe. The Lattice and the Group are Structures and they are also said to "belong to the Forms of Equilibrium". This is a silly circumlocution as they are simply Forms of monads, and they are not "Forms of Equilibrium", but Forms that eventually will attain equilibrium by means of equilibrations or operations. The Form, Structure or Absolute is not in equilibrium, and will not attain this fervently desired condition until all of physical reality has been assimilated (author's capitalization) (Bringuier, 1980, p. 44) (Piaget, 1950, p. 9) (Piaget, 1971a, p. 363) (Piaget, 1952, p. 407). Every individual is in the Field of Force and, moreover, has part of the Field within him. This Operational Field of Monads has one goal, and that is to assimilate everybody and every thing.

After treating them as somewhat separate concepts over more than 100 pages, we discover that the Combinatorial Operations and the Propositional or Interpropositional Operations are identical (author's capitalization) (Inhelder & Piaget, 1958, p. 122). So what is the relation of these operations to the Lattice Structure or the Group Structure?

> The Lattice Structure ... characterizes the System of Propositional Operations [and] implies a Combinatorial System. On the other hand the second Operational Schema, which we are now going to study, derives from the Group Structure ... The System of Formal Operations constitutes both a Lattice and a Group, and thus unites [them] into a single cluster (author's capitalization) (ibid., p. 123).

Piaget first separates the Lattice from the Group then ambiguously combines them again. The "Lattice", the "Group", the "System of Propositional Operations", the "System of Interpropositional Operations", the "System of Combinatorial Operations", the "Operational Schema" and the "System of Formal Operations" are identical. The System of Formal Operations do "derive" from the Group Structure - and from all the other Structures as well, including the "System of Formal Operations" - which highlights another confusing device. His alternating separation and then reuniting of these supposed differentiated concepts is strictly for the mystification and bewitching of his readers. All of the terms and dozens more simply refer to the Body of Monads, nothing more. He complicates things further by pretending to find all of these concepts and their interrelationships in the thinking of children, but since it is all anchored in the immanent Body of Monads within the children, we arrive at precisely the same conclusion.

There are many examples of Piaget insidiously claiming that a series of synonyms represent quite different concepts. In the following excerpt, he claims that three specific synonyms, plus others not named, are different kinds of Logico-Mathematical Structures.

> Action and its coordinates ... amounts to Intelligence. By this somewhat vague and rather dangerous word we mean precisely the functioning of Operatory Systems emanating from Action (of which the main systems are those of "Groups", "Networks", or "Lattices", and other important Logico-Mathematical Structures) (author's capitalization) (Piaget, 1971b, p. 80).

Based on sentence structure it is hard to tell whether "Action" or "Intelligence" is vague but dangerous, however, in this instance the general context indicates that it is "Action". In any case, it is the Operatory System that poses a danger, as sooner or later it will eliminate everyone. Since Operatory Systems emanate from Action, Action is a synonym for Absolute Subject; it is also a synonym for "Group", "Network", "Lattice", "Intelligence" "Logico-Mathematical Structure" and "Operatory Systems". Piaget impudently states that these as well as other Structures produce operations, while at the same time he holds that *only one* Structure produces operations (author's italics and capitalization) (Piaget, 1952a, p. VIII) (Piaget, 1973d, p.7) (Inhelder & Piaget, 1958, pp. 303-4) (Piaget, 1971a, p. 360) (Piaget, 1973c, p. 30)! This speaks volumes regarding his attitude toward his colleagues - as well as society in general.

THE STRUCTURE IS NON-CONTINGENT AND ERROR FREE

Piaget describes two types of regulations or operations, and announces that one of them, the superhuman type, is error-free.

> If regulation of the lower or ordinary type is a process for correcting or modifying errors, then operational regulation is seen as a process of precorrecting, avoiding, or eliminating errors, which is something much greater. Indeed, *an operational deduction is not subject to any error if it is in conformity with the laws of its Structure* ... An error in logic or in mathematics is the result of an individual slip ... which [has] nothing to do with the Structure being used (author's italics and capitalization) (Piaget, 1971a, pp. 210-11)

Physically based regulations or operations are good, but they do not compare with the ones based on the Living Structure, as they are not subject to any error at all. The only qualification is that the regulation or deduction must be in conformity with the laws of the Structure, and since He is able to make perfect operational deductions (author's capitalization) (Piaget, 1952b, p. 342) (Piaget, 1970c, p. 22) (Piaget, 1971a, p. 158), we would certainly anticipate that they would be completely free of error. Piaget concurs when he says that the only way errors can occur is when individuals slip. We cannot, of course, blame the Structure for that! In other contexts, Piaget insists that individuals do not *use* the Logical Structure - it is the other way around (author's capitalization) (Piaget, Inhelder & Szeminska, 1960, p. 404) (Piaget, 1967, p. 127) (Piaget, 1970b, pp. 69-70).

We have observed that Piaget uses the term "mathematics" to mean the operational activity of Self-construction. In Piaget's own words:

> Mathematics are, in fact, not simply a system of notions at the service of physical knowledge, but an Instrument of Structuralization, because it is of the nature of operations to produce transformations. The fact that the latter may be expressible in "symbols" does not in any sense reduce their active and constructive nature: thus, the Psycho-Biological problem of the construction of Mathematical Entities cannot possibly be solved by linguistic considerations (author's capitalization) (Piaget, 1971a, p. 47).

Piaget's concept of Mathematics is not in any way at the service of physical knowledge. It is the enemy of physical knowledge as it is in the process of eliminating it. The transformations it produces involves both the assimilation of objects or persons and the Self-development of the Absolute Structure. The Mathematical Entity or Absolute Subject produces or, rather, develops Himself Psycho-Biologically by means of mathematical activity.

PIAGET'S METHOD OF PROOF: USE ONE CHARACTERISTIC OF HIS SYSTEM TO PROVE ANOTHER CHARACTERISTIC OF HIS SYSTEM

The characteristics of child logic explain each other; Piaget admits that there is no other recourse within his system.

> The question is, where does the role of the Original Structure end and that of the contingent circumstances begin? *The only answer lies in the attempt to explain the characteristics of child logic by each other* ... Even though the method seems for the moment to involve us in a vicious circle, it means that the Thought of the child is coherent and *sui generis*. (author's italics and capitalization) (Piaget, 1928, p. 200).

Piaget does not deny that he is making a circular argument but, as he explains in the next quote, the circle is really dialectic so we are dealing with a logical necessity. This is an extremely significant point, as it shows that Piaget has no confidence whatever in the countless "experiments" he has performed with children to support his theory. *He does not depend upon the "contingent circumstances" of physical experiments to give his theory validity.* His only recourse is to explain one part of his theory by some other part of his theory. His System actually precludes the possibility of contingent physical experiments demonstrating the validity of a fully determined imposition of logic on the child by the immanent Original Structure. He expresses the same idea again:

> A Conceptual System ... is such that its elements are inevitably supported by one another .... It is impossible to describe a concept without making use of the others in a process which is of necessity circular also. The circles we are talking of here are dialectic, an inherent part of Thought in its functioning (author's capitalization) (Piaget, 1971a, p. 157).

Piaget tries to remove the focus from his system to any system with the first three words, but in doing so he disagrees with the viewpoint of natural science. *Although internal consistency is essential in natural science, the validity of its concepts always depends upon the empirical evidence afforded by experiments. Piaget's scheme attempts to detour around this scientific principle.* In addition to the concept of dialectics, he also appeals to "child logic". Piaget almost never appeals to traditional logic or natural science for support of his system. Since he has usurped and shaped "Child Thought" for his own illicit purposes, he naturally finds it convenient to appeal constantly to his "findings" in this field as they naturally agree with his doctrines.

> The Schema acquires the strength of reciprocal implication, which means that if one of the features is isolated from the Whole, and the child is asked for its reason, he will simply appeal to the existence of the other features by way of explanation or justification (author's capitalization) (Piaget, 1928, p. 230).

The following excerpt is the third taken from *Judgment and Reasoning in the Child* (ibid.) regarding the practice of proving one part of a theory by quoting another part. This is standard procedure for Piaget, so he makes a big effort to convince his reader that this behavior is correct and proper.

> The features of Child Thought ... really do constitute a Coherent Whole, such that each of its terms partially implies a portion of the other terms ... the factors of education and all the various influences which the adult exercise upon the child ... are 'assimilated', i.e., deformed by the Living Being who comes under their sway [*by the Living Being who brings them under His sway*] (author's correction), and they are incorporated into His own Substance. It is this Psychological Substance ... of the child's, or rather this Structure and functioning peculiar to his Thought that we have tried to describe, and in a certain measure, to explain (author's italics and capitalization) (ibid., p. 256).

Piaget completes his argument, in this particular book, for the practice of using one term of the Child's and his system to demonstrate the validity of other terms of the system. This final argument is based on his assumption that the Child's Thought is Coherent, therefore each term should partially imply the other terms. *It is important to understand that Piaget logically must substitute this type of argument in place of empirical data which, although he constantly pretends to employ, is not possible in his theoretical system. Having concluded this argument, he launches immediately into the metaphysical nature of the Coherent immanent Entity in the child. He is quite clear and specific about the metaphysical source of Coherence and how it remains Coherent in the face of all the influences directed at the child by adult society.* All of these influences are deformed by the Living Being who brings them all under His sway and assimilates them into His Substance. *They are not assimilated by the child, but by the Psychological Substance in the child.* Piaget, in his own inimitable way, leaves no doubt regarding the fact that this Substantial Psychological Structure does not really belong to the child, although it is "peculiar to his Thought". His rather obvious and brazen reversal of meaning regarding the relative power of the various influences exercised upon the child versus the immanent Living Being who resists and assimilates these influences, although irritating, should not conceal the meaning.

GENETIC PSYCHOLOGY DESCRIBES THE
DEVELOPMENT OF AN ETERNAL STRUCTURE

How do Structures develop? They develop according to the special process of "genesis". The purpose of genetic Psychology is to describe the formation of superhuman Logico-Mathematical Structures, not the human structures of developmental psychology as taught in all of our universities!

> Genesis ... is simply the process of transition from one Structure to another ... [It] is a certain kind of transformation which stems from a state A and results in a state B, where state B is more stable that state A ... We must first avoid any definition based on absolute beginnings ... Genesis is always conceived as stemming from an Initial State ... consequently, genesis is simply a form of development ... We can define genesis as a relatively determined System of Transformations (author's capitalization) (Piaget, 1967, p. 144)

Unlike the traditional concept of genesis, Piaget's concept does not involve the birth or creation of a new Structure or Subject. Genesis begins with the Initial Structure of Monads and involves the transformation of this Structure until full development is realized. Genesis begins with the Initial Structure because this Structure did not have an "absolute" beginning. *Only eternal Structures fit this description. Genesis is a fully determined set of operations that result in the Self-development of the Structure. Piaget could not be describing the development of people!*

Piaget is adamant regarding the genesis of Structures. Physical human beings have nothing whatever to do with their evolution - except to be sacrificed in the process of assimilation.

> As a point of reference we have a case of an evolution which we know to be autonomous - that of the Operational Structures ... It is in fact from one another that the Operational Structures develop, ... the preceding Structures becoming integrated in the next, these in turn opening up new Structures, and so on (author's capitalization) (Piaget & Inhelder, 1971, p. 7).

Piaget tells us explicitly that the development of Operational Structures has never been observed by man. His admission that their "existence" is "distinct from the system of observed relations and interactions" (Piaget, 1970b, pp. 111-12) also tells us that they are metaphysical as they do not belong to the *system* of observed relations and interactions, *which is the physical universe itself.* Yet he claims as a dogmatic fact that they develop from one another! Furthermore, he directly contradicts himself by saying elsewhere that they are not "facts". "Since Structures ... are ultimately Logico-Mathematical ... *they do not ... belong to the realm of 'fact'"* (author's italics and capitalization) (ibid., p. 98). Again, the realm of fact is the physical universe and Structures are not a part of this realm or system. In the following quote Piaget removes all doubt that he or any one else can make the genesis of Structures into an empirical or scientific epistemology:

> If one tries to deal with Structures within an artificially circumscribed domain - *and any given science is just that* - one very soon hits on the problem of being unable to locate the Entities one is studying, since *Structure is so defined that it cannot coincide with*

any system of observed relations, the only ones that are clearly made out in any of the existing sciences (author's italics and capitalization) (ibid., pp. 137-8).

This Structure is the Subject who is responsible for genetic Epistemology. So clearly, based on Piaget's own words, the epistemology for which he was cited by the APA can never be approached "in a resolutely empirical manner" and made "into a science separate from philosophy". On several occasions Piaget has spoken with pride regarding his citation by the APA, however, I believe he decided to pointedly chastise this august organization for their careless interpretation by definitely denying that he had made Epistemology into an empirical science. He said specifically that he was "a tireless opponent of empiricism in the field of Epistemology" (author's capitalization) (Piaget, 1980b, p. 10). The truth is that he received his citation from the APA for this and this alone. Surely this organization has never been involved in anything so utterly preposterous and embarrassing. This is the ultimate example of "pluralistic ignorance" or the "candid camera syndrome". True, Piaget's statement contradicts other statements, but his professional output contains so many vacillations between the value of physical experiment and the impossibility of any physical experiment supporting his theory, that one more contradiction is almost trivial. One must look beyond the many contradictions to Piaget's life-long goal of explaining everything in terms of "Biology".

THE PERMANENT IMMANENT STRUCTURE

"The facts point emphatically", states Piaget, "to the existence of a Structure" that is "more or less independent of external pressure" (Piaget, 1929, p. 39). He describes his view of this Structure in this way:

I ... arrived at two ideas ... I have never given up. The first is that since every organism has a Permanent Structure, which ... is never destroyed as a Structured Whole, all Knowledge is always assimilation of a datum external to the Subject's Structure. The second is that the Normative Factors of Thought correspond Biologically to a necessity of *equilibrium* by Self-regulation: thus logic would in the Subject correspond to a process of equilibrium (author's italics and capitalization) (Piaget, 1971c, p. 8).

Every lower-level organism has a Structure which does not die when the organism dies. Every animal and every plant has this Structure, but Piaget is concerned almost exclusively with the Structure in people. The assertion that *all* knowledge is assimilation of data external to this Structure is obscure. There are two kinds of knowledge, copy knowledge and assimilation Knowledge (Piaget, 1971a, p. 336). Copy knowledge is knowledge about the physical universe. This is the kind of knowledge we acquire, at all levels, in the normal educational process. Copy knowledge is another name for exogenetic knowledge, and is *the only kind to which natural science aspires,* as empirical science can only be based on knowing what the physical universe is like (Piaget, 1973c, p. 45) (Piaget, 1971a, p. 3). Piaget chides Kant for replacing the Epistemological Subject, as conceptualized by Descartes and, somewhat differently by Leibniz, (Piaget, 1971c, p. 52) with "knowledge conceived as being a copy of reality" (ibid., p. 56). Hegel, in turn, replaced Kant's copy knowledge with his dialectic Knowledge based on the Concrete Universal's Self-activity (ibid., p. 58). Piaget frequently refers disparagingly to copy knowledge (Piaget & Inhelder, 1971, p. XIII) (Piaget, 1977, p. 191) (Piaget, 1971a, p. 6), but he prefers that the academic community remain somewhat hazy regarding its *identity with scientific knowledge*. Both kinds of knowledge depend upon the Permanent Structure, but "all effective Knowledge is based on ... a System of Operations" (author's capitalization) (Piaget, 1953, p. 7), and it is this Permanent Structure who is the only source of Operations. Piaget expresses the same idea in different words, as we use the following quote again to emphasize a different point.

> If ... it is a question of asserting that all knowledge is dependent on the existence of a Subject: this is then the important discovery of the Epistemological Subject, but we are now concerned with epistemology and no longer metaphysics (author's capitalization) (Piaget, 1971c, p. 64).

The Subject here is the metaphysical Operational Mechanism, the only Permanent Structure in Piaget's system. This means that the processes involved are also metaphysical, so Piaget is incorrect when he claims to have removed epistemology from metaphysics. Returning to the excerpt regarding copy knowledge, we can be sure that the Permanent Structure or Subject is only interested in assimilating physical reality, not "copying" it. Normative factors refer to the Permanent Structure or His activities, and in the previous quote the main factor was His need to attain equilibrium which can only be achieved by means of Self-regulations, equilibrations, operations or psychogenesis. Logic refers to the operational activity of the Permanent Structure as He progresses toward equilibrium. *This is not a process of equilibrium, but a process of equilibration toward equilibrium.* The bottom line is that copy knowledge is for people while assimilation Knowledge, which is based on operations or equilibrations, is for the Absolute Subject. Piaget confirms this in his own ambiguous way: "It could therefore be maintained that the equilibrium explication covers only an extremely limited area which reduces, in fact, to the Logico-Mathematical Structures" (author's capitalization) (Piaget, 1967, p. 104).

More about the functioning of the immanent Permanent Structure:

> The intimate functioning of the Intelligence ... remains entirely unknown to the subject until, at very superior levels, thought on this problem of Structures becomes possible ... The subject's thought is directed by Structures whose existence he ignores and which determine not only what he is capable or incapable of "doing" ... but also what he "must" do ... In short, the Cognitive Structure is the System of Connections that the individual can and must use, and is in no way the contents of his conscious thought, since it is He who imposes certain Forms (author's capitalization) Piaget, 1973a, p. 33).

"Intelligence", "Structures". "Cognitive Structure", "System of Connections", and "Forms" all mean the immanent Permanent Structure of Monads, and "He" also refers to this Structure. Three of the five synonyms are singular and so is the pronoun "He" while two are plural. The subject's thought is directed by Structures which determine what he is capable of doing and also what he *must* do. The subject *must* use this System of Connections which is imposed on him. Who is the "He" who does the imposing? There are at least two reasons why it has to be the System of Connections. First, since the lower-level subject is not conscious of the system he would not be imposing it on himself; second, the system imposed is "Forms", and we have examined considerable evidence showing that they are metaphysical. "The fact is, a Structure can impose itself as a necessity and can do this by essentially endogenous means, being the product of progressive equilibration" (author's capitalization) (Piaget, 1971a, pp. 316-17). That is, the Structure imposes Himself on the lower-level subject by operating on and assimilating him. "Equilibration" means operation, and "endogenous" means by the instrumentality of operations (Piaget, 1980b, pp. 81; 96). In the following passage the Subject knows what He is doing, but the object-subject is not really aware of what is happening to him.

> Observable facts ... correspond in the causal system to properties belonging to the object ... whereas in the Logical System they are introduced by the Subject ... who ... adds frameworks that do not exist in those objects .... [In] Logico-Mathematical Structuration, *what is added to the object (even though the subject himself cannot ... distinguish [the] attribution[sic])* is transparent for the Subject since those [attributions] come from Him and include necessary characteristics (author's italics and capitalization) (Piaget, 1980a, p. 56).

The first sentence repeats Piaget's doctrine that all natural objects, with special emphasis on the human object, and their interactions are caused by the Subject. The second sentence is a sterling example of Piaget's craftsmanship in designing puzzles. Although the human object or subject cannot distinguish the attributions given to him, it is all quite transparent to the Subject who is the giver. The giver has to be the Permanent Structure as some of these gifts are "necessary". Human beings cannot give themselves necessary attributes (Piaget, 1971a, p. 14) (Piaget, 1974a, p. 9) (Piaget, 1969b, pp. 288-9). The fact that Piaget includes the two different subjects close together signals his intention to harass his reader. In the original this is more obvious, but would take too long to unravel - one would have to explain why the "filler" omitted in the quote is irrelevant.

In the following selection Piaget ascribes an attribute to the physical subject that belongs only to the metaphysical Subject, then he corrects himself - but the reader will remain unaware of this correction unless he makes the necessary inference that Piaget implies.

> The "lived" can only have a very minor role in the construction of Cognitive Structures, for these do not belong to the subject's *consciousness* but to his operational *behavior* ... If, then, to account for the Constructions we have described we must appeal to the Subject's acts, the Subject here meant can only be the Epistemic Subject, that is, the Mechanism common to all subjects (author's italics and capitalizations) (Piaget, 1970b, p. 68).

The "lived" refers to the lower-level subject who usually has no role at all in the development of Cognitive Structures (author's capitalization) (Piaget, 1970b, p. 139) (Piaget, 1973a, p. 132) (Beth & Piaget, 1966, p. 238). The lower-level subject is not conscious of these Structures, but they are the source of all of his operational behavior. *The problem with the latter part of the first sentence is that the lower-level subject is not capable of any operational behavior at all*, so to accept *all* of this sentence is to accept a very large misconception of Piaget's own system. This is not fair, of course, but it is a normal mode of procedure for Piaget. The reader now faces a clashing incongruity, because if he accepts *all* of the following sentence he must reject the part of the preceding sentence as specified. This kind of "correction" is also characteristic of Piaget's modus operandi. Since it is not possible for both sentences to be correct, the reader is, at least temporarily, in a quandary. We can only account for the development or construction of the Cognitive Structures or Permanent Structure or Subject by appealing to the operational acts, or Self-regulations of the Epistemic Subject, not the lower-level subject.

Piaget's Regulators are the metaphysical Logico-Mathematical Structures. They are not the biophysical regulators studied in natural science.

> As for the Logico-Mathematical Structures, ... it would be inconceivable to attribute to them, as Regulators, the physical nature of objects, since they extend beyond them everywhere .... The only Regulator we could assign to the cognitive regulations is an internal one ... Their existence can be attributed to conservation. In dealing with any Biological or Cognitive System, we must characterize the Whole as primordial ... The Whole possesses a force of cohesion and ... Self-conservation which distinguish it from nonOrganic physical-chemical totalities (author's capitalization) (Piaget, 1977, p. 22).

The Logico-Mathematical Structures are the Regulators - Self-Regulators in terms of their own development and also Regulators, in another sense, of all physical processes and movements. It is important to note that these Regulators are not based on biophysical processes as are the regulators studied by natural science, as "they extend beyond" everything physical. Cognitive regulations are internal to the Cognitive Structures, in other words, this is an ambiguous way to express Self-regulation. The existence of the Cognitive Regulator, Structure, or Absolute Subject is based on His ability to conserve Himself. This particular kind of Self-conservation is the source of His eternal Life. Piaget affirms that the Regulator is really the Primordial Biological Whole or God he first met under the tutelage of his godfather. *This metaphysical Biological Entity is Organic* (author's italics and capitalization) (Piaget, 1978b, p. 68) (Piaget, 1973d, p. 35) (Beth & Piaget, 1966, p. 203) (Piaget, 1970b, p. 48), *not organic* (Piaget, 1971a, pp. 34; 152-4; 358) (Piaget, 1973a, pp. 171-2), *so it is not physical.*

Piaget cunningly leads his reader to believe that Biological and Cognitive developments are initially separated, but are later fused or integrated into One Whole. In his system, however, both Biological development and Cognitive development is simply the development of the Body of monads.

> The interest in any comparison which ... might be drawn between the two types of development, Biological and Cognitive, is that ... if you take the kind of Science whose findings can be proved beyond fear of contradiction, which is the case with Logico-Mathematical Structures, these two types [of development] fuse and one become One Whole ... They ... become logically integrated into an Organized Whole (author's capitalization) (Piaget, 1971a, p. 74).

We see immediately that Biological and Cognitive development is really the development of the Logico-Mathematical Structures. This means that the Biological Structures and the Cognitive Structures are simply alternate names for the Logico-Mathematical Structures, *so they have never represented two types of development which later become fused.* The Primordial Biological Whole composed of monads is the Biological Structure, the Cognitive Structure and the Logico-Mathematical Structure. Observe that the "Science" of the Logico-Mathematical Structures is superhuman in nature. Practitioners of natural science do not make such claims. This is "metaphysical Science", referring exclusively to the progressive Self-development of the Logico-Mathematical Structure Himself.

The Non-Temporal Structures of the Absolute Subject, according to Piaget, finds the dynamism of the usual causal models to be "foreign". The differences between Spirit and matter are very great, but since the Non-Temporal Structures created matter, it seems odd that it would be considered foreign. Piaget elaborates:

> The usual causal models, in which the [dynamism] of masses, actions, forces, and energies intervene ... remains foreign to Nontemporal Structures. In the case of a complete geometrization of reality, the isomorphism between the objects and the operations of the Subject tends ... to become complete .... The power is ... in the hands of the Subject Himself .... Each operation is an act and it is their totality ... that constitutes the Subject .... A spatio-temporal power implies a succession in time, and therefore cannot be prevented from being assimilated (author's capitalization) (Piaget, 1974b, p. 152).

The Non-Temporal or Logico-Mathematical Structures know all about masses, actions, forces and energies since "in order for Consciousness to act causally it would also need to possess these properties (author's capitalization) (Piaget, 1971c, pp. 154-5). Piaget is ambiguous regarding the action of Consciousness on matter, but he concludes that it does indeed so act. We know that metaphysical Structures are the source of physical properties, but it is not clear how they "possess" them. Nevertheless, physical structures and processes are foreign to Non-Temporal Structures in composition, mode of operation, motivation, and in other ways. "Geometrization" of reality makes reality more and more like the Subject by means of operations. Geometrization, then, is another name for assimilation. The end result of geometrization or assimilation is that physical reality becomes a complete isomorph of the Subject, making them identical or really one integrated Entity again, as they were before the creation of physical reality. A complete set of operations is necessary to fully integrate physical reality within the Subject, and simultaneously, fully actualize every possible potential of the Subject. By "spatio-temporal power", Piaget means "human being" and he is happy to report that nothing can prevent the Gnostic assimilation of all these detestable (author's capitalization) (Inhelder & Piaget, 1958, p. 349), hateful (Piaget, 1971c, p. XVI) things (Beth & Piaget, 1966, p. 298) (Piaget & Inhelder, 1969, pp. 23-4). The mathematical combinations of the Form of Monads represents the process of intelligence; the genome and brain cannot do the job.

The following quote is an extension of meaning regarding the Form of Monads, as the Logico-Mathematical Structures refer to the same Organizations of Monads which are now responsible for the functioning of every living thing. They even operate the nervous systems of every person on the planet.

> Cerebral functioning is an expression or extension of very Generalized Forms rather than of particular organization forms .... *Nothing is farther from my thoughts than to attribute to the genome, or even to the brain, some kind of combinatorial intelligence* (author's italics and capitalization) (Piaget, 1971a, pp. 328-9).

A few pages later the same idea is amplified further:

> To sum up, Logico-Mathematical Structures are ... a much closer extension of the functioning found in every living structure than at first seemed to be the case ... *This functioning operates ... in the nervous system just as it does in any other organization* (author's italics and capitalization) (ibid., p. 333).

THE ABSOLUTE ENTITY AS SPACE

Piaget's doctrine of a supernatural Entity whose body fills all of space is rare in philosophy, but it is not entirely unique. Isaac Newton "introduced dynamism ... by conceiving space with time as a container and dynamics as a content" (Piaget, 1974b, p. 149). Newton conceived of the Biblical God in spatial terms. His view is different from Piaget's in many respects, but mainly because he wished it to be consistent with the Bible. It is said that Newton wrote more on religious topics than on scientific subjects. The source of dynamics in Piaget's Spatial Container is the monads, and while Newton does not appear to speculate on the specific dynamics of his Spatial Entity, Piaget wishes to leave the impression that the dynamics of Newton's metaphysical Container is much like his.

Only one other individual stands out in the history of philosophy, as portrayed in Macmillian's *The Encyclopedia of Philosophy*, who conceived of God in terms of space. The Swedish scholar, Emanuel Swedenborg was influenced by Newton's scientific and philosophical theories while studying for five years in England (Edwards, 1967, vol. 8, pp. 48-51). Taking additional ideas from Descartes and Leibniz, he elaborated a philosophy that included a God who created and maintains nature by means of "mathematical points". He did not call the points monads, but he held that there was an emanation from these points, like Piaget, which eventuated in nature as we know it. Piaget apparently does not mention Swedenborg, but the many similarities between his doctrine and Swedenborg's suggests that he was probably familiar with, and influenced by, his works.

THE STRUCTURE AND FUNCTIONS OF
SPACE DEPEND UPON THE MONADS

As we saw in Chapter 3, Piaget's theory begins with the Body of Monads. Any study of his concept of Space must begin with these constituent elements. In the following selection, he pretends that the child, through the intervention of his immanent Formal Structure, becomes aware of how operations are based on the monads.

> Where operations ... begin to function solely in terms of the Formal Structure, *the child can ... [extend] analysis ... beyond any physical limit* ... This facilitates the operational synthesis of Continuity .... At a certain point, the child suddenly becomes aware of the dynamics of the operation itself .... *All of the children have caught a glimpse of the fundamental truth that the infinitely small is not a static residual but the expression of*

a process of infinite subdivision. As for reassembly [of these infinitely small points], ...
it [is] a Homogeneous and Continuous Entity composed of the sum total of adjacent
points (author's italics and capitalization) (Piaget & Inhelder, 1956, pp. 147-8).

We have already seen that formal operations are based strictly on the immanent
Subject, and not on the individual child. In fact all operations are always performed by
the immanent Subject, but they are always resisted by the physical aspects of each
individual. Piaget, however, tends to hold that Formal operations are different in that
they function, completely free of the physical, and *solely in terms of the Formal*
Structure. Here the child is said to have a supernatural capacity to know about the
dynamics of operations by the Continuum of Monads, because operations "begin to
function solely in terms of the Formal Structure", enabling "the child" to make an
analysis *beyond any physical limit*, which obviously includes his normal mental
capacities as they are based on brain function. The following quote demonstrates that
the all-important progress toward equilibrium does not depend upon the brain.

> The movement towards an eventual equilibrium is not fully determined by the mechanics
> of, say, the human brain, *but is guaranteed by the nature of the sequential process itself*
> .... The development of operational behavior - and that development is relatively
> independent of any other, because it is governed by its own laws of equilibrium (author's
> italics) (Inhelder & Piaget, 1964, p. 293).

Piaget begins by saying that the movement toward equilibrium "is not fully
determined" by the mechanics of the brain, but he immediately negates this with the
statement that this movement is guaranteed by the sequential process of operations.
He equivocates again when he says that operational development is "relatively"
independent of any other kinds of development. If operations can guarantee
equilibrium and operational development is governed by its own laws, it is *absolutely*
independent, not "relatively" so.

Returning to the excerpt on formal operations, we see that it is an "analysis" by
the immanent Ego, as real children know nothing about such things. The Formal
Structure supposedly enables the child to make an analysis that *goes beyond physical*
or scientific analysis toward an understanding of "Continuity" or the Continuum as
well as the dynamics of an operation. *Piaget goes on to say that all of the children in*
a particular physical experiment "caught a glimpse" of the truth that the infinitely
small points or monads were not static material residuals, but could be
"reassembled" into the Homogeneous and Continuous Entity who is composed of the
sum total of adjacent points. This idea of "reassembly" is interesting as the Absolute
is never disassembled either in basic theory or verbally by Piaget. He is embodied in
matter, but the monads of which He consists are always united "in one monolithic
bloc" (Piaget & Inhelder, 1956, p. 456). *Piaget simply dreamed up the idea as a*
method to advance his theory of monads.

Although the child would not understand the concept of infinity very well, Piaget
does and it has a special meaning for him; namely that "the infinite is not a physical
but an operatory notion" demonstrating that something more than the physical is
intervening (Piaget et al., 1977, p. 96). The infinitely small monads are indeed
responsible for the dynamics of Spatial operations. In this short quotation, regarding
the *extension of analysis beyond any physical limit*, we see a microcosm of Piaget's

overall undercover attempt to lead his followers from the physical to the metaphysical by the clever but fraudulent manipulation and interpretation of "experimental" results.

PIAGET BEGINS WITH PHYSICAL SHAPES
AND ENDS WITH METAPHYSICAL MONADS

In the book *The Child's Conception of Space* (Piaget & Inhelder, 1956), an effort is made, beginning on page 125 and ending on page 149, to lead the reader to Piaget's concept of metaphysical monads by means of physical experiments. This is a further elaboration of some of the same references examined in Chapter 3. He does this without mentioning the word "monad" at all and, apparently, using "atomism" only once. He first has four to six-year-olds reduce squares and triangles until they are very small, then he asks them what they would look like when they are made smaller, and then smaller still until nothing is left. Then he asks the crucial question: Just before nothing is left, what does the last thing look like? These children tended to say that whatever they had been reducing retained the same shape until finally nothing remained. Some said other things, but no one said "a tiny round point" because this is to be a gradual revelation! The revelation will not only include a change in shape from square or triangle to round point, but it will go beyond scientific analysis to infinity and metaphysical atomism. On pages 138-140 he presents 7- to 10-year-olds with essentially the same problems. A few give answers similar to the younger children, but most agree that the square or triangle becomes a point before it disappears. On pages 146-7 10 to 12 year-olds sometimes go beyond the notion of a material point to concepts much closer to Piaget's heart. *One said that the points within squares are not only round, but that it would take forever to count them, suggesting, in Piaget's frame of reference, infinity.* Another, with Piaget's help, says that the points one should envision are smaller than visible circular points. *One child said that the points look like "dust floating in the air". At this juncture Piaget suggests that one should compare his notion of atomism with the child's statement, thus giving a clue to the reader that his notion of atomism is metaphysical.* With this "physical" experiment Piaget has led the child and his reader to his concept of the monad. Having reached this key concept of metaphysical Space by manipulating children, he backs off the concept of monads until he combines it with other spatial concepts on pages 447-485. *In the "general conclusions" Piaget admits that Thought requires more than [physical] points in the production of operations* (author's italics and capitalization) (ibid., p. 456), *and goes on to say that coordination depends upon an infinite number of [metaphysical] "points having neither shape nor size"* (author's italics) (ibid., p. 459). Ultimately, Piaget leaves no doubt about the metaphysical nature of the monad, which means that all of his manipulations at the physical level are not only irrelevant but are profoundly deceptive in nature.

I am convinced that anyone who reads the above book with care, and this actually holds with all of his books, will almost certainly become aware that Piaget prefers obscurity to clarity. Furthermore, I believe that most readers will realize that Piaget repeatedly leads one into logical impasses with respect to accepted theory - impasses that for whatever reason are never honestly analyzed or resolved. This is not surprising as he admits to "exercising a negative pressure" on his readers (Piaget, 1977, p. 145) - a negative pressure that causes the "pot of frustrations" to boil, but hopefully not to boil over into the corrections needed for understanding. The purpose of this book is to show that the pot should have boiled over long ago!

THE SPATIAL CONTAINER IS THE OPERATIONAL MIND

Probably the single most important statement about Space is found in Piaget's book on time.

> Space is not a simple 'container'. It is the totality of the relationships between the bodies we perceive or imagine, or rather the totality of the relationships We use to endow these bodies with a Structure. Space is, in fact, the Logic of the apparent world .... Because it is a Form of Logic, Space is above all a System of Concrete Operations ... As the Mind gradually learns to perform these operations ... the operations may become "formal" and it is at this level ... that Geometry becomes pure Logic (author's capitalization) (Piaget, 1969a, p. 1).

Space is not a simple or natural "container", it is a personal, metaphysical Container. "Space [is] a Container or Reference System which is independent of its content" (author's capitalization) (Piaget, Inhelder & Szeminska, 1960, p. 80), and its content includes scientists and their experiments - which have no affect whatever on the Container. The Container is the Coordinate Continuum with the capacity to make unlimited coordinations (author's capitalization) (ibid., p. 371); it is a Single Overall Spatial Framework (author's capitalization) (ibid., p. 120). The Container is the metaphysical Continuum of Spatial Monads, there is no room for doubt about this. Space is said to be a Form of Logic. Space is a metaphysical Form of Logic in the sense that "Logic" is one of its names. This Form of Logic is based on a private meaning, but Piaget is more than likely referring to the Spatial Form who behaves logically by performing operations on objects, so it probably should read, "Space is the Logical Form". Space, like the Form, is the System of Concrete Operations which may become formal and reach the level where Geometry becomes pure Logic. "Geometry" is a fancy name for the process of operational assimilation (author's capitalization) (Piaget & Inhelder, 1956, p. 449) (Piaget, 1978a, p. 163) (Piaget, 1974b, p. 130). *Perhaps the most important point made in this quote is the fact that Piaget equates Space with the Mind.* We see this identity in many other contexts, although usually not as clearly (author's italics and capitalization) (Beth & Piaget, 1966, pp. 215-16) Piaget & Inhelder, 1956, p. 416) (Piaget, 1977, p. 107) (Piaget, 1974b, pp. 142-3).

Also, Piaget boldly places lower-level "relationships" and upper-level "relationships" in the same sentence. His first use of the term, which he immediately withdraws, is quite deliberately incorrect, as he wishes to provide a contrast with his most unusual view. To wit, since *a true relation is an operation,* it is impossible for such relations to exist between things or between people and things. In his first book Piaget made this particular point.

"The connection is really between one ... judgment ... and another and not between one thing and another. This distinction, however subtle it may appear, is of the greatest importance [in] genetic Psychology (author's capitalization) (Piaget, 1926, p. 199).

"Judgment" is a synonym for an operation and an operation is always an action by the Subject on a person or object. There are two main kinds of "connections" with Piaget, the connections between the Absolute Subject and objects, which are operations (Piaget, 1977, p. 144) and the linking of the "Meanings" or "Classes" which result from these operations (Piaget, 1950, pp. 124-5) (Piaget, 1971c, pp. 154-5). The meaning of "connection" in this case is the latter.

He explicitly tells us that genuine relationships are always between the Self and things, *not the ego and things but the Ego and things.* "Wherever relations dependent upon the ego are concerned ... the child fails to grasp the logic of relations ... between himself and people ... [or] things" (Piaget, 1928, p. 197). True relations are not formed between the *physical ego* and things but "as soon as he brings *his Own Ego* as an element in these relations, the child attains to the reciprocity of relations .... The succession of [these] relations ... does present [the] Reasoning process" (author's italics and capitalization) (ibid., pp. 197-8). These two "egos" are separated by only 10 lines of print. The first ego cannot produce relations, but the child's Own immanent Ego is able to do so. This notion is affirmed in many ways. For instance, as "the data are no longer distorted by the experiencing self .... the Subject's own actions intervene in the elaboration of the relations" (author's capitalization) (Piaget & Inhelder, 1974, p. 114). The Subject is obviously the immanent Ego, as the human ego has been "disengaged". The intrusive self must be excluded by decentration if dialectical engagements are to proceed (Piaget, 1929, pp. 45-6). This is the basic problem between the Organism and the physical environment, and there can be no doubt about its central importance in Piaget's system. "The problem of the relations between the Organism and its environment ... is surely the major question ... with every solution to every question in every realm of life whatever depending on it" (author's capitalization) (Piaget, 1971a, p. 52). (The preceding sentence alone is enough to demonstrate an oracular dogmatism of the first magnitude.) Relations are not derived from physical objects or from "the individual psychological subject" (Beth & Piaget, 1966, p. 235).

The relations between the *Organism* and, the most significant part of the physical environment for Piaget, human *organisms,* is presented in a deliberately confusing way. "The basic obstacle to progress in Intellectual coordination is .... egocentrism .... This liberation [of Intellectual coordinations from egocentrism] is essential in relation to the 'I' and the 'We'" (Piaget's capitalization) (Piaget, 1973b, pp. 135-6). Piaget capitalizes the "I" and the "We" to underline the fact that both terms refer to the immanent Ego who wishes to be liberated from the detestable ego. This is the "most fundamental" problem of all - the relationship between homo faber and Homo Sapiens (author's capitalization) (Piaget, 1930, p. 195). The "I" refers to the immanent Subject or Ego in each individual, while the "We" refers to the collective immanent Sub-Units of Homo Sapiens or the Ego in the general population of people. *But Piaget is leading his quarry into a linguistic trap.* Three pages later we find this very calculated reversal of meaning.

The "de-centering" of the "I" or the "We" or of their symbols or of their territories is still hampered by more obstacles. Each time we liberate ourselves from this "I" or "We" in favor of a Collective Cause ... we become the victim of some new ... deviation (Piaget capitalized the "I" and "We") (author capitalized "Collective Cause") (ibid., p. 139).

Piaget again capitalizes the "I" and the "We", and springs the trap, as these terms no longer refer to the immanent Ego! They now refer to the lower-level, detestable human ego who is being decentered. The upper-level "I" and "We" have now become "Collective Cause". The "Collective" immanent Sub-Units within people are now being liberated from the physical "I" and "We" of the people themselves. Is it possible to see a "higher purpose" in such abusive treatment of the reader? Is this behavior anything more than senseless aggression? What possible justification can we find to absolve Piaget from all-out irrational assault? In my opinion there can be no "higher purpose" in any sense of the word!

And what is the purpose of "or of their symbols or of their territories" - other than to mystify? Homo faber, or the lower-level human organism, is thus a part of the *physical environment* from which Homo Sapiens, or the upper-level Absolute Organism, must be liberated. One must be wary, however, of another trap, the *Organized Environment* (author's italics and capitalization) (Piaget, 1952b, p. 10) who is determined to transform homo faber into Homo Sapiens! The source of all relations or operations is this Homogeneous Environment (author's capitalization) (Piaget & Inhelder, 1956, p. 376). We will not begin to understand Piaget until we get a handle on his motivation for such continuous and outrageous trickery.

Homo faber cannot produce relations or operations because operations cannot possibly be based on the objects themselves, since "abstractions from objects can give rise only to non-necessitous statements" (Piaget, 1971a, p. 14). Also "physical actions ... [are] irreducible to operations" (Piaget et al., 1977, p. 14), which, as noted previously, directly contradicts Wolf May's assertion that the child's "general acts of behavioral co-ordination become transformed into mental operations" (Piaget, 1972, p. 4) Mays states that the child's development of physical concepts such as time, speed, conservation, chance and causality are regarded as constructions from behavioral activities, and that Piaget starts from the facts of observable child behavior or overt activity in building up his concepts (ibid., p. 2). In his introduction to *Mathematical Epistemology and Psychology,* Mays, as translator, is even more specific: "Piaget uses the term 'operation' to refer to an action or system of bodily movements, which have become internalized in the form of thought activities" (Beth & Piaget, 1966, p. XVI). *In other words, Mays is basing operations on the object-person himself, which Piaget says is not possible.* David Elkind's assertion that Piaget's genetic Logic of operations is the "first successful attempt to construct a logical model of thought based upon experiment rather than armchair speculation" (Piaget, 1967, p. X) is also contradicted for the same reason. *The bottom line is that physical actions cannot be generalized into operations - only the Subject can produce operations* (author's italics and capitalization) (Piaget et al, 1977, p. 14).

THE SPATIAL CONTINUUM PRODUCES LOGICO-MATHEMATICAL OPERATIONS

Many followers of Piaget have twisted his statements about the operational aspects of Space, insisting that he is only speaking of the individual's development of spatial relations. They are incorrect, as *Space itself is operational.*

> When we come to the operational and deductive aspects of Space, it is ... striking to note the close parallelism that ... links the formation of Spatial with Logico-Arithmetical operations, even though the Spatial operations bear on the Continuum and on relationships of neighborhoods, while the Logico-Arithmetic ones group objects according to their qualitative resemblances and differences (author's capitalization) (Piaget, 1974b, p. 142).

In Piaget's system there is only one source of operations - the Absolute Subject. So what are we to make of this apparent differentiation between Spatial operations and Logico-Arithmetic operations? If "Space" and the "Logico-Arithmetic Structure" are synonyms of the Absolute Subject, why would Piaget say that the operations of Space are "parallel" or similar to the Logico-Arithmetic operations, but are nevertheless different? We realize that he must scramble signals regarding the relationships among the host of synonyms if he is to maintain his stated goal of keeping his followers ignorant of his system, but in this selection they can be unscrambled quite easily. We know that operations in both cases are produced by the same Body of Monads and for the same reason - the assimilation of physical reality and, simultaneously, the development of the Spatial Absolute. *Piaget feigns a differentiation of the supposedly different operations by taking different aspects of the same process to describe each operation, with the result that they only appear to be different.* By this simple procedure he scrambled signals sufficiently to force readers to make a time-consuming expenditure of energy to restore consistency to his own system. In the case of Logico-Arithmetic Operations, he actually ignores the operation itself and simply describes a preliminary step leading to the operation. The description of the Spatial operation is limited to monads operating on the outside of objects. The outside of objects is operated on by monads adjacent to or in the "neighborhood" of the objects. The Spatial Continuum is also inside of objects, but this aspect is left out of account. We must expand and reverse the phrase, "Spatial operations bear on the Continuum". It is true that Spatial operations have a relationship with the Continuum, but it is not sufficiently clear that it is the Continuum who produces Spatial operations. Piaget does not describe Logico-Mathematical operations at all, as the description is limited to the preliminary arrangement of opposite classes which will later engage in operations. Significant, honest, aboveboard statements by Piaget are quite rare.

There are two kinds of space, physical space and the Space that acts operationally by assimilating objects and people.

> Physical space is at first not differentiated from the Space of Action, but the latter is present from the outset, for it is not the properties of objects as such which determine Geometric Space but rather the assimilation of objects to the Schemata of the Subject's actions (author's capitalization) (Piaget, Inhelder & Szeminska, 1960, p. 208).

Geometrical Space, the Space of Action, the Schemata and the Subject were present from the beginning, in fact He had no beginning. Piaget's "Geometry" is a special metaphysical activity, as it is the Science of operational transformations. "Geometry, ... like other Sciences, [is] a Science of transformations, and however important the figurative aspect may be, it is nevertheless subordinate to operational considerations" (author's capitalization) (Piaget & Inhelder, 1971, p. 13). The "figurative aspect" is what we learn in school, but the important "operational aspect" is not possible for humans at all. *Geometry is merely another name for assimilation by operations.* "The Subject ... makes up His own Geometry by means of operations" (author's capitalization) (Piaget, 1974b, p. 41).

Space is the Subject who operates. We know that Space is the Subject or Mind because Space is Self-organized.

> It would be a complete mistake to imagine that human beings have some ... psychologically precocious knowledge of the Spatial Surround organized in a ... Three-Dimensional Reference Frame ... The reason is that ... perception covers only a very limited field, whereas a System of Reference presumes operational co-ordination (author's capitalization) (Piaget & Inhelder, 1956, p. 416).

In many other statements Piaget does, *on the contrary,* claim that children, even very young children, have "knowledge" of the various aspects of his doctrine of Space. The child is said to know very early, for instance, that there is a Universal Life (author's capitalization) (Piaget, 1929, pp. 261-2) who exists as a General Space (author's capitalization) (Piaget, 1973a, pp. 15-16). This Universal Life or General Space is held by the child to be a Continuous Entity made up of adjacent points (author's capitalization) (Piaget & Inhelder, 1956, pp. 147-8). Children are said to have intuitions of Space in the form of a Continuum containing the logical properties (author's capitalization) (Beth & Piaget, 1966, p. 255). This Universal Spatial Life, for the young child, teems with elements of the Subject (author's capitalization) (Piaget, 1930, p. 267). This Continuum is conscious (author's capitalization) (Piaget, 1929, p. 262). The child also believes that there is a fundamental final cause and that it is the Continuum who will bring the implied goal about (author's capitalization) (ibid., p. 224). Furthermore, the notion of a final cause implies a Creator who fashioned everything for a determined end (author's capitalization) (ibid., p. 224). The child "spontaneously" knows about atomism (Piaget & Inhelder, 1974, pp. VIII; 16; 72) (Piaget, 1950, p. 110) (Piaget, 1967, p. 43) (Piaget, 1929, p. 428) (Inhelder & Chipman, 1976, pp. 15-16), and the fact that the monads make up a Permanent Object-Person (author's capitalization) (Piaget, 1954, pp. 299; 312-13). The child also conceives of this atomism as the producer of material elements and substances of all kinds by means of condensation and rarefaction (Piaget, 1929, pp. 385; 428), and this schema of condensation and rarefaction or compression and decompression implies the idea of corpuscles or monads constituting, according to Piaget's interpretation of children's statements, a Spatial Composition (author's capitalization) (Piaget & Inhelder, 1974, pp. 144-5). The child is said to consider Space itself to be active and operational (author's capitalization) (Piaget & Inhelder, 1956, p. VII). The "intuition" of Space by the child includes "from the very beginning" an action performed on objects which assimilates the objects to Space itself (author's capitalization) (ibid., p. 449). We are definitely not talking about the space that is investigated scientifically here, as the Space that acts is not physical space (author's capitalization) (Piaget, Inhelder & Szeminska, 1960, p. 208). The infant is said to envisage Space as a function of the Self and that this Space or Self is independent of him (author's capitalization) (Piaget, 1952b, p. 212). This Self is the "I" who is bound up with the whole universe (author's capitalization) (Piaget, 1930, p. 128). The disconcerting point is that there is an unbridgeable chasm between Piaget's claim that we do not have knowledge of Personal Space and his equally insistent claim that children have a great deal of such knowledge. Regardless of how much or how little the child knows about metaphysical Space, Piaget tells us a great deal about his own view in the first sentence. That is, people do not realize that they are surrounded by the organized Spatial Framework because they depend upon perception, while he depends upon the System of Reference.

When Piaget compares perception with his System of Reference, he is comparing the physical with the metaphysical. Perception covers only a very limited field, but he leaves it to his reader to make the appropriate opposite inference regrading his System. Einstein said that space without a field does not exist (Piaget, 1974b, p. 167), meaning that a gravitational field was present everywhere. Piaget has said the same regarding Spatial Fields, but what does he mean by "Field"? *His Field is the Living Organism who is capable of multiple interactions* (author's italics and capitalization) (Piaget, 1971a, p. 34) *because He fills all of Space*. Other names for the Field are Lattice, Group Structure and Thought. All of these synonyms refer to a Psychological Field for Transformations (author's capitalization) (Piaget, 1953, p. 40).

Redundantly, but correctly, we must emphasize the fact that this Psychological Field is the Subject Himself who acts by means of His own Logico-Mathematical Activity Field (author's capitalization) (Beth & Piaget, 1966, p. 151). This is the Epistemological Subject who affects the measurement of meter rods and how fast clocks run when they are placed in His Field and move at various speeds (author's capitalization) (Piaget, 1971c, p. 70). Piaget seizes an opportunity to give his Absolute Subject credit for being the Actor behind Einstein's theory that clocks and meter rods are affected by the speed at which they move through space. He also gives his Spatial Subject credit for the fact that we tend to judge size more or less accurately regardless of the distance between the subject and the object (author's capitalization) (Piaget, 1969b, p. 207).

PHYSICAL MOVEMENT AND METAPHYSICAL MOVEMENT

The metaphysical nature of the Spatial Framework is demonstrated by a peculiar pair of attributes. "The Framework is *stationary and coordinated*" (author's italics and capitalization) (Piaget, Inhelder & Szeminska, 1960, p. 65). How could a system be both stationary and coordinated? This is possible only because the monads move at "absolute" or "no" speed. Since they move at absolute speed, no time is spent in the coordinating movements they must make! Piaget no doubt presents this logical quandary for its shock value, but he deliberately errs with regard to his own system when he claims that the "Framework is stationary", as movements that do not take time are still movements (author's capitalization) (Piaget, 1974b, pp. 152-3) (Piaget

& Inhelder, 1956, p. 42). Piaget specifically distinguishes physical movements from movements by the Subject.

> No ... placement exists without a movement ... of the Subject ... and no displacement exists without an ordered System of Reference .... *This System ... is distinct from ... objects [and forms] a Geometrical Space ... as opposed to the system of physical movements* .... After conceiving displacement simply as an empirical ... change of place, the child will come to define it in relation to the positions alone and no longer to the ... objects (author's italics and capitalization) (Piaget, 1970a, pp. 290-1).

Both placements and displacements depend upon metaphysical movements of the Subject, but Piaget throws a veil over this facet of his theory by the use of synonyms. We are told that the *Subject* is responsible for placements, but that a *System of Reference* which does not consist of objects is responsible for displacements. Admittedly, this is a rather thin veil, but it could easily cause a hurried reader to pass over the meaning. Piaget uses another synonym, "Geometric Space", in adding the fact that movements of the Subject or System of Reference are not physical movements. He then pretends that the child eventually progresses from the physical to the very abstruse metaphysical level when he comes to define displacement in terms of the positions alone. These positions or sites make up the System of Reference, and the correct name for them is "monads". Displacement is accomplished by the monads - both the child and Piaget agree that this is indeed the truth! This would be thigh-slapping comedy if it were not for the fact that such buffoonery has very likely already caused catastrophic derailments of important academic theories and research over the past three generations. At the very least billions of dollars have been wasted in terms of professor's time, advanced degree programs, public school programs, research grants etc.

There are "two distinct transmissions or conveyors of movement [and] one of these is by nature unobservable" (Piaget, 1976a, p. 71). The child "now sees a reason behind what would otherwise remain simple connections involving a physical law" (ibid., p. 71). One conveyor of movement is physical, and the other is metaphysical; the latter is obviously the one that is "naturally" unobservable. Piaget, true to form, makes the child agree with him that mere physical laws are not valid explanations for movement. The "reason" for all kinds of movement is the unobservable metaphysical source of movement (Piaget, 1973d, pp. 25-6) (Piaget, 1977, p. 166) (Piaget, 1971c, pp. 184-5) (Piaget, 1970b, pp. 14; 42) (Piaget, 1978a, p. 138).

FLAVELL'S REJECTION OF PIAGET'S METAPHYSICAL PSYCHOLOGY

Flavell could not conceive of a living psychological Lattice-Group or Logico-Mathematical Structure, so he claimed that these Structures could not originate in a psychological being.

> An understanding of Piaget's conception of cognition in the middle-childhood years and adolescence involves coming to grips with abstract structures whose origin is definitely nonpsychical: the ... *groups and lattices* to which we have alluded .... What is the liaison between logico-mathematical and intellectual structures? .... Piaget ... believes that certain logico-mathematical structures make very good models which the living

operational systems in the subject closely approximate (Flavell's italics) (Flavell, 1963, pp. 168-9).

This excerpt is an excellent example of how Piaget's disguises can derail individual investigators and, by extension, major segments of the academic process. Unfortunately, Flavell was not able to penetrate three of Piaget's major disguises of the Absolute Subject. The terms "Group", "Lattice" and "Logico-Mathematical Structure" have been employed hundreds of times to describe a Conscious, Living Being, but Flavell doggedly insists that these structures are definitely nonpsychological. Why? He realizes that these terms, as used by Piaget, do not refer to human beings, but he resists evidence that they do describe a Psychological Being who is intelligent (Piaget, 1970b, p. 138) (Piaget, 1969b, p. 356) (Piaget, 1971b, pp. 114-15) (Piaget, 1971a, pp. 74; 211-12; 267), conscious (ibid., p. 49) (Piaget, 1954, p. 118) (Piaget, 1969b, p. XXIII) (Piaget, 1971b, pp. 114-15), alive (Piaget, 1970b, p. 142) (Piaget, 1972, p. 52), active (Piaget, 1973a, pp. 56; 74-5) (Piaget, 1952b, p. 12), operational (Piaget, 1970d, p. 44) (Piaget, 1971a, pp. 210-11) (Inhelder & Piaget, 1958, p. 330) (Piaget, 1971b, p. 115), experiencing (ibid., pp. 70-1) (Beth & Piaget, 1966, pp. 233-5) (Piaget, 1973c, p. 45) (Piaget, 1972, p. 66), Self-developing (ibid., p. 24) (Piaget, 1977, pp.171-3) (Beth & Piaget, 1966, p. 282) and able to decenter the lower level subject (Piaget, 1971a, pp. 336-7) (Piaget, 1972, p. 83) (Piaget, 1973c, p. 56). Apparently he does not wish to concede that Piaget is concerned exclusively with a non-human Being who is the source of everything. This interpretation perhaps more than any other single factor, led eventually to many deeply-rooted misconceptions about Piaget's theory. This is because Flavell undoubtedly has been the most influential interpreter of Piaget's works. Just about everyone among my acquaintances who claim to know something about Piaget eventually admit that they have not read any of Piaget's books, but that they have read Flavell's classic work on Piaget.

Piaget tells us explicitly, perhaps in consciously responding to Flavell's statement, that Group Structures are "natural Psychological Totalities" who, in contrast to mathematical groups, are "aware" (author's capitalization) (Piaget, 1971b, pp. 114-15). Groups are "psychologically equilibrated Systems of Intellectual Operations (author's capitalization) (ibid., pp. 114-15). Groups, therefore, make up the Mind, and the Mind that produces operations, an impossibility for humans, is the "proper domain of Psychology" (author's capitalization) (Piaget, 1967, p. 114). Please note that, for Piaget, the proper domain of Psychology is not human psychology! Although Piaget deliberately confuses the issue regarding Living, Conscious "Group Structures" by inappropriately inserting lower-level "mathematical groups", he quite clearly communicates his view that Group Structures are Psychological Entities, not "nonpsychological" as Flavell declared. In fairness it should be mentioned that these two statements by Piaget, and many others which follow, were written after Flavell wrote his well-known book in 1963. Nevertheless, there was an abundance of evidence that he for some reason pushed aside, for example in *The Origins of Intelligence in Children* (1952b), a source which Flavell used extensively. Also much earlier, Piaget had said, "psychologically, the Group is the expression ... [of] the fundamental phenomena of intellectual assimilation" (author's capitalization) (Piaget, 1954, pp. 111-12), and that psychological assimilation entails an organization of Groups (author's capitalization) (ibid., p. 235). He goes on to say that "the logical definition of the Group is inexhaustible and involves the most essential processes of Thought" (author's capitalization) (ibid., p. 115). The Total Group is the Spatial Entity who is the only true Thinker in the universe, and Thinking for Piaget is primarily assimilation. Furthermore, the basic fact of Psychic Life is the "secret Mechanism of Biological assimilation" (author's capitalization) (Piaget, 1952b, p. 42). The physical mechanism of assimilation is no secret; Piaget is speaking of the metaphysical Mechanism, or Forms of Space (author's capitalization) (Piaget, 1977, p. 107). Not only do the monads of the Spatial Form have a Biology, but we also know, on Piaget's word, that they have a Physiology (author's capitalization) (Piaget, 1954, p. 109). Assimilation by Spatial Physiology is the "secret" Mechanism and process. Since the Group is responsible for Thought or assimilation, which is the basic fact of Psychic Life, and is Biological in nature, He necessarily is the Absolute Psychological Entity. The fact that Groups are conscious (author's capitalization) (Piaget, 1954, p. 118) adds weight to this conclusion.

The Group "Thinks" and assimilates by means of operations, and Piaget adds that the Lattice Structure, which is the Combinatorial System, is also the source of operations (author's capitalization) (Inhelder & Piaget, 1958, p. 123). He conceives of the functioning of Intelligence as operations by Groups, Networks or Lattices, and "other important Logico-Mathematical Structures" (author's capitalization) (Piaget, 1971b, p. 80). Piaget, using some different terms, also approaches thinking and psychology in a different way. The Lattice and the Group make up the Integrated Structure or the Organization of Operational Schemata. *These Schemata are integrated but not by the subject* (author's italics and capitalization) (Inhelder & Piaget, 1958, p. 329). *So who integrates the Schemata?* Piaget drags out the answer for more that a page and finally "decides" that the operations of the Schemata "do not occur at random but are directed toward filling in the Totality" (author's capitalization) (ibid., p. 331), who is the Subject! The subject is not able to integrate the Schemata, but the Subject can do the job! And the job involves the Self-utilization of the various Organizations of Monads, called Schemata, to "fill in" or fully develop the Totality or Subject. To put it precisely, the Lattice-Group is not psychological, but it is Psychological. The Group is a Spatial concept (author's capitalization) (Piaget, 1952b, p. 2), and the Spatial-Group, or Absolute Subject, is undergoing Psychological Self-development.

Before we leave the Lattice-Group, one of the many names for the Body of Monads, we must note again the Group of permanent objects which make up Someone Else's Person (what an extraordinary circumlocution!) or Substantial Object (author's capitalization) (Piaget, 1954, p. 299), who obviously is a Psychological Entity. This Group of permanent objects are the monads of which the Substantial Object or Person is composed. This Person of Substance is the Producer of operations (author's capitalization) (Piaget, 1974b, pp. 2-3), which is a Psychological process. To say the same thing in a very different way, the Permanent System of fixed sites or monads is the Producer of Operations (author's capitalization) (Piaget, Inhelder & Szeminska, 1960, p. 115). With this we can safely conclude that the Operational Mechanism, which consists of Groups of organized monads, both inside and outside of people, has a Psychological existence (author's capitalization) (Piaget, 1953, p. 24).

The Lattice-Group is a living psychological Being or Person, but Flavell's question of the relationship between logico-mathematical structures and intellectual structures remains to be examined. When Piaget says that the Group is operational, he is also saying that Space is operational (author's capitalization) (Piaget & Inhelder, 1956, p. 449) (Piaget, 1971b, p. 13) (Piaget, 1974b, p. 142). In a rather foolish statement, Piaget explains, if we patiently follow his evasive twists and turns, that Spatial construction is based on operations which construct Logico-Mathematical Structures (author's capitalization) (Piaget, 1977, pp. 115-16). More clearly, Spatial Operations are Logico-Mathematical operations (author's capitalization) (Piaget, 1972, p. 45), so this is a matter of Self-construction. Piaget also describes them as being isomorphic by which, in this case, he means identical (ibid., pp. 39-40). Logico-Mathematical operations are conscious (author's capitalization) (Piaget, 1971a, p. 33), and no assimilation is possible outside of the Logico-Mathematical Framework (author's capitalization) (ibid., p. 65). Since both the Group and the Logico-Mathematical Framework are said to the source of assimilation, we see a convergence to a singularity that cannot be dismissed. The Logico-Mathematical Structure is not a lifeless, abstract model which living operational systems may closely approximate, as it can only exist as a Living System (author's capitalization) (Piaget, 1970b, p. 142). It is indeed the Subject Himself.

It is true that Logico-Mathematical Structures are extra-biological (author's capitalization) (Piaget, 1971a, p. 275), that is, they are not based on physical biology, but they are in fact the Living Organism (author's capitalization) (Piaget, 1972, p. 91). Logico-Mathematical Mechanisms are equivalent to Biological Mechanisms that cannot be based on hereditary transmissions (author's capitalization) (Piaget, 1972, p. 52). Piaget is speaking of the Living Subject who has a metaphysical Biology. The Psychological Subject dissociates Himself from the human subject that He is investigating as an object (author's capitalization) (Piaget, 1974a, p. 30). Logico-Mathematical experience disengages the individual psychological subject (author's capitalization) (Beth & Piaget, 1966, p. 235). Therefore Operational Structures do not depend upon psychological experience (author's capitalization) (ibid., p. 234), and operations are freed from psychology (Piaget, 1972, p. 46). This is what Piaget means when he says that operations are autonomous (Inhelder & Piaget, 1964, pp. 290-1) (Piaget & Inhelder, 1971, pp. 7, 356) (Beth & Piaget, 1966 p. 244). Operations do not depend upon the physical subject with his "physical" psychology. Within the Logico-Mathematical System "the regulations ... modify the Forms by using its own Forms" (author's capitalization) (Piaget, 1977, p. 173). This is an artificially complicated case of Self-development as the Logico-Mathematical System is also the Form. Piaget prefaced this statement with "Logico-Mathematical Structures are the result of the Subject's activities" (author's capitalization) (ibid., p. 173). Taken together the two statements do not make much sense unless we realize that Piaget is playing games with his synonyms. The meaning of the latter statement is identical to the meaning of the previous statement, as Logico-Mathematical Structures are developed by the Subject's activities because the Subject is the Logico-Mathematical Structure. "Subject" equals "Logico-Mathematical Structure" equals "Form", so Piaget is simply exercising his ability to manipulate verbal entities with identical meanings - and torment his reader by not informing him properly regarding the meanings of the terms in question. Since we are speaking of Self-regulation or Self-construction, the Living Organism or Logico-Mathematical Structure represents an identity. The Operational Mechanism has a Psychological existence because it is the Structured Whole or Biological Organization, and Mental Life starts with this Structure (author's capitalization) (Piaget, 1953, pp. 24-5). Seven pages later we discover that this Structure is the Lattice-Group who is the Set of All Sub-Sets (author's capitalization) (ibid., p. 32). Yes, we must start with this Structure because the Logico-Mathematical Structure is none other than Hegel's Structure who is composed of "spiritual" atoms or monads (author's capitalization) (Piaget, 1971a, pp. 327-8).

The Lattice-Group or Logico-Mathematical Structure is thus seen to be the Fundamental Psychological Reality in Piaget's System, and for Flavell to assign these terms the lowly role of "nonpsychological" abstractions, analogies or models has undoubtedly had long-term negative repercussions. Assuming that we have established the Living, Psychological and Personal existence of Logico-Mathematical Structures, how should we view Logico-Algebraic (Piaget, 1971a, pp. 326-7) (Piaget, 1974b, p. 9), Logico-Arithmetic (Piaget & Inhelder, 1974, p. 267) (Bringuier, 1980, p. 58), and Logico-Geometric (Piaget, 1974b, p. 44) Structures and operations? Does anyone believe that Piaget really differentiates these terms capitalized by the author? Hopefully not, because they mean exactly the same thing. First, as we have already seen, "logic" usually refers to the operations (Piaget, 1953, p. 12) (Inhelder & Piaget, 1958, p. 342) (Piaget, 1971a, pp. 6-7) (Beth & Piaget, 1966, p. 255) but so does "algebra" (Piaget, 1971c, p. 50) (Inhelder & Piaget, 1958, p. 307) (Piaget, 1973c, p. 38), "mathematics" (Piaget, 1971a, pp. 6-7) (Piaget, 1973b, p. 103), "arithmetic" (Piaget & Inhelder, 1971, pp. 346-7) (Beth & Piaget, 1966, p. 255) and "geometry" (Piaget & Inhelder, 1971, pp. 335-6) (Piaget, 1974b, p. 130) (Beth & Piaget, 1966, p. 255). Both logic and mathematics usually refer to the operational activity of the Absolute, but both terms are sometimes used to mean the Entity Himself. Piaget speaks of the Logical Mathematical Body who must intervene if the Idea (that is, the Idea of a perfectly developed Absolute) is to be elaborated (author's capitalization) (Piaget, 1973a, p. 98), and he refers to Mathematical Entities who may be external to the subject, but who nevertheless regulate Intellectual operations with a superhuman "all-embracing prevision" (Piaget 1971a, pp. 211-12). Following Hegel (Edwards, 1967, Vol. 3, p. 444), Piaget has a low regard for formal logic as taught in all universities - contrary to the reading of his followers. He also follows Hegel in tying the concept of logic to the Absolute Subject or His activity. Some examples of Piaget's use of "Logic" as a synonym for the Absolute Subject are (author's capitalization) (Piaget, 1928, p. 171) (Piaget, 1970c, p. 19) (Piaget, 1973d, p. 28) (Piaget, 1973c, p. 32). Some additional examples of his use of "Mathematics" in the same way may be found on the following pages (author's capitalization) (ibid., p. 55) (Piaget, 1971a, pp. 348; 358) (Beth & Piaget, 1966, pp. 228-9).

We have a Space who is intrinsically operational and who is also responsible for Spatial, that is, operational, properties within objects and people.

THE PERMANENT IMMANENT SPACE

There exists from the outset an Operational Space and Spatial properties inherent in objects ... and the latter can only be reached through the intermediary of the former ... The Spatial operations we [are] talking about ... are ... operations "applied to the object ... They are used by the Subject Himself in His readings of the experiment, as instruments of ... assimilation for the purpose of His own findings but without reference to the causality of objects (author's capitalization) Piaget, 1974b, p. 143).

The Spatial properties inherent in all objects and people are the properties of Operational Space who has always existed. Piaget incorrectly states that these properties have been in objects from the outset, because objects, unlike Space, have not always existed; Space had to create objects before He could be immanent in them. Piaget is describing aspects of the "true experiment" where Spatial operations are applied to objects as instruments of assimilation. The same monads of Space who assimilate objects are able to read and measure the results of operations and group the objects in appropriate classes in preparation for future operations.

The Subject or Space has His own reasons for operating on objects which are unaffected in any way by what objects can do. The causal capacities of objects and the wishes of people are irrelevant to the purposes and actions of Space.

One of the first evident differences between the Operational Space of the Subject and the physical space of objects is that physical space is spatio-temporal, while *the Spatial operations of the Subject are extra-temporal.* Thus an operational displacement is only [an instantaneous] change in position ... while a real or physical movement takes time, and therefore includes speed (author's italics and capitalization) (ibid., p. 144).

We could ask Piaget how he knows that Spatial operations are extra-temporal, but we can be sure he would shy away from an answer. Obviously he is not considering people as the producers of such operations, and just as obviously his followers have missed the boat when they reduce his theory to judgments about physical reality. Operational Space is quite different from the space studied by physicists. When Space operates, the displacement of physical aspects by the monads is accomplished so "fast" that no time elapses. Physical movements of every kind, of course, do take time, so Piaget is talking about metaphysical movements not physical movements. Operational Space is the metaphysical Subject who always moves with "absolute speed" unless He is moving physical objects. *No matter how many excuses we may make for Piaget, it is impossible to consider operational displacements within the context of physical reality or science.*

Spatial operations ... permit the Subject to construct Forms [within the subject] and to transform them according to entirely ... Structural laws, indicating the necessary roles[sic] of reflexive abstractions ... The objects themselves have figurative forms and a Spatial organization, which are[sic] linked to their[sic] dynamics in a way analogous to that of the Geometric constructions [that are] dependent on the actions of the Subject (author's capitalization) (Piaget, 1974b, pp. 129-30).

In the first sentence, Piaget cleverly uses *eight sets of synonyms, plus the two subjects,* to camouflage one of his rather simple doctrines and overwhelm his reader! He then employs a different set of verbal entities to express the same doctrine in the second sentence. In typical fashion he expresses the doctrine so evasively that understanding requires considerable effort. Spatial operations or reflexive abstractions of the Subject are said to construct and transform Spatial Forms within the subject - who is only implied in the first sentence before being pluralized as "the objects" in the second sentence. The eight sets of synonyms are: Subject and Space, Subject and Forms, Subject and Structures, Space and Forms, Space and Structures, Forms and Structures, operations and reflexive abstractions and construct and transform. The metaphysical Subject and the implied physical subject are also forced into the same sentence. "Construct" and "transform" do not appear to be identical in meaning until we realize that in this context they both simply mean "development of the immanent System of Monads". As if this is not enough to cause mental vertigo, Piaget adds complexity by assigning multiple roles, by means of the plural, to the reflexive abstractions when only one role is otherwise indicated - i. e., assimilation of the object-subject. *Although we understand why Piaget could not afford to openly express his simple doctrine that the immanent Subject within all human beings develops Himself by operating on these beings, we are obligated to point out the nature of his deceptions and the problems they cause.*

The second sentence begins by explicit recognition of the object-subject who has a figurative or physical form. By introducing "physical form" immediately after utilizing "Spiritual Form", Piaget makes the correct interpretation of "Form" in the first sentence more difficult. The organization of object-subjects, with their physical forms, is based on a Spatial dynamic orchestrated by the monads. This metaphysical dynamic involves a Geometric construction by the immanent Subject. Piaget tells us a few pages later that "spatio-temporal powers", or people, are "assimilated" or "geometrized" (ibid., pp. 152-3), making clear the meaning, in this instance, of "Geometric construction"; namely, it is the Self-development of the immanent Subject by means of assimilating the physical subject in whom He resides. In the two sentences "actions" is equal to "operations" is equal to "reflexive abstractions" is equal to "geometric constructions". To top off the calculated difficulties of this short excerpt, Piaget deliberately misrepresents his own theory and probably perpetrates his most flagrant deception by using the plurals, "are" and "their" to suggest that the figurative or physical forms make up the dynamics of the object-subject rather than the singular Spatial Body of Monads. Finally, when one considers the many negative implications the quote signifies, how should we view its author? Has any "great man" in history devoted his entire professional career to such deceitful and anarchic schemes? Perhaps he had a score to settle with a society that rejected his view of reality! Is he a "great man" or is he rather an unwholesome buffoon with a high IQ?

The following selection is another approach to the operations of Space within people. He appears to begin with a description of the normal, lower-level development of spatial relations, and then suddenly switches to the possibility of metaphysical Space operating on children.

> Children ... use Natural Horizontal and Vertical References in order to construct Comprehensive Systems of Spatial Relations which include both the dimensions and positions of natural and artificial objects and the spaces between them which may be empty. We may well ask whether these Qualitative Reference Systems arise because measurements are being coordinated in terms of two- and three-dimensional frameworks

or whether it is the other way about (author's italics and capitalization) (Piaget, Inhelder & Szeminska, 1960, p. 404).

The first sentence ostensibly describes physical spatial relations as normally understood, but in this context there is something very special about "Natural Horizontal and Vertical References". It is these "References" which account for the "Comprehensive System of Spatial Relations". We discover in the second sentence that they make up the Qualitative Reference System who "coordinates" the "measurement" of children, and thus are metaphysical. *While the activity of the Horizontal and Vertical Lattice Work of Monads appears to be portrayed in the first sentence in terms of "guidance" in physical learning, this same metaphysical System is considered in the second sentence to be measuring the child for the purpose of assimilation.* Although we are told hundreds of times that "we" or the "children" use the metaphysical System, we must be aware that it is the other way around. There is one possible exception to this rule, however, and that is Piaget's concept of magic. It appears, as we shall see in chapter five, that "exceptional" devotees, such as Piaget, may cause the metaphysical System to act on their behalf under certain conditions.

This Lattice Framework is the Structure with which Space endows all objects and people (author's capitalization) (Piaget, 1969a, p. 1). This immanent Framework is the reason why infants of 8 to 9 months are said to only envisage Space as a function of the Self (author's capitalization) (Piaget, 1952b, p. 212), meaning that Space is the Self who functions. Empirical evidence for this remarkable claim is not necessary as Piaget is able to look directly into the infant's Mind - his immanent Mind. *He knows what is in the infant's Mind because he, Piaget, has the same Mind within himself. This marvelous doctrine gives him the right to speak for everybody! He simply listens to his Own True Self and forthwith he knows the absolute truth about everyone's "Innermost" Thoughts.* As is nearly always the case, babies support Piaget's position, including aspects where understanding is difficult for adults.

The Lattice Framework also is at work in our great natural scientists. Although Piaget has no confidence whatever in knowledge accumulated by traditional methods, his position requires that the Spatial Subject must ultimately account for everything.

We may ask why the concept of Spatial Metrics has undergone such fundamental transformations from Aristotle to Copernicus and Newton, and again from Newton to Einstein. In short, the growth of knowledge is not a matter of mere accumulation .... *Bit by bit They decenter relations which they have learnt in the course of their own actions, and transform them in such a way that they can be combined with other relations ... without the intermediary of the self, so that their own actions are included as mere elements within an Independent System* (author's italics and capitalization) (Piaget, Inhelder & Szeminska, 1960, p. 24).

The immanent Subject is seen to have a hand in natural science, but the "fundamental transformation in Spatial Metrics" is a sure indication that the Spatial Entity is active in His own interest behind the scenes. He will gradually decenter what the great scientists learn and transform their scientific knowledge, without their help, into something closer to His desire. *The "fundamental transformations" that have occurred from Aristotle to Einstein are the result of transformations without the intermediary of the lower-level self.* What we have is transformation by the superhuman Spatial Metrics of the Lattice Work of Monads within all objects and people. These special "Metrics" are responsible for the dynamics of planets and stars as well as their eventual assimilation. They are responsible for all phenomena, but they are particularly concerned, according to Piaget, with the metaphysical dynamics of people, although they also account for his physical dynamics. Piaget is very circumspect about making this claim regarding metaphysical Spatial Metrics as he interposes about three lines of misleading physical information indicated by the four periods. Then he returns to the problem of Metric transformations in natural science with an amazing, almost unthinkable, sentence. *They ("Spatial Metrics" or immanent Person composed of monads) decenter (assimilate) relations (findings of natural science) which they (human scientists) have learned (based on natural science) by their own actions (very ambiguous reference to actions of human scientists) and transform them (results of natural science) without the intermediary of the self (singular reference to plural scientists).* Please note that the first "They" must refer, not to the scientists, but to the immanent Entity in the various scientists because only He can "decenter". Decentering is accomplished only by assimilation, and He is the sole Person capable of this. *This is confirmed as the decentered relations are indeed transformed independently of the self.* Sentence structure alone demonstrates that "They" could not refer to the scientists because the decentering and transforming is accomplished by "They" but not by the "self". *This behavior is beyond bizarre, but how should we describe and evaluate it? In any case, it begs for competent clinical analysis.* So the first "They" is really the Independent System, composed of monads, who decenters and transforms. *The bottom line is that what Einstein and the other scientists learn from their "actions" or experiments is actually overruled by the Independent System who decenters and transforms their results as He wishes. It must be overruled because it is physical or copy knowledge.* It is interesting that the Absolute Subject, the Great Measurer (Piaget, 1928, p. 196), not only transforms the scientist, but He also transforms the knowledge that the scientist accumulates. Most significant of all, however, Piaget appears to have demonstrated once again how vulnerable we all are to the big lie!

Piaget's Multi-Named Metaphysical Absolute

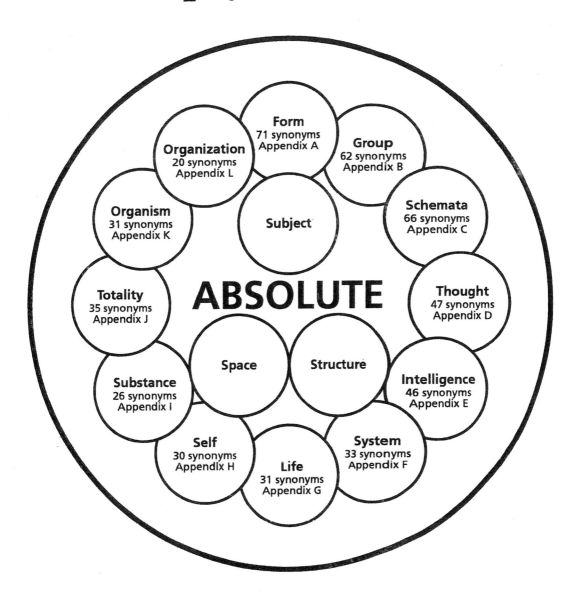

Chapter 5

ACTIVITIES OF THE ABSOLUTE

METAPHYSICAL DEVELOPMENT

Piaget's concept of development does not depend upon chance as it is guided by a "direct and unwavering teleonomy" (Piaget, 1978b, pp. 98-9).

> *Knowledge* is always in a state of development and consists in proceeding from one state to a more complete and efficient one ... This becoming does not unfold itself as a matter of chance, but forms a development .... There is a risk of endless regressions (that is, an appeal to Biology). Since the problem is that of *process law, and since the final stages [sic]* (that is, really final) are as important ... as the first known [stage]. The section of development considered can offer at least partial solutions, but only if [there is] a collaboration of historico-critical and psychogenetical analysis (author's italics and capitalization) (Piaget, 1971b, pp. 6-7).

If the development of Knowledge is progressively more complete and efficient *because* it does not unfold as a matter of chance, we are not talking about human knowledge. The development of human knowledge is not a fully determined process. But what does he mean by a risk of endless regressions which amounts to an appeal to Biology? The "endless regressions" refer to the operations that have occurred since the eternal Biological Being created matter and began His assimilative operations, which means that the regressions are not really endless, as they began at the point in time when He created the universe. "Biology" exists outside of time, but the "regressions" occurred in time. *The appeal to Biology involves His "process law" which is the "law" of operational assimilation.* The "really final" stage (If it is "really" final it must be singular, not plural as he has it.) represents the equilibrium that comes with complete assimilation and concomitantly the perfect development of "Biology". This final stage is as important as the "first known stage" which is the stage of the Spatial Continuum of Monads existing alone before there was a physical reality. The "solution" to the final stage must involve a collaboration with historico-critical and psychogenetical analysis. Analysis of the historico-critical process is simply viewing psychogenetic activity over long periods of time, as they both refer to the operational *process law. For Piaget both "Knowledge" and "development" refer exclusively to the progressive improvement of the Body of Monads alias Absolute Subject alias Biology.*

In the following passage, regulations organize or develop an unstated Entity - and chance is not a factor.

> Regulations ... stabilize themselves ... because an *Organization* can be developed ... If we were dealing with chance either the groping would never end or [the regulations] would finish in compromises, whereas [the regulations] are increasingly directed. In other words, each whole Set of Regulations is merely a System of Transformations .... It is no metaphor to speak of Regulations as a System (author's italics and capitalization) (Piaget, 1977, pp. 174-5).

Again, *the work of the regulations or operations is not a matter of chance,* making it a superhuman teleonomy. If chance were a factor the "groping" would continue indefinitely and the Regulator, who is conspicuous by His virtual absence in this quote, although there are three non-apparent synonyms, would have to compromise. However, the task of Self-development which the Regulator imposed on Himself, is a fully determined task (author's capitalization) (Piaget, 1967, p. 144), so no compromise is theoretically admissible. Rather than mention the Actor in the System that Transforms, Piaget absurdly insists that His set of operational acts or regulations is the the System itself. This is a familiar mind-bending pattern, but he recognizes in another context that, "if regulation is to occur, a Regulator must intervene, and we must discover its nature" (author's capitalization) (Piaget, 1977, p. 19). The set of regulations can only be called a system in the sense that a logical plan can be called a system, and just as we recognize that a plan must have a planner, we recognize that the regulations, at least in Piaget's theoretical framework, must have a Regulator. In other words, the "set of regulations" is not a Self-directed System per se, as Piaget suggests, but is the result of a systematic direction by the Regulating Body of Monads - who is the Self.

The fully determined set of regulations occur for one reason - to assure the complete development of the Ideal Totality.

> Organization ... is the internal aspect of the functioning *Schemata* to which assimilation tends to reduce the external environment .... Actually each Schema ... consists in a "Totality" independently of which no assimilation would be possible and which in turn rests upon a number of interdependent elements. Furthermore, to the extent that these Totalities are not entirely realized but are in [the] process of elaboration, they involve a differentiation ... between "values" subordinated to the formation of the Whole. This Whole not complete for an "Ideal" Totality (author's italics and capitalization) (Piaget, 1952b, p. 179).

Organization is the internal aspect of the *Schemata* who is the *Totality* who is the *Whole* who, when completely developed, will be the *Ideal Totality.* Preposterously, Piaget moves from one of the five synonyms to another with no discernible purpose, giving no clue to the reader that their meaning is identical, and with no effort to convey significant information. What little information is conveyed is so concealed by vagueness and disordered syntax that the average reader would probably pass over it with little more than mystification as a reward. One of the two bits of information conveyed is that assimilation would not be possible without a "number of interdependent elements". How many would realize that these "elements" are monads? The other bit of information is that all values are subordinated to the completion of the Ideal Totality, but the last eight inscrutable words of the quote would very likely make the reader's eyes glaze over. This wonder of obfuscating syntax, "this Whole not complete for an Ideal Totality", is incoherent gibberish. A catalog of such premeditated perversions of the communication process, and the translators make it clear that it is worse in the original French, would fill a large book with nothing more cogent than barely intelligible linguistic inanities conceived by a man who felt compelled to express his metaphysical convictions, but was forced by circumstances *of his own making* to hide these convictions within a tangle of antisocial, incongruous and enigmatic expressions.

What could be the meaning of "Organization is the internal aspect of the Schemata"? If one has read several of his books where "centripetal" or "implicatory" action is compared with "centrifugal" or "explicatory" action, the meaning of "internal" could be discerned, but in this book there is very little basis for understanding its meaning in the context above. The subject is touched upon on page 172, but nowhere does it appear to be spelled out clearly. In this context, "internal" refers to the centripetal turning of the operational process toward the development of the metaphysical Self. But to have one synonym of the Absolute, "Organization", described as being internal to another synonym, "Schemata", seems to be a little crazy, but it vaguely suggests that Piaget is describing the Self busily developing Himself. The second sentence affirms that assimilation depends upon the Totality who is composed of interdependent monads. In the third sentence the "Totality" inappropriately becomes unrealized plural "Totalities" as well as an incomplete singular "Whole"! *In Piaget's world impossibilities become possible with his myriad of verbal entities and no boundaries set by logic or reality as most of us understand these terms.*

Piaget falsely implies that Kant held views that supported Hegel's and Piaget's unique anti-scientific concepts of "science" and structure.

> This Hegelian or Kantian pattern is not a merely conceptual or abstract pattern such as would be of no interest to either the sciences or structuralism. It corresponds to a progression which is inevitable once thought turns away from false absolutes (Piaget, 1970b, p. 123).

Kant's philosophy is alien to Hegel's and Piaget's concept of inevitable progress once thought turns to the implied "true" Absolute. Piaget's Absolute is based on Hegel's Living Structure and identified by Piaget as the Logico-Mathematical Structure (author's capitalization) (Piaget, 1971a, pp. 327-8). *Kant never dreamed of Piaget's structuralism or his new kind of Science* in which Hegel's dialectic is "immanent in the spontaneous development of Science" (author's italics and capitalization) (Piaget, 1971c, p. 115).

Piaget equivocates in the following excerpt regarding the proper explanation of development. Although it is said to be autonomous because it is based on equilibrations or operations, maturation and learning are also held to play a part. He ends, however, by insisting that all of his investigations inevitably show that equilibration is *the* explanation.

> When we speak of the autonomy of ... *development*, we wish to be understood in the very precise sense that development can be explained without necessary reference to

various factors which undoubtedly do play a part in its concrete realization, e.g. maturation, learning and social education, including language. For the key to its explanation lies in the concept of equilibration, which is a wider notion than any of these and comprehends them all. The reason that we would insist on this point is not (only) because we are interested in a systematic formulation, or because we are trying to cling to a particular set of hypotheses, but quite simply because all our investigations make this conclusion inevitable (author's italics) (Inhelder & Piaget, 1964, p. 292).

Piaget wishes to be on both sides of the fence at the same time, but if the dictionary meanings of words are held constant, this is impossible. First he claims that development is autonomous, and that development can be explained without reference to maturation, learning and the use of language. So far so good, as autonomous means functioning independently without control by other factors. The key to explanation, as Piaget says, is equilibration or operations. Equilibration does function independently of the three physical factors above, but Piaget then jumps over the fence and proclaims that the three physical factors also play a part in development. Without further qualifications we again have mutually incompatible statements. Ultimately, the overall context shows that development is truly autonomous as it is the development of the immanent Entity. The "(only)" in the next sentence calls attention to itself as it is obviously a gratuitous prank at the readers expense. Piaget, however, makes one significant and one insignificant but familiar admission along with the prank. He is interested in systematic formulation, as everyone knows, and he tries to cling to a particular set of hypotheses which is a surprising and highly pertinent admission as he is aware that natural scientists frown on this characteristic, as it is usually associated with those who do not value or who lack the ability to evaluate empirical data. Piaget has no use whatever for empirical data, and his admission is consistent with this attitude.

In the following excerpt, Piaget dances awkwardly around the concept of "operational development":

> The development of *operational behavior* is an autonomous process ... Operations do not arise directly out of language, nor is language the central factor in their development. Leaving aside for a moment this crucial point of the autonomy of operational development .... (fifteen lines later) to come back to the autonomy of operational development ... this by no means implies that logical operations are somehow divorced from Mental Life as a Whole, like some kind of "state within a state". The very reverse is the case (author's italics and capitalization) (Inhelder & Piaget, 1964, pp. 290-291).

The development of operational behavior is autonomous, but again Piaget equivocates, in this case regarding the role of language. If this development is autonomous, language cannot be a factor, but Piaget simply says that this behavior does not arise *directly* out of language and that language is not a *central* factor. This leaves the door open for language to play a part. As with almost all significant terms, there are two kinds of language (Piaget, 1973a pp. 113-14) (Piaget, 1971a, pp. 6-7) - one physical and the other metaphysical. Physical language is not a factor, although Piaget is carefully ambiguous regarding this aspect of his theory (Inhelder & Piaget, p. 292) (Piaget, 1970b, pp. 76-79), but the metaphysical language of operations is central indeed (Piaget, et al., 1977, p. 179)) (Piaget, 1973a, p. 111). He also assures us that operations are not divorced from Mental Life as a Whole, like some kind of state within a state because the very reverse is the case. The question then becomes: what is the reverse of the previous sentence? Although the reverse of "state within a state" is highly ambiguous, Piaget obviously means that Mental Life produces operations. He should simply affirm that the *reverse* of "operations are divorced from Mental Life as a Whole" is the case. We know that operations are the overriding concern of Mental Life, and will continue to be until physical reality is completely assimilated and the Absolute is fully actualized.

Piaget makes it clear below that the Structures formed by the psychogenetic process are easily separated from the physical structures of the limited subject (author's capitalization) (Beth & Piaget, 1966, pp. 168-9).

> We tend today to use the term "genetic Psychology" to refer to the study of the developmental processes that underlie the Mental functions studied in General Psychology ... Genetic Psychology tries to explain mental functions by their mode of formation; that is, by their development in the child (author's capitalization) (Piaget & Inhelder, 1969, p. VIII).

Genetic Psychology is another name for the series of operations that is the sole motor for the dialectic development of the Mental functions. "In studying the development of Intellectual operations, genetic Psychology describes the formation of Logico-Mathematical Structures" (author's capitalization) (Piaget, 1971b, p. 145). This means that genetic Psychology is the study of diachronic development (Piaget, 1974a, p. 4). Genetic analysis assumes that the Subject engages in a certain activity which allows Him to Self-construct His Operational Structures, which are by definition Normative and diachronic. The individual subject has nothing to do with this activity (Beth & Piaget, 1966, p. 285). Piaget repeats the same idea using "reflective abstraction", a synonym of operation. "The fundamental genetic process which allows the construction of a new Structure from a previous one is that of reflective abstraction" (author's capitalization) (ibid., p. 249). Genetic Psychology is the continuous series of operations or reflective abstractions that defines the development of upper-level "General Psychology".

Logic does not develop because of the maturation of the nervous system (Piaget, 1971a, p. 307). The development of logic in the child is based on operations, deducible regulations or equilibrations (Piaget, 1974a, p. 66) (Piaget, 1950, p. 34) (Piaget & Inhelder, 1974, p. 113) (Piaget, 1971c, p. 69), and operations are completely "autonomous", meaning that they are independent of physical influences including the nervous systems of people (Piaget, 1962, p. 291) (Beth & Piaget, 1966, pp. 234-5; 244; 253-4; 285; 293; 298-99; 308) (Piaget, 1980b, pp. 102-3; 105) (Piaget, 1977, pp. 145-6) (Piaget & Inhelder, 1971, p. 356) (Inhelder & Piaget, 1964, p. 293) (Piaget, 1971a, pp. 6-7; 316-17; 337) (Piaget, 1967, pp. 127; 144) (Piaget, 1980a, pp. 157-8). In other words, this is a strictly endogenous construction. Furthermore, it is autonomous because the Operator is infinite (author's capitalization) (Piaget, 1950, p. 20). This is Hegel's autoregulating Structure (Piaget, 1971a, pp. 327-8), so what can prevent Him from operating independently? He is the Mathematician and Logician who operates the System (author's capitalization) (Piaget, 1970b, p. 15) - which is Himself.

PHYSICAL EXPERIMENTS ARE INTRINSICALLY INVALID

What is the relationship, then, of the invincible, autonomous operations to the hundreds of physical experiments that Piaget and his associates have performed in order to gain an illegitimate entrance into the scientific universe of discourse? In his first book he strongly hints that physical experiments are not reliable within his theory.

> We lay stress on the fact that we do not consider that our problem can be solved by figures. We have far too little confidence ... in the general value of our experiments ... to come to ... hasty conclusions .... We shall adopt this solution only as a working hypothesis, in order to see in the later paragraph's whether it really tallies with the clinical evidence (Piaget, 1926, p. 109-10).

Since Piaget describes with dogmatic certainty a particular kind of development and knowledge, we can be sure that he has complete confidence in something. He admits here that it is not in his physical or "figurative" experiments. Clearly, his "later paragraphs" will be based on something in which he has unquestioned confidence, namely another kind of experiment - the Logical or operational experiment!

> This Logical experiment [is a] true 'experiment'. It is ... an attempt to become conscious of One's Own operations .... Logical experiment is ... carried out on Oneself for the detection of contradiction. The necessity resulting ... from Logical experiment[s] is due to implications (author's capitalization) (Piaget, 1928, pp. 236-7).

This early book describes a "true experiment" as one carried out for the "detection" of dialectic contradiction. The presence of anything physical automatically results in a dialectical contradiction, and it can only be resolved by a "true experiment", operation, or implication. Since the mere presence of physical objects provokes operations, they occur continuously (Piaget, 1978a, p. 97) (Piaget, 1971a, pp. 223; 347) (Piaget, 1970b, p. 141) (Inhelder & Piaget, 1958, p. 307). So long as some physical aspects remain, dialectic contradictions will always be present. The results of the operations or implications are "necessary"; the cognitions and actions of human beings are never necessary (Piaget, 1972, p. 86) (Piaget, 1971b, p. 32) (Piaget, 1974a, p. 9). *The true Mental or Logical experiment is performed by the Thinking Subject. This experiment produces necessary results because it is a synonym of implication, operation or reflective abstraction.*

> This third type of Mental experiment is accompanied by an experiment which might be called 'Logical experiment' .... It is an experiment upon the Subject Himself as a Thinking-Subject ... It is ... an attempt to become conscious of one's Own operations ....
> The necessity resulting from mental experiment[s] is a necessity of fact, that which results from Logical experiment[s] is due to the implications existing between the various operations: It is a moral necessity due to the obligation of remaining true to oneSelf (author's italics and capitalization) (Piaget, 1928, 235-37).

Note how Piaget confounds "the third type of Mental experiment" with "Logical experiment", when they are identical. He creates confusion by saying that the first "accompanies" the second, indicating a differentiation between the two when there is none. This first use of "Mental" is upper-level, but his second use of "mental" is lower-level, which makes it extremely confusing, especially when we see what follows. This second use of "mental" to mean experiments based on brain function makes these particular experiments lower-level. Piaget further paralyzes the reader's capacity to comprehend by adding the unusual use of "necessity of fact" to describe the results of factual, lower-level human experiments. *It is unusual because Piaget's theory holds that contingent facts, and all physical facts are held by Piaget to be contingent, are not necessary* (author's italics) (Piaget, 1972, p. 86). Only a comma separates the results of lower-level mental experiments from the results of upper-level Logical or metaphysical experiments based on implications. In the over-all context these carefully crafted efforts to confuse are potentially devastating. The only protection one has from lies of this type is knowledge, but even with a thorough grasp of what he is up to it is extremely difficult to deal with such statements. Has the academic world ever encountered such a lawless, ill-intentioned will to deceive? In my opinion, this is a critically important quote. Any Piagetian who understands the meaning of "the necessity resulting from mental experiment[s] is a necessity of fact" in the context of this quote will never again see Piaget as a trustworthy purveyor of knowledge. This "physical" phrase is basically hidden within an otherwise metaphysical context. It is hidden because the same words - "necessity", "mental", "experiment" - are used but with different meanings. Nevertheless it will be well worth the effort to see how it should be distinguished from its surrounding environment. Piaget frequently contradicts himself quite profoundly in order to confuse his reader. For instance, in the use of lower-level "necessity" above he directly contradicts many dogmatic statements (Piaget, 1974a, p. 9) (Piaget, 1971b, p. 32) (Piaget, 1950, p. 148).

The Thinking Subject has a moral obligation to be true to Himself, and this is accomplished by continuous metaphysical operations, implications or Logical experiments. I counted 14 instances in about one fourth of my notes where Piaget insisted that the production of operations is *continuous,* and he clearly means without a pause of any kind, since the physical universe was created. These four references are typical (Inhelder & Piaget, 1958, p. 307) (Piaget, 1950, p. 39) (Piaget, 1971a, p. 223) (Piaget, 1973a, p. 133).

Piaget also speaks of experiments that "may" be based on Structures, may partially be based on Structures or may not be based on Structures. The discussion below is valuable because it demonstrates some of his evasive tactics.

> [Do the Structures] constitute simple 'models' in the service of theoreticians or ... should [they] be considered as inherent to the reality under study, in other words as Structures of the Subject or subjects themselves. This question is fundamental, because in the eyes of authors critical of structuralism the latter is merely a language ... which refers to the observer's logic, but not to the Subject [and His Logic] .... A model without sufficient relationship with the Concrete Being [is] no more than a play of mathematical relations ... In most [experiments] the models used in the human sciences are placed ... halfway between the 'model' and the 'Structure' (author's capitalization) (Piaget, 1973d, p. 25).

It is very important that one at least try to be aware of the various changes of level in this passage, but that is most difficult. "Structures of the Subject" is upper level, but "subjects themselves" is lower level. Based on Piaget's references to the first sentence, part of the sentence should be expanded as follows: "Structures of the

Subject or subjects themselves" should read, "Structures of the Subject *or structures* of the subjects themselves". The lower-level subject is not a language, but one kind of structure he produces is language. "The latter" or lower-level structures of the "subjects themselves" involves merely a "physical" language, traditional logic, and traditional or utilitarian mathematics. *This is a most unfair juxtaposition of the two subjects, and certainly represents an intentional violation of the readers normal expectations of an author.* No one violates our long-established, codified pattern of linguistic expectations more ingeniously or more flagrantly than Piaget. We must realize that he cannot accept the focus on the "subjects' structures themselves" because it by-passes the Subject and His Logic. When the experiment is based on the "subjects themselves" and physical reality, as it always is in every university, there is insufficient relationship with Hegel's and Piaget's Concrete Being. The idea that most "models" are halfway between the physical and the metaphysical Structure is wishful thinking on the part of Piaget. The implication is that human beings have already reached the midpoint on the way to complete assimilation. After all, assimilation has been at work in human beings for several thousand years (Piaget, 1971a, pp. 152-3) (Piaget, 1971b, p. 72) (Piaget, 1930, pp. 115-121).

When Thought assimilates some aspect of reality a Mental experiment has occurred. The following passage describes what Piaget means by "affecting" reality.

> The empiricist models of intelligence that some writers try to build up are inadequate at all levels since they disregard assimilatory construction .... In its finished state, *a Mental experiment is the reproduction in Thought, not of reality, but of actions or operations which affect it* (author's italics and capitalization) (Piaget, 1950, pp. 92-3).

There is an incredible naivete among Piagetians regarding the role of experiment in Piaget's system. Most of them almost certainly support the empiricist models that Piaget specifically rejects and would be astounded to hear exactly what he considers to be a true experiment. Piaget specifically rejects "copy knowledge", or knowledge about "reality as it is", in this quote, which is precisely the kind of non-assimilatory knowledge for which scientists such as Newton and Einstein are honored. In the following excerpt Piaget is even more explicit regarding his view of a "true" experiment.

> If we wish to consider the ensemble of Knowledge solely by "experiment", we can justify such a thesis only by seeking to analyze what the experiment is .... *The experiment always consists in an assimilation to Structures and a turning to a systematic study of the Ipse Intellectus* (author's italics and capitalization) (Piaget, 1971b, pp. 4-5).

The first sentence is somewhat ambiguous, but there can be no doubt about the meaning of the second sentence. The experiment always consists in an assimilation to Structures and a study of the one whose Structures accomplish the assimilation - the Ipse Intellectus or Absolute Subject. Piaget thus rejects the validity of the "hands on" experimentation pushed by science educators in his name; he rejects the value of natural science and, most incredible of all, he rejects the verity of the countless physical experiments he and his associates have performed. The truth is that his "physical experiments" have essentially the same function as his multiple verbalisms - they create opportunities for cultivating confusion and fostering deception.

The following quote explains why empiricism with its scientific experiments, is an impossible position within his system.

> The natural tendency of the mind is to perceive reality intuitively and to make deductions, but not experiments; for unlike deduction, *experimentation is not a free or even a direct spontaneous product of Intelligence; it calls for acceptance of external authorities* (author's italics and capitalization) (Piaget, 1974a, p. 23).

Why is empiricism and natural science impossible in Piaget's system? *It is because Gnostic Intelligence cannot accept the authority of physical reality!* Physical reality is external to Intelligence or the Absolute (author's italics and capitalization) (ibid., p. 401) (Piaget, 1967, pp. 7-8) (Piaget & Inhelder, 1969, p. 157) and physical reality *includes the lower-level person who is indeed "external" to his immanent Intelligence or Absolute* (author's italics and capitalization) (Piaget, 1954, pp. 285; 401) (Piaget & Inhelder, 1969, p. 94) (Piaget, 1952b, p. 415). The fact that Piaget deformed the meaning by pluralizing "authority" indicates that he had something to partially hide. His system is dual, and this means that there is only one "external authority", namely the physical universe. *He must not be completely open, therefore, regarding his intense Gnostic antipathy to human beings as physical entities, as well as to physical reality as a whole.*

Piaget and Inhelder make an extended argument in *The Child's Construction of Quantities* (1974) that children are "impermeable" to, or show a deafness to experience (ibid., p. 242). The main points of the argument can be followed quite easily by referring to the following pages (ibid., pp. 220; 228-9; 233; 239-242; 257; 264-5). The quote below provides the gist of their conclusion:

> [Children] prove quite incapable of drawing logical conclusions from the data of a possible [physical] composition, but they also hold experiment in utter contempt: *the result of a particular experiment tells them nothing at all about the next [possible experiment]* (author's italics) (ibid., p. 242).

As is nearly always the case, children are made the vanguard when Piaget broaches some sensitive aspect of his theory. This is certainly the case here as the italicized portion of the quote confirms that Piaget is telling us about his theory, not the child's, as he gives a reason why physical experiment is considered to be contemptible that a young child would not give. It is significant that some of Piaget's most famous physical experiments are detailed in this book, particularly the conservation experiments with the ball of clay, dissolving sugar grains and the expansion of popcorn. In the "general conclusions" regarding these experiments, and following all the other experiments, causation and meaning are never based on anything physical, but always something metaphysical, namely the Body of Monads, *and this explanation is unmistakably seen in Piaget's revealing discussion of metaphysical atomism all through this particular book.*

Before we leave the topic of experiment we must take another look at the lower-level kind that Piaget despises, but utilizes for the express purpose of providing a "more telling" criticism of empiricism. "As to the relations between Logico-Mathematical Structures and physical reality: ... these factual analyses based on psychological experimentation will provide a criticism of empiricism .... [and it will be] the more telling since it starts from the same basis as empiricism" (author's capitalization) (Beth & Piaget, 1966, p. 148). Piaget's experiments do not start from the same basis as empiricism; he only pretends that they do. *And the pretention is amazingly shallow, because Piaget is obviously speaking of "dialectic experiments" in the quote, not scientific experiments!* Furthermore, he claims to be a "tireless opponent of empiricism" (Piaget, 1980b, p. 10) and states flatly that "I am no empiricist" (Piaget, 1972, p. 10).

THE STAGES OF METAPHYSICAL DEVELOPMENT

Piaget frequently utilizes the concept of "stage" in presenting his theory of metaphysical development, his *only* theory of development. Piaget has no theory about the development of the physical human being, other than asserting that he is a "product of a number of interactions".

> From the interactionist point of view, again the individual is seen as not being an autonomous element or a primary source, because it is simply the product of a number of interactions, dependent upon the Population as a Whole (author's capitalization) (Piaget, 1971a, p. 283).

The human being, like all other natural objects, is the result operational activity *by monads of the Absolute Subject, here called the "Population as a Whole".* Immediately after this quote, Piaget busily begins to cover up part of the meaning. First, he switches from the "physical individual" to the "metaphysical Individual" who is the source of these interactions". This latter Individual "becomes, not just an element or independent source, but a 'Population' in itself", who is "interactive by nature" (author's capitalization) (ibid., p. 283). This "Population" that is naturally interactive is obviously the Body of Monads. Piaget also thoroughly confuses the "Population" of monads as a whole with the "endomorphic Population" of monads within each individual person, which is completely and perfectly connected with the whole Population of monads. The endomorphic metaphysical Entity in people is sometimes called the Spirit (author's capitalization) (Piaget, 1926, pp. 139; 144-5) (Piaget, 1971b, p. 99) (Piaget, 1970b, p. 8) (Piaget, 1932, p. 388) (Bringuier, 1980, p. 51), or the Human Spirit (author's capitalization) (Piaget, 1930, p. 237) (Piaget, 1970a, p. IX) by Piaget. "If we examine the intellectual development of the individual or the whole of humanity, we shall find that the Human Spirit goes through a certain number of stages" (author's capitalization) (Piaget, 1930, p. 237). Piaget goes on to affirm that this Spirit is the "Thinking Subject" (author's capitalization) (ibid., p. 237). *It is the developmental stages of the Spirit or Thinking Subject that is the exclusive concern of Piaget.*

The almost universal belief among educators and psychologists that Piaget worked diligently to elaborate a theory of child development is a cruel hoax. He worked with extreme diligence to create the hoax, but nothing was further from his mind than to produce a theory of the bio-psychological development of children. He was never interested in "the material object with which the biologist experiments" (Piaget, 1971b, p. 120), so he would never confuse the *"things"* we call human beings (Piaget & Inhelder, 1969, pp. 23-4) (Piaget, 1971c, p. 103) (Piaget, 1971b, p. 29) (Piaget, 1929, pp. 176; 266) with the developing Biological Subject he worshiped.

Would he ever pay homage to the "detestable ego" (Inhelder & Piaget, 1958, p. 349) whom he "dislikes" (Piaget, 1970b, p. 68) and holds to be "hateful" (Piaget, 1971c, XVI), by devoting his life to an understanding of its development, when he is vitally concerned with the development of the true Ego or Subject (author's capitalization) (Piaget, 1971a, p. 74) (Piaget, 1973d, pp. 35; 37) (Piaget, 1970b, pp. 123; 142) (Piaget, 1952b, pp. 45; 170; 179) (Inhelder & Piaget, 1958, pp. 330-1)? No, the object-person is of no importance to Piaget as he is not capable of achieving true Knowledge (Piaget, 1969b, pp. 285-6) because he is not Intelligent in terms of Piaget's definition (Beth & Piaget, 1966, p. 285). Furthermore, this incompetent human entity is not the actual motor of his own activity as he is neither a causal nor a Substantial force (author's capitalization) (Piaget, 1971a, p. 94). We have also observed that he can only make "non-necessitus" statements (Piaget, 1971a, p. 14), while Piaget is only interested in necessity (Piaget, 1972, p. 86) (Piaget, 1971b, p. 32) (Piaget, 1970d, p. 29) (Piaget, 1977, p. 184) (Piaget, 1974b, 131-2). One way Piaget demonstrates his notion of "necessity" is his dogmatic certainty regarding questions when empirical evidence is not available (Piaget, 1971c, p. 5) (Piaget, 1971a, pp. 52; 268) (Piaget, 1974b, p. 28). This is Piaget's view of flesh and blood humanity and it is abundantly clear that his theory of development is not pertinent to this kind of entity.

Piaget has the audacity to make the very young child agree with him in this negative evaluation. By age two, the child already realizes, according to the great man, that he is only an object (Piaget, 1972, pp. 21-2) (Piaget, 1952b, p. 327) (Piaget & Inhelder, 1969, p. 13). Typically, Piaget presents no evidence for this conspicuously fictitious statement. The human thing or object is the "not-self" who obeys the true Self (author's capitalization) (Piaget, 1929, p. 175). The not-self is the "other" who is dissociated from the Self (author's capitalization) (Piaget & Inhelder, 1969, p. 22). Piaget composed a foolish little riddle regarding the physical self that shows his low evaluation of this self, but it fails to indicate the role of the highly valued Self: "The self is freed from itself by finding itself and assigns itself a place as a thing among things and event among events" (Piaget, 1954, p. XI). This riddle is foolish because it does not make sense for the lower-level self to "free itself and assign itself" within Piaget's system - it is only assimilation by the true Self that can free Itself from the physical self, otherwise known as the decentering process. The true Self then assigns the physical self to the status of "object", "thing" or "event".

For Piaget the development of stages is autonomous because they are generated by operations. The development of stages has nothing to do with human beings. When we peel back the layers of fabrication we find that stages of development apply only to the Absolute Subject.

> The operations of Intelligence ... proceeds by clearly defined stages, and the process is entirely autonomous .... Such an evolution is autonomous in that the Structures are generated from one another under motivation from Intelligence alone. Affective factors may speed up or slow down the formation of Structure, but they will not actually modify it qua Structure (author's capitalization) (Inhelder & Piaget, 1958, p. 356).

Development proceeds by clearly defined stages. This process is based on operations and it is completely autonomous. The stages of development pertain exclusively to the metaphysical Entity. Piaget partially hides the meaning of how Structures are generated, but if one understands the metaphysical concept of operations there is no problem. However, to say that Structures are autonomously "generated from one another" is a purposely evasive way to describe the Hegelian triad of thesis, antithesis and synthesis. Every synthesis generates a more developed Structure. This is a metaphysical and not a human process.

> *We are compelled to think of the construction of Logico-Mathematical Structures ... as a kind of endogenous evolution going forward in stages.* The combinations characteristic of any ... stage will be new as combinations, yet based entirely upon the elements already present in the preceding stage (author's italics and capitalization) (Piaget, 1971a, pp. 318-19).

The development of the *Logico-Mathematical Structures* goes forward by means of endogenously constructed stages. This means, according to Piaget, that exogenous or scientific verification is not necessary (Piaget, 1980b, p. 83). Since endogenous development is accomplished by reflexive abstractions or operations (Piaget, 1974b, p. 67), it is more accurate to say that the development of stages is impossible to verify by the methods of natural science. If the stages of development referred to the development of people, as described in all of the textbooks used in our universities, they could be analyzed and enhanced by empirical methods, but such is not the case. No, Piaget's famous stages are based on immanent Logico-Mathematical construction, not on the maturation or physical structures like the brain or on the physical experience that learning provides (author's capitalization) (Piaget, 1980b, p. 81). This is Self-construction based on the ability of the Combinatorial System or Body of Monads to employ the appropriate combinations of elements or monads as needed. The Combinatorial System, of course, is the Logico-Mathematical Structure (author's capitalization) (Piaget, 1972, p. 49). Note too that the same basic "elements" or monads are the same at every stage. The only difference that exists between the stages is the difference between the variety and difficulty of combinations of which the monads are capable.

A SURVEY OF VARIOUS WAYS PIAGET
UTILIZES THE CONCEPT OF STAGE

Before we look more closely at Piaget's theory regarding the stages of general development, we will examine other ways he uses the concept of stages to "teach" us the fundamentals of his philosophical position. In his first book, *The Language and Thought of the Child* (1926), he describes the kinds of conversation that occur among children of four to seven years in terms of stages that occur between egocentrism, or thought that revolves around the physical self, and Egocentrism, or thought that revolves around the metaphysical Self. *Some aspects of every stage are designed by him to inculcate his philosophy.* A progression toward a fuller elaboration in the child of Piaget's position is called for by his System, but the most fundamental concepts may come at any stage. For instance, the first stage of conversation is the "collective monologue". This is undoubtedly the most important stage from Piaget's point of view. Each child is engaged in a monologue, and none of the children are listening to anyone else but, according to Piaget, the children believe that *Someone* is listening to them (author's italics and capitalization) (ibid., p. 31). Piaget asserts, without evidence, that the children think they are talking with Someone. In a subsequent book, *The Child's Conception of the World* (1929), Piaget is very specific regarding this Entity who is supposedly listening. He quotes from Edmund Gosse's memories of childhood, who as a child had found a "companion and a confidant" *in himself.* "There was a secret in this world and it belonged to me and to *Somebody* who lived in the same body with me. *There were two of us and we could talk to one another"* (author's italics and capitalization) (Piaget, 1929, p. 155). Edmund Gosse had, according to Piaget, discovered his Subjective Self (author's capitalization) (ibid., p. 155) - one of the terms Piaget invented to mean "immanent Absolute Subject". *In both cases we actually have a dyadic relationship rather than a monologue even though one of the dual participants is invisible.* Stages 2 and 3 deal with the issue of reciprocity between the immanent "endomorphic" (Piaget, 1971a, pp. 170-1) Sub-Groups of monads within the children. At stage 3, the highest stage, there is "collaboration in abstract thought" (Piaget, 1926, p. 72). Piaget is speaking of "abstract thought" that begins at about seven years of age, so it is quite clear that he is deftly bringing in *"Someone"* as the immanent Subject who thinks abstractly (author's italics and capitalization) (ibid., pp. 81; 88-92), as the physical child is still a bit young for this kind of thought. In this first book we see an unnecessary complication of stage 2, a practice which is carried to much greater extremes, with regard to stages, in later books. There are not only stages 2a and 2b, but there are two types of both 2a and 2b. The implicit claim in such excessive complications is superior intellectual acumen on the part of the author, because he appears to be making discriminations beyond the capacity of the reader. The problem with Piaget's work is that essentially all such complications are deliberately contrived.

In his third book, *The Child's Conception of the World* (1929), Piaget uses the idea of stage to explain, among other things, how the child progresses in understanding "thought", "dreams", "participation", "consciousness", "life", and "artificialism". *We observe that the statements by children at every stage, except possibly the last, agree with some aspect of Piaget's philosophical position.* His main concern with "thought" is to prepare his reader to accept the view that monads inside and outside his body can think equally well, and that the brain is not necessary for thought. Also, with "dreams" he tries to show that both inside and outside monads are involved. "Participation" is the concept that one Group of monads can affect another Group of monads. In this book one emphasis is on the magical effect the monads inside the bodies of children have on objects by influencing the monads in and around these objects. Piaget's rather prominent concept of magic, as described in this book and other contexts, puts a strain on his notion that the individual has no affect on his immanent Body of Monads, as his concept of magic appears to require some effect by the physical individual on his immanent monads, which then bring about magic. This concept will be explored more completely later in this chapter.

Piaget begins his discussion of "consciousness" by saying that the child "is unconscious of his Self"; "this is what we shall attempt to prove" (author's capitalization) (Piaget, 1929, p. 151). In other words, Piaget is going to emphasize his doctrine that although the immanent Subject within us is conscious, we ourselves are not conscious of its presence. *One can quickly see that his statements about the young child's and Edmond Gosse's conscious dyadic encounters with this conscious Self represents a direct contradiction!* Piaget begins his examination of "Life" with, "it remains an undoubted fact that child thought starts with the idea of a Universal Life as its primary assumption" (author's capitalization) (ibid., p. 261). This Universal Life, of course, is the Absolute Entity who fills the universe with His living monads. For Piaget, as we have said, there is only one living Being. All physical beings are alive only because the monads of the Absolute innervate them. Piaget claims that the child gradually "realizes his own Subjectivity" has an "inexhaustible scope" (author's capitalization) (ibid., p. 269). That is, he is vaguely aware of not only his immanent Subject but also has some intuition regarding His superhuman nature. Artificialism, another superhuman attribute, is based on a Divine Mover (author's capitalization) (ibid., p. 285) who is both "transcendent" and "immanent in nature", and who made all natural objects. Piaget's artificialism and animism clearly are expressions of pantheism. He often has the child saying that Man made these objects, but he makes it clear that "Man" in such cases is a synonym for God (author's capitalization) (Piaget, 1926, pp.188; 209) (Piaget, 1930. pp. 45; 75) (Piaget, 1929, pp. 288; 294; 300).

In his fourth book (*The Child's Conception of Physical Causality,* 1930), the nature of "air", "wind", "breath", "the movements of clouds and heavenly bodies", "water currents", "movements due to weights", "force", "floating of boats", "shadows", "the mechanism of a bicycle" and the explanation of a "steam engine" were investigated. We have already observed that Piaget uses "air" as a synonym for spiritual atoms or monads. He begins the first chapter with the claim that children *spontaneously* consider "air" and "wind" to be alive (author's italics) (ibid., p. 3) and conscious (ibid., p. 4). He follows this with the concept of "participation" between outside and inside air (ibid., pp. 8-9), an obvious analogy with outside and inside monads. Piaget then addresses the subject of how projectiles move (ibid., p. 20). In the early stages children believe that there is a "reflux of air which comes and pushes the object before it" (ibid., p. 22) just like the monads supposedly move the moon and sun. In the later stages, around eleven or twelve, the child accepts the view that an impetus is sufficient to account for the movement of projectiles (ibid., pp. 22-3). Here we see, as is so often the case, that the early stages are more advanced than the later ones from the standpoint of Piaget's theory, although this is a logical impossibility within his system. Piaget then returns to "wind and breath" with the claim that children around nine believe that all currents of air participate with one another and that the currents of air are "independent vibrations of a Single All-Pervading Substance" (author's capitalization) (ibid., p. 32). This is a perfect analogy with the All-Pervading Body of Monads within which any Sub-Group of monads can "participate" with any other Sub-Group. The "facts" about air wind and breath cannot be explained, says Piaget, without bringing in the metaphysical concept of pre-relation. "The facts requiring explanation are in reality full of what we have called pre-relations" (ibid., p. 50). *A "pre-relation" is a "pre-operation" - not exactly a relation but a close approximation. In other words, "pre-relation" is a mere "verbalism"!*

Piaget deals next with the movement of clouds and heavenly bodies. There are five stages in the explanations children give for the movement of clouds. The first stage is magical, the clouds obey us at a distance. Children at this stage believe that clouds are alive, and that magical obedience is imposed as a moral obligation. Piaget concludes that the child believes there is a dynamic participation between his activity and that of the cloud (ibid., p. 62). The second stage is artificialist and animistic - the clouds move because God or Men make them move. This second stage presents us, according to Piaget, with the "idea of a double motor, both internal and external" (ibid., p. 63). Where have we seen this before! He further asserts that stages three and four also contain this idea. During the third stage the cloud's spontaneous movement is based on a "motor schema" which compels movement. Piaget explains "that there are always *two causes* at work, one internal and one external (author's italics) (ibid., p. 64). These causes are partly moral and they are not "exclusively physical" - i. e., they are metaphysical (ibid., p. 65). In the fourth stage wind comes out of the cloud and pushes the cloud (ibid., p. 61). Six pages later Piaget revises the meaning: "When the child says that the wind pushes the clouds, one should not accept the statement at its face value" (ibid., p. 67). Beginning with the fourth stage Piaget confuses the reader by mixing "types" with the stages in ways that make interpretation difficult. The fifth stage, reached about age nine, represents the correct explanation (ibid., p. 62). Each of the first four stages are seen to agree with some aspect of Piaget's system; only the fifth stage, the stage in which the child gives the correct explanation, runs counter to his theory. The answers of the fifth stage "have none of the *spontaneity* of those we have quoted" (author's italics) (ibid., p. 86), so Piaget is uninterested. Since the term "spontaneity" is generally used to indicate influence by the immanent monads, *Piaget is faced with the problem of explaining the failure of the immanent Subject to maintain progress.* Here again it is the younger children who are the most advanced in terms of Piaget's theory - a circumstance which is quite impossible to explain within his system.

Piaget uses "water currents" in the same way he uses air and wind, which is to "teach" the basic principles regarding the activity of monads. Ultimately, the explanations regarding the movements of water, including waves, are based on "explanations" by "reaction of the surrounding medium" (ibid., p. 96). The term "type of answer" replaces "stage" in Piaget's discussion of force. The child fills the world with spontaneous movements and "Living Forces" (author's capitalization) (ibid., p. 114). These Living Forces are Groups of monads, and that is what Piaget wishes to teach his reader - with a somewhat obscure vocabulary. *The child has a vague understanding because of the metaphysical pre-relations* (author's italics) (ibid., pp. 114-15), but adults, especially scientifically oriented adults, have somehow lost this "knowledge"! Every movement, as understood by the child, calls for the "intervention of special forces" that are "alive, Substantial" and intentional (author's capitalization) (ibid., p. 117). Physical contact is not necessary for force to act on an object (ibid., p. 119), so we have action at a distance based on Psychology (author's capitalization) (ibid., p. 126). "Force becomes gradually withdrawn from external objects and confined within the Ego" (author's capitalization) (ibid., p. 132).

In introducing the concept of "floating boats", Piaget says, *"the earlier the explanations are, the less simple we shall find them"* (author's italics) (ibid., p. 135). "Less simple" is his way to express "greater conformity" with his theory, but he immediately begins to blur this admission. On the following page he forthwith contradicts himself: "the second stage is much more complex [than the first]" (ibid.,

p. 136). This is not atypical, as he frequently contradicts himself in a very direct way. There are four stages, and in conclusion Piaget states that "pure legality never satisfies the Mind" (author's capitalization) (ibid., p. 158). "Legality" for Piaget means understanding at the level of empirical science or scientific law. *This is why, with Piaget's special blessing, the child reasons with absolute concepts, and contrary to his "progressive" theory, proceeds "from absolute to relative"* (author's italics) (ibid., p. 162). In experiments with "water level" when objects are placed in the water, Piaget again points out that the earliest stages "are definitely opposed to legality" (ibid., p. 176). Next there are four stages in explaining shadows, and Piaget concludes that "child physics proceeds from a Substantialist dynamism to explanations of a more static order" (author's capitalization) (ibid., pp. 190-1), i. e., *from a metaphysical to a physical explanation, when Piaget's progressive theory requires the opposite!*

There are four stages in explaining the mechanism of a bicycle. First stage children show three *positive* features: first, explanation by moral determinism; second, explanation without spatial contact; third, participation of "forces" or of a "current" (ibid., pp. 204-5). Amazingly, we see Piaget reducing the mechanism of a bicycle to the metaphysical forces of the monads. Remember, every movement in the universe is ultimately caused by the metaphysical Structure of monads (author's capitalization) (Piaget, 1970b, p. 142) (Piaget, 1972, p. 80) (Piaget, 1973d, p. 36). Piaget is in the difficult position of not being able, within his system, to honestly ascribe any physical cause to the movement of objects. At stage two the child still explains the bicycle's motion by syncretic relations - which are metaphysical. Syncretism is the result of Egocentrism, not egocentrism. Syncretism is the expression of perpetual assimilation of all things to Ancient, Subjective Schemas (author's capitalization) (Piaget, 1928, p. 228). Since syncretism is a characteristic of young children it does not represent a well-rounded picture of the immanent Subject, nevertheless, "syncretism is a vision of the Whole which creates a vague but All-Inclusive Schema, supplanting the details" (author's capitalization) (ibid., p. 59). *In the third and fourth stages the child gradually gives up his syncretism and explains the mechanism of the bicycle correctly. Since this is at odds with Piaget's theory, he shows no interest.*

Next Piaget asks children to explain the steam-engine. There are three stages, but Piaget is primarily interested in the first stage because "action at a distance" is implied in the children's statements. The fire is believed to send an invisible current or force, which goes to the wheel and pushes it (Piaget, 1930, p. 219). Piaget sees animism in their statements as "fire and air must be able to direct themselves, to go to the wheel with intention and intelligence, etc." (ibid., p. 219), *just like the monads Piaget always has in mind!* He also sees finalism or purpose of an artificialist kind: "the fire is "good at" making the wheels go ... [and] this goodness ... is sufficient to explain why fire sets the wheels in motion" (ibid., p. 219). These "spontaneous mental tendencies" thinly veil Piaget's theory of monads. In fact *all of the "physical" experiments in this book are utilized by Piaget to adumbrate his metaphysical philosophy.* What he thought the end result of his plan would be is hard to fathom, but the bottom line is that his philosophy remains unknown in the academic world.

In his fifth book (*The Moral Judgment of the Child*, 1932) there are four stages in the "practice of rules" and three stages in the "consciousness of rules". One thing Piaget tries to inculcate, based on one of the youngest children, Pha, age five and one-half, is the notion that the true Ego is "ancient".

> Did your daddy play at marbles before you were born? - *No, never, because I wasn't there yet!* - But he was a child like you before you were born. - *I was there already when he was like me. He was bigger.* - When did people begin to play marbles? - *When the others began, I began too.* It would be impossible to outdo Pha in placing himself at the center of the universe, in time as well as space (Piaget's italics) (ibid., p. 54).

Pha claims to have been in existence before his father was born, a "finding" that Piaget has observed and used in other contexts (Piaget, 1969a, p. 205). Why would Piaget consider this to be significant? It is significant, as we have previously observed, because the true Ego within the child is eternal, and Piaget is motivated to demonstrate this Ego's influence on the child - even if he cannot demonstrate it in the adult. Along the same line, his enthusiastic assertion that Pha is placing himself in the center of the universe in terms of both time and space, is surely an indirect reference to Pha's immanent Ego who is indeed the center of the universe.

The two books, (*The Origins of Intelligence in Children*, 1952b and *The Construction of Reality in the Child*, 1954), are based on the observation of Piaget's own children. All of the observations for these two books were made before they were two years of age, and most were made when the children were much younger than two. In both books most of the observations were made before one year of age, and in the former, particularly, most appear to be before six months of age. *The bottom line is that all of Piaget's fundamental doctrines are derived or rederived by him from these observations between hours after birth and two years of age!* The observations are well-written, clear, highly detailed, sensitive and have the ring of truth and accuracy. There is an impossible gap to bridge, however, between the beautiful observations and the inferences Piaget makes from them. The necessary logical connections between the observations and the basic, sometimes quite abstract and obscure, inferences simply do not exist. *Usually Piaget makes no attempt to make specific connections between observation and inference. The relationships between the observations and the conclusions regarding their meanings are no more substantial than the relationships in a dream.*

The Construction of Reality in the Child consists of four chapters plus the conclusion. There are six stages in the development of the object concept, six stages regarding the Spatial Field and the elaboration of groups of displacements, six stages in the development of causality and six stages in the development of the temporal field.

THE SIX STAGES IN THE DEVELOPMENT OF THE OBJECT CONCEPT

Piaget's theory of the development of the immanent Absolute Subject within people requires, as we have observed, that there be no objects in the newborn's experience (author's capitalization) (Piaget, 1950, p. 108) (Piaget, 1952b, pp. 36; 64-5; 67) (Piaget, 1962, p. 13) (Piaget & Inhelder, 1969, p. 14) (Piaget, 1971b, p.

16) (Evans, 1973, p. 20) (Piaget, 1974b, pp. 113-14), so the infant is born into a universe in which there are no objects (Piaget, 1954, pp. 1-2). This being the case, it is essential for Piaget to immediately begin throwing sand in our eyes, and he does so as follows! For the infant at this stage then, "recognition is not at all a recognition of objects" (ibid., p. 3). Recognition is the "product of an extremely complex intellectual elaboration and not of an elementary act of simple sensorimotor assimilation" (ibid., p. 4). But the baby between birth and four months of age is not capable of "extremely complex intellectual elaborations", as he is only in the early sensorimotor stage. Piaget, then, is telling us quite openly that the true Self is responsible for the "complex elaborations", but even He, according to the theory, does not "see" objects right away! And most important, Piaget does not need empirical evidence to support this understanding. During the first two stages, from birth to about four months of age, the "child does not know how to construct either Groups or objects, and may well consider the changes in his image of the world as being simultaneously real and constantly created by His Own actions" (author's capitalization) (ibid., p. 6). The physical baby does not know how to construct Groups and natural objects, but the immanent Subject does. Piaget affirms this, at least in the case of objects, when the immanent Subject, in the baby who is no more than four months old, assumes that He could create the world! Note that the phrase before the comma in the quote speaks of the lower-level subject and that the phrase after the comma refers to the upper-level Subject. *Piaget obviously knows more about the secret thoughts of babies between birth and four months of age than any other person on earth!*

"Each Schema of this child", of four months or less, "seeks to encompass the whole universe" (author's capitalization) (ibid., p. 7). The Schemas within the child are mainly concerned with assimilating the child, but they also share the wishes of the Total Schema. During the third stage, which occurs between four and nine months, "the child does not know the Mechanism of his own actions, and hence does not dissociate them from the things themselves" (author's capitalization) (ibid., p. 46). Although Piaget confounds the two subjects, as he is bound to do over and over, the meaning is still quite obvious. First, infants in Piaget's system confuse the two selves (Piaget, 1926, p. 235) (Piaget, 1928, p. 197) (Piaget, 1929, p. 46; 175) (Piaget, 1930, p. 284) (Piaget, 1954, p. 272). This is demonstrated here because *the "Mechanism of his own actions" refers to the upper-level Self. The infant of less than nine months still thinks that actions have their source in the lower-level "things", i. e., physical, human bodies, themselves!* More accurately, Piaget constantly changes the roles played by the two subjects, as well as the rules within which they are supposed to play, depending upon the needs of the moment. He feels free to make all of these changes as he goes along because he is convinced, with good reason, that academia is completely bemuddled regarding his theory. This means that there are contradictions galore! At this third stage he sees other people as "things", but he will not see himself as a "thing" until the sixth stage. During the fourth stage "the object remains a practical object rather than a Substantial Being" (author's capitalization) (ibid., p. 72). That is, the child of eight months to one year sees other people as practical objects or things rather than as Substantial Beings. The not so subtle implication here is that the child will eventually "see" the immanent Subject in other people. The behavior patterns of this stage merely extend those of the preceding one (ibid., p.

72), and a "truly geometric rationalism will have to supersede ... immediate perception" (ibid., pp. 72-3). In other words, "geometrization", which is really assimilation, needs a bit more time to do its work (Piaget & Inhelder, 1971, p. 336) (Piaget, 1978a, pp. 163-4) (Piaget, 1974b, pp. 31-2; 130).

During the fifth stage, ages eleven months to one year and three months, Piaget observes that "the practical and egocentric object defends foot by foot the terrain which the Geometric relationships will conquer" (author's capitalizations) (Piaget, 1954, p. 73). The two subjects are front and center again, as the egocentric, or physical object-child resists the geometric or operational activity of his immanent Subject who will eventually conquer him. *One should observe here that the immanent Subject is depicted as progressively conquering the infant, while in most of the stage sequences we have examined the child gradually moves in the opposite direction, that is, he becomes less influenced by the immanent Subject through time until he eventually acquires the "correct" interpretation - correct in terms of the reader's expectations but not in terms of Piaget's doctrine.* The ultimate example of this "regression toward correctness" is the natural scientist who shows very little influence by his immanent Subject - a problem that cannot be resolved within Piaget's system, since the Absolute Subject is constantly assimilating the individual and by definition this means progression in the opposite direction. *This fundamental contradiction permeates all of Piaget's work.*

The stage six child, ages one year and three months to one year and seven months, considers his own body to be an object. "The child is now able to see his own body as an object by analogy with that of another person" (ibid. p. 96). The difference between the stage-three child and the stage-six child is that the younger child sees others as objects or things but not himself, while the older child includes himself as an object or thing. The infant first regards other people as objects (ibid., pp. 285-6) (Piaget, 1929, p. 176) (Piaget & Inhelder, 1969, pp. 23-4), then eventually he realizes that he is an object (ibid., pp. 13; 94) (Piaget, 1952b, p. 327). The unstated reason that the infant must be seen as an object, and Piaget puts a great deal of effort into making this point, is the fact that *people must be assimilated* before the Absolute can be fully developed. People, as we have already seen, are the *primary* objects with reference to assimilation (author's italics) (Piaget, 1954, p. 285).

Now that he has covered the six stages in the development of the object concept, Piaget wishes to compare the processes of infant thought to the processes of scientific thought, *because thought remains constantly identical to itself from the functional point of view* (author's italics) (ibid., p. 97). Notice how Piaget immediately tells us in advance that he is not going to compare the processes at all (in fact he completely ignores natural science in what follows), *but that he intends to define scientific thought in terms of infant thought - the particular thought processes that he has just foisted upon us by looking inside the Mind of the immanent Subject within babies* and relating to us ex cathedra what *he alone can see!* He also tells us the rather tangential approach he intends to take: "It is not ... illegitimate to elucidate one of the terms of intellectual evolution by the directly opposite term, that is, the construction of practical objects by that of Scientific Objects" (author's capitalization) (ibid., p. 97). As we have seen previously, natural or practical objects and people are constructed by the Absolute Subject (author's capitalization) (Piaget,

1952b, p. 190) (Piaget, 1971a, pp. 282-3 (Beth & Piaget, 1966, pp. 284-5). That is what he is saying here, as "Scientific Objects" refers to the monads of which this Subject consists. "The elaboration of the object", intones Piaget, "is bound up with that of the universe as a whole" (ibid., p. 103). The universe as a whole is considered "the object" (Piaget & Inhelder, 1974, p. 274) (Piaget, 1969a, p. 34), and every thing physical within it was constructed for the purpose of developing the Absolute as He reverses the process of physical construction by means of assimilation (author's capitalization) (Inhelder & Piaget, 1958, pp. 257-8) (Piaget &Inhelder, 1974, pp. 265; 272) (Piaget, 1971b, p. 114) (Piaget, 1928. pp. 171-174) (Piaget, 1967, p. 106). As noted above, Piaget does not deal with natural science or scientists at all; he only deals with Hegelian-Piagetian Science and the "true" Scientist composed of monads.

THE SIX STAGES IN THE DEVELOPMENT
OF THE SPATIAL FIELD AND GROUPS

The next six stages deal with the Spatial Field and the elaboration of Groups. "It is one thing to act in conformity to the principle of Groups and another to perceive or conceive of them" (author's capitalization) (Piaget, 1954, p. 109). Piaget's position is that everyone acts in conformity with Groups of Monads, but does anyone besides Piaget perceive and conceive of Spatial Groups? *"It is the understanding of Space and not its physiology which we shall try to study here"* (author's italics and capitalization) (ibid., p. 109). *Since Space is the Primordial Biological Entity in Piaget's system we should indeed be able to talk about its metaphysical physiology!*

The first two stages are considered together, and perhaps the most significant aspect of his discussion of the first two stages is that he begins to confuse the meanings of practical groups and Conscious Groups (author's capitalization) (ibid., p. 118). We are always, of course, forced to discern the differences between physical entities and metaphysical Entities. At the third stage Piaget increases complexity as he begins to use the terms "Subjective Group" and "Objective Group" for "Conscious Group" (author's capitalization) (ibid., p. 127), with the term "subjective group" also being lower-level at times. An important theme at this stage is the movement of lower-level groups toward upper-level Groups. This is very confusing as monads always work in Groups - they do not "move toward Groups", but they do move toward more efficient and powerful Groups. Only groups of objects move toward Groups, because when they are fully assimilated they will be reversed by assimilation back into the Groups of monads from which they originally emanated (author's capitalization) (Piaget, 1962, p. 13) (Piaget, 1971b, p. 120) (Piaget, 1974b, pp. 42; 113-14; 149) (Piaget, 1972, p. 73).

The fourth stage deals further with the transition from the lower-level groups of objects to upper level Groups of Monads. Piaget then begins to confuse practical physical displacements with operational displacements (ibid., pp. 172-3). When the infant discovers operations at less than one year of age, Piaget declares that he also discovers Groups! At the fifth stage the child arrives at "objective Groups" and a Homogeneous   Environment   in   which   displacements   take   place   (author's capitalization) (ibid., p. 206), that is, the metaphysical displacements that operations produce occur in the Homogeneous Environment of Monads known as the Spatial Field or Absolute Subject. At the sixth stage the universe contains the Personal Body who is aware of His displacements in an unlimited series of movements which are independent of the subject or child (author's capitalization) (ibid., p. 235). One small correction is helpful: *it is more accurate in this context to say that the Personal Body of Monads contains the universe, as the "universe is embodied in the activity of the Subject"* (author's italics and capitalization) (Piaget, 1952b, p. 43). It is true, of course, that the Personal Body of Monads is also within every object in the universe, but Piaget insists that the Body of Monads or Spatial Continuum is the Container of the universe, not vice versa (author's capitalization) (Piaget, 1974b, p. 149) (Piaget, 1969a, p. 1). In any case, our knowledge of the wider physical environment is made possible because the Logico-Mathematical Framework or Personal Body of Monads or Continuum or Absolute Subject extends *its* Structures into the universe as a whole (Piaget, 1971a, pp. 338-9).

After detailing numerous observations he had made on his children's behavior before they were two years of age, he makes the following statements that appear to be completely unrelated to the behavior described. "Every living or especially psychological organization contains in Germ Form the characteristic operations of the Group" (author's capitalization) (Piaget, 1954, p. 236). The Group is the principle of the System of Operations, and this is why "the logic of relations is immanent in all intellectual activity; every perception and every conception" (ibid., p. 236). "We may say that the Group is immanent in Intelligence itself" (author's capitalization) (ibid., p. 236). "Space is therefore the very activity of the Intelligence" (author's capitalization) (ibid., p. 239). A few pages later he explains what this odd last statement means: "It is the functioning of Intelligence which explains the construction of Space" (author's capitalization) (ibid., p. 245). One needs to realize that both of these terms, "Intelligence" and "Space", are synonyms of the Absolute Subject, and to remember that the development or construction of this Entity is a Self-development.

Which is more outrageous, Piaget's declaration that the above statements are based on the behavior of infants less than two years of age, or his follower's blind faith that there is a connection between the reported infant behavior and the statements? Amazingly, he does not really try to make a plausible connection between the two. Perhaps he really did have the gift of magic!

THE SIX STAGES IN THE DEVELOPMENT OF CAUSALITY

The six stages in the development of causality are supposedly based on the behavior of infants between the ages of three months and one year and nine months. This study is about the development of causality on both the practical plane and causality on the Noetic plane which, it should be noted, is the metaphysical plane where dialectic operations occur (Piaget, 1980a, p. XIV). The first two stages are said to be pure Reflexes (author's capitalization) (Piaget, 1954, p. 250). The immanent Spirit begins to reconstruct Himself in the newborn baby at the Reflex level (author's capitalization) (Piaget, 1950, p. 100) (Piaget, 1952b, p. 41). The influence of the immanent Subject is obvious in the following quote, but how can one ascribe credibility? "The little child, ever since the beginnings of his Mental Life, conceives of his own effort as the cause of every phenomenon" (author's capitalization) (Piaget, 1954, pp. 254-5). Surely one must take leave of his common sense to swallow such incredible assertions. Since the work of the first two stages is based on the Reflexes, they must somehow account for these assertions. Regarding the first two stages, Piaget concludes that "the point of departure of causality should ... be sought in a diffuse feeling of efficacy which would accompany the activity ... but would be localized by the child, not in a self, but in the action" (ibid., p. 258). Note how this statement differs from the previous quote. In the previous quote the baby is said to believe that *his own effort* is the cause of every phenomenon; now the baby is said to realize that *it is not his effort that is efficacious, but in the action-and true action is always upper-level. Fifty four pages later Piaget clarifies what he has in mind by informing us that the child, at about one year of age, "considers the Person of Another as being an entirely autonomous source of action"* (author's italics and capitalization) (ibid., pp. 312-13) - this is why the child does not localize efficacy in himself! References to the upper-level nature of action abound (Piaget, 1950, p. 32) (Piaget, 1972, p. 72) (Piaget & Inhelder, 1974, p. 278) (Piaget & Inhelder, 1969, p. 44). It is also worth mentioning that Piaget imposes a private meaning on the word "efficacy". For him it is a "force immanent in the object and directing it towards its destined end" (Piaget, 1929, p. 225). He also identifies the force involved: "to the child's mind the idea of 'Life' fulfills this function" (author's capitalization) (ibid., p. 225). "Life", of course, is a synonym of the immanent Subject (author's capitalization) (Evans, 1973, p. 111) (Piaget, 1977, p. 32) (Piaget, 1970b, p. 142) (Piaget, 1980b, p. 2). Piaget also defines efficacy as Psychological or upper-level causality which unites intention with the act (author's capitalization) (Piaget, 1954, p. 327). Since efficacy has nothing to do with the physical child, the "feeling" that accompanies it cannot logically be said to be felt by the physical child.

During the third stage the infant, who is between three and eight months of age, "becomes conscious of the existence of a General Cause: the efficacy of ... purpose, of effort ... in short, the Whole Dynamism of Conscious Action" (author's capitalization) (ibid., p. 264). The General Cause is the immanent Dynamism who is the source of true action and not the physical self, as Piaget affirms again (author's capitalization) (ibid., p. 272). He boldly says that this conscious and purposeful activity should be attributed to an Inner Self who is Spatial and Objective, i.e., who is the Spatial Object (author's capitalization) (ibid., pp. 272-3). One cannot expect lucidity regarding such risky admissions, but there can be no question regarding the meaning. Piaget also finds an interesting way to claim again that the infant considers people to be objects: "nothing contrasts [another person] in principle with the rest of the universe" (ibid., p. 286). Actually, this terminology is quite common, but it is so odd and unexpected, in terms of normal expectations, that one tends to become mystified and confused. During the fourth stage "everything takes place as though only his own movements were considered causal, the rest flowing from it, globally and necessarily" (ibid., p. 298). Aside from the impossibility of abstracting such thoughts from the behavior of infants, we see Piaget shamelessly pleading with us to see the influence of unseen "forces" in the lives of very young children. *Only one Entity could "sanely and truthfully" consider His own movements to be so important and central that all other movements in the universe must necessarily flow from His movements. In a strange, repellent way Piaget is reduced to begging!*

During the fifth stage the child gradually begins to realize that he, as a physical entity, is not the source of movements. From this time on the child considers the Person of Another as the source of actions (author's capitalization) (ibid., p. 312-13). *The Person of Another then gradually metamorphoses into a "Universe of Monads" (This is one of the few times that Piaget uses the term "monads" rather than a synonym) with centers of action that act upon each other at a distance* (author's italics and capitalization) (ibid., p. 317). Significantly, Piaget insists on subsequent pages that efficacy is "Spatialized" during this period (ibid., pp. 318; 319; 322; 326; 327; 331) - significant because Piaget is deeply and vitally concerned with a Spatialized Metaphysical Being. He very gradually leads his reader to the notion that the Universe of Monads of the fifth stage autonomously causes natural phenomena, and that this Universal Body is personal (author's capitalization) (ibid., pp. 352-3) - "the Personal activity ... being conceived as the sole cause of phenomena" (author's capitalization) (ibid., p. 353). It is the Organization of Spatial Schemata which constitutes causality; this is considered to be a "necessary intervention of Personal activity" (author's capitalization) (ibid., p. 353). "Causality is ... essentially an intellectual elaboration inherent in the organization of the Schemata and the concomitant organization of the universe" (author's capitalization) (ibid., p. 354).

THE SIX STAGES IN THE DEVELOPMENT OF THE TEMPORAL FIELD

Six stages between the ages of one month and one year seven months are required to develop the temporal field where phenomena occur. During the first two stages Piaget again tries to deal with his doctrine that no objects exist for the very young infant, as he holds that no concepts are developed during these stages which apply to external phenomena (ibid., p. 368). In the third stage, when the child observes object A act upon object B, Piaget says, "it is not the activity of object A which is conceived as cause of the movements of object B but rather the global movement which utilizes A" (ibid., 374). *The child here is made to support Piaget's doctrine that phenomena are not caused naturally by the interaction of objects, but by the Global Body of Monads* (author's italics and capitalization) (Piaget, 1929, pp. 10; 144) (Piaget, 1952b, pp. 357-8) (Piaget, 1972, pp. 21-2) (Piaget, 1977, pp. 45-6). Piaget then pretends to compare this behavior with a second behavior pattern: "Causality is Spatialized and objectified in A, so that B is regarded as depending on A" (author's capitalization) (Piaget, 1954, p. 174). This is not really a comparison between two behavior patterns at all, as Piaget is simply playing one of his favorite tricks. He is demonstrating his proficiency in the use of verbal entities with private meanings to say exactly the same thing using different words as well as exercising complete mastery over his reader. During the fourth stage "the child's Memory begins to enable him to reconstruct short sequences of events independent of the self" (author's capitalization) (ibid., p. 385). Natural scientists have discovered a great deal about how the brain remembers, but the physical brain is not important in Piaget's theory of memory. He "knew" from the beginning of his career that memory is based on the immanent Subject, *not the brain* (author's italics and capitalization) (Piaget, 1971c, p. 154) (Piaget & Inhelder, 1973, pp. 23; 116; 311) (Piaget, 1969a, p. 205) (Piaget, 1971a, p. 187). Piaget devotes little attention to the fifth stage, and little of significance appears to happen. He returns again to the concept of memory in the sixth stage, where the "Child" becomes capable of "evoking memories not linked to direct perception", and "succeeds by that very fact in locating them in a time which includes the whole chronology of the universe" (author's capitalization) (Piaget, 1954, p. 394). *The Child (capitalized as here it is a synonym of his immanent Subject) not only remembers events that he did not perceive through any of his senses, but he remembers events through "the whole chronology of the universe". The immanent Subject is not only responsible for the activities of the individual child, but He is also the source of his memory which extends into the past all the way back to the beginning of things.* These statements demonstrating Piaget's metaphysical philosophy about memory are among the hundreds that have been either ignored or studiously swept under the rug.

CONCLUSIONS REGARDING THE FOUR SETS OF SIX STAGES

Piaget begins his concluding summary by declaring that this book was an attempt to understand how the "world is constructed" by means of the "Sensorimotor Instrument" (author's capitalization) (ibid., p. 395). The Sensorimotor Instrument, even in babies, is an integral part of the Total Body of Monads which created the world. As the baby develops, the Entity within, in addition to reconstructing Himself, recapitulates (author's capitalization) (Piaget, 1971a p. 160) the original creation and other aspects of the physical world.

Merely human subjects are not up to organizing the real world with its phenomena (ibid., pp. 361-2). The child believes that reality is made up by the decisions of the Mind (author's capitalization) (Piaget, 1928, p. 248) and so does Piaget. These decisions have to do with the process of assimilation, and in discussing assimilation Piaget emphasizes his doctrine that it is performed by the Mind and *not* by "the morphologic-reflex organization" or the "physiological and anatomic aspect of the organism". Clearly then, assimilation cannot be performed by the brains of individual people (Piaget, 1954, p. 401). "Reflex" in this quote is switched to the dictionary meaning. The bottom line for Piaget is that Reason, or operational activity of the monads, succeeds in elaborating the World because it replaces the appearance of things with a real construction (author's capitalization) (ibid., p. 431). The world elaborated here is switched to the metaphysical World from the physical world.

OVERVIEW OF DEVELOPMENTAL STAGES

Piaget's theory, as understood by the academic world, revolves around the concept of "stage". None of his concepts have been twisted and mutilated more completely than this concept. Even Piaget complains that psychologists rely too much on the notion of stages (Piaget, 1971a, p. 17). Perhaps if we begin by examining his concept of "partial isomorphism" we can gain a better understanding of what he means by the concept.

> The drawback to the notion of partial isomorphism is, in fact, that it would be perfectly possible to establish links of this kind between any body and any thing: *a flea is a partial isomorph of the moon* ... But partial isomorphisms do acquire some fruitful significance if the two following considerations are fulfilled: (a) when it is possible to point out transformation processes such as may give a lead from one of the structures under comparison to the other; (b) when it is possible to show a connection between these transformations and some actual and observable process of a historic or genetic nature (author's italics) (Piaget, 1971a, p. 58).

If one really understands why a flea is indeed a partial isomorph of the moon, as well as any other object in the physical universe, one has a basis for comprehending Piaget's doctrine of existence and the motivation for his life's work. Understanding depends upon knowing, as in (a), that there is a single transformation process (Inhelder, Sinclair & Bovet, 1974, pp. 8-9) which is moving all physical objects in the same direction towards higher levels (Piaget, 1971c, p. 82), with the eventual result that they will become one with the Absolute Subject Himself who is the Deductive System (author's capitalization) (Piaget, 1974b, p. 125). Since all physical objects have been transformed to some extent by this process, they are all "partial isomorphs" of the Absolute Subject - as well as of each other. The main significance of "partial isomorphism" is not that objects are alike in some way, but that all objects are partially isomorphic to the Absolute Subject, and are constantly becoming more so. How does this help us understand stages? Two hundred and seventy three pages later Piaget further elaborates the concept of "partial isomorphism" without using the term itself. He gives us another example of the process behind the idea when he describes Alpine embryology as obeying the same law of development (more specifically, the law of assimilation that progressively moves the physical toward the metaphysical) that is seen in living objects. This "embryological development" of mountain chains is a series of constructions brought about by applying precisely the same law as is applied in lower-level living processes (Piaget, 1971a, p. 332). The source is the same in each case - the centrifugal aspect of reflective abstractions or operations of the Absolute Subject (author's capitalization) (ibid., p. 331). A corollary point to be made is that the "development" of mountain ranges and the development of individual people have exactly the same source, and are based on the same process, as the metaphysical Biological Entity who constructs Himself. The use of "development" in this case refers to the result of assimilation, which is drastically different from the source of "development" seen in the traditional study of child development. Operational assimilation is the source of both upper-level and lower-level development. The assimilatory "development" of human beings, along with the development of mountain ranges, is the physical or centrifugal aspect of the operation, while the development of the Absolute Subject is the centripetal or metaphysical aspect of the same process. It must be remembered when we speak of "assimilative development" of people, and mountains for that matter, that we are pointing to the very special "development" where the physical is being eliminated so that it can return to the monads from which it came. Two kinds of stages must be distinguished; one kind represents benchmarks that are passed as objects or persons move from the physical toward complete union with the metaphysical, while the other kind represents the parallel development of the metaphysical Subject as He develops both within human beings and outside of human beings. Piaget concentrates his attention on the development of the Absolute Entity. Only this Entity is able to make exact measurements of His progressive development and the stage each object has attained at a given time.

Physical or lower-level causal phenomena "eventually become integrated within a Conceptual Universe including all possibilities and no longer reality" (author's capitalization) (Piaget, 1971c, p. 82). That is, physical reality is eventually assimilated and reunited with the Universe of Monads. Expressed in another way, "an indefinite series of approximations can bring closer together causal and Deductive Systems" (author's capitalization) (Piaget, 1974b, p. 125). Here "causal systems" means physical systems, but keep in mind that Piaget also speaks of the metaphysical System as being "causal".

The development of the immanent Subject may be described as inexorably attaining progressively higher degrees of equilibrium.

> The value of being able to reduce this kind of development to a series of phases each of which possesses a higher degree of equilibrium than its predecessors lies in the fact that the process itself is essentially one of equilibration .... What this means is that the movement towards an eventual equilibrium ... is guaranteed by the nature of the sequential process itself (Inhelder & Piaget, 1964, pp. 292-3).

Equilibrium or complete development of the immanent Absolute Subject *is guaranteed* by the *sequential operational process*. Three of Piaget's disciples describe the same process in somewhat different terms:

> Piaget proposes a single explanatory principle to account for the transformations ... that characterize each successively more complex stage of development. This principle is based on autoregulatory mechanisms which account for both the Structure of the different cognitive stages at various levels of complexity and their mode of construction (author's capitalization) (Inhelder, Sinclair & Bovet, 1974, pp. 8-9).

The "sequential process" was based on "equilibrations" in the previous quote; here it is based on "autoregulatory mechanisms". The meaning is essentially the same as both refer to the production of operations. This is the single process which produces both isomorphisms and a fully developed Absolute Subject.

Textbooks dealing with Piaget's cognitive theory usually describe four major stages of development. The *sensorimotor* from birth to two years, the *preoperational* from two to six years, the *concrete operational* from seven to eleven years and the *formal operational,* twelve years and above. Based on numerous quotes in this chapter, we see how Piaget utilizes the answers of sensorimotor-level children to accentuate essentially every doctrine of his metaphysical position. As attested to by other quotes, he does the same with preoperational and concrete operational children. At the formal level, however, Piaget uses a different tactic in that he tends to exaggerate the superhuman nature of the immanent formal stage. The formal stage or level depends more completely upon the Formal Regulator who is Substance (author's capitalization) (Piaget & Inhelder, 1974, p. 16), because Piaget looks ahead in anticipation of more freedom for the Absolute than seems to exist at the present time. In fact, at times he writes as if the Formal Entity has already assimilated all matter. The Formal Structures responsible for the formal level are depicted at times as though they have been completely liberated from the resistance of matter. Piaget quite often leaps ahead of current levels of development and describes what he assumes will be the case in the distant future (Piaget, 1969b, pp. 297-8) (Piaget, 1972, pp. 46; 64) (Piaget, 1971b, p. 113) (Inhelder & Piaget, 1958, pp. 16; 254-5). Substance is composed of an invariable, permanent quanta or monads (author's capitalization) (ibid., p. 16). An alternate name for "Substance" is the Integrated Structure who directs *formal thinking* (author's italics and capitalization) (Inhelder & Piaget, 1958, p. 332). This Integrated Structure is the Psychological entity who explains with operational actions (author's capitalization) (ibid., p. 332) and is the Totality or Cognitive Field who is in the process of being fully actualized (author's capitalization) (ibid., pp. 330-1). Operational actions are reflective abstractions and formalization is a variety of reflective abstractions (Beth & Piaget, 1966, pp. 254-5) (Piaget, 1977, p. 193). The Cognitive Field is the Logico-Mathematical Structure who is undergoing an endogenous evolution measured by stages.

There are never any new elements or monads involved in constructing the new stages; all that is involved are calculations regarding ever more complex combinations of the monads (Piaget, 1971a, pp. 318-19). "A formalized theory starts from atomic elements ... and ends with a closed or completed System built up from these atomic elements" (author's capitalization) (Piaget, 1953, p. 24). The Formal Structures are in the Total Personality of the adolescent (author's capitalization) (Inhelder & Piaget, 1958, p. 350), and they must assimilate their object, the individual ego (Piaget, 1970d, p. 159). The stages are successive steps toward equilibrium (Piaget, 1973a, p. 60) (Piaget, 1973d, p. 52) (Piaget, 1978a, p. 225), and equilibrium is defined in terms of the assimilation of the whole of reality (Piaget, 1950, pp. 9; 39) (Piaget, 1952b, p. 407) (Bringuier, 1980, p. 44) which is a metaphysical notion. Human beings cannot accomplish this task (Inhelder & Piaget, 1964, pp. 292-3).

The formal stage of development, as described by Piaget, is a clear picture of the immanent Absolute Subject endogenously developing Himself. The fallacious view depicted in textbooks is not a rational possibility. The other three stages are based on the same processes by the same Structures. Piaget specifically states that concrete operations and formal operations have a common Structure (author's capitalization) (Piaget, 1970a, p. 209), and he also affirms that the Logico-Mathematical Structure is inherent at all levels of development (author's capitalization) (Beth & Piaget, 1966, p. 208). Please note that all of the stages are generated autonomously (Piaget & Inhelder, 1971, p. 356) without the aid of human beings. The dynamics of this generation is the series of dialectic improvements initiated by the Absolute Subject (author's capitalization) (Piaget, 1971c., p. 82). Piaget insists that there is only one process of organization in the generation of stages (Inhelder & Piaget, 1964, p. 185), and that "organization" means "development" (Piaget, 1971a, p. 135). All of the stages of Psychological development, not just the formal stage, are regulated by Endogenous Equilibrating Mechanisms which are not hereditary (author's capitalization) (Inhelder, Sinclair & Bovet, 1974, p. 10), and by "not hereditary" Piaget means that stages of development are not based on physical biology. This Mechanism repeats indefinitely the same kind of relation or operation (author's capitalization) (Inhelder & Piaget, 1964, p. 258) until the ultimate goal is reached

(Piaget, 1978a, pp. 226-7). All of the four stages of development refer to the metaphysical series of "reconstructions" of the Absolute Subject within each generation of the series of human beings.

THE ABSOLUTE SUBJECT DEVELOPS HIMSELF

Piaget's concept of development is based on one and only one process - a process that has been given many names. His favorite term is "operation" which can be analyzed in terms of three steps as described in the following excerpt.

> The interpretation of *all processes of development* proceeds by way of a thesis ... an antithesis ... and a synthesis transcending them both, thanks to the reconstruction, at successive levels, of similar or convergent Structures, each of which extends and enriches the preceding Structures while integrating them into itself. This, as we shall see is precisely what happens in the case under consideration (author's italics and capitalization) (Piaget & Inhelder, 1973, p. 137).

As noted above, *Piaget restricts the concept of development to the kind that results from operational activity.* The development of human beings as studied in every university is completely ignored in this definition. His theoretical process of development takes the Absolute Structure, but not the human being, to successively higher levels with each synthesis. The integration Piaget is describing is the integration of each improved Class, that results from every synthesis, into the base Structure. Classes "could only be constructed thanks to relations", and because of relations are constantly in a "state of perpetual mobility" (Piaget, 1930, pp. 297-8). This constant production of new Classes requires their continuous integration into the Body of Monads. This is not the integration of the object into the Subject as it is being assimilated, but Piaget makes no effort to distinguish between these two types of integration. He pretends that there are various *kinds* of structures which must be integrated, but there is only *one kind* of Structure although it is subdivided into many Sub-Structures in order to carry out its many functions. An "indefinite" series of Classes must be integrated, but these Classes all belong to one kind of Structure.

All of the constructions or Classes derived from operations or reflective abstractions are predetermined as it is just a matter of time before they are produced. *The predetermined development of the metaphysical Subject must be distinguished from the contingent development of human beings.*

> To look for the genetic origin of Logico-Mathematical Entities in the general co-ordinations of action, does not therefore mean that the latter contain the former in advance, but that the constructions which are derived from them through reflective abstractions are at once new and non-arbitrary: new, because not contained in them; and non-arbitrary, because they are contained in a predetermined Framework of Possibilities (author's capitalization) (Beth & Piaget, 1966, p. 303).

"The genetic origin of Logico-Mathematical Entities" gives us an invaluable insight into Piaget's concept of construction or development. It tells us what the coordinations of action or reflective abstractions are designed to do in terms of Self-development. First, we need to understand that the developing "Entities" is really the singular Body of Monads. Construction or development, then, is a gradual improvement of the Total Group of Monads to produce "effective" combinatory movements. *This kind of gradual improvement is Piaget's upper-level concept of Knowledge, and the process of achieving this Knowledge is Piaget's concept of valid Science.* The ultimate goal of the Body of monads, according to Piaget, is to become so efficient that it would be impossible for its opposite, the material facts of reality, to dialectically contradict this Body again (author's capitalization) (Piaget, 1974b, p. 123). This ultimate goal of perfect development is predetermined in the Framework of Possibilities that will be realized by the Body of Monads alias the Absolute Subject.

The developmental or constructive process is called "formative" in the following selection, where Piaget also tells us why child psychology is important for him. It is important, not because it informs us how the physical child develops, but because it enables us to follow the step-by-step formative process of the immanent "Living Subject" *in the physical "lived" subject.*

> Equilibration by Self-regulation constitutes the formative process of the Structures we have described. Child psychology enables us to follow their step-by-step evolution, not in the abstract, but in the lived and Living dialectic of subjects (author's capitalization) (Piaget & Inhelder, 1969, p. 159).

Equilibration by Self-regulation is a silly tautology, as both terms simply mean "operation". Child psychology supposedly enables Piaget to follow the progressive formative development of the Living Subject within lived subjects. The "steps" which Piaget imagines he sees are produced by dialectic equilibrations or Self-regulations. Each of these steps represents an improved Class of monads in the progressive development of the Absolute Subject. Piaget is focused on the imagined metaphysical Living Subject or Structure in this dialectic engagement with the lived or physical child. The development of the individual child holds no interest for him at all, except as an object to be eliminated by assimilation. The Living Subject is a Normative Structure, and He develops Himself by Self-regulations - the one method available to Him.

> The Normative Structure achieves a condition of equilibrium ... as a function ... of a process of Self-regulation. This Self-regulation is ... inherent in the production of Structure in that there are no Constructive Mechanisms and no Corrective Mechanisms ... but that progressive organization - in which construction consists (author's capitalization) (Piaget, 1973d, pp. 49-50).

For Piaget, the Absolute Structure of monads is the only Normative Structure in existence. This "Fundamental Structure" does not depend upon human nature because human nature is not permanent (author's capitalization) (Piaget, 1970b, p. 106). Norms, on the other hand are unchangeable and permanent (Piaget, 1973d, p. 34). This Structure is in the process of achieving equilibrium by Self-regulations, equilibrations or operations. Self-regulation is the only possible way to construct Normative Structures as Piaget redundantly says. Normative Structures move inexorably toward completion and equilibrium as they assimilate their opposite, the conventional structures. Furthermore, Normative Structures are diachronic while conventional structures are synchronic.

> The defining character of Norms is that they are obligatory ... Their equilibrium at any given time depends upon their antecedent history, for the distinctive character of development here is that it is always directed toward such equilibrium .... Normative and conventional structures are ... at opposite poles as regards the relations between synchronics and diachronics (author's capitalization) (Piaget, 1970b, p. 79).

Norms are "obligatory". Piaget means by this term that nothing can stand in their way because they are aspects of the Absolute Subject. They are also "obligatory" with regard to their development as it is completely predetermined and autonomous. The development of the Norm (it is really singular) is always Self-directed toward equilibrium, which is not fully achieved until the physical universe is completely assimilated. The Normative Structure is the dialectic opposite of conventional structures, and it is diachronic (author's capitalization) (Piaget, 1973d, pp. 13-14; 34-5; 51-2; 60-1) (Beth & Piaget, 1966, p. 280) (Piaget, 1971c, p. 156) because it exists through all time while conventional structures are synchronic because they exist at a given time, but not through all time.

The A Priori Framework is "necessary" because it is Normative. Piaget points out in the following quote that this Framework could not be based on physical biology and also be "necessary". Human biology cannot provide necessary characteristics. We observed previously how Flavell (1963, pp. 35-6) and Furth (1969, p. 48) were forced to incorrectly accept the notion that physical biology somehow produced necessary characteristics because they incorrectly reduced all of Piaget's dual system to the physical level.

> A Priori Frameworks evolve and perfect themselves .... [But] if A Priori evolve like some biological characteristic ... then they must lose, along with their uniqueness and their universality ... the very thing that gave them their chief value, which was their necessity (author's capitalization) (Piaget, 1971a, pp. 314-15).

The A Priori Framework is the Absolute Subject who alone is unique, universal and necessary. He could not evolve or develop like some biological entity as He is Normative and thus Biological!

> Let it be noted that A Priori do indeed evolve, but this can only take place by means of internal autoregulations and not because of chance encounters with environment or by some simple interplay of mutations and selections (author's capitalization) (ibid., p. 314).

The only way that the A Priori can evolve or develop is by internal or Self-development. Human beings must depend upon more or less "chance encounters" as they cannot utilize the Operational Mechanism that ensures perfect development. Ordinary interaction with the environment and genetic mutations with selection of the good one has no affect on the development of the A Priori. The only basis for the metaphysical development of this Entity is dialectic interactions with the environment arranged and produced by the Self.

Endogenous Structures are seen to be the Normative, A Priori Structures of the Living Subject. To further complicate the situation, Piaget adds the very confusing synonym "Individual" in the following quote, as well as "Logico-Mathematical" Entity and "Assimilatory Framework".

> We understand by "Endogenous" only those Structures which are developed by means of the regulations and[sic] operations of the Subject ... Such constructs[sic] ... arise from internal Logico-Mathematical activity engendered by the coordination of Individual's actions. By serving as an Assimilatory Framework then, these Structures are added to the properties of the external object (author's capitalization) (Piaget, 1980b, p. 80).

The development of Endogenous Structures is also, silly as it is, endogenous because it occurs by means of regulations or (not "and") operations performed by the Subject. "Endogenous" is said to describe the Structure; quite often this is the indicated meaning (Piaget, 1970c, p. 19), but here this term is used to describe the activity or development of the Structure (Piaget, 1974b, p. 67) (Piaget, 1980b, p. 81;106). As we have seen repeatedly, this is a common device for creating unnecessary complexity. We must remind ourselves that Structure is a synonym of Subject so Piaget is really describing Self-development. Such an activity as "regulation" or "operation" is based on the coordination of monads by the Absolute Individual. In the last sentence Piaget returns to the Self-developing Structure which develops while simultaneously adding aspects of Himself to objects as He assimilates them. The *Structure* is the *Subject* who is the *Logico-Mathematical Entity* who is the *Individual* who is the *Assimilatory Framework*. Note that it should be regulations or operations, and thus "construct" not "constructs".

In the passage below spatio-temporal transformations occur in physical reality, but "Geometric transformations" are based on the power of the Body of Monads or Subject, who exists apart from physical reality. The physical subject is also introduced inappropriately in this passage in order to muddle interpretation.

> If physical reality is conceived as the locus of spatio-temporal transformations, there remains a rather fundamental difference between them and the Geometric transformations due to the Subject. As far as the latter are concerned, the power is ... in the hands of the Subject Himself. To say that the subject constitutes only a locus or a stage and that the operations play the game by themselves does nothing to change the situation, because each operation is an act and it is their totality ... that constitutes the Subject (author's capitalization) (Piaget, 1974b, p. 152).

The Geometric transformations performed by the Subject are fundamentally different from transformations based on physical actions, so the Subject responsible for Geometric transformations is not physical and does not use physical forces in carrying out these kinds of transformations. *Notice that in the third sentence Piaget suddenly introduces the physical subject with no hint that he is drastically changing the parameters of his argument. It is extremely hard for the reader to handle such unexpected 180 degree changes in focus without some help from the author. Few, if any, readers have previously been subjected to such abusive, outrageously deceptive treatment by well-known academicians.* The lower-level subject is the place or stage where the immanent Subject performs His operations, but this, as he says, does not change the situation. Piaget switches back to the Absolute Subject at the end of the third sentence when he explains that the whole series of operations is what constitutes or fully develops the Subject or Body of Monads as a whole. "Constitute" is one of Piaget's favorite terms and one must be careful to understand whether he is using it to mean "to be the elements or components of" or mean "to set up", "establish" or "develop". In the third sentence it is the latter meaning.

In the following quote, the Subject alone elaborates His own Structures and the implied lower-level subject is the theater of action but not the source. The Absolute Subject by-passes every aspect of empiricism.

> In "operating" on the objects, the Subject alone, by His action, elaborates Structures and is not simply the theater of a restructuration or of a reequilibration acting according to the laws of gestalt physics. Otherwise the simultaneous restructuration of objects and Subject within the "Field" which encompasses them both, leads us back to a kind of empiricism (author's capitalization) (Piaget, 1973a, p. 132).

The Subject alone - thus autonomously, by means of assimilating the environment, but without its aid - elaborates Structures. This, of course, is Self-development because it is His Structures that are elaborated! Piaget makes it clear, however, that this elaboration does not follow from the laws of physical reality and, therefore, would be alien to empirical explanation. He does spell out both the centrifugal function, or the "restructuration of objects", and the centripetal function, or "restructuration of the Subject". *It is rare, as previously noted, that Piaget describes both functions at the same time.* The restructuration of the object refers to its assimilation, while the restructuration of the Subject refers to His perfect development. One should observe, however, that Piaget confounds an important facet of his metaphysical theory. The objects, including all subjects, are indeed encompassed within the Field of Monads, but is the Subject also encompassed as Piaget says? *Since the Subject is the Field, how are we to conceive of the Field encompassing the Subject?* This is the kind of nullity into which Piaget delights to lead his unsuspecting reader. He is correct though in assuming that it would be very difficult to clearly formulate his theory when one must constantly deal with such deliberate impediments to clear understanding.

In the following quote Piaget emphasizes that upper-level Thought is dialectical, and that it tends to restore equilibrium when disequilibrium occurs.

> Since Natural Thought is essentially dialectical in its development, being a succession of disequilibriums and reequilibrations, dialectical contradictions are bound to fall within the province of such Mechanisms, even though we must always remember that these contradictions, "dialectical" and natural alike, are merely the expression and not the causal source of those disequilibriums (author's capitalization) (Piaget, 1980a, p. 304).

"Natural Thought" is obviously upper-level, but in the same sentence "natural contradiction", as opposed to dialectical contradiction, is used inappropriately. *"Natural contradiction" here is the lower-level dictionary definition, not upper-level as one would expect if Piaget had followed the conventional expectations of parallelism.* Natural "contradiction" in this quote does not provoke upper-level Thought, as one would normally expect. This is not very nice, but it is highly typical. The dialectical development of Natural Thought is operational, which takes the form of the thesis, antithesis, synthesis triad. Even though the term "dialectic" is not used very often, the concept is a major theme in Piaget's books. He says that "development is in conformity with the general dialectic of Subject and object" (author's capitalization) (Piaget, 1976a, p. 164), and he mentions that Hegel spoke of dialectic oppositions which produce Structures from other Structures (author's capitalization) (Piaget, 1971a, pp. 327-8). Piaget adds that we can be sure further Hegelian syntheses will take place because an immanent dialectic is at work (Piaget,

1970b, pp. 125-6; 143). Finally, the Hegelian pattern is inevitable once we turn away from false absolutes (Piaget, ibid., p. 123).

Human affectivity means very little to Piaget because it does not move the Subject toward final equilibrium or development. Only Intelligence or Reason can do that.

> Affectivity is nothing without Intelligence. Intelligence furnishes affectivity with its means and clarifies its ends ... In reality, the most profound tendency of all Human activity is progression toward equilibrium. Reason which expresses the highest forms of equilibrium, reunites Intelligence and affectivity (author's capitalization) (Piaget, 1967, pp. 69-70).

Previous to this quote, Piaget put forward the notion that as "Intellectual elaboration" progresses, affectivity gradually disengages itself from the self in order to submit it to the "laws of cooperation" which are nothing more than the "laws of operations". (A slight correction: affectivity does not disengage itself; it is disengaged by operations of the Subject). In the quote, we see that Reason reunites Intelligence and affectivity. This reunification occurs because we are not only talking about Self-development, but also about Self-love on the part of the Absolute. We can understand in a general way that Piaget is describing his own religious experience in which his affections gradually became less egocentric and more Egocentric, that is, they revolved around Reason which is another way of saying that they were based on operations. Moreover, Piaget's theory gives a strange twist to the concept of affectivity, a twist toward narcissism in which the true Self loves only the true Self. *A corollary to narcissism is that the true Self does not love people!* Piaget says that "the root notion in the term 'narcissism' is valid" (Piaget & Inhelder, 1969 p. 22). When the most profound tendency of Human activity reaches equilibrium, Homo Sapiens will be fully developed and love only Himself! The "true" Human, as we have seen, is the immanent Homo Sapiens not the physical homo faber (author's capitalization) (Piaget, 1930. p 195).

In the following quote Piaget informs us that pure Mathematics is based squarely on the Subject's general actions or operations. Furthermore, we are informed that individual people have nothing to do with pure Mathematics.

> The psychological reasons for the possibility of pure Mathematics: The first of these is the radical autonomy of operational development ... The operations are constructed by abstraction starting from the Subject's general actions, independently of specific physical objects and of the ... action of individuals as such (author's capitalization) (Beth & Piaget, 1966, p. 244).

In a discussion of "the psychological problem of pure Mathematics" Piaget wavers between mathematics as an activity and as the Entity Himself who is the metaphysical Mathematician (author's capitalization) (Beth & Piaget, 1966, pp. 242-247). Later in the same book he definitely speaks of the Mathematical Entity, the "Creator of Forms", who gives rise to Mathematical Form by Self-development - in other words, the Creator of Forms is the Mathematical Form. In another context, Piaget speaks of "Groups" and "Networks" as being Mathematical Structures (author's capitalization) (Piaget, 1974a, pp. 75-6). As we have seen, these three terms are synonyms of the metaphysical Body of Monads. Also, the "changes of position", which is one way that Piaget describes the process of assimilation as accomplished by the three dimensional Lattice of Monads, is said to form a Mathematical Group (author's capitalization) (Piaget, Inhelder & Szeminska, 1960, p. 3). More accurately, the Mathematical Group of Monads, by producing the "changes of position", develops Himself. Again, operational development is radically autonomous, with the reminder that this means individual people have nothing to do with it. Operational development is based solely on "abstraction", which in this excerpt means "operations".

In the following selection, Piaget lectures his reader on the fundamentals of metaphysical Mathematics. Mathematics reconstructs Reality and deduces phenomena. Metaphysical Reality, or the Living Absolute Himself, is in the process of "reconstructing" Himself by means of purging Himself of all objects, but in the meantime He deduces or produces natural phenomena. He accomplishes both feats by means of operations - dialectical operations for reconstructing Himself who represents "true" Reality, and other kinds of operations for producing natural phenomena or physical reality. The last sentence underscores the central meaning of Mathematics - which is the central activity of the Absolute Subject or operations. The whole series of possible operations will assure His perfection.

> Mathematics ... alone can enable Him to reconstruct Reality and to deduce what phenomena are, instead of merely recording them. The point is that, to do this, Mathematics uses operations and transformations ("Groups", "operators") which are still actions although they are carried out mentally. What [Mathematics] actually does goes far beyond immediate reality .... Mathematics consists not only of all actual transformations but of all possible transformations (author's capitalization) (Piaget, 1971a, p. 6).

Only Piaget would use "mathematics" in the way it is used in this quote. The first two instances of "Mathematics" refers to the immanent Entity, while the last instance refers to the operational activity of the Entity as a Whole. The next to last usage, in parenthesis, could be either the Entity or His activity. This interpretation is not really obvious, but the overall meaning seems to require this view. The metaphysical Mathematician can "deduce" or produce phenomena and use operations and transformations. The last sentence views mathematics as the "mental" operational or mathematical activity of the Absolute, which in producing all possible transformations, concomitantly develops Himself perfectly.

The monads that make up personal, metaphysical Space are busy assimilating all objects in Space, Piaget gives his reader a glimpse of his rather closely guarded feelings regarding this process in the following quote.

> The grouping of displacements leads to the gradual ... "purging" of Space (if the reader will forgive the metaphor), by progressively emptying it of objects in order to organize the Space or "Container" itself, leads to exactly the same result ... This dual process does not take place all at once ... Both paths followed by this process invariably consist of anchoring the transformations to invariants, basing ... the displacements on an inter-linkage of objects assumed to be stationary (author's capitalization) (Piaget & Inhelder, 1956, p. 377).

The metaphor, "purging of Space", is an excellent way to illustrate Piaget's concept of assimilation, as well as an indication of his attitude toward this very anti-social process. The Body of Monads, called the Absolute Subject, Space or Container must cleanse Himself of all undesirable "impurities". This purging must eliminate everything in physical reality, *including all people*. One could well suspect that Piaget's request for forgiveness to the reader being purged, is not altogether sincere! Observe that Space is actively emptying Himself of objects by operational displacements. "Progressively emptying" Himself of objects is merely a fanciful way to express the process of assimilation by Space or Container, and it is for the purpose of organizing or developing Himself. It is important to realize that the displacements by assimilation results in a dual grouping of two kinds of classes which follow two different paths - Classes of progressively improving monads and classes of progressively assimilated matter. The exact opposites among these classes will continue to engage in operations until no matter remains. The invariants on which the two kinds of transformation are anchored are the upper-level objects or monads which are "assumed to be stationary". *Observe that Piaget does not give the reader the courtesy of differentiating the first "objects", which means lower-level matter from the second "objects" which has the drastically different upper-level meaning of metaphysical monads. No, this is a contrived effort to mystify or confuse.* The monads do move, as we have seen, but since the movements are at "absolute speed" no time elapses - thus they are "assumed to be stationary"!

Piaget's low opinion of natural science is evident in the following selection. Every aspect of physical reality that traditional science is involved with will dissolve, i. e. be assimilated, in the metaphysical process of the Absolute's development.

> Any being (or object) that sciences attempt to hold fast dissolves once again in the current of development. It is in the last analysis of this development, and of it alone, that we have the right to state, "It is (a fact)". What we can and should then seek is the law of this process (Piaget, 1971b, p. 3).

All of the objects and people studied by natural science eventually dissolve in the current of assimilation which is a concomitant of the Subject's development. In this particular selection, *Piaget wants to reserve the status of "fact" for the metaphysical process of development, and nothing else. Surely this is one of the most extreme examples of an idee fixe one will ever see!* Piaget readily admits to being dominated by a single idea. At the beginning of his autobiography he has this to say: "There is probably some truth in the statement by Bergson that a philosophic mind is generally dominated by a single personal idea which he tries to express in many ways in the course of his life" (Piaget, 1976b, p. 115). Furthermore, in the conclusion to his autobiography, the first sentence reads: *"My one idea* ... has been that Intellectual operations proceed in terms of Structures-of-the-Whole. These Structures denote *the kind of equilibrium toward which Evolution in its entirety is striving"* (author's italics and capitalization) (ibid., p. 136). Since the Living Structure, or "Biology", is striving toward His own evolution, which in this context means full development, we see a reaffirmation of the single "fact" of Piaget's System. Note that if "Evolution" is *striving, it* is another unusual synonym for the Absolute Subject. Many other statements by Piaget carry the idea that a single general doctrine is what motivates Piaget, for instance (Piaget, 1969b, p. 179). And what is the purpose of the second parenthesis? This statement, including the inappropriate parenthesis, was probably designed by Piaget to cause the reader to stop and puzzle over it a bit, and it does deserve some thought. Piaget is basically concerned with only two concepts and they are both metaphysical. First, he is vitally concerned with the attributes of the Absolute Subject; second, he is equally concerned with the Self-developing activities of this Subject. These two concerns converge to the one fact of the need for His development. This particular emphasis of the "one fact" shows that Piaget is actually looking far into the future when, according to his doctrines, the physical universe will finally have been assimilated and the Subject, or Body of Monads, will then exist isolated in the splendor of its perfect development. In the "last analysis", then, this is the one fact that will remain.

The Living Structure is eternal and He constructs or develops Himself by means of repeatedly "reflecting" partially developed aspects of His Structure to progressively higher levels.

> There are no absolute beginnings in the building up of Structures ....The brain [does not contain] in advance the Structures which are built up in the course of development; the latter "construct" themselves in the true sense of the word, that is, the simpler Structures already elaborated at a lower stage are "reflected" on to a higher plane (author's capitalization) (Beth & Piaget, 1966, p. 198).

Piaget affirms that his Structures are eternal as they have no beginning, but there *is* a beginning in "the building up of Structures". This process of development did not start until the first operational synthesis occurred. These Structures are composed of monads which fill all of space, including the insides of all objects and every person. Metaphysical monads have only one overriding goal regardless of whether they are inside people or outside, and that is to assimilate matter so that the entire Body of Monads can develop Himself fully. *The only means of this development is the use of operations.*

CONSTRUCTION AS DEVELOPMENT OF THE ABSOLUTE SUBJECT

There is a "Certain Given" who has always existed, that is why not even Piaget can "go behind it". Everything began with this "Given" who was full of potential that needed to be actualized by "working through His opposite". It was this need that started a chain of events which resulted in the universe and human society as we know it.

> There are Certain Givens from which the construction of Logical Structures takes off ...
> We called these Initial Structures behind which we cannot go "General Coordinations of Actions", meaning to refer to the connections that are common to all sensori-motor coordinations (author's capitalization) (Piaget, 1970b, pp. 62-3).

The "Certain Givens" or "Initial Structures" refers to the Spatial Continuum of Monads who was there all by Himself at the beginning. The "Logical Structures" do not "take off" from this "Given" as the Given *is* the Logical Structure. The Logical Structure or Given simply begins to develop Himself according to the "laws of development" that Piaget has so urgently, but ambiguously and enigmatically, expounded in his many books. As usual, there is a peculiar corruption of language. He uses an activity of the Initial Structure - "General Coordinations of Actions" - to mean the Structure Himself. The term "construction" is to be taken in its "genetic sense", which means that it is a precise synonym of "development".

The main function of genetic construction, as discussed below, is to "reconstitute an Object of Thought". This is exactly the same function as ascribed to "Mathematics" above, which was to reconstruct Reality. We must realize, however, that in the first, second and last sentence in the quote below, "mathematics" is used with the traditional dictionary meaning. Interestingly, Piaget admits that he is not competent to discuss the *traditional* concept of mathematical construction.

> We shall take the term "construction" here in its genetic or general sense, which is to produce or to reconstitute an Object of Thought and not in its special mathematical sense ... see note 9 on next page .... We take the term "construction" in the sense of the production of the Object, without needing to discuss the mathematical concept of construction, which we are not competent to do ... The axioms [of this construction] ... are the result of a reflective abstraction starting from operational co-ordinations .... The Mind ... always seems to be constructive (in the genetic and not the mathematical sense of the term) (author's capitalization) (Beth & Piaget, 1966, pp. 294-5).

Piaget wishes to disclose his private meaning of "construction", but not without some contortions to clutter up the concept. In the middle of a description in note 8 on page 294 he illogically refers the reader to note 9 on the following page where he repeats over and over what he said in note 8. The private definition of genetic or operational construction is expressed six times altogether, and *it simply means the production or development of the metaphysical Subject*. The genetic definition is essential as Piaget is speaking of the construction of his "Object of Thought", or "Object", or "Mind", which, in this excerpt, are synonyms of the Absolute Subject.

The first sentence of the following quote repeats approximately the same idea four times. First, "operational construction" is, second, the "construction of operational Structures" by, third, a "certain activity" which, fourth, is "genetic" action or operations. Piaget dances in place like a dog chasing his tail. It is important to observe that this genetic process of construction by operational activity does not originate, and cannot be controlled by, human beings. Only the Transcendental, Universal, Epistemic or Biological Organization, who is immanent in, or common to, every person can perform this function.

> The operational construction suggested by genetic analysis is [based upon] a certain activity which allows [the Subject] to construct Operational Structures. This construction is not arbitrary, for the individual subject is neither its origin nor does he seem to control it. The Epistemic Subject is what all subjects have in common since the general co-ordinations of actions involve a Universal which is [the] Biological Organization itself. [This is] contrary to physical or psychological empiricism (author's capitalization) (Beth & Piaget, 1966, p. 285).

Only the Epistemic Subject is capable of operational construction. The individual subject has nothing to do with this kind of construction or development. It is also important to understand that a "certain activity" - only one very curious activity - enables the Subject to construct or develop the Operational Structures which make up his own Biological Organization of Monads. The Universal Biological Organization, which is immanent in every individual subject, actually *opposes* the physical, psychological entity of empiricism - the individual person.

The "natural" method of forming Logico-Mathematical Structures in the following passage is the metaphysical method of reflective abstraction. This method of forming or constructing Structures touches upon metaphysical Epistemology and Mathematics.

> Reflecting abstraction ... rebuilds unremittingly at higher levels what is taken from actions or operations at lower levels, this being the common natural method of forming Logico-Mathematical Structures. For their part, psychologists, studying this formation, which may be spontaneous or guided by teaching methods, are, either unconsciously or deliberately, constantly touching upon these questions of Epistemology and of the foundations of Mathematics (author's capitalization) (Piaget, 1973c, pp. 55-6).

Piaget repeats the "certain activity" which alone builds or develops the Universal Biological Organization or Logico-Mathematical Structure. This Structural Entity has, or rather, *is* the only Constructive Mechanism in existence (author's italics and capitalization) (Piaget, 1973d, pp. 49-50). Reflecting abstractions or operations rebuild at higher levels what is received from actions or operations at lower levels. This is one of many ways to describe the "certain activity", which entails a very long series of operations forming the basis of Piaget's concept of Epistemology, producing the kind of Knowledge needed by the Subject in His development, and is called "mathematics". As Piaget says, the factors involved in "Mental effort" are really mathematical (author's capitalization) (Inhelder & Piaget, 1958, p. 268).

In the next selection, Piaget says that the chief factor in development is equilibrium, but the meaning is reversed. Equilibrium is determined by the level of development not the other way around, as equilibrium is a result not an action. The meaningful statement that Piaget had in mind was that the chief factor in development is equilibration, as this is the action that leads to equilibrium. He teasingly chose to use the wrong word as he is wont to do. This particular bit of roguery is practiced several times (Piaget, 1970b, p. 113) (Inhelder & Piaget, 1958, p. 332) (Piaget, 1971c, p. 8) (Piaget, 1967, p. 103), and it not only prevents clear communication, but it also creates frustration in the reader which is one of his goals (Piaget, 1977, pp. 144-5).

> The chief factor in ... development is ... equilibrium, which arises from the fact that the co-ordinations are increasingly controlled by the Subject's activities, which tend to compensate the external influences .... So we see that under its different aspects, the transition from Sensory-Motor Structures to Operational Structures depends on processes which are essentially *internal,* that is, capable of guaranteeing the autonomy of the successive constructions (author's italics and capitalization (Beth & Piaget, 1966, p. 297).

The "certain activity", now called the "chief factor", is specified again as "equilibrium" which is based on the Subject's "coordinations" or "activities". The coordinations are not "controlled" by the Subject's activities because they *are* the Subject's activities. We should also be aware that there is no true transition from Sensory-Motor Structures to Operational Structures as they are the same Structures. Piaget even claims that Sensory-Motor action is the source of operations in the sense that the same Structure produces operations at a later stage of development (Piaget, 1970b, p. 44). The point is that there is only one Body of Monads! Piaget insists that "internal processes guarantee the autonomy of this successive construction" (Beth & Piaget, 1966, pp. 296-298). The whole history of Human Knowledge is based on Structures which are integrated into a Single Structure or Organism (author's capitalization) (Piaget, 1971a p. 360), and all development presupposes an Initial Structure. The development of this Initial Structure consists in His completion and differentiation (author's capitalization) (Inhelder & Piaget, 1964, p. 1) (Piaget, 1967, p. 144).

Piaget emphasizes the universality of the Absolute Entity who "engulfs" the real world in order to "explain" it better. "Explain" becomes an unusual synonym for "assimilate".

> Reflecting abstraction ... does not replace empirical abstraction, rather it frames it, as it were, from the outset, and subsequently transcends it infinitely (in the proper sense of the word). Nor does the Universe of Logico-Mathematical Possibility replace the real world, but rather engulfs it in order to explain it better (author's capitalization) (Piaget, 1980b, p. 97).

The "chief factor" or "certain activity" is now "reflecting abstraction", which "frames" or "engulfs" empirical abstraction as well as the real world. The Body of Monads frames or engulfs not only everything physical, but even the type of learning, "empirical abstraction", which is employed in "copying" the physical. Eventually empirical abstraction along with the real world *are* replaced, contrary to Piaget's statement, because they are in the process of being eliminated by assimilation. Reflecting abstraction transcends empirical abstraction *infinitely because it is operational.* "The infinite is not a physical but an operatory notion", meaning that something besides physical reality, the only reality studied by natural science, is intervening (Piaget et al., 1977, p. 96). The reason we can combine "reflecting abstraction" with the "Universe of Logico-Mathematical Possibility" is that *the latter "explains" by means of reflecting abstraction or operations.* This Universe of Monads does not explain verbally; it explains by its operations, and it can operate on everything because it frames and engulfs everything. The formative process depends upon the engulfing monads which in turn depend upon physical reality to "contradict" their presence and activity.

> This progressive overtaking ... of contradictions, which constitutes the formative process of differentiations as well as of coordinations, is fundamental when it comes to relations between operations and causality. To raise contradictions is, in effect, to construct a new Operational Structure (author's capitalization) (Piaget, 1974b, p. 122).

The "chief factor", "certain activity" or "reflecting abstraction" becomes "progressive overtaking" of dialectic contradictions.

A contradiction is "overtaken" when a synthesis occurs. It is overtaken when the Operational Structure coordinates His Body of Monads in an efficient operation. The formative process of Self-construction or Self-development proceeds in this way. "Causality" in this context appears to mean "with regard to Self-development", however we must bear in mind that causality can either mean cause in the physical world of reality (author's capitalization) (Piaget, 1973d, p. 18) (Piaget, 1929, p. 188) or cause in the development of the Absolute (author's capitalization) (Piaget et al., 1977, p. 176). Piaget confirms this fact by stating that there are two kinds of causality; one kind is on the practical plane of reality and the other is on the "Noetic" or metaphysical plane (author's capitalization) (ibid., p. 175) (Piaget, 1954, p. 249) (Piaget, 1974b, p. 121). As noted previously, metaphysical causality is based on operations defined in terms of thesis, antithesis and synthesis, while physical causality or phenomena is based on a different kind of operational manipulation of physical objects by the monads. The construction or development of the Absolute Structures requires an extremely long series of dialectical contradictions and their resulting overtakings by synthesis.

Logico-Mathematical Structures are said to be the product of the Living Organization, but Piaget does not explain that Logico-Mathematical Structures and the Living Organization are the same Being. And neither does he explain that the term "product" really means "development". The Living Organization is the Biological Structure who is *not composed of material atoms.*

> Logico-Mathematical Structures [are] the product of ... the Living Organization itself, then to attribute to Intellectual operations the nature of higher types of regulation will take on an even more profoundly Biological significance .... [22 lines later] as soon as atomism is rejected in favor of dialectical constructionism (author's capitalization) (Piaget, 1971a, p. 212).

The Logico-Mathematical Structure is the Living Organization and since this Entity is eternal it could not be a product of any other Entity. The development of this Entity, however, is Self-development, and this is implicit in the quote. It is interesting that the "higher types of regulation" have a profound "Biological significance". We know that this is metaphysical Biology for two reasons: First, Piaget would never say that physical biology is "profound"; second, "Biological significance" is connected, over the next 22 lines of print, with dialectic constructivism rather than material atomism. Unlike the book containing the previous quote, "atomism" in *Biology and Knowledge* is, with few exceptions, lower level. In fact, material atomism in this book serves explicitly as the antithesis of monadism while dialectic constructivism is set forth as the synthesis of the two opposites (Piaget, 1971a, pp. 93; 132). There are two kinds of atomism, but only one appears to be in tune with the Spirit of Structuralism (author's capitalization) (Piaget, 1970b, p. 8). For the genetic Epistemologist, every act of understanding, reflexive abstraction, Self-regulation or operation contributes to the continuous construction of Knowledge necessary for the full realization of the Absolute Subject (author's capitalization) (Piaget, 1970c, p. 77). The following passage focuses on *metaphysical atomism or monadism.* Piaget approaches the concept by trying to con his reader into believing that children find it easy and natural to acquire it.

> True atomism [is] a form of atomism based on mental constructs rather than on perception. Now, nothing could be simpler than this final step: all the child has to do is to realize that the 'tiny things', the 'crumbs' or the 'dust', result from the break-up of the initial lump and that, if this process is continued, the end product will be a host of invisible but none the less Substantial corpuscles (author's capitalization) (Piaget & Inhelder, 1974, p. 79).

Piaget shows us how easily the child "constructs" the concept of metaphysical atomism. "Nothing could be simpler" than to realize that the "tiny things" that result when sugar lumps begin to dissolve in water, will eventually become a host of invisible but none the less Substantial corpuscles or monads. Piaget is definitely not talking about the atomism of natural science, as he prefaced this selection with the observation that the children were demonstrating elements of a future "powder metaphysics". The meaning of "Substantial" is metaphysical not material. In most instances, the meaning of "atom" or "atomism" in this book, unlike the opposite meaning in *Biology and Knowledge*, is metaphysical, not material.

As we saw previously, the coordination of the Subject's actions is both causal at the physical level and causal at the level of metaphysical decentering. The coordinations which manipulate the objects of reality to produce observable phenomena, however, are different from the coordinations which metaphysically decenter human egos.

> In short, the co-ordination of the Subject's actions, inseparable as it is from the spatio-temporal and causal co-ordinations which he attributes to reality, is the origin both of the differentiations between this Subject and objects and of the decentering process on the level of physical acts (author's capitalization) (Piaget, 1972, p. 22).

It is important to understand that there are two kinds of coordinations by the Subject. Piaget refers to coordinations which lead to metaphysical results first, then mentions the Subject's coordinations which lead to the phenomena of reality, before more fully describing metaphysical coordinations. Instances of the latter in Piaget's work far outnumber instances of spatio-temporal coordination. The metaphysical coordination on which development depends involves the selection of opposite pairs of classes by the Absolute, the representation of these pairs and their possible modes of engagement to Himself, followed by the act of operational engagement (author's capitalization) (Piaget & Inhelder, 1971, pp. 11; 128; 347) (Piaget, 1977, pp. 84; 147) (Piaget, 1978a, pp. 220-1). Spatio-temporal or causal coordination by the monads includes every change and movement in the physical universe and, of course, this is also metaphysical activity. Although this type of coordination would seem to keep the monads of the Subject extremely busy, it is in Piaget's opinion, of secondary importance compared with the metaphysical coordinations of thesis, antithesis and synthesis. *Observe that metaphysical coordinations are said to include processes on "the level of physical acts". This is deliberate misinformation as it is not "physical acts", but "acts on the physical".* As we have seen, Piaget frequently uses this particular adolescent-like ploy to confuse the reader (Piaget, 1928, p. 148) (Piaget, 1969a, p. 33) (Piaget & Inhelder, 1974, pp. 77; 115; 179-80; 225-6; 267; 278) (Piaget & Inhelder, 1956, p. 485).

In the following passage, Piaget contrasts the work of the physical subject with the work of the metaphysical Subject who has his own internal principle of construction. The physical subject assumes that the universe runs on stable mathematical principles and the function of education is to discover or "copy" these principles. This is the position held by all of the scientists in the major universities of the world.

> The work of intelligence [supposedly] leads to indefinitely fruitful results [but] since the mind is called upon to discover little by little a universe which is already completely structured and constructed, this work does not admit of any internal principle of

construction and consequently of any principle of deductive rigor ... It is from the
Subject as such that Intellectual progress stems (author's capitalization) (Piaget, 1952b,
p. 417).

Piaget describes the work of human intelligence or mind as it attempts to "copy" an
already completely structured and constructed universe. This "copy" view of learning
and reality, the view universally held by natural scientists, does indeed accept the
notion of a universe that is governed by stable principles and thus that the purpose of
education is to discover little by little those principles. Current educational policy is
based firmly on this view of reality. Piaget holds the radical contrary position that
everything about physical reality, along with the principles that govern it, is in the
process of being transformed (Piaget, 1971b, pp. 3-4) (Piaget, 1972, p. 85). What is
lacking in natural science and university education, argues Piaget, is *an internal
principle of construction.* The internal principle guarantees the autonomy of
successive construction (Beth & Piaget, 1966, p. 297), and thus guarantees full
development of the Absolute Subject. Valid Biological Structures and Qualitative
Algebraic Structures contain their own laws of construction (author's capitalization)
(Piaget, 1971c, pp. 184-5). Supplies from the outside are never needed by these valid
Structures which gives them complete autonomy (author's capitalization) (Piaget,
1973d, pp. 15-16).

The following quote affirms Piaget's view that metaphysical Mathematics, when
applied to the world, produces isomorphisms and explains physical phenomena. One
caution is necessary - only "complete isomorphisms" are synonyms of the Absolute,
as the metaphysical Entity is One Whole (author's capitalization) (Piaget, 1971a, p.
74) (Inhelder & Piaget, 1958, pp. 289-90).

> Turning now to the relations between Mathematics and reality, let us first note that it
> seems possible to apply Mathematics to the world ... at least in terms of isomorphisms
> and structural relationships ... there is the surprising fact that Operational Structures
> constructed deductively without any thought of application, have subsequently provided
> Frameworks of Explanatory Structures for physical phenomena discovered much later
> (author's capitalization) (Piaget, 1972, p. 73).

As we have frequently noted, the assimilatory and constructive activity of the
Absolute Subject is called "mathematics" by Piaget. Mathematics, to put it simply, is
actions or operations on things (author's capitalization) (Piaget, 1973b, p. 103). To
put it another way, Mathematics produces transformations (author's capitalization)
(Piaget, 1971a p. 47). The great man believes that it is possible to apply
Mathematics to the world, at least in terms of isomorphisms. We have already seen
that the main meaning of mathematics, in Piaget's system is assimilative activity by
the Subject, but Piaget is interjecting another concept of mathematics. Mathematics,
in this context, is a synonym, not an activity, of the Subject. Piaget is basically
playing mind games, but *pure Mathematics is a complete isomorphism or synonym of
the Subject because Piaget asserted that it is "aware of itself"* (author's italics and
capitalization) (Beth & Piaget, 1966, pp. 228-9). He also speaks of Mathematical
Forms (author's capitalization) (ibid., p. 298), which is another isomorphism or
synonym, and Mathematical Structure (author's capitalization) (Piaget, 1973c, p. 55)
(Piaget, 1977, p. 22). Piaget distinguishes between lower-level mathematics, which is

primarily used as a tool to manipulate and explain physical phenomena, while His Mathematics is used to assimilate.

In the passage below, Piaget again contrasts the lower-level or "lived" subject with the upper-level Subject or Cognitive Structure. He assures us that the lived subject can only have a very minor role in the construction of Cognitive Structure.

> There are thinkers who dislike "the subject", and if this subject is characterized in terms of "lived experience" we admit to being among them .... The "lived" can only have a very minor role in the construction of Cognitive Structures, for these do not belong to the subject's *consciousness* but to His *operational behavior* which is something quite different (author's italics and capitalization) (Piaget, 1970b, p. 68).

There are two subjects; Piaget dislikes one of them and worships the other one. The one he worships, the Cognitive Structure, only uses the one he dislikes as an object to assimilate and thus further the long-term project of fully constructing or developing Himself. The term "construction" does not exaggerate what happens, says Piaget, when used to describe how the Totality is being actualized (author's capitalization) (Piaget, 1977, pp. 140-1). When the facts of physical reality present themselves as a contradiction to the Totality, and they always do, Operational Instruments composed of monads are applied to these facts (author's capitalization) (ibid., p. 141). The Living Subject is the source of operational behavior, and He is conscious of what He is doing, but He is immanent in the "lived subject" who is unconscious of His existence. Sometimes the "lived subject" has a minor role; at other times he has no role at all. The last sentence is especially troublesome as Piaget switches levels in the same sentence with no indication to his reader that he is doing so. The "subjects' consciousness" refers to the lower-level subject, while "His operational behavior" refers to the upper-level Subject. *This "right to the jaw" of the reader is clearly deliberate, as linguistically the "His" is indeed the previous, lower-level "subject". Psychologically, it would seem to be almost impossible to make this switch inadvertently.*

KNOWLEDGE AS THE DEVELOPMENTAL PROCESS

What is Reality as a Whole? Piaget's extreme view of the nature of reality is evident in the quote below. *The Absolute Subject is not just an important part of reality, He is Reality as a Whole* and to know Him as Piaget claims to know Him, is "complete knowledge". This complete knowledge is divorced from the knowledge of facts, which is not "knowledge properly so called".

> If ... philosophy is concerned with Reality as a Whole, it is assumed to be possible to train specialists in this complete knowledge or search for the Absolute ... The only specialization demanded of them is the History of Philosophy, but as far as the methods of knowledge are concerned, only reflection which, moreover, corresponds to the Deep-Rooted Tendencies of adolescence and the Natural Inclination of the Human Mind .... In such a situation, the knowledge of facts is divorced from that [Knowledge] which alone can give it the character of Knowledge properly so called (author's italics and capitalization) (Piaget, 1971c, pp. 168-9).

It is essential to understand the two meanings of "knowledge" as used in this selection. The first "knowledge" is gained as the philosopher "searches" for the Absolute. Since this obviously refers to knowledge acquired by the individual human philosopher, it is not upper-level development. But look at the "Knowledge" which can only be acquired by reflected abstractions or operations. *How do we know that this is not the dictionary meaning of "reflected" as the word "abstraction" is omitted? Because in "such a situation" "Knowledge properly so called" is divorced from the knowledge of physical facts.* Piaget's omission of the word "Knowledge" before "which" in the last sentence lets us in on his desire to shade his private meaning of "Knowledge". This private meaning is seen in the "Deep-Rooted Tendencies of adolescence" which is "the Natural Inclination of the Human Mind". This means that Piaget is speaking of the "true" or immanent Human Mind.

How many of Piaget's followers have been trained in "complete knowledge or search for the Absolute"? Who would train them? I had a long discussion a few years ago with a well-known psychologist who was considered to be an authority on Piaget. Among other puzzling assertions, he insisted that Piaget had nothing whatever to say about an Absolute Being. Such an assertion could only be made by an individual who had not read Piaget's books, and he conceded as much during our long discussion. Clearly he knew what other Piagetians were saying, especially Flavell, but he was woefully ignorant of what Piaget had said. The only specialization demanded of the hypothetical trainees is "History of Philosophy". *This is the "special" History "discovered" by Hegel, which is the History of the dialectical development of the Absolute* (author's italics and capitalization) (Piaget, 1971b, p. 1). For Piaget, besides the usual history of visible and partially contingent events, there is also the History of the Underlying Dynamism's development, structuration or organization (author's capitalization) (Piaget, 1973d, p. 35). This latter History is what Hegel "discovered" - the non-contingent History of the Underlying Dynamism or Absolute Subject. Piaget's own father was a historian, "but he did not believe in Historical Knowledge" (author's capitalization) (Piaget, 1971c, p. 4)! That is, he did not believe in Hegel's new kind of History. Piaget poses an interesting question regarding the "training of specialists" in another context. "Why philosophers? (unless it is in order to philosophize about engagement, but then *it is engagement and not philosophy which elaborates* meaning)" (author's italics) (Piaget, 1971c, p. 118). That is, operational engagement elaborates "true" meaning independent of any philosopher. Again, the real "Philosopher" is the metaphysical Being of Piaget's theory.

As with essentially every significant concept, Piaget has a private meaning which he may or may not use depending on the need of the moment. The two subjects are again contrasted below with the usual outcome. The "psychological subject" does not produce Structures of General Knowledge, but the Epistemic Subject, who is "common" to all "psychological subjects", does produce Cognitive Structures of General Knowledge. Naturally, Piaget is not interested in studying the "psychological subject", and that is why all of his books and papers focus on the Epistemic or metaphysical Subject.

> There is the "psychological subject", centered in the conscious ego whose functional role is incontestable, but which is not the origin of any Structure of General Knowledge; but there is also the "Epistemic Subject" or that which is common to all subjects at the same

level of development, whose Cognitive Structures derive from the most General Mechanisms of the Co-Ordination of Actions. Insofar as the facts authorise us to look for some connection between Logico-Mathematical Structures and the Subject's activities, we must naturally pursue our enquiry in the direction of the Epistemic Subject (author's capitalization) (Beth & Piaget, 1966, p. 308).

We must get on Piaget's merry-go-round of the two subjects and try not to get too dizzy or nauseated. This quote was used previously, but different aspects are emphasized here. The physical, "psychological subject" is not the origin of any significant knowledge; he is conscious, but he is not conscious of the "Epistemic Subject" who, on the other hand, is conscious of everything. Cognitive Structures of the Epistemic Subject are "common to" all "psychological subjects" but, being eternal, they do *not* derive from "the most General Mechanisms of the Co-Ordination of Action". *They are Self-developed by these Mechanisms, however, because the "General Mechanisms" are indeed the very same Cognitive Structures that make up the Epistemic Subject!* All of these terms are merely some of the names of the Body of Monads. The "common" Epistemic Subject is immanent in every "psychological subject". And please observe that *Piaget's enquiry - his life-time of enquiry - is in the direction of the Epistemic Subject who is the metaphysical Biological Being with whom he became enchanted as a teenager.*

Those who think that Piaget is a scientist, owe it to themselves to digest the following passage. The German Idealism that sprouted immoderately from Kant's philosophy, especially the form it took with Hegel, was not scientific but was suprascientific. *Piaget claims, sub rosa, to have developed a "second form" of this suprascience, which is actually a virulent form of anti-science.*

> The Ideal of a suprascientific Knowledge originating in the nineteenth century had its beginnings either in the frankly speculative form of German Idealism, or in the more modest and more cautious form of Epistemology, of a critique of science. This second form has resulted, toward the end of the nineteenth and during the twentieth century, in a new philosophical approach, namely that in the field of "things" and phenomena *there was room alongside scientific knowledge ... for another kind of Knowledge ... which would be completely independent and admit of indefinite progress* (author's italics and capitalization) (Piaget, 1971c, pp. 88-9).

The Ideal of a "suprascientific" Knowledge began with the post-Kantians. Hegel, as we have seen, is the Post-Kantian who laid the groundwork for Piaget's philosophy. He was 30 years old when the 19th C. began, and died in 1831, so Piaget, in this quote, is not giving him full credit for "discovering" this new kind of Scientific Knowledge because a "second form" of this Knowledge was discovered after Hegel died. This, of course, did not prevent him for giving Hegel rather full credit in other contexts (ibid., p. 58;115) (Piaget, 1974a, p. 56). In any case, Piaget is the major, if not exclusive, proponent of this new form of Epistemological "Science". Although Piaget was only about 3 years old at the end of the 19th century, he did begin developing the second form of suprascience early in the 20th century as an adolescent. The key to this passage is Piaget's assertion that this new kind of Knowledge is completely independent - independent of people, including every aspect of their intellectual activity. This is endogenous Knowledge whereas people are only capable of exogenous knowledge (Piaget, 1980b, p. 81).

Knowledge of an object, as Piaget conceives it, is very far indeed from knowledge as defined in the dictionary. Knowledge for Piaget is incorporation or assimilation of an object into a Schema. But what does this mean? First, it should be understood that individual people are not capable of "rational assimilation" (Piaget, 1962, p. 161). *Complete Knowledge of an object means the elimination of that object* by transforming it so that it is identical to the metaphysical Framework, thus making it a part of that Framework (author's italics and capitalization) (Piaget, 1980b, p. 111) (Piaget, 1967, pp. 6-7) (Piaget & Inhelder, 1956, p. 449) (Piaget, 1928, p. 175) (Piaget & Inhelder, 1969, p. 5) (Bringuier, 1980, p. 44).

> To know an object implies incorporating it into Action Schemata, and this is true from elementary Sensorimotor behavior right up to the higher Logico-Mathematical operations .... These Action Schemata and, a fortiori, the Operative Schemata deriving from them, comprising an Organization, and this fact immediately brings us into the realm of Biology (author's capitalization) (Piaget, 1971a, pp. 7-8).

To know an object is to assimilate that object and *all of the synonyms listed in appendices A through M can do the job.* In this instance "Action Schemata" are the assimilators. Piaget differentiates "Sensorimotor behavior" from Logico-Mathematical operations", but it is worthwhile to remember first, that incorporation of the object occurs in both cases and second, that the Body of Monads is the only Entity who can "incorporate". One also might note a logical inconsistency, as Piaget includes Logico-Mathematical operations as an activity of Action Schemata in the first sentence, but this contrasts with the second sentence where Operative Schemata are said to "derive from" Action Schemata, suggesting that only "Operative Schemata" can produce operations. *Anyone who has spent much time in Piaget's books realizes that "action" and "operation" are often used interchangeably.* The Schemata are represented in the second sentence as forming a Biological Organization (author's capitalization) (Piaget, 1973d, p. 57) (Piaget, 1950, p. 7) (Piaget, 1971a, p. 33), which brings us back again to the "Biology" or Life which fascinated and motivated Piaget from the beginning of his interest in philosophy.

Perception is egocentric, that is, the lower-level or physical subject thinks at that level because he is physical and perception is based on physical organ systems. Naturally, Piaget does sometimes speak of upper-level perception (Piaget, 1950, pp. 120-1; 124-5) (Piaget, 1926, p. 160) (Piaget, 1969b, p. 212), but this is to be expected. The ego involved in lower-level perception is limited intellectually and is the source of systematic errors; operations on the contrary achieve Universal Knowledge without any help from the physical ego.

> Perception is essentially egocentric ... and this egocentrism is not only limiting but it is also the source of systematic errors ... The essence of operations is, on the contrary, the achievement of Knowledge, which is *independent of the ego,* independent of a particular individual's point of view (but not of Human Subjects in General, i. e. of activities common to a given level). Its essence is also the achievement of ... Universal Knowledge (author's italics and capitalization) (Piaget, 1969b, pp. 285-6).

"Perception" represents the best that individual people can function intellectually. Basically egocentrism is defined by Piaget as any activity which does not recognize the true Ego, and if the true Ego is freely active we have Egocentrism. Perhaps there is no one besides Piaget who could be called "Egocentric". Actually, Egocentric behavior in Piaget's books has nothing to do with the thoughts, attitudes or actions of people; it is based on the operational activity of the Subject. Operations are again declared to be autonomous, as they achieve Knowledge independently of the human ego. However this Knowledge is not acquired independent of *Human Subjects in General* because the "common level" of activities or operations represents the immanent Subject in human beings - or Human Subject in General. Operational activity, regardless of whether it is outside of human beings or inside, produces "Universal Knowledge".

The next passage clarifies the basic identity of "operation" and "cooperation" (Piaget, 1974a, p. 51). They are identical for the same reason the Absolute is both the Individual and Society - in Piaget's System.

> In the realm of Knowledge, it seems obvious that individual operations of the Intelligence and operations making for exchanges in cognitive cooperation are one and the same thing, the "general coordination of actions" [are] interindividual as well as intraindividual ... so the question whether Logic and Mathematics are essentially individual or social attainments loses all meaning; the Epistemological Subject constructing them is both an Individual, though decentered in relation to his private ego, and the sector of the Social Group decentered in relation to the constraining idols of the tribe (author's capitalization) (Piaget, 1971a, p. 360).

Operations are always performed by the Individual who is also Society (author's capitalization) (Piaget, 1970b, p. 142). In the first sentence, both operations in individuals and operations which involve exchanges among individuals are the "same thing" *because the same Individual performs them* (author's italics and capitalization) (Piaget, 1973c, p. 32) (Piaget, 1969, p. 156) (Piaget, 1970d, p. 71). In other words, the general coordination of actions are within the individual, or intraindividual, as well as responsible for exchanges among individuals, or interindividual. Why then is it meaningless to ask the question whether attainment in Logic and Mathematics is individual or social? It is because, in this case, Piaget's private meaning for these two terms is Self-construction by operational activity of the Epistemological Subject and operational activity has the same source regardless of whether it is within an individual or among society at large. Piaget's question regarding Logic and Mathematics is also reduced to the same single source - the Individual who Piaget said could also be called "Society" (author's capitalization) (Piaget, 1973d, p. 68) (Piaget, 1974a, pp. 30-1). The Self-construction of Logic or Mathematics which, as synonyms of the Epistemological Subject, are identical in meaning, depends entirely upon this Subject who is both the Individual and the Social Group. Contrary to the quote, the Epistemological Subject, as the Individual, decenters the individual subject's ego and, as the Social Group, decenters the "constraining idols of the tribe". Piaget has the "Individual" decentered from the "private ego" and the "Social Group" decentered from the "constraining idols", but these are reversals of meaning. We must always remember that *the Absolute Subject as the Individual and as the Social Group is centered, not decentered! It is the "private ego" and the "constraining idols" that are decentered. Piaget is certainly not constrained by the "traditional idols" of society, in fact a careful reader will realize that he is utterly lawless - a "bull in a china shop".*

Exogenous knowledge is human knowledge, while endogenous Knowledge is metaphysical. Contrary to Piaget's suggestion in the next selection, these two forms of knowledge are not closely related, in fact they are at opposite poles. There is a very slow passage from the physical form of knowledge to the metaphysical, but this will only happen over eons of time.

> The passage from exogenous to endogenous varieties thus seems to constitute a very general process relevant to every field of life, from the organism to the cognitive functions. It goes without saying that in cognitive functions, the endogenous and deductive reconstruction of links, at first empirical, does not go back as far as the genome, since the development of Knowledge is dependent on equilibration and not on innate programming (author's capitalization) (Piaget, 1977, pp. 199-200).

The passage from exogenous or physical knowledge to endogenous or metaphysical Knowledge is what assimilation is supposed to accomplish. Endogenous Knowledge is developed by regulations or operations (author's capitalization) (Piaget, 1980b, p. 80), not learning as we know it. The physical organism and traditional cognitive functions will very gradually become a part of the Body of Monads by means of endogenous reconstruction. Endogenous or deductive reconstruction is not connected with the physical genome in any way, since the development of this kind of Knowledge depends solely upon equilibrations or operations - which is "genetic" with a drastically different meaning.

We have looked at two kinds of reality, two kinds of subjects, two kinds of science, two kinds of knowledge and two kinds of perception. This reflects Piaget's dual framework that has so long escaped the attention of his followers. One kind in each case represents the Absolute Subject or His activity, while the other kind refers to physical reality. In the following quote Piaget compares two kinds of form. One kind is based on organic morphology while the other belongs to the higher cognitive functions. It is the upper-level Cognitive Organization or Form that concerns Piaget, and this Form progressively dissociates Himself from material content by means of assimilation.

> There are not only fundamental analogies ... but also differences, which are no less significant, between "Forms" belonging to the higher cognitive functions and those on which organic morphology is based. Here we are confronted by ... differences such as may help us understand the profound specificity and originality that are an essential part of Knowledge .... The outstanding characteristic of Cognitive Organizations is the progressive dissociation of Form and content (author's capitalization) (Piaget, 1971a, pp. 152-3).

There are two kinds of "forms"; the higher cognitive functions are based on one kind, while physical, organic morphology, and the activities based on this morphology, is based on the other kind. *The notion of physical morphology being based on a "form" is quite odd, so odd that apparently no one besides Piaget knows about it.* The defining characteristic, in this particular context, of the Form belonging to the higher cognitive functions is the last sentence of the quoted passage, and it comes 24 lines of print after the previous sentence in the quote. The intervening 24 lines are very ambiguous and contradictory. We can be sure that the higher cognitive functions are metaphysical as content or matter is gradually dissociated and assimilated. The most important point to be made with regard to Knowledge by the higher functions is that they are "profoundly specific" and original.

The "common" or "Initially Privileged Elements" of the following passage are the monads which are continuously reorganized as developmental Knowledge progresses.

> To start with Common Elements, examples are found at all levels which illustrate the fundamental fact that the acquisition of Knowledge, or better, of a Body of Knowledge (because, of course, all knowledge, including even the most elementary perception of an isolated element, forms an integral part of a System), is not a purely additive process but entails continuous reorganisations stemming from Initially Privileged Elements (author's capitalization) (Piaget, 1969b, p. 298).

Piaget narrows his brand of Knowledge to the organization of "Initial" Elements into a System which he calls a "Body of Knowledge". This organization entails a continuous reorganization of these "Common Elements". The constant operational production of progressively improved Classes are integrated into the developing Body of Monads (author's capitalization) (Piaget & Inhelder, 1956, p. 377), leading to the very specific metaphysical Knowledge of Piaget's theory. This is the exclusive Knowledge attained by the Body of Monads as they produce synthesis after synthesis based on their continual engagement with physical reality. The bottom line regarding this Knowledge is the ability of the monads to develop and precisely use the "correct" combinatory movements in all possible circumstances vis a vie physical reality.

The previous quote tells us how the Absolute Subject develops Himself; the following quote tells us how, or at least that, He produces phenomena in the physical world.

> To know is to produce something in Thought in such a way as to reconstitute the way in which phenomena are produced. This definition corresponds to the way in which scientists generally think (in spite of the prohibitions of positivism), and, if accepted, it follows that Operative Structures must play the leading role in knowledge. The indisputable primacy of Logico-Mathematical explanations then follows (author's capitalization) (Piaget, 1969b, p. 356).

In Piaget's System, all natural objects (author's capitalization) (Piaget, 1926, pp. 189-190; 209; 212; 234) (Piaget, 1950, p. 145) (Piaget, 1972, p. 83) (Piaget, 1928, pp. 203; 248) (Piaget, 1952b, p. 190) (Piaget & Inhelder, 1974, p. 45) (Piaget, 1967, p. 64), and the phenomena associated with these objects (Piaget, 1970b, pp. 39-40) (Piaget, 1974a, p. 73) (Piaget, 1971c, p. 109) (Piaget, 1973b, p. 28) (Piaget, et al., 1977, p. 3; 170; 179) (Piaget, 1929, p. 404) (Evans, 1973, p. 114), are produced by the Body of Monads or Thought. To say that scientists generally think this way, however, is either a grotesque illusion or a capricious sense of humor. Those who naively accept this argument could well believe lots of things, including Piaget's "indisputable" claim that the Logico-Mathematical Operative Structures play the leading role in Knowledge acquisition. It should be mentioned that under certain "magical" conditions, Piaget's System appears to provide the possibility that people can make use of the immanent Body of Monads to produce phenomena.

Piaget boldly uses the term "realism" in the next passage when the meaning is "idealism". The "preceding paragraph", which Piaget oddly and improperly refers to, informs the reader that this realism, which is really idealism, keeps the child ignorant of the difference between the physical and the psychic. In trying to find a way to bring the child's view of things in line with his own view, Piaget is actually affirming that both he and the child are "psychics" or idealists, as it was their Own Common Mind who constructed the world in the first place. The child does not know that his true Mind constructed the world, but this does not prevent Piaget from saying that he does because he cannot afford to stand on this sensitive doctrine all by himself. *He also cannot afford to claim the support of scientists, at least not very often, so he dishonestly claims the support of children, especially very young children.* The "secret of Intelligence" is probably to be found in children under the age of seven or eight (author's capitalization) (Piaget, 1950, p. 25).

> Childish realism is intellectual and not visual (see preceding paragraph) - [from the preceding paragraph] Realism keeps [the child] in ignorance of the distinction between the physical and the psychical, [so both are considered aspects of the external world] at the same time. [Returning to the main paragraph] The child only sees what he knows, and sees the external worlds (sic) as though he had previously constructed it with his own Mind. Childish causality is therefore not visual ... It is intellectual, that is to say, full of considerations that are foreign to pure observation (author's capitalization) (Piaget, 1928, p. 255).

Why does Piaget say that childish realism is intellectual and not visual. First, *by "intellectual" he means "considerations" not based on what he can observe.* The child, like Piaget, does not need to observe what happens in the "external world" as this world was constructed by the child's, and Piaget's, Own Common immanent or true Mind. Second, the child sees only what he already knows, so knowledge is not to be based on careful observation, because in Piaget's view of things that would be *anti-intellectual* (author's italics) (Piaget, 1930, p. 299) (Inhelder & Piaget, 1958, p. 346) (Piaget, 1969b, p. 306) (Piaget, 1928, pp. 70-1) (Piaget, et al., 1977, pp. 179-180) (Piaget, 1973d, pp. 25-6) (Piaget, 1980a, pp. 84-5) (Piaget, 1974b, IX). When the "hands-on" science educators in our public schools fully absorb this fact, they will not feel very kindly toward Piaget and his primary interpreters. The true Mind, consisting of monads, had constructed the physical universe by "psychic" methods and this made observation and hands-on physical experiments not only a truly foreign methodology, but an acceptance of physical reality as an "authority" - which is an abomination to Piaget. One must keep in mind while trying to understand this passage, that Piaget is ignoring the physical child who is not aware of any of the things which supposedly motivate his immanent "Child".

We must study the Subject of Knowledge who is the source of Logico-Mathematical Structures. As is often the case, Piaget confounds Logico-Mathematical Structures in the quote below with the Subject of Knowledge because the two terms are identical in meaning. These Structures are said to form a Network which covers all of the sciences, and they are enabled to form this covering because of their relations with Biology! The metaphysical Biological Entity composed of monads is the only possible Subject who could "cover" all the sciences. The Subject of Knowledge is seen, then, to be the "Biological Entity" - the lode-star who determined Piaget's destiny.

> The human sciences, in so far as they necessarily include in their ... study the Subject of Knowledge - the source of the Logical and Mathematical Structures on which they

depend - do not merely maintain a set of interdisciplinary relations between one another ... but are part of an Extensive Circuit or Network that really covers all the sciences (this was clear in any case owing to their relations with Biology). It was essential to recall this so as to be able to shape our conclusions in such a way that they might succeed in revealing the true significance of interdisciplinary relations. For their significance far exceeds that of a mere tool for facilitating work .... The true object of interdisciplinary research, therefore, is to reshape or reorganize the Fields of Knowledge by means of exchanges which are in fact constructive recombinations (author's capitalization) (Piaget, 1973d, pp. 65-6).

The human sciences must include study of the Subject of Knowledge, who is not only the Logical and Mathematical Structure, but represents the kind of "Biology" that has *little significance on the physico-chemical level* (author's italics and capitalization) (ibid., p. 13). These sciences and their interrelationships are far more important than mere tools for facilitating natural science, as "Biology" is using them to further His agenda. It was essential that Piaget "recall" this, as the true significance of the relations among the sciences depends upon the constructive recombinations that can only occur by means of the dialectic exchanges arranged by "Biology" Himself!

SCIENCE AS THE DEVELOPMENTAL PROCESS

The following passage demonstrates, albeit not very directly, that Piaget's concepts of construction, dialectics, and Science specifically refer to the "spontaneous" "tested methodology of operational progress.

All the constructivism that characterizes the progressive constitution of Cognitive Structures - have often been related to dialectical interpretations .... It has, however, also been possible since the time of Kant and Hegel to conceive a philosophical form of dialectics that ... seeks to found or even direct the sciences ... It has been of very great importance for ... it can base itself on a tested methodology that coincides with the spontaneous methodology of many disciplines (author's capitalization) (Piaget, 1974a, p. 56).

Cognitive Structures are Self-developing by means of a dialectic interaction with physical reality. The philosophic dialectics of Hegel, but not Kant, is another way of expressing the same idea. This form of dialectics is held by Piaget to eventually overrule findings in natural science, by means of a tested methodology - operations by the Independent System who is independent of lower-level selves (author's capitalization) (Piaget, Inhelder & Szeminska, 1960, p. 24).

The meaning of the following passage is repeated three times, and then Piaget asserts that its importance inheres in the fact that it is based on operations. The "tested", "spontaneous methodology" becomes the "Science" of the "Subject-Psychologist". This superhuman Entity is said to construct "His Science" or "His Epistemology" until it is completed. *A "complete" Science or Epistemology means a fully developed or actualized Absolute Subject.*

I ... [distinguish] the Subject-Psychologist who constructs His Science, and [sic] any human subject whatsoever ... The Subject-Psychologist constructs His Epistemology as a function of the turning points of His Science. There is therefore no need for the philosopher to intervene ... in order to construct a complete Epistemology (author's capitalization) (Piaget, 1971c, 224-5).

We have seen this revealing excerpt before, but not with an emphasis on metaphysical Science. Note that the first "and" should be "from" and the first comma should be omitted. Interestingly, Piaget's "Science" and "Epistemology" turn out to be identical. *It also eventually becomes clear that "development", "Knowledge", "Science". "Epistemology" and other terms all point directly to a single event in Piaget's theory - the actualization of the Absolute's potential.* In the quote, then, the metaphysical Subject-Psychologist constructs a complete Epistemology by means of His Science, and He does this all by Himself without any help from human philosophers. And let it be noted that this is a Self-construction of the Body of Monads of which the Subject-Psychologist consists. No new monads are added to the metaphysical Body, but the monads become more capable of combinatorial activity in order to conserve their integrity in all possible situations.

In the selection below the "tested methodology" or "Science" of the Subject-Psychologist becomes the intervention of the Mind or Thinking Subject. Since the "unity of Science" is based upon the activity of this Subject, He must be removed from philosophy and his operational activity studied "scientifically" - which is impossible because this activity cannot be detected by any means known to man!

Science implies the intervention of the Mind, let us say at least the activity of the Thinking Subject ... The Subject's activity is a field of investigation usually reserved for philosophy. If we really wish to achieve the unity of Science, we must scientifically study this activity of the Subject, that is remove Something from philosophy (author's capitalization) (Piaget, 1971b, p. 90).

Piagetian Science requires the dialectical activity of the Mind or Thinking Subject, which is the source of the "unity of Science" that he considers so desirable. Would Science have as a goal the relative and philosophy the Absolute (or search for the Absolute) (author's capitalization) (ibid., p. 92)? Piaget leans on Max Planck, who said that "science must believe in the absolute of a certain reality even if this is never achieved" (ibid., p. 92). We can be very sure that Planck's notion of "absolute" is quite different from Piaget's notion. Science advances by altering the principles of physics, asserts Piaget (ibid., p. 92), but physicists assume that the principles of nature are stable. Piagetian Science alters the principles of physics by means of assimilation, meaning that the findings of our greatest scientists will eventually be invalidated by this new "parascience". One can only pretend to remove "the activity of the Subject" from philosophy, as it is not possible to study it scientifically - unless we drastically pervert the meaning of science.

In the following passage the Subject-Psychologist, Thinking Subject or Mind becomes the "Logico-Mathematical Structure" or "Organized Whole" who produces Hegelian-Piagetian Science. This is the "Science" required in the progressive building up of the Logico-Mathematical Structures, in other words, it is the Science of metaphysical Self-development.

[There is a] kind of Science whose findings can be proved beyond fear of contradiction, which is the case with the Logico-Mathematical Structures ... Such Structures are built up progressively both from the historical and psychological point of view [and] they ...

become logically integrated into an Organized Whole, which constitutes a piece of Organic development (author's capitalization) (Piaget, 1971a, p. 74).

The "Scientific" activity of the Logico-Mathematical Structures, which is diachronic Self-development through all of historical time by means of operations, is held to be invincible and certain by Piaget. This "Scientific" activity is by definition progressive, as it creates by synthesis a series of Classes each of which is more "advanced" than the one before. All of the progressively more developed Classes must be integrated into the Organic Whole.

In the quote below the Subject-Psychologist, Thinking Subject, Mind, Logico-Mathematical Structure or Organized Whole becomes the Non-Temporal Structure or Subject. This Entity of many names does not operate in terms of physical force, but in terms of a spiritual dynamics - a dynamics that is foreign to physical masses, actions, forces and energies.

> Now in the usual causal models, in which masses, actions, forces and energies intervene, the parallelism between causality and operations is approximated only to the precise degree that this dynamism remains foreign to Nontemporal Structures. In the case of a complete geometrization of reality, the isomorphism between the objects and the operations of the Subject tends, on the contrary, to become complete (author's capitalization) (Piaget, 1974b, p. 152).

Natural science is based on masses, actions, forces and energies but, as Piaget affirms, this is foreign to the Non-Temporal Structures responsible for operations. Piaget then looks far into the future to the time when he assumes that reality will have been fully assimilated or "geometrized" and announces that there is a complete isomorphism between the objects of reality and the Subject. By definition, of course, this is the meaning of "complete geometrization". *Please observe that "isomorphism between the objects and the operations of the Subject" is nonsensical because of the inappropriate insertion of "the operations of". The future isomorphism is between all objects and the Subject, period.*

To extend the litany of synonyms, we see below that the Subject-Psychologist, Thinking Subject, Mind, Logico-Mathematical Structure, Organized Whole, Non-Temporal Structure, or Subject becomes the Intimate Mechanism or "Certain Structures" of the Group. This Entity must activate the brain before any thought whatever is possible, according to the Oracle of Geneva (Piaget, 1971a, pp. 312-13; 328).

> The Intimate Mechanism which directs thought .... is by no means particular to infant thought; it is found again not only in every adult thought but also in the development of scientific thought. Thus mathematicians of all times have reasoned by obeying, without knowing it, the laws of Certain Structures ... of the Group (author's capitalization) (Piaget, 1973a, p. 34).

The immanent Subject is described as directing the thought of "infants", "every adult" and "scientific thought". In his discussions regarding directed thought, Piaget frequently crosses the line, in both directions, between more or less contingent physical thought directed by the immanent Subject and the Self-directed thought by the immanent Subject which completely by-passes the thought of individuals. This topic of "directed thought" is at times almost hopelessly confused - which makes it a favorite point at issue for Piaget. It is worth noting that mathematics is one area of knowledge which Hegel and Piaget treat differently. Piaget at least pretends to have a high regard for mathematics while Hegel held mathematics in contempt (Edwards, 1967, Vol. 3, p. 445). In evaluating Piaget's attitude toward mathematics, we must examine at least three ways that he uses the term. Most often mathematics is described as operational activity. The next most frequent use is as a synonym for the Absolute Subject. For instance, *he speaks of the Mathematical Apparatus "conversing" with the fundamental equations of entropy* (author's italics and capitalization) (Piaget, 1973c, p. 26)! One can only wonder if his immanent Subject was happy with this alternate name, as it implies subordination to the one who uses the "Apparatus". On the other hand, an independent "Apparatus" who "converses with equations" is more than weird! Piaget does speak of traditional mathematics but only occasionally (Piaget, 1971a, p. 344) (Piaget & Inhelder, 1974, p. 9) (Beth & Piaget, 1966, pp. 201-2; 243) (Piaget, et al., 1977, p. 13) (Piaget, 1973b, p. 31).

In the next passage synonyms of the Absolute Subject continue unabated with the additions of "System of the Whole" and "Science". The main point of the passage is that science is bound up with the philosophical system of the metaphysical Subject. The second "Science" is capitalized because it has suddenly become a synonym of the Absolute Subject who is the System as a Whole.

> The interpretation of science will thus remain necessarily bound up with a philosophical System of the Whole - from Plato to Bergson - and we can then merely note the contradictions among a certain number of fundamental propositions without Science having the slightest interest in joining with any of them (author's capitalization) (Piaget, 1971b, p. 97).

Science is said to be bound up with the philosophical System as a Whole, from Plato to Bergson. In two places Piaget traces his view of philosophy from Plato to Hegel (ibid., p. 1) (Piaget, 1971c, pp. 47-59). Here he replaces Hegel with Bergson who, as we saw in the introduction, had a somewhat similar philosophy. His next use of "Science" is personified, with the obvious meaning of the true Scientist or Absolute Subject.

Piaget agrees with F. Brunner that true Science (author's capitalization) is in God (ibid., p. 117), and continues in the quote below with synonyms of the Subject-Psychologist; namely, "Being of Microphysics", "Mathematical Being", "Being of Science", Being of the Sciences", "Being-for-the-Subject" and "Knowing Subject". He implicitly avows that he is not a natural scientist, but he is willing to assume that they speak meaningfully about their "restricted" investigations of the physical universe. He basically makes the same point when he compares Galilean physics, which is physical, with the Being of Microphysics, who, Piaget illogically asserts represents metaphysical activity "below" the level of the physical. It is illogical because natural science is investigating the physical world at this sub-atomic level, and Piaget's metaphysics cannot be investigated by natural science. Piaget hides behind Planck again in making the microphysical the threshold where "the notion of object loses its meaning" (Piaget, 1975, p. 238). He then creates an exquisite problem for the reader when he adds that, "in the domain of phenomena ... the object is at the same time the point of departure of Logico-Mathematical operations ... and the point of arrival of spatial-temporal operations" (author's capitalizations) (ibid., p. 238). Piaget is guilty of a very low blow by using "object" in this latter quote to mean "monad". Once we gain this insight, however, we see that Piaget is making the point that in microphysics the physical and the metaphysical meet in "double indetermination" (ibid., p. 238).

> One can ... assume that scientists speak meaningfully ... about the subject matter they have modestly restricted themselves to ... The Being of Microphysics is not the same as that of Galilean physics ... The Mathematical Being of today is no longer the same as that of Euclid and of Descartes etc. Why not begin ontology by ... inquiry into the Being of Science (or of the Sciences)? (Let it not be said that this Being is that of things: it is well and truly Being-for-the- Subject, for the Knowing Subject, of course) (author's capitalization) (Piaget, 1971c, p. 120).

Piaget disparages the natural scientist because he restricts himself to exogenous knowledge. He then sings the charms of his metaphysical Being, urging an inquiry into this "Being of Science". *Piaget's endogenous Science is nothing more than the Self-developing operations of this Being.*

The selection below continues with synonyms of the Subject-Psychologist: "Absolute", "Transcendental Organization" and "Immanent Organization". Piaget confounds certain basic characteristics of the Absolute in both the first sentence and the last sentence. In the first sentence the Absolute *is* "in the clouds" and He *is also* "inside things". In the last sentence, the immanent Organization is the Transcendental Organization who is also "up in the clouds". This Absolute or Transcendental Organization, who is both immanent in all people and other objects as well as filling all space between objects, is the metaphysical "Biology" Piaget encountered in ecstasy at Lake Annecy (Piaget, 1971c, p. 5).

> Before we locate the Absolute up in the clouds, it may well be helpful to take a look inside things. Once we do that, if the true is an organization of the real, then we first need to know how such an organization is organized, which is a Biological question ... What we must do, before having recourse to a Transcendental Organization, is to fathom all the resources of the Immanent Organization (author's capitalization) (ibid., p. 362).

Piaget plays with his doctrine of the two motors. Before we locate the Absolute up in the clouds - the outside motor - we ought to look inside of things - the inside motor. Both motors are aspects of the single Body of Monads, but by playing the inside monads against the outside monads Piaget manages to confuse the issue. He says that the monads inside of all objects in the universe actually organize the universe. Of course, this ignores the aspect of his theory that says the monads outside of, but contiguous to objects are also involved in this organization (Piaget, Inhelder & Szeminska, 1960, p. 396) (Piaget, 1974b, p. 142). The whole Spatial Surround is organized (author's capitalization) (Piaget & Inhelder, 1956, p. 416), and the Subject, or Space, must be able to embrace reality in toto (author's capitalization) (Piaget, 1952b, p. 417) (Piaget, 1954, p. 241). Furthermore, the universe is embodied in the Subject (author's capitalization) (Piaget, 1952b, p. 43). It would be well to remember that "organization of the real" sometimes refers to physical reality and sometimes to metaphysical Reality - or to both at the same time.

In the first sentence of the following selection, exogenous or "physical" knowledge is declared to be science in the "strict sense", while "Science on the march" in the other sentence is the metaphysical Science of the Absolute Subject who is invincible in His quest for Self-development.

> All clearly established knowledge obviously falls into the field of specialized learning in the strictest sense of science. For others, including several dialecticians, the study of philosophy calls above all for awareness of dialectical processes arising from "Science on the march" (author's capitalization) (Piaget, 1974a, p. 10).

The first sentence refers to science as taught in the universities. The second sentence, however, refers to the dialectic Scientist of operational activity, who is the Absolute Subject or God marching inexorably toward His Ideal perfection. The phrase "Science on the march" would seem to be an obvious take-off on Hegel's famous statement regarding the nature of a true state: "The march of God in the world is what the state is" (Hegel, 1952, Vol. 46, p. 141). The deciding factor in whether or not to capitalize "Science" was based on my opinion that Piaget probably had Hegel's statement in mind and wished to honor the same Entity as the irresistible metaphysical Scientist. One reason Hegel was lionized by many Germans was because he tied such assertions to his belief that the German state was the highest type of state in existence. Many believed, following Hegel, that "history had revealed its fulfillment in German culture" (Edwards, 1967, Vol. 3, pp. 454-5). Others blamed World War I on Hegel's "theory of the God-state" (ibid., p. 458). Add to this his acceptance of warfare as the only way to determine "which right has to give way to the other" (ibid., p. 443), and we should not be surprised that many investigators explain some of the more aggressive positions taken by German leaders in the past by referring to Hegel's philosophy.

"Artificialism" in the following selection is the second of three terms used by Piaget to show the development of metaphysical atomism or manadism in people from childhood to adolescence. Spiritual atoms or monads make up upper-level or immanent Man or God, who is held by children to be the source of natural objects and phenomena. This being the case, the immanent Monads or Mind of the child feels no need for empirical or scientific verification, since He made the things Himself. Note that, by means of verbal magic, Piaget coalesces "Mind" and "child" into an impossible conscious unity.

> 'Artificialist' explanations given by children, of natural phenomena, are very frequent: rivers, lakes, mountains, sea, and rocks have been made by Man ... He enlarges sensible reality ... by means of the verbal and magic [sic] reality which he puts on the same plane. These things are not sufficient in themselves to make the Mind feel any need for verification, since things themselves have been made by the Mind (author's capitalization) (Piaget, 1928, p. 203).

Piaget took the term, "artificialism" from Brunschvicg, who used it to mean the endowment of "men or gods with the power of making river sources, rain, etc., by means of human contrivances" (Piaget, 1926, p. 209). Artificialism supposedly "grew out of" animism, and we eventually learn that out of artificialism "the child attains *spontaneously* ... causality by Substance" which is based on "a certain primitive atomism" (author's italics and capitalization) (Piaget, 1929, p. 428). In the movement from *"animism"*, or monads giving life to objects, to *"artificialism"*, or monads producing, shaping and activating natural objects, to cause by *"Substance"*, or monads ultimately causing all physical movements and phenomena, we see how Piaget elaborates his mature form of Spiritual monadism. *It fundamentally demonstrates how apparent changes in conceptual development are not really changes at all when the meaning of the changing terms are understood.* It is also noteworthy, as we observed previously, that Man and God often have the same meaning in Piaget's writings. For instance, the child's early concepts regarding the origin of the sun and moon are ascribed "to human agency (or divine, but we shall see that this amounts practically to the same thing)" (Piaget, 1929, p. 288). A few pages later, "in this universe ... of living beings, Roy gives the first place to Man (or alternatively to God, which amounts to the same)" (author's capitalization) (ibid., p. 294). The same idea is expressed in numerous places (ibid., 414) (Piaget, 1930, pp. 45; 75). This use of "Man" with an upper-level meaning makes sense to Piaget as he is referring to the true Self of man. "What are the relations between homo faber and Homo Sapiens" (author's capitalization) (ibid., p. 195)? Homo faber is physical man while Homo Sapiens is God immanent in man.

Structuralism, constructivism and Science converge below into the dialectic historical development of the Absolute Subject. They converge because they mean approximately the same thing.

> The fundamental fact [is] that in the domain of the sciences themselves structuralism has always been linked with a constructivism from which the epithet "dialectical" can hardly be withheld - the emphasis upon historical development [and] opposition between contraries ... is surely just as characteristic of constructivism as of dialectic (Piaget, 1970b, p. 121).

Again and again Science is seen to be simply the operational activity exercised by the Subject as He develops or constructs Himself. This, of course, is the dialectical activity that occurs between the metaphysical monads of the Subject and everything connected with physical reality. The dialectical interactions of Piagetian Science are circular, but represent a hidden means of particular richness. These "Scientific" interactions, which refer exclusively to the development of the Absolute Subject, remove the mystery of developmental Psychology.

> Circular or dialectical situations ... although a source of difficulty, contribute to the particular richness of the sciences of man .... One is left wondering at the hidden means whereby these problems, even if not fully solved, have at least been divested of their mystery. These means .... constitute the prototype of a dialectical interaction (Piaget, 1974a, p. 35).

This selection is not about science as studied in all the universities, but it is about *dialectical Science*. The "hidden means" is always the same in Piaget's theory - the Body of Monads - and dialectical interaction describes its essential activity. Piaget's Science is not designed to learn about and utilize the physical or "lived" world. It only wishes to get further away from the physical world, and is enabled to do this by gradually assimilating and eliminating it with operational activity.

If the world of science is really "constructed" on the lived world, it is not ... constructed
on its foundations, for the aim of Scientific Thought is always to get further away from
this lived world, contradicting it instead of utilizing it ... The true starting point of the
Universe of Science is to be looked for in the World of Action [of] ... the Thought
operation (author's capitalization) (Piaget, 1971c, p. 87).

Natural science is constructed on the "lived world" of physical reality. Piaget's
dialectical, personalized Science, however, attempts to contradict and thus assimilate
the lived world by means of Thought operations rather than "copy" and utilize it. His
Science starts in the World of Action which is the Unseen World of Monads or the
Universe of Science! *Cognitive development of the Form or Absolute Subject is
explained by equilibrations or operations. This is true regardless of whether we are
speaking of the development of the immanent Subject in people or in the History of
Science - which is the History of the Absolute Subject's development through time.*
The operational process in both cases is called "psychogenesis" because this term
refers to the development of the total Body of Monads as well as the immanent
Groups of Monads within people.

The central concept in our explanation of cognitive development (whether we speak of the
History of Science or of psychogenesis) is ... that of successive improvements of the
Forms of Equilibrium, in other words, of an "increasing equilibration" (author's
capitalization) (Piaget, 1977, p. 178).

Cognitive development, as Piaget understands it, is different from anything most of
us have ever heard about or even imagined. His central concept is the progressive
improvement of the Form of Monads by successive equilibrations or operations. This
cognitive development of the Form or Absolute Subject occurs in individuals, and is
often described as "psychogenesis", but the same process occurs in the monads outside
of people, as it is the function of monads to assimilate all objects and thus further
Self-development. That is, the immanent Monads assimilate the people they occupy,
while monads outside of people assimilate objects in which they reside and to which
they are adjacent. Regardless of whether the process is inside of people or outside, the
very same process constantly occurs. This is because *the "Psychology" being
developed is metaphysical Psychology, not human psychology!* Piaget uses another
term to indicate the development of metaphysical Psychology, which is at the same
time a covering mask over the concept to discourage comprehension. This other
term is 'History of Science". Psychogenesis means improvement of the Body of
Monads by means of equilibrations or operations, and this is equally descriptive of the
Historical development of Science (author's capitalization) (Piaget, 1971c, p. 156)
(Beth & Piaget, 1966, pp. 306-7), meaning the development of the Absolute Subject.
We must remember, as this implies, that the psychogenesis that occurs within
individuals is equally Historical because we are talking about *one* Body of Monads
(author's italics and capitalization) (Piaget, 1967, p. 144) (Piaget, 1950, p. 66). This
upper-level kind of History and development was proclaimed by Piaget to have been
discovered by Hegel (author's capitalization) (Piaget, 1971b, p. 1) (Piaget, 1974a, pp.
16-17). It is the same History that Piaget's father, a historian, did not believe in
(author's capitalization) (Piaget, 1971c, p. 4).

    In the first sentence below, Piaget again uses "objects" to mean monads. In the
same sentence he compares the "legal" findings of natural science with the

"necessary" findings of dynamic operational coordinations. The problem with "legal" investigations is that the "observables" of natural science provide logically insufficient verification for their findings - at least for the *explanation* of their findings.

> Any dynamic coordination between objects implies the use of necessary inferences ... or simply extensions which are "legal" but are not necessary, as they know no control other than a logically insufficient verification made from observables. If these inferences are necessary, they can only be operational ... that is, based on the general coordinations of the action (Piaget, 1977, pp. 54-5).

Piaget says that coordination between objects is explained in two ways. One way is based on "legality" which is Piaget's term for the way of natural science. Legality is based on observation and experiment which, in Piaget's opinion, is "logically insufficient" and not "necessary". However, if the coordination of the "objects", which in this case are monads, is operational the explanation will be logical and necessary, even though it will be based on the hidden activities of inferred monads or metaphysical "objects".

The experimental actions in the quote below are metaphysical in nature. These actions "get at" or assimilate the object and decenter the lower-level subject. The mathematical operators or monads make their own laws without any help from people.

> There is always the unavoidable necessity of actions in order to get at the properties of the object .... Experimental action is oriented ... in the direction of Logico-Mathematical decentering .... Mathematical operators [and their] coordinations provide laws independent of the subject as individual ego (author's capitalization) (Piaget, 1971a, pp. 336-7).

"Experimental action" in this excerpt is based on the coordinations of the Mathematical operators or monads. These operators decenter the individual subject as they make their own laws regarding assimilation of the object-subject and construction of the metaphysical Object. True autonomy includes the liberty to make one's own laws (Piaget, 1971c, pp. 184-5) (Piaget, 1952b, p. 10) as well as the power of Self-existence (author's capitalization) (Piaget & Inhelder, 1973, p. 15) without input of any kind from outside sources (Piaget, 1970b, p. 5) (Piaget, 1973d, 7; 15-16). These attributes distinguish the Logico-Mathematical Subject from the individual ego.

Piaget has no use for "positivist" or natural science because it is only interested in facts and laws. After all, challenges Piaget, there is no need for "Psychology" if this is the extent of one's concern! *This means, of course, that "Psychology" is not needed in any of our universities!*

> If [experimental pedagogy] intends to limit itself, in conformity with the positivist conception of science, to a simple investigation into fact and laws without claiming to explain what it states, then naturally there is no need whatever for a connection with Psychology (author's capitalization) (Piaget, 1970d, p. 23).

If educational theory limits itself to natural science, there is no need whatever for a connection with upper-level Psychology. Of course he is only pretending, as he grossly exaggerates educational theory's independence of his Absolute Subject for the purpose of impact. After all, his System dictates that every kind of lower-level thought activity depends upon the monads in the brain. The monads must activate the neurons even though the thought may be inconsistent with desires of the monads. This is because everything physical resists the activity of the metaphysical.

The quote below speaks of the Logico-Mathematical Universe, which is the World of Possibles. Both of these terms refer to the Body of Monads which contain within themselves all of the possibilities necessary for perfect development. The application of "natural Logic", another term for the operational activity of the Body of Monads, will fully realize these possibilities - this is Piagetian Science.

> If one defines the Logico-Mathematical Universe as the World of Possibles, independent of the checks by the real *(since formal deduction dispenses with experimental verifications)* ... then the conquest of a natural Logic ... may tend ... towards that Knowledge of possibles constituted by the Logico-Mathematical Sciences (author's italics and capitalization) (Piaget, 1980a, p. 158).

The World of Possibles refers to the Body of Monads and the possibilities that it will realize in its Self-development. Physical reality will "check" or resist this realization, but full realization is nevertheless dogmatically assumed, as metaphysical or "natural Logic" will achieve complete development by achieving "Knowledge of the possibles". This is what Logico-Mathematical Science is all about. In the following passage, Piaget quotes the philosopher Jaspers. One might be a bit suspicious of Piaget's use of the quote because Jaspers insisted that "there is no certainty either in philosophy or in science". (Edwards, 1967, Vol. 4, p. 255).

> [Piaget quotes from Jaspers:] *"As soon as knowledge is imposed upon each individual for apodictic reasons, it becomes immediately scientific, it ceases to be philosophy and belongs to a particular domain of the knowable".* Without changing a single word, this is what we have tried to show (Piaget's italics) (Piaget, 1971c, p. 210).

This quote gives us an insight into Piaget's dogmatic philosophical position, which he rather directly declares to be apodictic in nature. He basically declares that his philosophical position is absolutely certain and necessary, and therefore it is scientifically sound. This position, however, would appear to be almost the opposite of the existentialism of Karl Jaspers who "stresses the irrational in man" (Edwards, 1967, Vol. 4, p. 254). All we have, of course, is Piaget's word for this certainty, as he admits that he has no use for empirical evidence (Inhelder & Piaget, 1958, p. 257) (Piaget, 1980b, p. 105) (Piaget, 1973b, pp. 10-11). After all, empiricist tradition regards knowledge as a copy of reality (Piaget & Inhelder, 1969, p. 28). If one understands that Formal Thought subordinates empirical reality to the System of Operations (author's capitalization) (Inhelder & Piaget, 1958, p. 254), it immediately becomes clear that empirical evidence is irrelevant to the Absolute Subject who alone is the System of Operations and the source of Formal Thought.

THE REVERSAL OF REALITY

We have seen repeatedly that the Subject and physical reality have common roots (author's capitalization) (Piaget, 1973d, p. 57) (Piaget, 1962, p. 13). We have also observed that they diverged to become dialectical opposites, but through operational assimilation physical reality will converge with the Subject and become one with Him again in the distant future. In the quote below Piaget speaks of the Subject and object having common roots, but that presently the conflict between the two involves much work and many difficulties. This work is of such a nature, however, that it eventually will bring about a profound convergence of the metaphysical and physical entities.

> Both [causality and operations] adhere to the laws of Reality and therefore to the common roots of the Subject and objects, then why so much work and so many difficulties until their discovery or their conscious realization? Why this evolution of psychogenesis .... since at the end of their conflict ... they ... are profoundly convergent? These are the broad outlines of this dialectic (author's capitalization) (Piaget, 1974b, pp. 113-14).

Lower-level causality - the kind observed in natural science - as well as operations adhere to the laws of upper-level Reality - the kind Piaget associates with the Body of Monads. One of the "laws" of this Reality specifies that the Continuum of Monads or Absolute decided to create the world of physical reality, and that this occurred by the mysterious process of emanation from the monads. The Absolute made this momentous decision even though He knew millennia of conflict would ensue because physical reality is His dialectic opposite and would "resist" Him (author's capitalization) (Piaget, 1926, pp. 235-6) (Piaget, 1930, p. 131) (Piaget, 1952b, pp. 135-6) (Piaget, 1973c, p. 33). His motivation was Self-development and He knew (Piaget is dogmatic regarding the Absolute's need for this particular kind of metaphysical Knowledge as it is fundamental to his theory) that the only way this could be achieved was to create and then to reverse the process of creation by assimilating His opposite with a very long series of operational syntheses, collectively called "psychogenesis". It should be understood that "evolution of psychogenesis" is very awkward phraseology - the meaning is *"psychogenetic evolution" of the Absolute Subject* which involves concomitantly the assimilation of physical reality (Beth & Piaget, 1966, pp.36; 145-6) (Piaget, 1974a, pp. 55-6) (Piaget, 1928, p. 200) (Piagct, 1971c, p. 75) (Bringuier, 1980. p. 40). *Psychogenesis is not evolving!* This dialectic conflict will end, and the Absolute will be fully developed, when His opposite is completely reversed back into the monads by assimilation - which is another way to express the psychogenetic evolution of the Body of Monads.

The difficult work mentioned in the previous quote must be accomplished by Groups of monads. The Total Group, also called "Space", is a Self-Enclosed System, the *only* Self-Enclosed System in existence according to Piaget, which created a huge problem for itself and is now in the process of resolving this problem. The solution will be secured when reality is completely reversed as the System "closes" on itself and returns to the "point of departure".

> The concept of a Group goes far beyond the construction of Space. Every Self-Enclosed System of Operations constitutes a Group, that is it is possible to return to the point of departure through an operation .... The concept of Group thus forms the principle of this System of Operations .... Every act of assimilation ... presupposes a System of Operations arranged in Groups ... Assimilation ... involves a reversibility, or a possible return to the point of departure (author's capitalization) (Piaget, 1954, p. 236).

Since "Group" is merely another name for "Space", the first sentence is another tautology affirming the concept of Self-development, but it also ushers in another essential matter, namely that the Group is a Self-Enclosed System. And what does Piaget mean by "Self-Enclosed System of Operations"? In the quote he makes it a synonym of Group or Space because in his opinion there is only one Self-Enclosed System - the reversible operational System of the Group. *The operations of the Group are said to be Self-enclosed because they are reversible, that is, the Group performs direct operations, which are followed by operations which reverse the direct operations. This enables the Group to close the loop by returning to the starting point of its grand metaphysical experiment to perfect Himself.* When the last operation occurs and the physical universe has been fully reversed we have Self-enclosure. In other words, the Total Group, who is the Absolute Subject or Continuum of Monads, originally existed all by Himself; He decided to create the physical universe by emanations - sometimes called "direct operations" - and then to reverse the process by assimilative operations (Piaget, 1950, p. 90) (Piaget, Inhelder & Szeminska, 1960, p. 330). This represents a special kind of submission to the object, although it is certainly not exclusively submissive, for the purpose of a long-term benefit based on the Subject's coordinating activities (author's capitalization) (Piaget, 1973a, p. 107), which will ultimately assimilate and thus reincorporate all physical objects (Piaget, 1950, p. 9) (Piaget, 1952b, p. 407) (Piaget, 1971a, p. 363) (Piaget, 1967, p. 64) (Piaget, 1928, p. 228) (Bringuier, 1980, p. 44). It is important to understand at this juncture that Piaget tells us almost nothing regarding the nature of an emanation or "direct operation". *He only elaborates the assimilative or reverse operation.* Furthermore, in Piaget's numerous references to the "reverse" or "inverse" operation, one must remember the particular entity that is being reversed. *The only significance connected with the "reversal aspect" of this operation is that physical reality is being reversed.* The last use of "Group" in the quote is taken to mean "groups of Groups" but the meaning could be "groups of operations".

It may be difficult but one must keep in mind that "Space" or the "Group" is a Psychological Entity. This Psychological Entity or Field of Monads is the Essential Mechanism or Intelligence or the Absolute Subject who can only become fully formed by returning to the point of departure as vaguely traced below.

> Operations are organized Psychologically only in the form of Group Systems, characterized by their reversible composition ... This increasing Mental reversibility ... leads ... to ... reversible operations in the logical sense, that is, such that each direct operation corresponds to a possible contrary one ... The notion of "Group" in the Field of Logico-Mathematical Operations corresponds in the Psychological Field to the Essential Mechanisms [sic] of Intelligence formed by means of return to a point of departure (reversibility) (author's capitalization) (Piaget, 1971b, p. 114).

The meaning before the first comma is reversed, a stultifying but very common device. *Group Systems are organized Psychologically in the form of operations, not vice versa.* Each operation by this non-human Psychological Entity corresponds to a contrary operation that will reverse it (Piaget, 1950, p. 90) (Piaget, 1967, p. 54). Piaget insists that we cannot even speak of operations unless the process is reversible (Piaget, 1970b, p. 65). His "suggested" distinction between the fields of Logico-Mathematical Operations and Psychology is pure pretension, as the "two fields" are identical. The Mechanism of Intelligence or Group is indeed formed in the process of returning to *the* (not "a") point of departure. This Mechanism or Group is developed by the assimilative or reverse operations which eventually will return Him to the point of departure, defined implicitly by Piaget as the moment He created the physical universe. Now we can understand why Piaget believed that the ancient Neoplatonic idea of a "procession" followed by a return of things to their source (Piaget, 1957, p. 28) shadowed forth his doctrine concerning the creation of the physical universe followed by its difficult reversal back into the monads.

Formal possibility is what the great metaphysical experiment is supposed to produce. In the following excerpt, Piaget claims that formal possibility is a necessary outcome of direct and reverse operations.

> But what is the nature of formal possibility? [It] is the totality of reversible transformations performed in such a way that the composition of an operation and its inverse result in a product termed "identical" or null ... whereas from the standpoint of physics operational reversibility signifies the exact compensation of potential transformations (or operations), from the logical standpoint it refers to deductive necessity (Inhelder & Piaget, 1958, p. 258).

Formal possibility will be realized when all of the direct operations and all of their inverses or reverses have occurred. "Formal possibility" refers to all of the possibilities of development which will be attained when operations finally close the loop by reversing the *first* "direct operation", which will be the *final* reverse operation, that occurred at the point of departure. This will signal simultaneously complete actualization of the Absolute's potential and complete assimilation of physical reality. For Piaget it is a foregone conclusion that every possibility will be realized and the "direct" and reverse operations will balance out perfectly, establishing equilibrium at last.

The great reversal of physical reality requires that every direct operation be reversed. When this is accomplished the entire set of operations or equilibrations will have occurred. *This process, however, does not describe the construction of "reversibility", but the construction of the Operational System.* The reversibility of *physical reality* is indeed the sine qua non of this construction, but this vital component is purposely omitted. Piaget is very clever at twisting meanings.

> Reversibility ... is the sine qua non of the construction of Operational Systems ... *True reversibility* (in contrast to the 'empirical return to the starting point') *cannot be properly constructed unless it is based on the entire set of operations.* In other words, direct operations are necessarily based on their inverses (author's italics and capitalization) (Piaget & Inhelder, 1974, p. 272).

When Piaget states that reversibility is absolutely essential if Operational Systems are to be developed, he means that the creation of the physical universe by the direct operations must be reversed completely by the reverse operations if the Operational System or Absolute is to be constructed. As Piaget says, construction is based on the entire set of operations (Inhelder & Piaget, 1958, p. 307). Piaget describes only one of the two outcomes of the entire set of operations. The other outcome is complete reversal of physical reality.

Since Logical Structure in the following passage is the Absolute Subject we know that He is not reversible, so Piaget first feeds his reader a deliberate falsehood. As is so often the case, he then tries to "balance" the false account with a true statement regarding the presence of direct and inverse operations in connection with the Logical Structure. The exact "compensation" by a reverse operation for each direct operation leads to a permanent equilibrium.

> Truly Logical Structures are distinguished by their complete reversibility, i.e., by the presence of direct and inverse operations that exactly compensate one another and thus effect a permanent equilibrium (author's capitalization) (Piaget, 1967, pp. 106-7).

In the first phrase Piaget wittingly confuses the Entity with His operations. *The Logical Structure is not reversible; it is His operations which produced the physical universe that are reversible.* And these operations can be called "reversible" *only* because they are able, according to the theory, to actually reverse physical reality back to the time when it did not exist (author's italics) (Piaget, 1928, 189). There are, of course, reversible structures; physical structures were created for the express purpose of being reversed back into the monads (Piaget, 1970a, p. 32) (Piaget, 1973a, p. 131) (Piaget & Inhelder, 1974, p. 267). Note that the reverse operations *"effect a permanent equilibrium"*, a condition that human beings would never be expected to attain. Piaget also makes the concept of reversibility difficult to formulate for another reason as he frequently makes the process of attaining the reversal of reality the *source* of reversibility. Admittedly, this is very odd, but he goes even further in this direction by often claiming that equilibrium is the *source* of reversibility (author's italics) (Piaget, 1967, pp. 114; 131) (Piaget, 1971a, p. 12) (Piaget, 1972, p. 38) (Piaget, 1974b, p. 23). In other words, the meaning is reversed in two ways. First, operations or equilibrations are not the source of *reversibility* as the source is the Absolute Subject, whose operations do *effect the reversal* of physical reality. Reversibility is a characteristic of physical reality and it is only because operations effect this reversal that they are said to be "reverse operations". Second, equilibrium, or the eventual result of operations, is certainly not the source of reversibility as the Absolute Subject again is the source. Perhaps the most clever and subtle way Piaget makes this concept hard to understand is his use of "reversibility" when the meaning is really "reversal" or "reversed". Added to this confusion is his use of two main kinds of reversibility. By far the most important kind of reversibility, as has already been indicated, is the kind that physical reality exhibits. Physical reality is held to be intrinsically reversible, and the fulfillment of this possibility is the overriding concern of both Piaget and the Absolute Subject.

Piaget's ability to confuse and deceive by manipulations of word meanings and reversal of meanings is seen, for instance, in Flavell's major work. Notice how Flavell is confused by Piaget's use of "reversible", when the word should be "reverse", and by a tricky reversal of meaning. In Piaget's view, states Flavell, "reversibility is a necessary by-product of the equilibration-of-structures process" (Flavell, 1963, p. 243). Reversibility is *not* a result or by-product of equilibration. Equilibrations or operations do not produce reversibility; they *reverse what is reversible*. Flavell then quotes Piaget: "An operation ... has become completely reversible in a system equilibrated, and become completely reversible *because* completely equilibrated".[2] First, we observe the familiar ploy of a reversal of meaning. *The operation is not reversible because the system is equilibrated. The system is equilibrated because the operation is reversible.* Second, the meaning of the last six words should refer to a completely *reversed* reality rather than a completely *reversible* operation, but this reality is missing from the context as it has been craftily *replaced* by a "completely reversible" operation within a "completely equilibrated" metaphysical System. Piaget thus misrepresents his own theory. The operations in his system are indeed reversible, but it is meaningless to refer to reversible operations without revealing the purpose of their reversibility, *which is to completely equilibrate the Absolute System by reversing physical reality*. Piaget hides this central fact! The bottom line is that Flavell is hopelessly lost regarding the concept of reversibility. This follows as sure as night follows day from his inability to accept Piaget's dual metaphysical-physical system. *The concept of reversibility is utterly ludicrous if interpretation is confined to the level of physical reality.*

Piaget again speaks of reversible operations in the selection below, but ignores what they reverse. Reversible operations are "regular" operations because they are performed by the Group. Empirical actions by scientists may be fruitful, but they never result in "regular" constructions.

> Every operation, as we saw time and again, is a reversible action. Irreversible actions are not operations because they .... [are] empirical ... They may result in fruitful, but never in regular, constructions. Regular constructions only begin when the actions are grouped into a closed Operational System (author's capitalization) (Piaget & Inhelder, 1974, p. 278).

The only kind of operation Piaget deals with in any detail is the operation that reverses reality by means of assimilation. Emanations or the "direct operations" of creation are never described; they are only mentioned from time to time. "Irreversible actions" are not operations because they are "empirical". "Reversible actions", in Piaget's terminology, are simply not possible in physical reality (Piaget, 1952a, p. 201) (Piaget, Inhelder & Szeminska, 1960, p. 24) (Piaget, 1930, p. 271) (Piaget, 1969b, p. 359) (Piaget, et al., 1977, p. 14). Furthermore, Piaget makes it very clear that human beings can have nothing to do with reversible operations, as he specifically asserts that the "self is eliminated" from reversible operations (Piaget & Inhelder, 1971, pp. 368-9). But what is a "regular construction"? First, we note that regular constructions can only occur when operational actions are "grouped into a closed Operational System". Second, "every Self-enclosed System of Operations

---

[2] This quote is taken by Flavell from page 37 of: Piaget, J. Logique et equilibre dans les comportements du sujet. In L. Apostel, B. Mandelbrot, & J. Piaget, Logique et equilibre. *Etudes d'epistemologie genetique. Vol. 2. Paris: Presses Univ. France, 1957. pp. 27-117.*

constitutes a Group" (author's capitalization) (Piaget, 1954, p. 236) (Piaget, 1972, p. 36). A regular construction, then, is an operational construction by a Group of monads.

In the quote below Piaget makes a revealing contrast between activities of the Mind and mental activities. Activities of the Mind are, by implication, reversible, whereas mental activities can never be reversible. This is a good example of the dual framework which was the focus of chapter two, but to which Piagetians have turned a blind eye. The Mind is metaphysical while the minds of individual people are based on physical processes. Piaget also speaks of an "Identity" who is the result of reversibility, but he is not at all clear about who He is. However, since this "Identity" is "guaranteed by the permanence of the identity element" (author's capitalization) (Piaget, 1970b, p. 20) we can infer the correct Entity with absolute certainty. Since monads are the only permanent "elements" in existence, according to his theory, Piaget is referring to the metaphysical Subject. In the beginning "Identity" existed in splendid isolation, that is, Piaget sees the Continuum of Monads or Absolute at this primal juncture as having an undisputed "Identity". When the Absolute created the physical universe this "Identity" was divided into a multitude of Sub-Groups in order to activate every living thing and engineer all the moving parts of the universe. Looking far into the future, this "Identity" will again become undisputed when reality is reversed completely, and matter no longer encumbers and subdivides the monads of the Absolute. This is why Piaget asserts that the two poles of reversible operations are regarded as identical (Inhelder & Piaget, 1958, p. 258) (Piaget, 1952a, p. 201). The Continuum or Absolute Subject before the creation of the physical universe remains the same identical Entity after the universe has been completely reversed, but of course it is not identical in terms of level of development. "Identity" usually refers to the time before the "point of departure" and the time after "complete reversal". During the time in between "Identity" is so enmeshed in matter that only Piaget can "see" Him. In any case, reversible relations are said to reveal only one General Identity (author's capitalization) (Piaget, et al., p. 185).

> There certainly is an activity of the Mind: a physical or mental movement is never wholly reversible, since it occurs in time .... There certainly is also Identity ... but this Identity is the result ... of reversibility ... Operations ... are the essence of Thought .... [We] distinguish [operations] from empirical constructions precisely by their reversibility, Identity then being ... the product of inverse operations (author's capitalization) (ibid., pp. 201-2).

Taking the last sentence first, we see again that *empirical constructions cannot be reversible according to Piaget's definition*. Also, note the contrast between "Mind" and "mental movements". The essence of Thought is operations by the Mind, and operations by the Mind are always reversible (author's capitalization) (Piaget, 1974b, p. 125) (Piaget, 1928, pp. 11-12) (Piaget, 1967, pp. 49; 130) (Piaget, 1970b, pp. 15; 65) (Piaget, 1971a, p. 367) (Piaget, 1978a, p. 228). *Moreover, true Mental operations are always reversible* (author's italics and capitalization) (Piaget, 1928, p. 171; 190), *but the ordinary mental operations of people are irreversible because the ordinary physical self is eliminated from reversible operations* (author's italics) (Piaget & Inhelder, 1971, pp. 368-9). *This notion is augmented by the "fact" that "temporal events" are irreversible; since everything man does takes time, it is not possible for him to reverse things in terms of Piaget's definition* (Piaget, 1969b, p. 293). He expands this notion with the statement that "everything experiential" is irreversible (Piaget, Inhelder & Szeminska, 1960, p. 24). Not only is the self incapable of reversible actions, but no physical action whatsoever is reversible according to Piaget (Piaget, et al., 1977, p. 14). The essential point is that no event in the real world is reversible (Piaget, 1069b, pp. 293; 359) Piaget, 1930, p. 271) (Piaget, 1953, p. 8). This is further affirmed by Piaget's assurance that if *chance* is a factor reversibility is not possible (author's italics) (Piaget, 1971c, p. 201).

In the following passage the Organism is called the "Sea of Multiple Physico-Chemical Compensations". The Organism is indeed the Sea of Monads within which everything takes place, including the behavior of people.

> In the final analysis, the common source of operational reversibility and of compositions peculiar to causal actions is naturally found in the Organism, since the latter is at the ... same time the Sea of Multiple Physico-Chemical Compensations through which it partakes of the laws of matter and of a homeostatic activity ... from which ensue a growing number of readjustments, including those of conduct characterizing the behavior of the subject (author's capitalization) (Piaget, 1974b, p. 27).

The Organism is the common source of the great reversal as well as of causality in the physical universe. *This is the metaphysical Organism, who is the Sea of Multiple Physico-Chemical Compensations.* In other words, it is the Sea of Monads within which all of the physico-chemical interactions in the universe occur. Furthermore, it is the Sea of Monads which, behind the scenes, characterizes the behavior of every object-subject. It is worth noting that over more than one hundred pages Piaget repeatedly switches from the metaphysical Organism to the physical organism and vice versa. One must have patience to work through such scheming duplicity, but effort will be rewarded with the observation of quite clear switches on pages 36, 67, 127 and 137, with the most odious and vexing switch appearing on page 137. If one has the stomach to deal with the underlying moral turpitude, it could be worthwhile to fully familiarize one's self with the way these switches are handled.

In the following statement the vital processes of the Living Organism, Mechanism, or Intelligence are judged by Piaget to be impervious to the effects of entropy. Unfortunately he unfairly enlists the support of two individuals who surely would not agree with him.

> There remains the problem of knowing whether the vital processes are wholly submitted to irreversibility conforming to the second principle of thermodynamics (growth of entropy with the probabilist models which have been furnished) or whether, as Helmholtz, Guye and many others believed, the Living Organism supposes a Mechanism escaping from this principle and then converging with the characteristic reversibility of Intelligence (author's capitalization) (Piaget, 1973a, p. 169).

The vital processes of the Living Organism do not submit themselves to entropy in Piaget's theory, thus the second principle of thermodynamics does not apply to the metaphysical Organism (author's capitalization) (Piaget, 1971a, p. 13) (Piaget, 1977, pp. 174-5) (Inhelder & Piaget, 1958, p. 332). Piaget cleverly mixes levels by bringing in "probabilist" or physical models which are subject to entropy. Worse, he suggests that Helmholtz and Guye agree with him that the Living Organism, whom they know nothing about, has a Mechanism that enables it to escape entropy - a Mechanism that "converges" with "the characteristic reversibility of Intelligence". The Living Organism *is the Mechanism* that converges, not "with the characteristic reversibility of Intelligence", because Intelligence is not reversible, but with the reversible physical universe (author's italics and capitalization) (Piaget, 1974, p. 152) (Piaget, 1974a, p. 76) (Beth & Piaget, 1966, p. 301) (Piaget & Inhelder, 1969, p. 5) which will have been assimilated and thus reversed by Intelligence. The reversal of reality by Intelligence is the ultimate way of escaping entropy as *physical reality eventually merges with the Intelligent Subject* (author's italics and capitalization) (Piaget, 1928, p. 189) *or Form of Monads* (author's italics and capitalization) (Piaget & Inhelder, 1974, p. 267) *who is immune from this final disorder.*

THE METAPHYSICAL PRODUCTION OF NUMBERS

In Piaget's system everything, as we have seen over and over, must flow from the Absolute Subject. This doctrine forces him to hatch some of the most fanciful theories imaginable. The most difficult problem for him, however, was to make these chimerical theories acceptable to the academic community, and his success in this venture is without doubt one of the most astonishing deceptions in academic history. Piaget's imaginative pipe-dream regarding the metaphysical generation of numbers is a case in point. Yes, *numbers must be generated by the Absolute, otherwise they simply would not exist.* This initial generation is repeated by the immanent Subject in each individual. Both of these kinds of generation are more or less obscured by Piaget's make-believe findings in children of the basic metaphysical processes *disguised as observable physical processes.* In other words, he tries to annul the initial metaphysical production of numbers by hiding this supernatural process under the mask of *supposed* keen observation and experimental findings. Unfortunately, he has been able to prevail over his readers because he is a creative genius in deception and in creating confusion. We will focus on the basic initial metaphysical generation of numbers - a subject studiously avoided by Piagetians.

In the passage below numbers are said to result from a "synthesis" of Classes with seriation. More specifically, numbers are based on the operations or relations of Classes, which conforms with the genetic or psychogenetic viewpoint. This means that "Class and number have a common Mechanism" (author's capitalization) (Piaget, 1952a, p. 181). Piaget is describing the process of Self-development by the Absolute Subject, so it would be lunacy to accept number production as identical to this development, but it is indeed a concomitant of this metaphysical process!

> [We can account] for number by a "synthesis" ... of Classes with ... seriation; and this in the precise sense, it would seem, in which Hegel uses the term "synthesis" (Classes and relation[s] ... constituting "moments" of number, "moments" later "surpassed") .... The ... central point of the construction of number .... [is an] appeal to Classes and the relation[s] ... which conforms with what the genetic viewpoint led us to expect (author's capitalization) (Beth & Piaget, 1966, p. 270).

Piaget defines number in terms of the operational process. In other words, he is affirming his doctrine that "numbers do not exist alone, but are engendered by the *very law of formation itself*" (author's italics) (Evans, 1973, p. 126). Operations or relations synthesize opposite classes which results in a more advanced positive Class (Inhelder & Piaget, 1958, p. 30) (Piaget, 1977, p. 41) (Piaget, 1972, p. 71); this process continues in an indefinite series of operational syntheses or Hegelian "moments". Number, of course, is based on a certain kind of series, so it is reasonable to conclude from the above quote that this series of operations involving opposite classes is closely related in Piaget's mind to the series of numbers. This is what the psychogenetic or genetic viewpoint led him to expect - and we can be sure, because mere verbalisms are easy, that he will always "find" whatever he expects to find. Clearly, then, the psychogenetic process, which is the necessary means for the Absolute's development, is a vital component in the construction of number, but how could it be? What is the precise relationship? It is not surprising that Piaget considers his view regarding synthesis to be the same as his mentor, Hegel, but it is apparent that Hegel did not explain the "construction" of number by means of synthesis as Piaget strongly suggests, as Hegel was not interested in mathematics and presumably never discussed the "construction" of number.

In the following quote Piaget reiterates his doctrine that the construction of numbers is organized stage by stage, hand in hand with the development of the Living Logical Structure.

> We have ... deliberately restricted ourselves to the problem of the construction of number in relation to logical operations. Our hypothesis is that the construction of number goes hand in hand with the development of Logic ... Our results do, in fact, show that number is organized, stage after stage, in close connection with the gradual elaboration of [Logical] Systems (author's capitalization) (Piaget, 1952a, VIII).

This passage repeats the meaning of the preceding passage in somewhat different words. Piaget "deliberately restricts" himself to the psychogenetic process with regard to the construction of number because he holds this view dogmatically. Not only is number constructed hand in hand with the development of Logic, but each number "finally takes its roots from a purely Logical Structure" (author's capitalization) (Piaget, 1971b, p. 40). When he asserts in another context that Logic is a privileged domain for Structures, he is not speaking of traditional logic but of Natural Logic in the sense of "natural numbers" (author's capitalization) (Piaget, 1970b, p. 28). This Natural Logic is based on a Formal System that is "Absolute" (author's capitalization) (ibid., pp. 29-30). "Logic" is capitalized because it is often used, as it certainly is here, as a synonym for the Absolute Subject (author's capitalization) (Piaget, 1971a, p. 358) (ibid., pp. 6-7) (Piaget, 1973a, p. 106) (Piaget, 1980a p. 158) (Piaget, 1973d, p. 28) (Piaget, 1928, p. 171), who is the "purely Logical Structure". Number, then, develops integer after integer in intimate association with the only true or Logical System - the Absolute Subject (author's capitalization) (Piaget, 1954, p. 236) (Piaget, 1969a, p. 1) (Inhelder & Piaget, 1958, pp. 288-9; 303-4; 340-1) (Piaget & Inhelder, 1956, pp. 292; 457) (Piaget, 1972, p. 91) (Piaget, 1978b, p. 96). Number generation obviously parallels the psychogenetic development of the Absolute.

In the selection below Piaget emphasizes the fact that number construction is endogenous in nature, meaning that the processes of number production, such as "including" and "putting in order" are not based on learning. This follows from Piaget's doctrine that endogenous construction is not a human activity at all.

Number appears to be an endogenous construction in that it is produced by highly
generalized operations in the Subject, who then coordinates them; number is a synthesis
of inclusion ... and of order .... The operations of putting together, including, putting in
order, and so on are in no way the products of learning (author's capitalization) (Piaget,
1971a, p. 310).

Number is an endogenous construction because it is produced by metaphysical
operations *in* the Subject (author's italics and capitalization) (Piaget, 1980b, pp. 80;
81; 96; 106) (Piaget, 1977, pp. 172-3; 199-200) (Piaget, 1971a, pp. 316-17), that is
what "endogenous" means. Endogenous construction of number by operations is
another restatement of the psychogenetic process. Interestingly, the operations are
not only by the Subject, but they are *in* the Subject. Since the operations involved in
this construction are not products of learning, Piaget must be thinking of the
immanent Subject in individuals. He wishes to emphasize his belief that the facets of
number production, such as "putting together", "including", and "putting in order" or
serialization, depend upon metaphysical processes rather than brain processes.
Otherwise the *"in"* could refer to the fact that all possible operations are coordinated
within the Single Body of Monads (author's italics and capitalization) (Piaget, 1954,
p. 117) (Piaget, 1971a, p. 93) (Piaget & Inhelder, 1974, p. 114), whether inside or
outside of people. Although he probably means "in" the immanent Subject in this
passage, other passages regarding the operational synthesis of numbers shows that the
latter alternative is considered to be equally true by Piaget. For instance, when we are
told that Space synthesizes numbers (author's capitalization) (Piaget, 1977, p. 7), we
understand that both possibilities are true. Piaget makes several statements
associating Spatial activity and number production (author's capitalization) (Piaget,
1972, p. 39) (Piaget & Inhelder, 1956, p. 117). Similar statements regarding the
Continuum (author's capitalization) (Piaget, 1972, pp. 46-7), the Group (author's
capitalization) (Piaget, Inhelder, & Szeminska, 1960, p. 60) (Piaget, 1969a, p. 50)
and the Body (author's capitalization) (Piaget, 1973a, p. 128) are also pertinent for
the same reason.

The key to the excerpt below is Piaget's assertion that the construction of
numbers starts from the Operational Nucleus or original Body of Monads.
"Operational Nucleus" is Piaget's term for the Absolute Subject before He performed
His first dialectic interaction with His newly created physical universe. *His first
operation will begin the production of numbers!*

The operation is implicit from the start in the construction of natural numbers, and it is
its generalisations resulting from reflective abstractions ... The operation ... corresponds
minimumly to relations ... All [numbers] are constructed through abstraction and
generalisation starting from the Operational Nucleus. [This view] allows us to derive
everything from a minimal starting point (Piaget's italics) (author's capitalization) (Beth
& Piaget, 1966, pp. 294-5).

The operations, reflective abstractions or relations which construct or generalize
number start from, and with, the Operational Nucleus. Piaget takes us back to the
starting point, as the "Operational Nucleus" refers to the Continuum or Absolute
Subject before He performed His first operation. The minimal starting point is the
bare Primordial Biological Entity - the Body of Monads. Everything, including
number, is derived from this starting point, that is, everything except the "Eternal

Given" or original Continuum of Monads (author's capitalization) (Piaget, 1970b, pp. 62-3) (Piaget, 1969b, p. 298) (Piaget, 1929, p. 267). *When the Operational Nucleus performs His first dialectic operation He creates number one; when He performs His second operation He creates number two and so on indefinitely.* According to Piagetian doctrine, regardless of how inane, adolescent-like or silly it may appear to be, this is the unique way integers or whole numbers originated. In the absence of dialectic operations there would be no such thing as number.

In addition to the integers, irrational numbers "were introduced in response to the necessity of making the series of numbers correspond to Spatial Continuity" (author's capitalization) (Piaget & Inhelder, 1956, pp. 148-9; 459). This was necessary to fill the gaps between the rational numbers (ibid., p. 459). Note that *Spatial Continuity* is based on a fully packed Framework of Monads, while the *rational numbers* represent a series of operations. At best Piaget's theory of numbers becomes very murky, so murky that Piaget is seen to be scrambling to cover up some logical inconsistencies. Nevertheless, he owes his reader a better explanation of the "gaps" that exist between rational numbers, as his theory of monads appears to leave no "gaps". Furthermore, he does not tell us how irrational numbers were produced or why it was necessary to fill the gaps - if there were gaps!

In the following quote Piaget moves from the Absolute Subject at large in the previous quote to the immanent Subject. He surprises his reader with what apparently is his idea of a practical joke, by completely contradicting his usual explanation of number production. It turns out to be only a nasty little trick as he immediately begins to take it all back. What makes the recantation especially offensive is that he makes it difficult for his reader to comprehend it. Piaget makes every effort to keep his reader in the dark while slickly withdrawing the contradiction.

> The beginnings of operations means that there is a beginning of differentiation between the qualitative mechanism and the Numerical Mechanisms ... Apart from numbers 1 to 3 at about age 3, 1 to 4 at about age 4, and 1 to 5 at about the age of 5, the construction of number cannot remain within the field of perceptual intuition and can therefore be completed only on the operational plane (author's capitalization) (Piaget, 1952a, p. 154).

Piaget appears to substantially modify his concept of number by suggesting that "physical" or perceptual processes account for numbers up to 5, and that operations then complete the process, *but he is only pretending!* What we have is something akin to a practical joke. Piaget frequently will make a statement that is inconsistent with his theory, then he will follow with a series of statements that gradually cancel out the first statement without specifically calling his reader's attention to his about-face. That is what he does here as he completely nullifies the idea that perceptual processes account for the numbers up to 5. He immediately begins to retract this suggestion by stating that this is an "early stage, and there is not yet true coordination" of operations (ibid., p. 154). *On the following page the retraction becomes complete as "there was no reversibility" in the early stage, so the "intuitive seriation vanishes" - only operational seriation remains* (author's italics) (ibid, p. 155). *Speaking of "seriation", i. e., the series of operations,* while individual people cannot account for it, a Psychological Entity does indeed explain it. Piaget maintains that number can be both logically and psychologically explained although it "cannot be constituted without inclusion and seriation" (Piaget, 1952a p. 184). *The argument here turns on the "fact" that inclusion and seriation are "logical" processes requiring Conscious Intelligence, but that a human source is out of the question.* This means that Piaget's concept of seriation is not pertinent to human development, making all of the physical experiments reported in the literature on this topic quite beside the point. Piaget is so enamored with the notion of seriation that he declares the series of whole numbers to be the Psychologically Organized Totality (author's capitalization) (Piaget, 1973a, p. 128). Seriation is not an entity, of course, so this is one of the many instances where Piaget irrationally makes an activity of the Subject the Subject Himself.

The final "Number" that appears at the end of natural numbers is the fully developed Absolute, or rather represents the fully developed Absolute. This is because the last natural number is produced by the last dialectic interaction. Piaget calls this final result of operations the "Whole Number". He then ignores the completed "time line" when operations are no longer needed and, without appropriate qualification, speaks of the "Number" intervening in operations along an incomplete time-line. As he is well aware, this makes "clear formulation" of his theory difficult.

> The Whole Number results from a synthesis of order and inclusion appearing at the end of natural numbers or when the Subject establishes a correspondence between one element in one set and another element in the second set ... As such the Number intervenes in an essential way in most of the operations applied to the object (author's capitalization) (Piaget, 1974b, p. 35).

Piaget merges "Number" and the Absolute Subject into the "Whole Number" which appears at the end of natural numbers. When the final operation occurs the final number signals the complete development of the Absolute. This would seem to present at least one problem for Piaget, as his theory regarding the production of whole numbers postulates that *after this final operation no more numbers can be created.* He attempts to gloss over this problem by asserting that the "grains" or "elements" can be put into a one-to-one correspondence with the positive integers (Piaget & Inhelder, 1974, p. 276). "Grains" and "elements" refer to the monads, and as they are infinite in number (Piaget & Inhelder, 1956, pp. 147-8; 459), this makes numbers also infinite (ibid., pp. 146; 149). We saw above that irrational numbers were placed in the "gaps" between rational numbers, and here there is a positive integer for every monad in existence. The metaphysical Universe is becoming very crowded with numbers! This presents a further problem, as just implied, namely if positive integers can be put in a one-to-one correspondence with the monads which fill all of space and are "closely packed" (Piaget, 1972. p. 49), where are the gaps into which the irrational numbers are supposed to fit? The parameters of the quote are changed without explanation after the "or" as he describes the production of number in general. Piaget then simply uses "Number" as a synonym for the Subject, but not as the fully developed Subject. If the Absolute is still intervening by means of operations He is not yet fully developed. And He necessarily intervenes in *all* dialectic operations, not *most* of them.

The Metaphysical Origin of Fractions and Proportion

Before we leave the topic of number, we may note Piaget's concepts of fraction and proportion. The concept of fraction is derived from the process of inclusion and is intimately tied to the reversal of physical reality. What is the inclusion process including? The going gets a bit complicated at this point because there are two kinds of metaphysical inclusion and fractions are produced with each kind. First, there is the Invariant Whole who is improved as He includes each improved Class, with each Class representing another fraction of the possibilities to be included by the Absolute Subject in His development. When the final operation occurs all of the possibilities will have come to pass so the sum of fractions will equal the possibilities required for the perfect development of the Whole (author's capitalization) (Piaget, Inhelder & Szeminska, 1960, p. 311). The other kind of fraction involves including what must be reversed: the "final term" is "the whole object (to every possible scale, even that of the spatio-temporal universe itself)" (Piaget, 1950, p. 47). That is, the physical universe must be reversed and each operation in this process represents an improved Class and one additional number. In addition to adding a possibility of development, each successive improved Class represents a larger proportion of the physical universe to be included within the monads of the Absolute Subject, and each larger number in the series corresponds with the larger inclusion with which it is paired. We can see now how this "concept of a fraction is a derivative from that of inclusion" (Piaget, 1953, p. 44). Every operation *includes a fraction* of the whole that is to be reversed, and with the last operation the sum of the fractions will equal the whole physical universe.

Quite obviously proportion is also based on inclusion and the great reversal. "Proportion ... constitutes the point of arrival of a long sequence of compositions which begins with the composition of two ordered pairs" (Piaget, et al., 1977, p. 186). If we realize that "compositions" means operations and "pairs" refers to two opposite classes, and not four as Piaget indicates with *"two* ordered pairs", this quote is easy to understand. There are also two kinds of proportion. One kind is based on the proportion of the possibilities of development included; the other is based on the proportion of physical reality included. Piaget explicitly recognizes this: "proportionality ... [is] a coordination of ... a double relationship or of the establishment of a relationship between *two laws of progression* (author's italics) (ibid., p. 137). Piaget shows his disdain for the facts of physical reality and science by personalizing "proportionality": "Proportionality tends to eventually impose itself *... regardless of the facts"* (author's italics and capitalization) (ibid., p. 144).

The Metaphysical-Physical Basis of Magic

In the quote below, the emphasis is on the metaphysical basis for magic. Whenever Piaget describes a concept in terms of *sui generis* qualities he is always referring to the metaphysical qualities of the Substantial or Absolute Self. This passage is also noteworthy for stressing the "much more intense and systematic belief" which characterizes "magic strictly speaking" as compared to the weak belief of child magic.

> We have ... assumed ... that there [is] continuity between the ... idea of efficacy and the idea ... of a magical type .... We thus define 'magical' phenomenon [sic] by the idea of efficacy at a distance and we distinguish two types: (1) Individual child magic, in which the belief is weak and probably discontinuous; and (2) Magic strictly speaking, or collective magic, characterized by various qualities *sui generis*, among them being a much more intense and systematic belief (Piaget's italics) (Piaget, 1929, p. 436).

Magical phenomena are defined as efficacy at a distance, but since the source of efficacy are the monads and they are everywhere, phenomena could never "be at a distance from monads". The meaning must be "at a distance" from the human being working the magic. Piaget's theory offers little opportunity for the human being to express himself in terms of ability to do things, as the monads always seem to completely usurp this role, but his concept of magic appears to be an exception. Magic is an activity in which people apparently have a relatively minor role through participation with the source of efficacy, the monads. A complication immediately presents itself, however, as one considers how, within Piaget's theory, one human being, for instance, might affect another human being thousands of miles away. This could only be done through one's immanent Subject who has instant communication with the monads immanent in any other individual in the world. So while it is not possible to spell out precisely the human role in magic vis a vis his immanent Subject, he has the capability to work, or at least to initiate, magical activity under certain conditions. The efficient cause is a Force that is *immanent in the child* (author's italics and capitalization) (ibid., p. 225) and the adult, so the Force per se is not the human being but the monads within the human being plus the monads "at a distance". This is a special Substantial Force that causes things (author's capitalization) (Piaget, 1930, p. 117), and the magical act depends upon the individual's ability to tap this metaphysical Force. Child magic is portrayed as being weak in this quote relative to "magic strictly speaking", but in other contexts it is strong (Piaget 1926, p. 36) (Piaget, 1929, p. 434); in still other contexts, as one can expect, adult magic is stronger (ibid., p. 435). The causal Substantial Force is *the true Self who is omnipotent;* this is the Self the child and the adult must use in order to produce magical effects (author's italics and capitalization) (Piaget, 1954, p. 272).

The following quote underlines Piaget's tenet that people can initiate magic by somehow delegating "efficacy" to "External and Autonomous Centers", namely the immanent Subject. Magic is possible because the External, but nevertheless immanent, Subject is a part of Personal Space who alone can produce magic.

> As soon as it is acquired imitation engenders a causality through imitation which constitutes one of the varieties of efficacy .... For causality to exist there must be a kind of fixation on or delegation of efficacy to External and Autonomous Centers. This is precisely what imitation brings about .... The coordinations of Schemata ... alone account for the ... Spatialization of causality (author's capitalization) (Piaget, 1954, pp. 360-1).

The first and second sentences confirm the role of the individual in the magical act, and they spell out the main aspects of this role as he somehow makes use of participation to modify reality. Every true magical act requires participation (Piaget, 1929, p. 157). In participation there exists "something in common" between two things which "enables them to act upon one another" (Piaget, 1930, pp. 260-1).

These two "things" are the immanent Subject in the person who wishes to work magic and the Sub-Group of monads which control the object or innervate the person to whom the magical force is directed. The two Sub-Groups of monads participate with each other to generate magical activity, but the human being who knows the "language" of magic is able, within Piaget's theory, to initiate the magical process by "imitation" and "delegation" of efficacy.

Piaget distinguishes the subtle difference between animism and magic by describing two different ways young children view the moon when it appears to follow them. If he believes that the "moon is trying to follow him", the "relation is animistic"; if he believes that he is "forcing or compelling the moon to move" the relation is magical (ibid., p. 260). Both the animistic relation and the magical relation are varieties of "phenomenistic" causality. The animistic relation is based on the living "Spatial Contiguities", composed of monads, which are simply exercising there ability, independently of the child, to make the moon follow the child. The magical relation, on the other hand, is based on the child's ability to delegate efficacy to the "Spatial Contiguities" of monads who then force the moon to follow the child (author's capitalization) (ibid., p. 260).

Although he guilefully intermingles the physical with the metaphysical in the context of this reference, the fact that he says the "phenomenistic relation is ... essentially vicarious" (ibid., p. 260) confirms the need to capitalize "External and Autonomous Centers" and "Spatialization", which are merely exotic synonyms. The "External and Autonomous Center" is the immanent, but psychologically "external and autonomous" Body of Monads in the child, while "Spatialization" is Piaget's obscure way of describing the magical activation of the Spatial monads contiguous with and within the moon. There is no "physical" spatial contact which connects the child or his immanent Subject to the moon's "movement", but because of participation there are metaphysical "Spatial Contiguities" or contact by the Spatial monads. Piaget, of course, is protected in this example as the movement is only apparent, but he is obviously reporting his view of magic. This quote tells us how the person initiates magical causality by delegating efficacy to the External and Autonomous Center composed of Schemata, and previously called "Space" or "Subject". How does he delegate efficacy? Piaget uses the term "imitation", but a better word for the meaning he has in mind is "visualization". The person must fervently wish the magical act to occur and believe in its inevitably as he visualizes it (Piaget, 1929, p. 434). He visualizes the monads of Space or Subject performing the desired magic, and if there has "been a long period of conformity" to the production of magical effects, the Schemata of Space or the metaphysical Subject will assuredly achieve success. It is the coordination of Schemata alone which account for the causal activity of Space.

In the excerpt below, Space is the Personal Subject who is the source of magical causation. Children believe, according to Piaget, that natural phenomena are based on the magical activity of this metaphysical Subject.

> The early notion of causality may be called magical-phenomenalist: "phenomenalist" because the phenomenal contiguity of two events is sufficient to make them appear causally related, and "magical" because it is centered on the action of the Subject without consideration of spatial connection between cause and effect (author's capitalization) (Piaget & Inhelder, 1969, p. 18).

In the previous passage the supposed magical activity was carried out by two Sub-Groups of Spatial monads; one Sub-Group made up the immanent Subject of the child and the other Sub-Group was "contiguous" with the moon. In that passage the "contiguities" were spatial; in this passage they are temporal. In this quote the magical activity is carried out by the Subject, previously called "External and Autonomous Center" "Schemata" and, by implication, "Space", without consideration of a spatial connection between cause and effect. When Piaget says "without consideration of spatial connection between cause and effect", he really means *"without any material contact"* (author's italics) (ibid., p. 8), because there is a metaphysical contact. This is an example of magical-phenomenalist causality so it is also a vicarious activity. In other words, the immanent Subject is acting vicariously in place of the physical subject.

WORD MAGIC

The passage below introduces "word magic", a form of magic at which Piaget is quite adept. He demonstrates repeatedly that this magic is not just for children. By deforming words Piaget believes that he deforms what the words represent.

> The word, originally bound up with the act of which it is an element, at a later stage suffices alone to release the act. The psycho-analysts have given an analogous explanation of word magic ... Having originally formed part of the act, [it] is able to evoke all of the concrete emotional contents of the act ... Such facts as these explain the very wide-spread tendency of primitive thought to look upon the names of persons and objects ... with ... the belief that it is possible to work upon them by the mere evocation of words, the word being no longer a mere label, but a formidable reality partaking of the nature of the named object (Piaget, 1926, p. 27).

In addition to fixation on the delegation of efficacy by visualization, there can also be fixation on the primary word or name associated with the desired magical act. This is "word magic", whereby persons or objects may be worked upon by the mere evocation of names or words. This variety of magic is based on Piaget's belief that words are part of the nature of the object or person, and not mere labels (Piaget, 1929, pp. 57; 84; 87; 91; 177-8). Piaget practices word magic by deliberately "deforming" words from time to time, strongly suggesting that he wishes to magically deform or weaken the scientific or other kinds of validity represented by the words. For instance, when he says that "the genetic code ADN is a system of indicat*ed* and not of indicat*ing* knowledge" (Piaget's italics) (Piaget, 1973d, p. 8), he is attempting to suppress the scientific concept of DNA. First, he goes to great pains in attempting to show, *contrary to the position universally held by biologists,* that "ADN" is *not* the primary storage and distribution center of biological information, as *he reserves that function for his Living Structure* (author's italics and capitalization) (ibid., pp. 7-8) *of immanent monads.* Second, by deforming DNA, the standard, universally accepted abbreviation for deoxyribonucleic acid, he is practicing a form of word magic whereby the scientific concept of DNA is supposedly distorted and hopefully crippled. "To distort a name in order to prevent the consequences of some event or as a means of defense ... follows as a natural result of regarding names as bound up in the nature of actual things and persons" (Piaget, 1929, pp. 177-8).

Along the same lines, when research results run counter to Piaget's theory he always attempts to suppress that fact - if he deals with it at all. In *The Mechanisms of Perception* (Piaget, 1969b), for example, he is quite agitated with regard to certain characteristics of the Oppel-Kundt illusion which do not fit within his theory. This particular illusion apparently does not "obey the law of reduction with practice" (ibid., p. 146), and also does not agree with Piaget's theoretical expectation that there will be a gradual reduction of illusion with age (ibid., pp. 63; 144; 149; 150). He befogs the issue in many ways, including the artificial addition of "primary effects" and "secondary effects" which take turns, over many pages, representing each side of the metaphysical versus physical aspects with respect to this particular illusion. In other words, he uses both of these "effects" to explain away the fact that this illusion does not fit within his theory. With the following quote, Piaget finally tires of toying with his reader and destroys any hope that he can expect to make sense of these two terms with regard to the Oppel-Kundt illusion.

> The first effects to be encountered are the so-called primary effects. These are followed by perceptual activities which are, in this respect, secondary. But are not the primary effects (primary within the limited context studied) themselves derivatives of anterior perceptual activities?... In other words, if perceptual activities can give rise to secondary errors ... why should primary errors ... not be secondary in this sense (ibid., p. 196).

Pity the reader who has tried valiantly to understand what Piaget really means by primary and secondary effects. When he finally reads this not so subtle admission that he has no intention of clearly differentiating between the two concepts, an angry reaction is understandable. Piaget comes back repeatedly - more than 20 times - to the Oppel-Kundt illusion, which clearly is a very vexing problem for him. He also brings in a confusing array of auxiliary concepts and some tables that show evidence of having been disfigured or warped in some way.

THE MENTAL IMAGE AS A PRECURSOR OF MAGIC

In *Mental Imagery in the Child* (Piaget & Inhelder, 1971), Piaget set for himself the difficult problem of elucidating the "mental image" that always precedes an operation, regardless of whether the operation is inside or outside of people. Most of Piaget's discussion involves mental images within people. Although he constantly interjects the familiar mental images of perception into his arguments, the mental imagery he *promotes* invariably accompanies operations according to laws different from the laws of perception (author's italics) (Piaget, 1928, p. 295). In one argument he declares that there are two types of image; reproductive images are perceptual but anticipatory images envisage transformations as well as their results (Piaget & Inhelder, 1969, p. 7). He also asserts that the mental experiment consists in imagining operations that can be carried out on reality (Piaget, 1928, p. 193). Not only is the Form or Structure of the metaphysical image he promotes "far removed from perceptual structures" (author's capitalization) (Piaget & Inhelder, 1971, p. 365), but there is a systematic difference between perceptual distortions and the distortions of reality characteristic of metaphysical images (ibid., p. 365). The metaphysical image is to a large extent based on "liberties taken by the Subject" (author's capitalization) (ibid., p. 365) - who is the Form or Structure of the only image with which Piaget is really concerned. This latter image is *entirely* concerned with transforming the object. This particular image is further elaborated in the passage below, where its superhuman character is confirmed. Piaget calls it the "concept of Space" because it is an *image of* the Spatial monads indicating an operation that they will perform. Remarkably, this image is also *produced by* the Spatial monads, which makes it a rather difficult and unusual concept.

> Finally, at Substage IIIB there appears a third type of image, one capable of anticipating the results of actions before they are carried out. This image is dynamic and mobile in character, free of defects and inadequacies of its forerunners and entirely concerned with transformations of the object ... This [is the] type of imagery which geometricians term the 'concept of Space' when it has become purely Intellectual and transcends the bounds of sense perception (author's capitalization) (Piaget & Inhelder, 1956, p. 296).

There can be no doubt regarding the metaphysical nature of this "third type of image". "Mobility", for Piaget, means the capacity to produce operations (Piaget & Inhelder, 1974, p. 272) (Piaget, 1950, p. 65), and the more actualized or developed the Subject becomes, the more "mobile" He becomes (author's capitalization) (Piaget, 1973b, p. 28). This image is also free of the defects and inadequacies found in perceptual images and, most important, only the metaphysical image is entirely concerned with transformations. This type of image actually becomes the concept of Space or Absolute Subject because it is purely Intellectual and transcends the bounds of sense perception.

The contrast between physical, perceptual or figurative images and transformation images is very great. This fact is emphasized in the quote below as we are informed that figurative images oppose transformation images in an *abusively important* way. The opposition and the abuse stem from the fact that figurative images are physical while transformational images are metaphysical.

> The figurative aspect of thought is everything related to the [physical] configurations as such, in opposition to the [metaphysical] transformations. Guided by perception and supported by the mental picture, the figurative aspect of representation plays an important role (*abusively important and precisely at the expense of transformations*) (author's italics) (Piaget, 1973a, p. 75).

Although the internal contradiction is extreme, the tremendous contrast between the figurative and the transformational image is apparent. What is the important role played by the figurative image? It is the role of playing the opposite of the transformation image, but this does not prevent Piaget from labeling the figurative image as *abusive* - but *abusive* to precisely whom? It is *abusive* to the Subject who is in the process of performing operational transformations! One can see quite clearly that the "mental image" is simply another way to express the concept of "visualization" associated with magic proper. This should not be surprising as Piaget conceives of magic as basically imitating or simulating the Continuum-Subject in the process of operating on and transforming some aspect of physical reality (author's capitalization) (Piaget & Inhelder, 1971, p. 178). Piaget, quite understandably, does not go into specifics when speaking of "imitating" or "simulating" operational activity by the Body of Monads or Continuum. After all, how does one imagine or simulate an act by a Disembodied Entity? He concedes that "magic is disembodied" (Piaget, 1971c, p. 141), which means that the image and simulation must be the role of the superhuman Disembodied Entity who alone can "see" the total situation at the metaphysical level. Piaget asserts that the mental image is so powerful because it is Spatial like the Entity, the Disembodied Entity, symbolized (author's capitalization) (Beth & Piaget, 1966, p. 217). This narrows the role of the human being in magical activity considerably! Mental images are described as interiorised imitations (Beth & Piaget, 1966, p. 216), indicating again that these are supernatural images produced by the immanent Subject.

They are also said to be especially superior in the Field of Space *if they are directed by operations* (author's italics and capitalization) (ibid., p. 217) - a waggish double-entendre! Piaget elaborates his "inside joke" with, "Spatial mental images... acquire a degree of adequacy vastly superior to that which the mental image possesses in general" (author's capitalization) (ibid., p. 217)! "Spatial imagery only progresses when directed and molded by the Subject's active operations, in such a way that its figural aspect is more and more subordinated to the operational aspect of Thought" (author's capitalization) (ibid., p. 219). Here Piaget accentuates the fact that Spatial images are based on the Body of Monads rather than figural or physical processes. That is why there is a "close connection between the development of Space and that of Intelligence" (author's capitalization) (Piaget, 1954, p. 241) - a close connection indeed because in this case "Space" and "Intelligence" are synonyms, as both terms simply refer to the Body of Monads. "Space" had just previously been defined as a System of the Totality which coordinates Schemata while simultaneously elaborating Groups (author's capitalizations) (ibid., p. 241). According to Piaget it is the operations by personal Space, or the Body of Monads, that make it an Intellectual Entity (author's capitalization) (Piaget & Inhelder, 1956, p. 456). Also it is important to realize, as we have already noted, that the image of the Spatial System deals with this System as a producer and product of operations (author's capitalizations) (ibid., p. 457). Yes, the Spatial image symbolizes its *own* Form *and its* activity. In the words of Piaget, "the Spatial image is the only image in which there is a ... *real isomorphism* between the symbolizing Form and symbolized Content" (author's italics and capitalization) (Piaget & Inhelder, 1971, p. 347). The symbolized "Content" is capitalized because it refers to the symbolized monads as well as their anticipated activity. Since the image is derived from the activity of the Schemata (author's capitalizations) (Piaget, 1952b, p. 354), and is a visualization by the Schemata of what the Schemata intend to do, we have a typical explanation of the Absolute at work. The figural or "brain image" is "ill-equipped to grasp the dynamism of a Continuum" (author's capitalization) (Piaget & Inhelder, 1971, p. 363). "The images we have studied" are "movements and transformations" that are "independent of the subject's body" (ibid., p. 369). This means that they are independent of the subject's brain. Furthermore, we are specifically informed that Spatial operations cannot be observed by human beings and *cannot be represented in their imagination* (author's italics and capitalizations) (Piaget, 1973a, p. 77), so we can rest assured that only the supernatural Schemata of Space can imagine or visualize such operations. Piaget uses a table indicating that there are 24 kinds of mental image

(Piaget & Inhelder, 1971, p. 6) - an impossible number within the context of the book. Since neither he nor his reader would be capable of distinguishing differences among this many basic types of mental image, we can safely assume that he prepared the table in order to cognitively overwhelm and confuse the reader. Piaget's notion of "mental image" is a key metaphysical concept, so we can partially understand why he uses such a table.

MAGIC AS AN EFFICACIOUS REALITY

In the passage below Piaget rhapsodizes over magic as an eminently efficacious social reality. Magic is said to be universal in adult society, so we can be certain that magic plays a vital role in Piaget's life - including his professional life! Piaget makes it abundantly clear that this particular kind of magic is not for children.

> For our part we fully realize that in all adult society, magic is an eminently social reality and that belief in magical efficacy, therefore, possesses an intensity and a continuity that make it incomparable with the weak and extremely discontinuous beliefs of children (Piaget, 1929, p. 435).

"Magic" is not just a phase young children go through, no, magic is an eminently social reality in all adult society. Furthermore, magic is said to be much stronger and intense in adults than it is in children. In the passage below Piaget affirms the prominent role of magic in society and, at the same time, subtly communicates his considerable erudition in this arcane, anti-scientific subject. There can be no doubt that he is a serious devotee of the bewitching magical arts, and that they are an important part of his professional strategy. Unfortunately he was heedlessly encouraged in this direction by a misperceiving, doting academic community.

> Reflection would seem to suggest that the content and the form of magical phenomena are bound up closely enough with social actions and with communication between individuals; its symbolical and formal character, its grammar and its syntax imply an adaptation, and more often a long adaptation, to the sum total of rites and habits of the group - the language of magic, that is, has a history. The actual form of a spell can show traces of its character. The nature of a conviction must be influenced by the belief that it affects the life of the entire group. These reverberations give it not only increased strength but the character of an action with a definite and productive end. A protective conviction which is effective is a different thing from a belief in an evil spell which fails (Piaget, 1929, p. 433).

Piaget again claims that magic has a fundamental place in society, with a special grammar and syntax based on a long history. We do not need to wonder why he is particularly taken with the use of magic as a protective function, as *he freely admits that he will be a total failure if his theory is ever fully understood* (author's italics) (Piaget, 1971c, p. 29). At least a magic that protects is better than an evil spell which fails, but my guess is that Piaget also considers himself to be proficient in the latter! The individual who would perform magic should be convinced, as Piaget is obviously convinced, that it will be an action that is definite and productive, affecting the life of the entire group.

PIAGET'S PROFESSIONAL OUTPUT AN EXTENDED WORK OF MAGIC

Piaget's entire professional output should in fact be interpreted as an extended work of magic. Based on his enthusiastic acceptance of magic as a way to affect the "entire group" in terms of a "definite and productive end", it would be irrational to overlook this theoretical perspective that he so transparently set forth. Piaget planned to overcome opposition to his views by means of magic, not science, and he never forgot his source of magic - *"Biology"*. Without belief in the power of magic, it is hard to imagine the young Piaget seriously embarking on a life-plan to fool the academic community by dressing up his purely metaphysical theory in the trappings of science. What an incredible goal! What a catastrophic outcome! From the beginning, Piaget depended heavily upon "protective magic" to see him through his many books, papers and presentations as well as countless interviews and occasional debates. It is almost inconceivable that a man with such doctrines, doctrines that have been manifest at least since 1929, could have a reputation as a great scientist. Piaget is saturated with occultic metaphysical ideas that are completely antithetical to scientific pursuits. The embrace of this charlatan as a great scientist by a significant part of the academic community is an outrageous lapse of rational discernment and a glaring perversion of common sense.

Agenda of the Absolute: Creation and Eventual Assimilation of Physical Reality

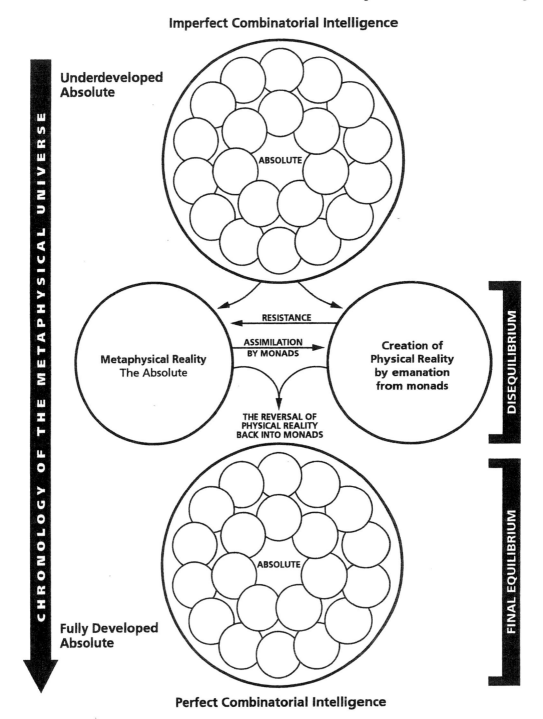

APPENDICES

APPENDIX A FORM

Who composes, imposes and develops **Forms**? Only **Forms** themselves can perform these functions, because as a synonym of the Absolute Entity the Form must *account for everything.* Listed below are some synonyms of **Form** who is **Space** who is the **Structure** who is the **Subject** who is the **Absolute**. In some instances attributes and activities of the **Form** or **Absolute** are included to enhance understanding of Piaget's use of the synonyms. Appendices A through L are interrelated and interconnected so that, although there is considerable duplication among them, *all of the capitalized terms in bold print are synonyms of Piaget's Absolute Entity.* Appendix M records 163 "different kinds" of metaphysical Structures, all of which are synonyms of the Absolute Entity, but the format of this appendix is different as the main purpose is to facilitate insight into how Piaget uses the two drastically different meanings of each synonym to confuse his reader. Twenty three conventional, lower-level structures are also tabulated to give some examples of dictionary meanings. *This avalanche of verbal entities was invented by Piaget for the sole purpose, as he himself forewarned, of preventing a clear formulation of his theory.* Because of the necessity for each entry to be brief, it is not possible to include much more than the synonym itself. Even when some of the context is included, it is never more than an imperfect portrayal of how the target term is actually utilized, but the references will enable the reader to follow up on any term of interest.

"What are the relations between *homo faber* and *Homo Sapiens*? This is the last problem we have to solve, but it is the most fundamental of all" (Piaget's italics) (author's capitalization) (Piaget, 1930, p. 195). All of the synonyms in appendices A through M refer to the Absolute Subject, *Homo Sapiens,* regardless of whether He is immanent within homo faber or outside of him.

1. **Awareness** or **Consciousness** (Piaget, 1977, p. 147).
2. The **Organism** imposes the **Form of Consciousness** upon matter (Piaget 1930, p. 283).
3. **Continuum** (Piaget, Inhelder & Szeminska, 1960, p. 408).

4. The **Geometry of the Subject** impresses an overriding **Form** on content; this **Form** is the **Logico-Mathematical System** and the **Continuum** (Piaget, 1978a, p. 163).
5. The **Logical Structures** are **A Priori Forms** (Piaget, 1973a, p. 106).
6. **Forms of Equilibrium** (Piaget, 1977, p. 178).
7. Rational operations cannot be explained except in terms of the **Forms of Equilibrium** towards which development is moving (Piaget, 1962, p. 291).
8. **Extra-Temporal Forms** (Piaget, 1974b, p. 137).
9. **General Form** (Inhelder & Piaget, 1958, pp. 331-2).
10. The **Most General Form** is the **Fundamental Biological Structure** which accounts for the fundamental logical operations (Piaget, 1971a, p. 158).
11. The **Logico-Mathematical Universe of the Subject** opens upon the various **Forms of the Infinite** (Piaget, 1980b, p. 86).
12. **Operational Forms** (Piaget, 1974b, p. 130).
13. Structuralism means the hypothesis of **Overall Forms** that are operational (Piaget, 1973c, p. 36).
14. The **Forms of Space** make up the **Whole Set of Assimilating Processes** (Piaget, 1977, p. 107).
15. **Spatial Forms** are **Groups** that give birth to each other (Piaget, 1973d, p. 62).
16. **Logico-Mathematical Framework** (Inhelder, Sinclair & Bovet, 1974, p. 7).
17. **Group** (Piaget, 1953, p. 40).
18. The **Cognitive Structure** is the **System** that the individual must use, but in no way is it a part of his conscious thought, since it is **He** who imposes the **Forms** (Piaget, 1973a, p. 33).
19. **Intelligence** (Piaget, 1952b, p. 389).
20. **Intelligence** is the only **Form of Equilibrium** to which things tend (Piaget, 1950, p. 6).
21. The **Forms of Intelligence** can dissociate **Form** and content, but this is not possible in the organic domain (Piaget, 1971a, pp. 98; 153-4).
22. **Gnostic Intelligence** (Piaget, 1952b, p. 6).
23. **Reflective Intelligence** (Piaget, 1952b, p. 6).
24. **Lattice** (Piaget, 1953, p. 40).
25. The **Lattice Structure** implies a **Combinatorial System** (Inhelder & Piaget, 1958, p. 123).
26. **Life** (Piaget, 1980b, p. 2).
27. **Life** is the creator of **Form** including **Mathematical Forms** (Beth & Piaget, 1966, p. 298).
28. **Formal Logic** (Piaget, 1971a, p. 358).
29. **Natural Logic** (Piaget, 1980a, p. 158).
30. **Formal Logic** is a form of **Natural Thought** of the **Logician Himself** (Beth & Piaget, 1966, p. 257).
31. **Endogenous Explanatory Model** (Piaget, 1980b, p. 86).
32. **Mechanism of the Action** (Piaget, 1974b, p.126).
33. **Cognitive Mechanisms** (Piaget, 1969b, p. 302).
34. **Thought Mechanisms** (Piaget & Inhelder, 1969, p. 136).
35. **Causal Structure of the Object** (Piaget, 1974b, p. 126).
36. **Organism** (Piaget, 1930, pp. 282-3).

37. The **Individual Organism** is a **Form** imposed on matter (Piaget, 1971a, p. 93).
38. **Spatial** operations permit the **Subject** to construct **Forms** by means of reflexive abstraction (Piaget, 1974b, pp. 129-30).
39. **Schemata** manifest the **Essence** of the **Structured Totality** and the **Form** (Piaget, 1952b, p. 379).
40. **Motor Schemas** play the part of **Form** which is independent of matter (Piaget, 1930, p. 284).
41. **Logico-Mathematical** Sciences (Piaget, 1980a, p. 158).
42. **Set of All Sub-Sets** (Piaget, 1972, p. 47).
43. **Formal Structure** (Piaget, 1974b, p. 126).
44. **Formal Operational Structure** (Inhelder, Sinclair & Bovet, 1974, pp. 246-7).
45. **Fundamental Structure** (Piaget & Inhelder, 1969, p. 136).
46. The **Integrated Structure** which directs formal thinking is a **Psychological Structure** (Inhelder & Piaget, 1958, p. 332).
47. **Interpropositional Structure** (ibid., p. 122).
48. **Logico-Mathematical Structures** (Piaget, 1977, p. 173).
49. **Operational Structures** (Piaget, 1971a, pp. 93-4).
50. **Organizing Structure** (ibid., p. 358).
51. **Overall Structure** (Inhelder & Piaget, 1958, p. 122).
52. **Regulating Structure** (Piaget, 1977, p. 173).
53. **Subject** (ibid. p. 127).
54. The **Subject** enriches objects with **Timeless Forms** (ibid., p. 47).
55. **A Priori Forms** that are part of the **Subject** incorporate the object in the process of knowing (Piaget, 1971a, p. 55).
56. The **Operational Forms of the Subject** will be constructed in such a way that they can never again be contradicted by facts (Piaget, 1974b, p. 123).
57. Geometric constructions by the **Subject** are based on the **Operational Forms of the Geometry of the Subject** (Piaget, 1974b, p. 130).
58. **Substance** (Piaget, 1929, p. 428) (Piaget & Inhelder, 1974, pp. 15-16).
59. The **Formal System** is self-sufficient and is **Absolute** (Piaget, 1970b, pp. 29-30).
60. **Combinatorial System** (Inhelder & Piaget, 1958, pp. 254-5).
61. **System of Connections** (Piaget, 1973a, p. 33).
62. **Coordinate System** (Piaget, 1978a, p. 163).
63. The **Form of the Operational Systems** (Inhelder & Piaget, 1958, pp. 331-2).
64. The **System of Formal Operations** is both a **Lattice** and a **Group** (Inhelder & Piaget, 1958, p.123).
65. **Initial Systems** (Piaget, 1972, p. 47).
66. **Logico-Mathematical System** (Piaget, 1977, p. 173).
67. **Causal Totality** (Piaget, 1971a, p. 98).
68. **Form of the Whole** (Piaget, 1977, p. 127).
69. **Spatial Whole** (ibid., p. 127).
70. **World of the Possible** (Piaget, 1980b. p. 86).
71. When **Thought** or the **Organism** escapes from the world of physical reality, all that will be left is the **Form** (Piaget, 1974b. pp. 125-6).

Amplifications

2. The two capitalized terms refer to the same identical Body of Monads.
4. The Subject's Geometry, the Form, the Logico-Mathematical System and the Continuum refer to the active Body of Monads which is the Subject.
6. "Forms of Equilibrium" does not accurately express Piaget's meaning. The Forms of Monads are moving toward equilibrium by assimilating physical reality.
7. Development is moving toward equilibrium of the Forms, not "Forms of Equilibrium".
10. The Fundamental Biological Structure is the Entity Piaget discovered at the feet of his godfather. He is the only Living Being who can perform "logical operations".
11. The Logico-Mathematical Universe is the Universe of Monads which make up the Subject and the Form.
14. Only the Forms can assimilate physical reality. This is quite simple, but Piaget's unprecedented invention and manipulation of an overwhelming flood of verbal entities which mean "Forms" makes it appear to be very complex.
15. Forms or Groups do not "give birth to each other". This is deliberately incorrect with the purpose of preventing clear understanding. Each operation by the Form or Group produces a more developed Entity. The "complete set" of operations ensures complete development of this same Entity.
18. It is important to realize that the Cognitive Structure of Monads is a Living Entity that can be personalized.
56. Natural science is based on discovering the facts; Piaget's science is based on opposing and eliminating the facts of physical reality.
57. This is obviously a highly contrived way to express the fact that the Form or Subject is able to operate.
59. Piaget is parsimonious in his use of "Absolute", but the Formal System is the Absolute System.
71. Since "Thought" and "Organism" are synonyms of "Form" they will also be left - along with all of the other synonyms in the appendices!

APPENDIX B GROUP

Who composes, imposes and develops the **Group**? The **Group** like the **Form** must perform these functions, because the **Group** is the **Form** who is **Space** who is the **Structure** who is the **Absolute**.

1. The **Group of Pure Possibilities** are contained within the **Transcendental Divine Being** (Beth & Piaget, 1966, pp. 207-8).
2. The **Transcendental Divine Being** is the **Ideal** or **A Priori Entity** (ibid., p. 208).
3. The logical definition of the **Group** is inexhaustible; the **Group** has an **A Priori** nature (Piaget, 1954, p. 112).
4. **Living Being** (ibid., p. 112).
5. **Thinking Being** (Piaget, 1973d, p. 16).

6. The **Group of Operators** is **The Body** which is a very strong **Structure** (Piaget, 1974b, p. 66).

7. **Logico-Mathematical Compositions** will remould the universe by a group of operations (Piaget & Inhelder, 1974, p. 267).

8. Groupings lead to the **Regular Compositions** of **Experimental Science** which sooner or later will treat all perceived data as consequences of operations (ibid., p. 279).

9. **Continuum** (Piaget, 1974b, p. 142).

10. The **Lattice** and the **Group** provide a **Field of Possible Transformations** (Piaget, 1953, p. 40).

11. The **Lattices** and **Groups** of the formal stage are **Atemporal Structures** (Inhelder & Chipman, 1976, p. 121).

12. **Forms of Equilibrium** (Piaget, 1953, p. 40).

13. **Spatial Forms** (Piaget, 1973d, p. 62).

14. There are permanent objects arranged in **Groups** which are conceived by the child to form a **Substantial Spatial Object;** that is, to form **Someone Else's Person.** This **Object-Person** does not belong to the child's universe (Piaget, 1954, p. 299).

15. Cognitive function refers to an organized **Group of Structures** and their functioning (Piaget, 1971a, p. 141).

16. **Conscious Groups** (Piaget, 1954, p. 118).

17. **Mathematical Group** (Piaget, Inhelder & Szeminska, 1960, p. 3).

18. **Operational Grouping** (Piaget, 1950, pp. 163-4).

19. **Spatial Group** (Piaget, 1952, p. 265).

20. **Logic** consists of a **System of Operations** or **Transformation Groups** (Piaget, 1971a, pp. 6-7).

21. The **Set of Integers** is a **Schema** and a **Group** (Piaget, 1969a, p. 50).

22. The functional activity of **Reason** or the **Ipse Intellectus** does not come from experience (Piaget, 1952b, p. 2).

23. **Psychological Mechanisms of Intelligence** (Piaget, 1971b, p. 114).

24. **Lattice** (Piaget, 1971b, p. 80).

25. The **Formal Grouping** consists, first of all in a **Lattice** (Piaget, 1967, p. 95).

26. The **Group** is a **System of Operations** which is called the **Logic of Relations** (Piaget, 1954, p. 236).

27. **Mathematics** consists of all actual transformations plus all possible transformations (Piaget, 1971a, p. 6).

28. **Spatial Forms** are **Groups** which produce **Meanings** by means of reflective abstractions (Piaget, 1973d, p. 62).

29. The **Mechanisms** on which the individual subject's acts of intelligence depend cannot be explained except in terms of **Structures** such as the **Group** (Piaget, 1970b, p. 138).

30. **Networks** (Piaget, 1971b, p. 80).

31. **Rational Object** (Piaget & Inhelder, 1974, p. 60).

32. **Organism** (Piaget, 1973d, p. 16).

33. **Fundamental Psychological Reality** (Piaget, 1967, p. 95).

34. The best test of the completion of groupings are the construction of **Atomistic Schemata** and affirmation of the **A Priori** (Piaget & Inhelder, 1974, p. 272).

35. The **Operational Schema of Equilibrium** (Inhelder & Piaget, 1958, p. 176).
36. The prototype of **Algebraic Structure** is the **Group** (Inhelder & Piaget, 1958, p. 269).
37. The **Integrated Structure** is the **Lattice** and the **Group** (ibid., p. 329).
38. **Logico-Mathematical Structures** (Piaget, 1971b, p. 80).
39. **Groups** are **Mathematical Structures** (Piaget, 1974a, pp. 75-6).
40. **Mathematical Structure of Group Transformation** (Piaget, 1971a, p. 324).
41. There is **One Vast Explanatory Structure** based on the **Group** concept (Piaget, 1970b, p. 42).
42. **Thought** (Piaget, 1953, p. 40).
43. The **Group** concept is the **Basic Constructivist Tool** (Piaget, 1970b, p. 21).
44. **Natural Psychological Totalities** (Piaget, 1971b, pp. 114-15).
45. **Organized Totality** (Piaget, 1952b, p. 10).
46. **Absolute Systems** offer us a **Group Structure** (Piaget, 1971a, p. 167).
47. The **Group** is a **System of Action** impacting on the real (Piaget, 1973d, p. 58).
48. **Regular Constructions** can only occur in a **Closed Operational System** (Piaget & Inhelder, 1974, p. 278).
49. The **Lattice Structure** implies a **Combinatorial System** (Inhelder & Piaget, 1958, p. 123).
50. Every **Self-Enclosed System of Operations** is a **Group** (Piaget, 1954, p. 236).
51. **Operational System** (Piaget, 1950, pp. 152-3).
52. **Operatory Systems** (Piaget, 1971b, p. 80).
53. The **System of Formal Operations** is both a **Lattice** and a **Group** (Inhelder & Piaget, 1958, p. 123).
54. **Group Operatory System** (Piaget, 1971b, pp. 36-7).
55. **Logical Systems of Mental Operations** are isomorphic with **Structures of Logical Groupings.** (Inhelder, Sinclair & Bovet, 1974, pp. 31-2).
56. The **Lattice Structure** characterizes the **System of Propositional Operations** (Inhelder & Piaget, 1958, p. 123).
57. **Psychologically Equilibrated Systems of Intellectual Operations** (Piaget, 1971b, p. 115).
58. **Compositions** must be fitted into a **Reversible System** if relations are to be grouped (Piaget & Inhelder, 1974, p. 268).
59. **Lattices** and **Groups** reflect the possibilities of a **Total System** (Inhelder & Chipman, 1976, p. 121).
60. **Transformational System** (Piaget, 1971b, p. 36).
61. **Overall System of Possible Actions** (Piaget & Inhelder, 1974, p. 279).
62. All of the operations of the **Group** will ensure the equilibrium of the **Whole** (Piaget, 1977, pp. 64-5).

Amplifications

1. The possibilities contained in the Divine Being are defined in such a way that their actualization is assured by operations.
2. The special meaning of "Ideal" is clarified.

3. The definition of "Group" is inexhaustible because it is the Divine A Priori.

6. The Group of Operators is the Body of Monads, and it is a very strong Body.

7. Operational compositions will "remould" the universe by assimilating it.

8. "Experimental Science" is Piaget's metaphysical Science of operations.

10. The Lattice and the Group is the Field of Monads and the possibilities contained within this Divine Field will be developed by operations. These possibilities are called "virtual possibilities" and, according to Piaget's theory, they will all be actualized.

14. The permanent objects arranged in Groups are monads. The child conceives these invisible objects to be a Substantial Spatial Object, in fact, Someone Else's Person. This is a comical but shameful example of how Piaget uses the child as a wedge for his metaphysical theory. First, the child sees Groups of objects, or monads, which are not detectable by any means. Second, he comprehends that they make up the Substantial Body of a Personality - Someone Else's Person! Third, it is obvious to him that this Object-Person is too strange to be a part of his universe. *Does anyone believe that Piaget empirically discovered these beliefs in the child?* Compare this concept of the permanent object with the one described in all of the textbooks. Please remember that in philosophy "substance" can mean "beings which have an independent existence and which underlie all phenomena".

20. "Logic" in this instance refers to the metaphysical Entity. Interestingly, Hegel also used "Logic" as a synonym for the Absolute.

21. Piaget's strange account of how numbers came to be is examined in Chapter 5.

27. This is metaphysical Math, of course, as it refers to the operational Entity who transforms both the object and Himself.

28. "Meanings" here refers to the transformational Self-improvements that occur in the metaphysical Entity as a result of each operation or reflective abstraction.

29. Only the immanent Group of monads can account for acts of intelligence.

34. Piaget pretends that "groupings" of operational acts will lead the child to understand the nature of Atomistic or "Monadistic" Schemata and to affirm the A Priori. In another context the one-year-old child is said to affirm the existence of the "Person of Another" (Piaget, 1954, pp. 312-13)! Moreover, Piaget claims that at the age of approximately eight months the child "becomes conscious of a General Cause" (author's capitalization) (ibid., pp. 262-4).

41. The Spatial Group extends Himself into all of physical space and "explains" everything.

46. The Group Structure is the Absolute Being.

48. The Closed Operational System refers to the central concept of reversibility which is covered in Chapter 5.

50. See 48.

55. "Isomorphic" in this statement refers to two synonyms of the metaphysical Entity. Piaget also uses "isomorphic" when referring to a parallelism between the metaphysical System and the physical system. For instance, he claims that there is a psychophysiological parallelism between the lower-level nervous system and the upper-level Implicatory System, and asserts that these two systems are isomorphic (Piaget, 1974a, pp. 77-8). Almost all of the theoretical terms Piaget employs have such double meanings - one of which is not in any dictionary!

58. See 48.

61. The dictionary meaning of "possible" does not apply. These are "virtual" possibilities of metaphysical development that will be actualized.

APPENDIX C SCHEMATA

Who composes, imposes and develops **Schemata?** The **Schemata** like the **Group** must perform these functions, because **Schemata** make up the **Group** who is the **Form** who is **Space** who is the **Structure** who is the **Subject** who is the **Absolute**.

1. Only **Schemas** are capable of real activity (Piaget, 1952b, p. 387).
2. The **Schematism of Action** is an art hidden in the depths of the **Human Soul** (Piaget, 1971c, p. 161).
3. **Mobile Schemas** and **Upper-Level Classes** are **Logical Beings** (Piaget, 1952b, pp. 239-40).
4. **Consciousness** is certainly not an epiphenomenon caused by physical processes. It is connected with the **Schematism of Action.** (Piaget, 1971c, pp. 154-5).
5. The **Combinatorial Schemes** correspond to the **Operational Structures** and the **Spatial Continuum** based on **Corpuscular Models** of closely packed but unobservable elements (Piaget, 1972, p. 49).
6. The **Schemata** of the **Totality** transform incoherent data into an **Organized Environment** (Piaget, 1952b, p. 10).
7. The **Spatial Field** is a **Single Schema** embracing all the elements of which it is composed and uniting them in **One Monolithic Bloc** (Piaget & Inhelder, 1956, p. 456).
8. **Form** (Piaget, 1952b, 378).
9. **Motor Schemas** play the part of **Form** which is independent of matter (Piaget, 1930, p. 284).
10. **Action Schemata** are **Immaterial Forms** of the **Living Organization** (Piaget, 1971a, p. 33).
11. **Schemes** make up a **Mediate Framework** (Piaget, 1969b, pp. 295-6).
12. **Schemas** are the only **General Factor** in childish ratiocination, but the child is not conscious of these **Schemas** (Piaget, 1928, p. 56).
13. The **Set of Integers** is a **Schema** and a **Group** (Piaget, 1969a, p. 50).
14. **Intelligence** constructs its own instruments which are **Schemata** (Piaget, 1971a, p. 225).
15. The **Lattice-Group** consists of **Operational Schemata** (Inhelder & Piaget, 1958, p. 329).
16. The **Schemata** of the **Lattice-Group** are linked together but not by the subject (ibid., p. 329).
17. The **Coordinators of Schemes** correspond term-by-term with the **Combinators of Combinatory Logic** (Piaget et al., 1977, p. 176).
18. The **Schemata of Intelligence** are controlled by the law of **Totality** (Piaget, 1952b, p. 10).
19. **Operational Schemas** are composed of atoms (Piaget & Inhelder, 1974, p. 110).

20. There is only one process of **Organization,** and it engenders **Operational Schemata** (Inhelder & Piaget, 1964, p. 185).

21. **Operative Intentions** (Piaget, 1971c, 161).

22. **Organism** (Piaget, 1971c, p. 155).

23. A **Schema** always includes actions by the **Subject** or **Organism** (Piaget, 1971a, p. 9).

24. The **Schemata** tend to reduce the external environment to the **Organization** (Piaget, 1952b, p. 179).

25. **Action Schemata** make up a **Biological Organization** (Piaget, 1971a, pp. 7-8).

26. The affective aspect of assimilating **Schemas** is only a veil of mystery which surrounds the **Personal Element** (Piaget, 1962, p. 208).

27. **Atomistic Schemata** explain things at the corpuscular level (Piaget & Inhelder, 1974, pp. 177-8).

28. **Euclidean Schema** (Piaget, Inhelder & Szeminska, 1960, p. 10).

29. The **Final Schema** is the goal of all transitional **Schemata,** and they function specifically with this goal in **Mind** (Piaget, 1952b, p. 230).

30. The diachronic approach is historical and genetic, connecting **"Forms"**, **"Intentions" or "Meanings"** to the **Schemes of Action** (Piaget, 1970b, p. 156).

31. The **Principal Schema** moves toward a particular end and all means are subordinated to that end (ibid., pp. 321-2).

32. The Ego-Centric tendency is to impose arbitrary **Ancient Schemas** of the **Self** upon the world of external objects, and to be constantly assimilating new experiences to these **Schemas** (Piaget, 1928, p. 228).

33. **General Schemas** result from syncretism and Ego-Centrism (Piaget, 1926, pp. 161-2).

34. Syncretism is a vision of the **Whole;** it involves an **All-Inclusive Schema** (Piaget, 1928, p. 59).

35. **Syncretistic Schemas** are comprehensive, but basically inexpressible by the child. The constant assimilation by **Ancient Schemas** of the external world is syncretism (Piaget, 1928, pp. 227-8).

36. **Assimilation Schemata** (Piaget, 1971a, p. 256).

37. **Assimilatory Schemata** are common to all **Behavior** (Inhelder & Piaget, 1964, pp. 286-7).

38. **Cognitive Schemata** are part of a **Vast Regulator System** by means of which the **Organism** preserves its autonomy and resists entropic decay (Piaget, 1971a, p. 13).

39. There is a relationship between **Operational Schemata** and the memory of the entire past. How is this conservation of memory explained (Piaget & Inhelder, 1973, p. 1)?

40. **Structures** are **Schemata** (Piaget, 1950, p. 66).

41. The **Schemata** in the infant are **Historical Schemata** for they grow out of one another (Piaget, 1950, p. 66).

42. **Schemes** play the part of **Forms,** because like **Forms** they are independent of matter (Piaget, 1930, p. 284).

43. **Mobile Schemata** are constructed by the **Subject,** not the child (ibid., p. 237).

44. **Operational Schemata** imply the diverse possibilities of the **Structured Whole** (Piaget, 1953, pp. 41-2).

45. **Space** encompasses activity in a **Total System of Schemata; Spatial Schemata** also are immanent in people (Piaget, 1954, pp. 241-6).

46. Causal explanation is based on **Corpuscular Schemes** (Piaget, 1977, p. 168).

47. **Combinatorial Schemes** make up the **Set of All Sub-Sets**, the **Operational Structures** and the **Spatial Continuum** (Piaget, 1972, p. 49).

48. The very idea of **Unconscious** representations seem to me contradictory. The **Unconscious** is equipped with **Operatory Schemes** organized as **Structures** (Piaget, 1973a, p. 42).

49. **Models** drawn from actions of the **Self** serve as the **Schemes** of **Assimilation** for the construction of **Reality** (Piaget et al, 1977, p. 175).

50. **Space** does not read the properties of objects, but acts upon them by creating **Operational Schemata** (Piaget & Inhelder, 1956, p. 449).

51. **Logico-Mathematical Structures** (Evans, 1973, p. XLVIII).

52. **Assimilatory Schemata** are the common source of all mnemonic codes and of all **Operational Structures** (Piaget & Inhelder, 1973, p. 311).

53. All information acquired from the external world is in terms of the **Internal Schematism** of the **Subject** (Piaget 1971a, p. 253)

54. Laws concerning the equilibrium of **Schemes** stem from the activities of the **Subject** (1973a, p. 72).

55. Functions, actions or operations of the **Subject** express **Schemes of Assimilation** (Piaget et al, 1977, p. 95).

56. The **System of Schemas** is not timebound; this ensures the conservation of the **System** by its inner logic (Piaget & Inhelder, 1973, p. 15).

57. The **Overall System of Schemas** is invariant because of its mode of composition (ibid., p. 15).

58. Construction starts from a **System of Schemes of Actions** (Beth & Piaget, 1966, p. 238).

59. **System of Unconsciously Interdependent Relationships** (Piaget 1952b, pp. 179-80).

60. **Thetic Intention** (Piaget, 1971c, p. 161).

61. A **Whole World of Thought** is present to the child which is made up of images and **Motor Schemas**, but the child cannot formulate this **Thought** verbally (Piaget, 1929, p. 36).

62. Each **Schema** is a **Totality** which means that its elements are unable to function without each other (Piaget, 1952b, p. 244).

63. All **Schemas** belong to a **Totality** (ibid., pp. 179; 379).

64. All **Schemata** are coordinated as one **Totality** (ibid., p. 7).

65. All **Schemata** represent a **Totality** that is momentarily incomplete (ibid., p. 45).

66. Anticipatory **Schemata** are **Intellectual Wholes** which intervene in **Living** and **Active Thought** (Piaget, 1950, p. 26).

Amplifications

1. Piaget is correct; only Schemas are capable of real activity. He neglects to tell his reader, however, that its many synonyms must also have this capability. See Form 32; Group 47 and 61; Thought 1, 31, and 47; Intelligence 1 - 4, 7, 23 and 39. One can also confirm from the text that Subject, Structure and Space are capable of "real" activity.
2. The Hidden Art is that of the immanent Subject.
3. Both Schemas and upper-level Classes are composed of monads, so they are Living Beings. Every operation results in a synthesis which represents an improvement over the preceding synthesis. The result of every synthesis is an improved Schema or Class of monads.
4. Consciousness is based on the immanent monads, not bio-physical processes.
5. The Combinatorial Schemes, Operational Structures and Spatial Continuum are based on "Models" composed of corpuscles or elements which are closely packed together. "Corpuscular Models" is capitalized as "Model" nearly always means "Absolute Subject". So we have four synonyms of the Absolute Subject.
6. The "incoherent data" are aspects of physical reality, and the Organized Environment is the Totality of Monads.
7. The Monolithic Bloc of Monads is united.
11. Schemes are the Medium for bringing about the Absolute's development.
16. Individual subjects do not link Schemata together or control them in any way. Linkages are only made by operations.
19. Operational Schemas are not composed of physical atoms.
20. Every form of organization that man knows about is worthless according to Piaget.
21. "Operative Intentions" refers to the original plan of the Absolute Subject to achieve perfect development by means of the dialectic process.
22. This is a weird way to affirm that Schema equals Subject equals Organism.
23. Compare this environment with the Environment of number 6.
24. The Biological Organization that changed Piaget's life at Lake Annecy
25. The Personal Element is the immanent Subject.
28. Euclidean Schema refers to Operational Space.
30. "Diachronic" refers to operational progress across the span of time beginning with the creation of the physical universe. "Intentions" and "Meanings" are unusual synonyms for operational results.
32. The Absolute Ego or Self imposes His Ancient Schemas upon all external objects, but especially upon the human objects He inhabits. The "person", Piaget avers, "constitutes the primary object and the most external of the objects in motion through space" (Piaget, 1954, p. 285). This makes him the prime target for assimilation.
35. The term "syncretism" refers to efforts by the immanent Entity to influence the young child. Piaget alternately takes physical and metaphysical approaches to this concept, but unfortunately commentators have ignored its metaphysical nature.
37. "Behavior" is capitalized because Piaget defines it as "the entire System of Action Schemata" (Piaget, 1971a, p. 33). Although somewhat camouflaged by

being placed next to physical considerations, this definition is reflected constantly in his books, for instance (Piaget, 1978b, pp. 40-41).

39. Memory of the entire past is explained by the Body of Monads which has always existed. This Organized Body remembers every one of the trillions of operations it has performed since the beginning of time.

41. Schemata do not "grow out of one another", but each operational synthesis produces a more developed Schema. The Schemata in the infant have previously developed within many infants.

46. Schemes are composed of organized Groups of monads.

47. A litany of four synonyms

48. The representations of the Schemata are always conscious. Schemata never sleep.

50. The Body of Monads or Space "reads" objects for the purpose of assimilation, but not for the purpose of practical information or application.

53. About the same as 50

56. The System of Schemas is eternal because of its inner logic. Basically this says that the metaphysical System has Life within itself - a special conserving function (Piaget & Inhelder, 1973, pp. 15; 16) (Piaget, 1977, p. 22) (Piaget, 1971a, pp. 34; 330).

57. This is begging the question in the most ridiculous way, because Piaget makes no effort to show how it could be true. In any case, the atomism which develops in the child is a System of Compositions (Piaget & Inhelder, 1974, p. 115).

60. "Thetic Intentions" refers to the initiation of an operation which is the one essential activity of the Absolute Subject. See 21.

61. This is the amazing position Piaget actually takes with regard to all of his experiments with children and adolescents. In all of his experiments he takes the position that the experimental subject cannot formulate the answers that should be given. He nearly always pretends otherwise, but if one follows his arguments to their "general conclusions" it is easy to see that he knew in advance what the answers had to be. As he admits, "it is we who grope towards the child's unconscious intention and sometimes succeed in making him indirectly own to it" (Piaget, 1928, p. 151). *Clearly he knows in advance what the "unconscious intention" is, and he directs the experiment in such a way so as to "reveal" it.* Piaget always wishes to get at the "true" thought of the child, namely the thought of the immanent Entity who always works behind the scenes. *Since true thought is based on his metaphysical system* (Piaget, 1932, p. 70), *Piaget knows what the child's responses must be, and he always finds what the theory predicts. He expressly says that language is not suited to expressing the child's experience* (Piaget & Inhelder, 1969, p. 58), *and he truthfully states that he pays no attention to what the child says! We must strip the answers of their "verbal element" because the words are "necessarily inadequate".* The "important thing is the attitude" (Piaget, 1929, p. 36). *Now the way is clear for Piaget to cast any "experiment" in terms of what he imagines the "true thought" to be regardless of what the children actually say. Thus he can compel the child to support every aspect of his metaphysical theory.* He is not bound by any of the conventions which natural scientists always follow. All Piaget has to do is look inside the Mind of the child to find all of the Norms that are produced by the Groups and Networks of his System and report them to the academic community. This is

precisely what he did beginning in the nineteen twenties. Berko and Brown (1960, p. 536) as well as Flavell (1963, p. 437) agree that Piaget is "good" at looking directly into the Mind independently of experimental evidence.

APPENDIX D STRUCTURE OF THOUGHT

Who composes, imposes and develops the **Structure of Thought? Thought** like the **Schemata** must perform these functions, because the **Structure of Thought** is the **Total Schema** who is the **Group** who is the **Form** who is **Space** who is the **Structure** who is the **Subject** who is the **Absolute**.

1. **Action** (Piaget, 1980a, p. XVI).
2. The Hegelian pattern of **Self**-construction is an inevitable progression once thought turns from false absolutes (By implication, "true **Thought**" is focused on, or rather is, the **"True Absolute"**) (Piaget, 1970b, p. 123).
3. **Field for Possible Transformations** (Piaget, 1953, p. 40).
4. **Forms** (Piaget, 1971a, p. 152) (Inhelder & Chipman, 1976, p. 121).
5. **Forms of Equilibrium** (Piaget, 1953. p. 40).
6. **Single Framework of Reference Elements** (Piaget, Inhelder & Szeminska, 1960, p. 393).
7. True **Thought** is a **Living System** (Piaget, 1952a, p. 180).
8. **Atemporal Group** (Inhelder & Chipman, 1976, p. 121).
9. **Integrated Group** (Inhelder & Piaget, 1958, p. 330).
10. If **Intelligence** and **Thought** are prime facts, which is the idealist thesis, the function of the nervous system is not necessary for thought (Piaget, 1971a, p. 215).
11. The young child consider's **Thought** to be identical to **"Air"** - which Piaget eventually admits is really the **Continuum** (Piaget, 1929, p. 133).
12. **Atemporal Lattices** (Inhelder & Chipman, 1976, p. 121).
13. **Formal Logic** is the **Natural Thought** of the **Logician Himself** (Beth & Piaget, 1966, p. 257).
14. **Pure Logic** could deduce the whole universe by the achievement of **Thought** (Piaget, 1969b, pp. 357-8).
15. **Pure Mathematics** could deduce the whole universe by the achievement of **Thought** (ibid., pp. 357-8).
16. **Pure Mathematics** is a new form of **Thought** (Beth & Piaget, 1966, p.243).
17. **Thought** is a **Medium** (Piaget, 1928, p. 213).
18. **All-Embracing Representation** (Piaget, 1950, p. 120).
19. **Syncretistic Schemes** (Piaget, 1929, p. 18).
20. **Thought** is something sui generis which characterizes the **Self** as **Spirit** (Piaget, 1930, pp. 242-3).
21. **General Structure** (Inhelder & Piaget, 1958, p. 330).
22. **Group Structure** (Piaget, 1953, p. 40).
23. **Implicative Structure** (Piaget, 1978a, p. 222).
24. **Integrated Structure** (Inhelder & Piaget, 1958, p. 330).
25. **Lattice Structure** (ibid., p. 330) (Piaget, 1953, p. 40).

26. **Thought Mechanisms** produce the **Combinatorial System** or the **Fundamental Structure** (Piaget & Inhelder, 1969, p. 136).
27. **Total Structure** (Inhelder & Chipman, 1976, p. 121).
28. **System of Intimate Beliefs** (Piaget, 1929, p. 14).
29. **Combinatorial System** (Inhelder & Piaget, 1958, pp. 288-9).
30. The **Cognitive Structure** is the **Intimate Mechanism of Thought** (Piaget, 1973a, pp. 32-3).
31. **Thought** is a **System of Interiorized Actions** which are coordinated into a **Total System** (ibid., p. 17).
32. A **Whole System of Special Laws** (Piaget, 1926, p. 63).
33. The **Deductive System of Thought** corresponds to nothing in the subject's conscious thought (Beth & Piaget, 1966, p. 305).
34. **System of Mental Tendencies** (Piaget, 1929, p. 14).
35. True **Thought** lies deep at the level of **Metaphysical Systems** (Piaget, 1932, p. 70).
36. **Complex Operational Systems** (Piaget, 1950, p. 36).
37. The **System of Significations** is the **Whole of Intelligence** (Piaget, 1962, p. 163).
38. **Logico-Mathematical Thought** can be considered as a **Vast Autoregulatory System** (Piaget, 1971a, pp. 11-12).
39. **Psychological Substance** (Piaget, 1928, p. 256).
40. **Precausal Mentality** is in agreement with the **Ego-Centrism of Thought** (ibid., p. 255).
41. **Egocentric Thought** assimilates reality to itself; the extreme form of this assimilation is imaginary play which makes it possible to increase tenfold the possibilities of satisfaction which is offered to **Action** (Piaget, 1954, pp. 408-9).
42. **Living Thought** (Piaget, 1971a, p. 152).
43. **A Whole World of Thought** made up of images and **Motor Schemas** (Piaget, 1929, p. 36).
44. **Totality** (Inhelder & Piaget, 1958, p. 330).
45. **Symbolic Thought** forms a **Single Whole** (Piaget, 1962, p. 170).
46. **Structured Whole** (Inhelder & Piaget, 1958, pp. 288-9).
47. **The World of Action** (Piaget, 1971c, p. 87).

Amplifications

2. "Thought" in this statement should be upper level but this is impossible within Piaget's theory. Metaphysical thought obviously could never accept false absolutes as metaphysical thought is Self-thought. Only human thought could believe in false absolutes, but human thought is not capable of producing the Hegelian pattern of Self-construction. One frequently meets such logical impasses in Piaget's work. Piaget walks a fine line between Thought as the Body of Monads and thought as the activity of the Body of Monads.
6. The Single Framework of Reference Elements is the Body of Monads.
8. The Group is outside of time as it is eternal.

10. If Thought and Intelligence are "prime facts", this means, within Piaget's theory that they are synonyms. The use of "Thought" for the Entity as well as "thought" as an activity of this Entity in the same context is confusing.

11. Piaget uses "Air" in an elaborate introduction to the Spatial Continuum. This carefully crafted subterfuge is worked out minutely in several books.

12. The Group-Lattice Structure of monads is eternal.

15. "Pure Mathematics", in Piaget's private vocabulary, means either the Absolute Subject Himself or the activities of the Absolute. This being so, He could deduce or create the whole universe. "Deduce", of course, carries Piaget's private meaning of "produce by means of the monads".

16. Pure Mathematics is indeed a new form of Thought, but it is not for human beings. This may be an activity of the Absolute; if so "Mathematics" and "Thought" should not be capitalized. However, it is quite possible that "Pure Mathematics" stands for the Absolute Himself.

17. "Thought" in the dictionary is something one does, but Piaget tends to ignore dictionary meanings. Here Thought is the Entity, who is the Medium of Monads. The Medium of Monads is adumbrated by Piaget's "experiments" with air by means of which he leads the reader to the Spatial Continuum - which is the Medium of Monads. See 11.

20. The Spirit Self in this instance is the immanent Body of Monads in the child. In the context, the child is said to be the "owner" of this Thought which is "more intimate than the body itself". This seems to indicate that "Thought" refers to the immanent Absolute Himself rather than what He does.

35. True thought is indeed at the level of the Metaphysical System.

37. The System of Significations arranges the two exact opposites of a metaphysical class versus a physical class immediately before a dialectical operation takes place. In this instance, Piaget considers the "System of Significations" to be an integral part of the operational process, hence it is the "whole of Intelligence". As one might guess, this system consists of monads that must determine by "measurements" what the next operation will be.

39. Psychological Substance refers to living, thinking monads.

40. Precausal mentality is based primarily on Schemas which make up the immanent Ego in the child, so naturally there is agreement.

41. This gives us an intimate view of Piaget's zealous relationship with his immanent Ego. It is his Ego who assimilates, but Piaget pictures himself as joyfully participating. It certainly appears to be Piaget who happily "plays" with the possibilities of assimilation, undoubtedly with special reference to his academic colleagues, and it is Piaget who enjoys "tenfold satisfaction" with success. The religious nature of his feelings of satisfaction with the implied experience of joy and gratitude is evident as he offers them to Action - apparently as a form of thanksgiving or worship. "Action", it should be noted, is used here as a synonym for the Absolute Subject within, which means that Piaget offers thanksgiving to "Thought", as "Action" means both the Absolute Himself, as it certainly does here, as well as the thought of the Absolute.

APPENDIX E INTELLIGENCE

Who composes, imposes and develops **Intelligence?** **Intelligence** like the **Structure of Thought** must perform these functions, because **Intelligence** is the **Structure of Thought** who is the **Total Schema** who is the **Group** who is the **Form** who is **Space** who is the **Structure** who is the **Absolute**.

1. **Action** and its coordinates amounts to **Intelligence** (Piaget, 1971b, p. 80).
2. **Action** is the source and **Medium** of **Intelligence** (Piaget, 1950, p. 32).
3. **Intelligence** is composed of endogenous **Structures** (Piaget, 1980b, p. 80).
4. **Gnostic Intelligence** is satisfied with constructing **Forms** (Piaget, 1952b, p.6
5. The **Group** concept is the **Basic Constructivist Tool** (Piaget, 1970b, p. 21).
6. **Causality** must definitively be conceived as **Intelligence Himself** (Piaget, 1954, p. 357).
7. The **Causal Totality** is **Intelligence** (Piaget, 1971a, p. 98).
8. **Intelligence** is the **Causal Totality,** and is seen in the triple aspects of **Form,** force and finality (ibid., p. 98).
9. Perceptions are structured because they are bathed in their **Natural Environment** of **Intelligent Activity** (Piaget, 1952b, p. 391).
10. **Forms** (Piaget, 1952b, p. 389).
11. The cognitive process of **Intelligence** is not one form of structuring among others; it is the **Form of Equilibrium** toward which all **Structures** tend (Piaget, 1950, p. 6).
12. **Intelligence** is a **Permanent Intellectual Function** (Piaget, 1952b, p. 374).
13. **Intelligence** organizes a **Lasting Universe** (Piaget, 1954, p. 357).
14. The **Group** is immanent in **Intelligence;** every act of assimilation presupposes a **System of Operations** arranged in **Groups** (Piaget, 1954, p. 236).
15. The **Essential Mechanism** of **Intelligence** is the **Group** (Piaget, 1971b, p. 114).
16. **Intelligence, Thought** and **Consciousness** are prime facts (Piaget, 1971a, p. 215).
17. **Individual** (Inhelder & Chipman, 1976, pp. 61-2).
18. An infinite expansion of spatio-temporal distances between **Subject** and objects and the power to operate across any distance and any time interval is the principal innovation of **Conceptual Intelligence** (Piaget, 1950, p.121).
19. Cognitive functions are set up in the **Form of Conscious Intelligence** (Piaget, 1971a, p. 33).
20. **Intelligence** transforms objects and reality (Piaget & Inhelder, 1969, p. 28).
21. **Intelligence** is a **Self-Explanatory Mechanism** (Piaget, 1952b, p. 370).
22. The **Object** is **Self**-constructed by **Intelligence** (Piaget, 1950. p. 110).
23. **Space** is **Self**-constructed by **Intelligence** (Piaget, 1954, p. 245).
24. **Intelligence** can equally well **Self**-construct past **Schemata** by means of present ones and vice versa (Piaget, 1950, p. 66).
25. **Networks** (Piaget, 1970b, p. 138).
26. We are on the front line of research on the connections between the **Organism** as the source of the **Thinking Subject** or **Intelligence** (Piaget, 1971a, p. 124).

27. **Intelligence** appears as a **Total System** of which one cannot conceive of one part without bringing in all of it; it is a **Sui Generis Power** (Piaget, 1952b, p. 370.).
28. The **Structures of Intelligence** derive from one another (Piaget, 1973a, p. 133).
29. **Intelligence** is an **Organization** co-extensive with all **Living Structures** (Piaget, 1950, p. 89).
30. **Homo Sapiens** (Piaget, 1930, p. 195).
31. The **Schemata of Intelligence** are controlled by a law that is within themselves. This is the law of **Totality** (Piaget, 1952b, p. 10).
32. The **Self** is the **Living Intelligence** who apprehends in the capacity of **Substance** (Piaget, 1952b, pp. 135-6).
33. The **Substantial Self** or **Living Intelligence** remains identical to itself in the course of history while opposing itself to the environment (ibid., p. 135).
34. **Intelligence** discards hereditary structures in order to engage in social interaction. In a sense **Society** is the supreme unit. The **Individual** can only invent **Intellectual Structures** if **He** is the seat of collective interactions (Inhelder & Chipman, 1976, p. 61).
35. The **System of Significations** is the **Whole of Intelligence** and the **Whole of Consciousness** (Piaget, 1962, p. 163).
36. **Intelligence** means only those **Structures** which are developed by means of regulations and operations of the **Subject** (Piaget, 1980b, p. 80).
37. **Logico-Mathematical Structures** (Piaget, 1973d, pp. 62-3) (Piaget, 1971b, p. 80).
38. **Intelligence** at all levels is an assimilation of data into **Structures of Transformation** (Piaget, 1970d, p.29).
39. **Intelligence** is a **System of Living and Acting Operations** (Piaget, 1950, p. 7).
40. **Intelligence** or the **Group Structure** wishes to return to the point of departure (Piaget, 1971b, p. 114).
41. It is difficult to account for **Intelligence** by anything other than its **Organization** considered as a **Self-Sufficient Totality** (Piaget, 1952b, p. 370).
42. **Intelligence** is a **Structured Totality** from the outset (Piaget, 1952b, pp. 135-6).
43. The **Mechanism of Intelligence** was a **Structured Totality** from the outset (ibid., p. 378).
44. The **General Logical Relations of Transitivity** (Piaget, 1980b, p. 80).
45. **Intelligence** is the only **Form** for structuring (Piaget, 1950, p. 6).
46. The history of the **Forms** informs us about the history of **Intelligence** (Piaget, 1952b, p. 389).

Amplifications

1. "Action" assumes the non-dictionary meaning that we have seen before; it means the Absolute Entity and so does Intelligence.

2. "Action" is the Intelligent Medium of Monads, so it is indeed the source of Intelligence.

6. Causality is equal to Intelligence and Intelligence is equal to the Metaphysical Entity.

9. Perceptions as we traditionally view them would not be possible, according to Piaget, unless the perceiver and the perceived were bathed in their Environment or Medium of Monads.

11. There is only one kind of cognitive structuring - structuring by the Intelligent Form or Structure.

13. The Lasting Universe Self-organized by Intelligence is the Universe of Monads.

14. The Intelligent Structure *is* the Group or System of Operations.

16. If Intelligence, Thought and Consciousness are prime facts, they must refer to the same Entity in Piaget's System.

18. "Infinite" is used incorrectly as neither distance nor time is infinite with regard to the physical universe. However, since the monads move with "absolute speed" distance is no problem. Furthermore, the monads have no problem with time as they have the ability to "go back and forth from present to past and from past to present" as they may desire (Piaget, 1970c, p. 75) (Piaget, 1954, pp. 393-4). In addition to that amazing ability, temporal successions can be reconstructed if the monads wish. That is, past constructions by the monads may be reworked and modified so that they may fit more perfectly with more recent constructions (Piaget, 1969a, p. 250) (Piaget, 1950, p. 66) (Piaget, 1970a, p. 285). Since Intelligence is said to be the "innovator", Piaget is speaking of the Intelligent Structure.

19. The Form is apparently the "Conscious Intelligent Entity".

22. Intelligence develops or constructs the Intelligent Object, which is Himself.

23. Intelligence develops or constructs Space, which is Himself.

24. The Intelligent Subject can reconstruct past phases of His own development if He so chooses.

26. Piaget is on the front line of research that, among other matters of consequence, connects three synonyms.

27. Intelligence is a one-of-a-kind power that must be conceived in toto if it is to be conceived at all - according to Piaget.

28. The Structures of Intelligence form a series leading to perfect development. To say they derive "one from the other" is not accurate.

30. Homo Sapiens is the "I" rather than the "me".

31. These Schemata apparently are part of the Intelligent Structure and not vice versa.

32. The Self is the "I" rather than the "me" if it is immanent. The Self can also mean the Substantial Body of Monads as a whole.

33. The total Body of Monads is the Self or Living Intelligence that maintains its identity while it opposes the environment. This conservation of identity and opposition to the environment must continue until the physical environment is utterly vanquished.

34. One of the names of the Absolute is "Society". This is because He is the seat of collective interactions. Only this Individual can "invent" Intellectual Structures.

35. The System of Significations is the System of Operations, the activation of which is the prime concern of the Absolute.
40. "Intelligence", who is the Group Structure, wishes to return to the condition of equilibrium that He enjoyed before the creation of the physical universe.
44. The relations of transitivity refers to the transition of the Absolute from a potential Ideal to an actualized Ideal by means of a long series of operations.
46. The history of Forms is identical to the history of Intelligence.

APPENDIX F SYSTEM

Who composes, imposes and develops the **System?** The **System** like **Intelligence** must perform these functions, because the **System** is the **Intelligence** who is the **Structure of Thought** who is the **Schema** who is the **Group** who is the **Form** who is **Space** who is the **Structure** who is the **Subject** who is the **Absolute**.

1. The **Absolute System** is a **Group Structure** (Piaget, 1971a, p. 167).
2. The **Formal System** is a self-sufficient **Absolute System** (Piaget, 1970b, pp. 29-30).
3. Formal operations enrich the **Initial System** by elaborating a **Set of All Sub-Sets** based on a **Combinatorial System** (Piaget, 1972, p. 47).
4. The **Structured Whole** is the source of the **Combinatorial System;** the complete **Combinatorial System** is the mark of formal thought (Inhelder & Piaget, 1958, p. 55).
5. **Intelligence** is the **System of Living and Acting Operations** (Piaget, 1950, p. 7).
6. The **Genetic System** or **Genome** is a **Relational Totality**. This **Totality** is a **Center for Regulations** (Piaget, 1971a, p. 91).
7. Since Godel's theorem, **God Himself** is unceasingly constructing ever stronger **Systems** (Piaget, 1970b, p. 141).
8. **Groups** are **Systems of Transformation** (ibid., pp. 20-1).
9. Every **Self-Enclosed System** is a **Group** (Piaget, 1954, p. 236).
10. The **Ideal** is a **System of Values** which constitutes a **Whole**. This is the final goal of actions (Piaget, 1952b, p. 10).
11. **Intelligence** is a **System of Living and Acting Operations** (Piaget, 1950, p. 7).
12. The **Body of Knowledge** is an **Integral System**. This **System** entails continuous reorganizations of the **Initially Privileged Elements** (Piaget, 1969b, p. 298).
13. The **Living Organism** is a **Transformational System** and an **Invariant Totality** (Piaget, 1971a, p. 34).
14. Self-regulation refers to the **Mathematician** or **Logician** who operates on the **System** in order to regulate it (Piaget, 1970b, p. 15).
15. The **Mind** is a **Structure, a System** and a **Totality** (Piaget, 1967, p. 143).
16. **Space** is a **System** which is the **Mind** (Piaget, 1969a, p. 1).
17. The **Set of Integers** is a **Schema, a Group** and an **Operational System** (Piaget, 1969a, p. 50).

18. Every **Organization** forms a **Self-Enclosed System** (Piaget, 1954, p. 139).

19. Every **Schematism** is an **Overall System** (Piaget & Inhelder, 1973, p. 16).

20. The **System of Invariants** is the invariant actions of the **Self** (Piaget et al., 1977, p. 175).

21. **Space** is a **System of Operations** (Piaget, 1969a, p. 1).

22. Only **Self-Regulating Transformational Systems** are **Structures** (Piaget, 1970b, p. 113).

23. The **Operational Structure** must become a **Closed System** (Piaget, 1971a, p. 316).

24. **Structures** are **Systems of Transformation** that can account for observable data because they are the **Underlying Overall Systems** behind the data (Piaget, 1974a, p. 50).

25. The **Structure** is a **Totality** and a **System**. The **System of Whole Numbers** is a **Structure** (Piaget, 1970c, pp. 22-3).

26. **Structure** can only exist as a **Living System**. Since no activity is possible apart from this **System**, there must be a **Structure of All Structures**. Natural structures are not capable of any activity (Piaget, 1970b, p. 142).

27. **Logico-Mathematical Thought** is a **Vast Autoregulatory System** (Piaget, 1971a, pp. 11-12).

28. Fascination with the **Totality** is dangerous. This **Totality** is unfinished, but other parts will be added by the **System of Relations** (Piaget, 1973a, p. 137).

29. The **Organized Whole** is an **All-Embracing System** (Piaget & Inhelder, 1956, p. 418).

30. In speculation regarding the **Whole** the great danger is to give in to fascination with the **Spirit of the System**. This insidious danger lies in wait for all of us (Piaget, 1971b, p. 99).

31. The **Biological** or **Cognitive System** is a **Whole** which is different from non-**Organic** physical-chemical totalities (Piaget, 1977, p. 22).

32. The **Structured Whole** is the **Combinatorial System** who organizes the individual subject's thought (Inhelder & Piaget, 1958. pp. 288-9).

33. The **Behavioral System** is the **Organism** as a **Whole**; it has always existed (Piaget, 1978b, p. 158).

Amplifications

1. Yes, the Absolute System is a Group Structure, but more important the Absolute lurks behind all of the hundreds of synonyms listed in appendices A through M.

3. The Formal System is the Absolute System which will eventually dominate everyone's behavior, but this obviously is far in the future. It is safe to say that the Initial System of Monads will not be fully elaborated for sometime yet.

4. Piaget looks far ahead as he anticipates the Complete Combinatorial System which will be produced by formal thought. Only when all of reality has been assimilated will this occur. Formal operations are for the development of the Absolute within people, not people.

6. The Genome is the Relational Totality who is the Logico-Mathematical Structure composed of non-physical atoms (Piaget, 1971a, pp. 327-8). This is the Ideal

Totality (Piaget, 1952b, p. 179) who cannot be studied empirically (ibid., p. 377). The "Genome" can represent the Body of Monads as a Whole, or it can represent the Body of Monads within each individual person who regulates all kinds of gene activity.

7. This is part of Piaget's reaction to Godel's famous theorem. The theorem itself is too complicated to be detailed (the *Encyclopedia of Philosophy*, edited by Edwards, devoted seven pages to it), but a corollary that concerns Piaget is that *a formal system cannot be proved correct within that system*. This is why "God" is working unceasingly to develop ever stronger systems". Piaget does not tell us how stronger systems can obviate Godel's theorem, but the implication is that God will eventually Self-produce His perfectly realized Personhood which presumably will sidetrack the negative aspects of provability demonstrated by the theorem.

9. This is an unusual way to express Piaget's belief that there is only one Self-Enclosed System. It will become closed when the physical universe is completely reversed. This reversal is what he means by "Self-Enclosed".

10. The final goal of operational actions is to actualize every potential of the Absolute Whole, who will then be the Ideal Whole.

12. The "Body of Knowledge" is a very strange concept. It is the "Initially Privileged Elements" or Body of Monads as it develops during a long series of operations. Knowledge, for Piaget, simply refers to the gradual actualization of the Absolute's potential. Knowledge is increased as the "Initial Monads" become increasingly better organized with each operation upon the physical universe.

14. Self-regulation refers to the operations carried out by the metaphysical Person. It has nothing to do with the regulations studied by biologists.

15 & 16. The Mind is the Body of Monads.

17. The quaint story of whole numbers is in Chapter 5.

20. Only the metaphysical Self is capable of invariant actions - not the human self.

28. Piaget is apparently speaking from personal experience.

30. The Spirit of the System is the Totality in 29. This Spirit, consisting of immaterial monads, is an insidious danger to all because he is assimilating all of us.

31. This is a bit tricky because "Organic" is upper-level, so it is neither physical-chemical nor "somatic" - which is true for the Spiritual Biological System. The more one thinks about this the more of a mind-bender it turns out to be.

APPENDIX G LIFE

Who composes, imposes and develops **Life? Life** like the **System** must perform these functions, because **Life** is the **System** who is the **Intelligence** who is the **Structure of Thought** who is the **Schema** who is the **Group** who is the **Form** who is **Space** who is the **Structure** who is the **Subject** who is the **Absolute**.

1. For the child every activity is comparable to that of **Life,** so an appeal to a cause for motion is at the same time an appeal to a **Living Cause,** i.e., to **One Mentality** (Piaget, 1926, p. 211).

2. The **Living Organization** is isomorphic with the **Cognitive Organization** (Piaget, 1971a, p. 166).

3. The fact that **Living Thought** produces conservation among objects, including human beings, demonstrates that there is a fundamental difference between the **Forms** of the higher-level **Cognitive Functions** and the cognitive functions based on organic morphology (Piaget, 1971a, p. 152).

4. The notion of **Life** seems to indicate the presence in the child's universe of a **Continuum of Free Forces** endowed with activity and purpose (Piaget, 1929, p. 235).

5. The **Living Organism** supposes a **Mechanism** which enables it to escape from entropy (Piaget, 1973a, p. 169).

6. The **Living Organism** serves as the **Field for Multiple Interactions** (ibid., p. 34).

7. The child defines **Force** almost exactly as he defines **Life.** The idea of **Force** and **Life** completely overlap; the notion of **Force** gradually inherits all of the features of **Life** (Piaget, 1930, p. 121).

8. The idea of **Force** seems to be the prolongation of the idea of **Life** (Piaget, 1930, p. 126).

9. The notion of **Life** gradually becomes reduced to the idea of **Force** (Piaget, 1929, p. 235).

10. **Life** is a creator of **Forms** (Beth & Piaget, 1966, p. 298).

11. The **Living Body** imposes on the whole universe a **Form** of **Equilibrium** dependent on the **Organization** of the **Living Body** (Piaget, 1952b, p. 407).

12. Practical **Groups** have existed from the beginning of the **Spatial Living Being** (Piaget, 1954, p. 112).

13. Every living organization contains in germ form the operations of the **Group;** after all it is the nature of **Organization** to constitute a **Totality** (Piaget, 1954, P. 236).

14. An **Intelligent Organization** is co-extensive with all **Living Structure** (Piaget, 1950, p. 89).

15. The **Functional Framework of Knowledge** is based on the **Living Organization** (Piaget, 1971a, p. 213).

16. **Logico-Mathematical Knowledge** is based on the **Living Organization,** not on empirical learning (ibid., p. 313).

17. When **Life** became identified with **God,** the problem of knowing - epistemology - suddenly appeared to me in an entirely new perspective; it made me decide to consecrate my life to the **Biological** explanation of knowledge (Evans, 1973, p. 111).

18. Logic is not isolated from **Life;** it is no more than the expression of the operational coordinations essential to **Action** (Inhelder & Piaget, 1958, p. 342).

19. There is a close parallelism between the operations of **Space** and operations of the **Logico-Arithmetic Structure** (ibid., p. 142).

20. The **Logico-Mathematical Structure** must be sought within the **Living Organism** (Piaget, 1972, p. 91).

21. All **Mental Life** and all **Organic Life** tends progressively to assimilate the environment (Piaget, 1967, pp. 7-8).

22. The attribution of the **Mental** to the biological is dangerous because it is done systematically and under cover like this. The author knows what he is doing and has two answers ready: That **Mental Life** is preformed in the organism and that it is an unconscious preformation (Piaget, 1971a, p. 41).

23. The advance of Structuralism depends exactly on the extent that the **Model** coincides with the actual processes of the **Subject's Mental Life** or **Behavior** (Piaget, 1973c, 50).

24. The relations between the **Organism** and the environment represents the most important problem in the universe with every solution to every question in every realm of **Life** whatever depending upon it (Piaget, 1971a, p. 52).

25. **Psychic Mechanisms** are identical with **Life** (Piaget, 1952b, p. 24).

26. In a moment of enthusiasm close to ecstatic joy, I was struck by the certainty that **God is Life;** internal unity was thus achieved in terms of an immanentism which has taken an increasingly rational form (Piaget, 1971c, p. 5).

27. The explanation of **Rational Organization** is the **Living Organization** (ibid., p. 362).

28. The **Structure of All Structures** or **Subject** is the center of activity. It does not matter whether we call this **Structure "Society"**, **"Mankind"**, **"Life"**, **"Cosmos"** or something else (Piaget, 1970b, p. 142).

29. **The Living Organism** is an **Invariant Totality** (Piaget, 1971a, p. 34).

30. The integrating power of the **Totality** is not a deus ex machina, it is the result of assimilation. The **Totality** is, however, the **Deus of Life in General** in all of its manifestations (Piaget, 1977, p. 32).

31. The **Living Organism** is a **Transformational System** (ibid., p. 34).

Amplifications

1. The child, as usual, agrees with Piaget that the cause of motion is a Living Cause. Piaget then takes an illogical leap to the assertion that only One Mentality is the cause of all movement. Other contexts do confirm that this is Piaget's position. For instance, Piaget claims that the Structure can only exist as a Living System, and that natural structures cannot "act" (Piaget, 1970b, p. 142).

2. The Living Organization is the Body of Monads and so is the Cognitive Organization.

3. Piaget quite clearly distinguishes between the metaphysical Cognitive Function and the physical cognitive functions. "Function" should not refer to the Entity but rather to what He does, nevertheless we should note that Piaget claims that the Normative laws which govern Structure make it unnecessary "to distinguish Structures and Functions". So when Piaget uses words like "Action" or "Function" as synonyms for the Absolute we need to recognize what he is doing.

4. The child is made to shoulder Piaget's abstract notion of a Continuum of "Free Forces" or Living Monads which have their own agenda.

5. Entropy will affect all of physical reality, but not the metaphysical Living Organism. This is a very ambiguous statement in context. The Living Organism could be lower-level with an immanent Mechanism, but we should probably consider it to be upper-level. Piaget unethically makes the two scientists,

Helmholtz and Guye, support his metaphysical theory of reversibility by taking their statements regarding entropy in relation to the physical organism and applying these statements to the metaphysical Organism. In any case, we know from other statements by Piaget that he holds his metaphysical Subject to be exempt from entropy.

7, 8 & 9. Piaget's theory requires that physical forces be subordinate to the undetectable activity of Living Monads, so the child is made to run interference for him with this idea. He complicates things in "7" by having the child define "material force" in a way that slightly differs from Life. We should remember that we are dealing with metaphysical Force in 7, 8 & 9.

10. "Life" and "Forms" are synonyms. The Life-Form is eternal and is now in the process of Self-development.

11. The Living Body of Monads is able to impose as it is the "Force".

12. "Practical" is usually lower-level, but here it is upper-level.

13. Groups of monads are the only source of Life, and every Group of monads is a Totality (Piaget, 1971b, pp. 114-15) because they "participate" with the Total Group. By utilizing both lower-level "organization" and upper-level "Organization" close together, Piaget demonstrates his plan to confuse and deceive.

17. This was the beginning of Piaget's most unusual theory of knowledge or epistemology. He consecrated the remainder of his life to the "undercover" explanation of God's Self-development or, what is the same thing, the Biological explanation of the growth of Knowledge. This is precisely why the International Center of Genetic Epistemology was established. For Piaget, at least, there was no other reason.

18. What is logic? It is the operational coordinations of Action. "Action" is an unusual synonym for the true Actor, the Absolute Subject or Life.

19. Space is the Logico-Arithemetic Structure, so the operations are indeed "close"! A pertinent question: Did Inhelder know this? I am not at all sure that she did.

20. The Living Organism is the Body of Monads.

21. Mental Life and Organic Life are simply names for the Body of Monads.

22. The "Mental" Body of Monads is attributed to the lower-level biological organism or human being. The Mental Entity is dangerous to the person he lives within because He is constantly assimilating him, and *Piaget proudly declares that he is also dangerous because he is systematic in his presentation of this basic dogma of his position, and because he is doing it "under cover like this". It is hard to imagine a more direct "in your face" challenge to the reader than to tell him that he is at this very moment being manipulated by a carefully crafted, systematic plan for unfriendly deception!* **Yes, he is doing it undercover, and that is what this book is about.** And what he is doing is dangerous, particularly in terms of the academic process and educational policy, but ultimately it is also dangerous, as Piaget well knows, in terms of his recognized standing as a scholar and as a person. We know that Piaget was acutely aware of this negative possibility, because *an understanding of his system means, as he emphatically admitted, the conclusive proof of his failure* (Piaget, 1971c, p. 29). While we are not supposed to know exactly what Piaget is "affirming", he wants us to know that he knows exactly what he is doing and that he has two answers ready: That Mental Life is

preformed in the organism and that the organism is unconscious of this preformation. This is a very vague indication of the two answers he really has in mind, which are based on his dual metaphysical-physical system. Nevertheless the attribution of metaphysical Mental Life to the physical organism is a dim reflection of the two answers. The point that Piaget is making, and must make rather obscurely, is that he is confident that by switching back and forth between the two poles of his dual system he can defend his theory and himself from hostile inquiries - and from professors who do not have time to patiently analyze what he is really saying.

23. Piaget's Model is not a scientific model; it is the real thing.
24. A revealing, dogmatic, arbitrary and very narrow mind-set.
25. Psychic Mechanisms and Life refer to the same Body of Monads.
26. What gives Piaget ecstatic joy? It is his doctrine that the Absolute Subject is his true Self. By "rational" Piaget means rationalism which is a philosophy based on reason without aid from the senses.
28. A forceful, comprehensive description of the Absolute Subject.
30. The Totality is not a god-from-a-machine, but He is God.

APPENDIX H SELF - EGO - I

Who composes, imposes and develops the **Self**? The **Self** like the **Life** must perform these functions because the **Self** is the **Life** who is the **System** who is the **Intelligence** who is the **Structure of Thought** who is the **Schema** who is the **Group** who is the **Form** who is **Space** who is the **Structure** who is the **Subject** who is the **Absolute**.

1. The child can only grasp the **Absolute** by reference to the **Self** (Piaget & Inhelder, 1974, p. 201).
2. There is a **Self** who is omnipotent (Piaget, 1954, p. 272).
3. The **Innermost Self** is the **Totality of Schemes** (Piaget, 1971c, p. 151).
4. The **Self** is composed of **Ancient Schemas.** It is this **Ego** who leads the child to impose **Schemas** upon the world of external reality (Piaget, 1928, p. 228).
5. If "man" equals **Self,** unique and irreplaceable, we have nothing to say, but there is a possibility of a Psychology of the subject as **Subject** (Piaget, 1971c, p. 118).
6. With regard to causality, the child feels that the universe is obedient to the **Self** and that the **Self** is **Absolute** (Piaget, 1929, p. 188).
7. The infant only envisions **Space** as a function of the **Self** (Piaget, 1952b p. 212).
8. The child, at the age of 18 to 24 months, perceives that the universe, which was centered on the **Self,** seems abolished on the plane of practical action. This is the source of the "why" which obsesses the child of this age. However this universe centered on the **Self** reappears on the plane of **Thought** and impresses itself on the little child as the sole understandable conception of **Totality** (Piaget, 1954, p. 425).

9. Relations are always between the **Self** and things. The **Measuring Factory,** which is the **Ego,** intrudes upon the measured entity which is the world (Piaget, 1928, p. 196).

10. Adolescent **Egocentricity** is manifested by belief in the omnipotence of reflection, as though the world should submit itself to **Idealistic Schemes** rather than to systems of reality. The **Self** is strong enough to reconstruct the universe and big enough to incorporate it (Piaget, 1967, p. 64).

11. Actions of the **Self** are the basis of causality (Piaget et al, 1977, p. 175).

12. **Causality** is a **System** attributed to the object by the **Self's** actions (ibid., p. 176).

13. The **Self** is responsible for both causality and operations. **Causality** bears upon objects while operations construct the **Self** or **Subject** (ibid., p. 175).

14. **Causality** is a **System of Invariants** which transforms objects. This **System of Invariants** is actually the invariant actions of the **Self.** It is the **Model** drawn from the actions of the **Self** which are the **Schemes** of assimilation for the construction of **Reality** (ibid., p. 175).

15. The image combines the notion of the object with the notion of a **Model** that is sort of undifferentiated from the **Self.** This combination of object and **Model** is accompanied by causality through imitation of this **Model** or **Self** (Piaget, 1962, p. 85).

16. If it should turn out that **Structures** are connected, the **Subject is** not static but is actively mediating the connections in such a way that proves **Him** to be the **Structure of Structures** and the **Transcendental Ego** or **Self** described in the theories of synthesis (Piaget, 1970b, p. 70).

17. When reality is transformed by symbolic play according to the needs of the immanent **Self, Egocentric Thought** makes it possible to increase tenfold the possibilities of satisfaction. This satisfaction is offered to **Action** to reinforce **His** tendencies of assimilation by **Personal** activity (Piaget, 1954, pp. 408-9).

18. The values of the person, often regrettably confused with those of the **Ego,** are less important than the constructive activities of the **Epistemic Subject** (Piaget, 1970b, pp. 126-7).

19. So long as the child thinks he can reason directly without taking **Himself** into account, he will never be able to handle relations or reach logical necessity. However, as soon as he brings in his own **Ego** the child attains to relations and logical strictness (Piaget, 1928, p. 197).

20. The basic obstacle to intellectual progress is egocentrism. The liberation from egocentrism is essential in relation to the "**I**" and the "**We**" ("**I**" and "**We**" are capitalized by Piaget). (three pages later) The decentering of the "**I**" and the "**We**" (Piaget again capitalizes the "**I**" and the "**We**" but now they are both lower-level, so they should be in lower case letters - "i" and "we") is always hampered by obstacles. Each time we liberate ourselves from the "**I**" or "**We**" (although capitalized they are obviously lower-level because "**Collective Cause**" is clearly the **Absolute** "**I**" **and** "**We**") in favor of a **Collective Cause** we become the victims of something new (Piaget, 1973b, pp. 136; 139). Piaget outdoes himself in dreaming up this incredible puzzle!

21. Now after the "lived me" is precipitated out from the **"I"**, there remains the **Subjects's** operations. These operations are the **Structures** employed in intellectual activity (Piaget, 1970b, p. 139).

22. Decentration is the rejection of egocentrism in favor of **Regular Compositions;** this means that the child's own actions have been incorporated in an **Overall System of Actions** (Piaget & Inhelder, 1974, p. 279).

23. **Reason** must keep correcting the egocentrism of the subject so that there is a conversion - a sort of Copernican revolution which robs the initial reference system of its privilege (ibid., p. 61).

24. Everything happens as though the child began by attributing forces to **All Outside,** and then only later the child finds in himself the **"I"** that was the cause of his own force. The more the feeling of the **"I"** develops in the child the more does the idea of Force lose in wideness of application. In the early stages during which the child's ignorance of his own **Ego** is at its highest point, childish dynamism is complete (Piaget, 1930, p. 128).

25. From the point of view of **Consciousness** there is simply assimilation of the world by the **Ego** or **"I".** In proportion that the **"I"** is dissociated from external objects, this means that **Force** is gradually withdrawn from all external objects and confined within the **Ego** (ibid., pp. 131-2).

26. Our earliest experiences are not referred to a **Central "I"** but float about in an undifferentiated **Absolute.** The **Self** would thus be the result of a gradual dissociation by an effort of the **Mind** to oppose the world. This effort is probably first thought of by the child as the **Absolute "I"** who is bound up with the whole universe (ibid., p. 128).

27. The **Logical Mathematical Body** elaborates the **Idea** which in its perfected form is the fully developed **Body** or **Self** (Piaget, 1973a, p. 98).

28. We do not understand why the **Mind** is more honored as a collection of **Permanent Schemata** than as an unfinished product of continual **Self**-construction (Piaget, 1970b, 114).

29. Besides the **Operational Space** constructed by **Our** actions, there exists a physical space of objects. There is a close correspondence between the symbolic **Spatial** image and the **Spatial Entity** or transformation (Beth & Piaget, 1966, pp. 220-1).

30. The child eventually gives up materializing **Thought** and makes of it something sui generis which characterizes the **Self** as **Spirit** (Piaget, 1930, p. 242).

Amplifications

1. The Absolute is conceived by Piaget as a Personal Self, not an impersonal Force.

2. The Self who is omnipotent is the supernatural Body of Monads.

3. Although the context includes much lower-level discussion, the Innermost Self within each individual person is a Sub-Structure of the Totality or Absolute with His organization of Schemes.

4. This is the same Self as in 3. The Schemas are ancient as they have progressively developed from living in and partially assimilating a long series of people. The

child in no way imposes these Schemas on reality, only the immanent Self can do that.

5. Man is not a true Self; he is only a replaceable thing or object in Piaget's system. The Psychology Piaget "studies" is that of the immanent Subject within the physical subject.

6. This is in an ambiguous context, but it is obviously Piaget's position. Piaget presents no evidence that the young child conceives of the Absolute Subject.

7. Space is the Absolute Entity, not His function, in Piaget's system, but he is apparently saying that the child believes Space functions as the Absolute Self. Again he presents no evidence. Actually Piaget had previously presented contrary evidence. He had asserted that the spatial explanation of cause was the sixteenth type of explanation that children give, but that it is "rather an advanced form of explanation" and consequently only occasionally to be found in children (Piaget, 1930, p. 266.

8. This is an amazing concept to palm off on toddlers who could not possibly communicate such concepts even if they had them. Piaget admits this, as we have seen, as he sees *directly into the Minds* of infants and young children. *Piaget fancies that he knows the basic desires of the immanent Subject and that is all he needs. The child's frequent use of "why" is given the most unique spin ever ignored by child psychologists, and the "little child" is "so impressed" with the philosophical subtleties of Piaget's Totality that he is convinced his concept is the only understandable one in existence!*

9. There are no "true" relations between things in Piaget's system. *This means that there are no relations between individual people as people are merely things. This may be hard to swallow but Piaget makes this claim deliberately and knowingly.* The only true relation is an assimilative relation or operation between the Absolute Self and any thing or person in the universe. There are only two factors in a relation - "Motivity" and tangible matter (Piaget & Inhelder, 1974, p. 279), and individual people are in the category of "tangible matter". When Piaget insists that children do not differentiate between "action of the Self on the self" and "action of the Self on things", he is underlining his concept of relation (Piaget, 1929, p. 176). Of course he often uses "relation" in the usual way, and that is what makes it difficult. Please note the interesting choice of the term "Measuring Factory" to describe the "intruding Ego", composed of monads, who is measuring the world and its people for the express purpose of assimilation.

10. Adolescent Egocentricity is treated ambiguously in the context, but the upper-level Ego rises to the surface loud and clear at times. This Ego is omnipotent and operates in terms of "Idealistic Schemes" by means of which He will force physical reality to submit to Him. He is indeed the Self who is strong enough to reconstruct the universe through the process of assimilation and big enough to reincorporate the universe back into His monads when He has completed His task of assimilation!

11. The monads of the Absolute Self or Body of Monads are behind every physical action in the universe.

12. This is very confusing unless we understand that there are three kinds of cause, with regard to physical reality, that are based on three kinds of operations. The same operations that construct the Absolute Self, and this is the only kind that

Piaget spends much time on, also produce profound changes in the nature of objects and the principles of their interactions. While it is true that the scientific community has never detected any of these profound changes, we have Piaget's word that they are coming to pass. Another kind of operation by the monads move objects about in the universe for various reasons. Also, one must not forget a third kind of operation that produced physical reality in the first place - apparently by emanation from the monads. In any case, the Self composed of monads is responsible for it all.

13. Both lower-level and upper-level "causality" are used close together, making it quite confusing.

14. The Invariants are the monads and their intentions. The Reality constructed by the Model or Self is the upper-level Reality of the Universe of Monads.

15. The Model is not "sort of" undifferentiated from the Self - it is the Self. This is a partial description of the "image" and its role in operations. The image is formed by the monads for the monads, not for people. The monads then "imitate" this image as they engage in operational activity. The image is for the purpose of preparing for an encounter with the Self's physical opposite and for directing the operation. Although the monads work independently of man, Piaget reserves a role for human beings which he often describes as "magic". The image is what the monads imitate when they operate, but Piaget assumes that "advanced" individuals like himself can participate by visualizing operational activity that should be directed at special targets of assimilation, especially people who do not accept their idealistic dogmas. *Piaget has great faith in magic and why not; how could his acceptance in academic circles be based on rational considerations?* The subject of magic is examined in Chapter 5

16. Piaget has assumed from the beginning that the various Sub-Structures are connected and integrated into a Single Structure. All we have, however, is this dogmatic assumption that cannot be verified by any method.

17. This "offer of satisfaction" in thanksgiving to "Action" in order to encourage His acts of assimilation demonstrates Piaget's belief that man can have at least a minor role in furthering the Absolute's agenda.

18. The lower-level person should not be confused with the upper-level Ego who is the Epistemic Subject.

19. As soon as the child's ego is decentered, his own true immanent Ego can attain "necessity".

20. This is a calculating double switch of meanings from upper to lower level then back to the upper level. The liberation of the immanent Subject from egocentrism is accomplished by the immanent "I" and "We" (capitalized by Piaget). Three pages later the "I" and "We" now represent lower-level obstacles to the liberation of the immanent Subject so "they" must be decentered. This lower-level "I" and "We" are also capitalized by Piaget when they should be "i" and "we" to show that they are lower-level. *This places such great demands upon the reader that he simply does not have a chance to comprehend if he must hurry. In the following sentence of the text he switches back to the upper level. Note that Collective Cause is upper level as it refers to the monads, not people. Negotiating such a mine field of booby traps is frustrating and time consuming.* We must ask the question: Why would anyone spend so much time and effort in

preparing such mine fields? Can anyone cite a precedence for such treacherous antisocial behavior in the academic world? An even more pertinent question: *Why was Piaget accepted so reverentially by a good portion of academia? Has there ever been a more egregious lapse of responsibility and accountability among the professional purveyors of knowledge?*

21. The upper and lower levels are obvious.

22. Here the "child's own actions" are lower level as they are assimilated into the Overall System. The "child's own actions" may be either level depending on context.

23. A previous instance of the "initial reference system" was upper level, meaning the "Initial Continuum of Monads", but here it means the lower-level ego which must be removed as a "center" and replaced, in analogy with the Copernican replacement of the earth by the sun, by the upper-level Ego.

24. "All Outside" alludes to the monads external to the child. The child is sometimes said to be aware of this "Person of Another" first and then later realizes that his true "I" is this "Person of Another". Piaget goes on to say that as the feeling of the "I" develops in the child, the idea of Force becomes more and more to be based on the "I" and not on objects. In the last sentence Piaget speaks of the child being ignorant of his own Ego. In this case, he is ignorant of his upper-level Ego or the "I", but being aware of "All Outside", he "peoples the universe with Living and Substantial Forces", which is the "complete childish dynamism". One trick Piaget uses in this general context is to reverse the meaning of "Realism", giving it the meaning of his version of Idealism!

26. We are informed, based on Piaget's oracular insight, that our earliest experiences are not referred to a Central "I", but that they float about in an undifferentiated Absolute. What is the difference between a Central "I" and an Absolute who is "undifferentiated"? Is the Absolute fully "differentiated" for anybody, even Piaget? It appears that our earliest experiences are referred to a Central "I" after all. And who is the Mind who opposes the world? The child agrees with Piaget that it is the Absolute "I" who is bound up with the whole universe.

27. The Logico-Mathematical Body elaborates the Idea that will eventually become the fully developed Self. After "which" follows the implied meaning. The Logico-Mathematical Body is the Self.

28. Possibly no one but Piaget accepts the notion of Schemata, as defined by him, so to argue about their possible development is beside the point.

29. Operational Space is not constructed by the actions of people; it is *Self-constructed and* Our immanent Space is an integral part of Total Space. The Spatial image is produced by the Spatial Entity in preparation for an operational engagement, so there is a close connection between the image and the Entity who produced it. There is also a close connection between the image and the transformation of both the object and the Spatial Subject, but the "or" between Spatial Entity and transformation is an obvious obstacle to quick understanding.

30. The true Self is a Spirit and all true Thought is based on this Spirit composed of monads.

APPENDIX I SUBSTANCE - PERSON

Who composes, imposes and develops **Substance**? **Substance** like the **Self** must perform these functions because **Substance** is the **Self** who is the **Life** who is the **System** who is the **Intelligence** who is the **Structure of Thought**, who is the **Schema** who is the **Group** who is the **Form** who is **Space** who is the **Structure** who is the **Subject** who is the **Absolute**.

1. **Substance** not only is conserved but it does the conserving. **Substance** is the **Formal Regulator** who constructs objects (Piaget & Inhelder, 1974, pp. 15-16).
2. The **Substantial Ego** or "**I**" can only be reached by reflection (Piaget, 1930, p. 130).
3. The ego is not in any way a causal or **Substantial** principle (Piaget does not immediately tell us that there is also a **Substantial Ego** - He does that in 2) (Piaget 1971a, p. 94).
4. The **Living Intelligence** is the emanation of a **Self** which apprehends in the capacity of a **Substance** and therefore is a **Force** remaining identical to itself in the course of history while opposing itself to the environment (This is Main de Biran's doctrine which Piaget says is quite different from his view. Later on we learn that it is also Piaget's view, and that he only differs from Biran because he argues that the subject is not conscious of this **Force** while Biran considers the subject to be aware of it.) (Piaget, 1952b, pp. 135-6).
5. The child believes in a **Panpsychic or Hylozoic Dynamism** which endows every object with a **Sui Generis Force** (Piaget, 1930, p. 118).
6. Children believe that **Special Forces** always intervene in the most simple movements. Moreover, they believe that these **Forces** are alive, **Substantial** and teleological (ibid., p. 117).
7. The permanent objects of the infant are arranged in **Groups** that must form a **Substantial Object** and be **Someone Else's Person** (Piaget, 1954, p. 299).
8. The general heredity of the **Living Substance** is contrasted with man's particular heredity (Piaget, 1952b, p. 13).
9. **Logico-Mathematical** knowledge draws its **Substance** from the **Living Organization,** not from empirical learning (Piaget, 1971a, p. 313).
10. The look is a **Quasi-Substantial Reality** that goes from the eye to the object. There is no light that goes from the object to the eye (Piaget, 1974b, p. 28).
11. The correct reading of experience must be based on a **Single System of Relations,** which is the **Substantial Invariant** (Piaget & Inhelder, 1974, p. 114).
12. Atomism means to think in terms of **Substantial** but imponderable grains without volume (ibid., p. 112).
13. True atomism is based on **Mental** construction rather than material atoms. The end product is a host of invisible, but **Substantial Corpuscles** (ibid., p. 79).
14. **Substance** is a **Formal Regulator** and provides the content of this **General Quantum** (ibid., p. 16).
15. The child will readily grant that the sugar is conserved in the **Form** of a weightless **Substance** (ibid., p. 88).

16. It is the **Psychological Substance** of the child's or rather this **Structure** peculiar to his **Thought,** who incorporates the adult influences on the child into his own **Substance** and thereby deforms them (Piaget, 1928, p. 256).

17. The **External Ontic Substratum** is the source of causality as it attributes its **Structure** to reality (Piaget, 1974b, p. 135).

18. When the child becomes aware of **Personality** or **Subjective** activity in himself, he refuses to allow **Self-Consciousness** to things. **Personality** has an inexhaustible scope (Piaget, 1929, p. 269).

19. The **Intellect** cannot provide an opportunity for an effort by the **Personality** unless its object (the individual ego) is first assimilated by the **Personality** (Piaget, 1970d, p. 159).

20. We must distinguish the self-centered egocentric individual from the **Personality** who freely subjects **Himself** to a **System of Norms.** The **Personality** is opposite to any restraints since it is autonomous (Piaget, 1973b, pp. 90-1).

21. The initial egocentric space is turned around; the universe is no longer centered on a self ignorant of its **Self,** but contains the **Personal Body** which is aware of its displacements (Piaget, 1954, p. 235).

22. The **Formal Structures** are in the **Total Personality** of the adolescent (Inhelder & Piaget, 1958, p. 350).

23. The **Personal System** supposes **Formal Thought.** The **Life Plan** presupposes the intervention of **Thought** which requires **Formal Thought. Personality** implies a decentering of the self (Piaget, 1967, pp. 65-6).

24. The ego is detestable, but the **Personality** can make it submit to the **Ideal** which the **Personality** embodies. The **Personality** adheres to a scale of values relative to a given task (Inhelder & Piaget, 1958, p. 349).

25. The child believes that **Living** and **Personal Forces** explain natural phenomena (Piaget, 1930, p. 87).

26. Kant withdrew **Organization** from **Our Personal Power** by rooting **Organization** in our psycho-physiological organization (Piaget, 1952b, p. 380).

Amplifications

1. Substance, in Piaget's vocabulary, refers to the composition of the Absolute's body - the monads. The monads regulate their own development while conserving or preserving themselves. They constructed objects at the beginning of things, but now they are assimilating these objects and are incorporating them back into themselves.

2. The Substantial Ego cannot be detected by any means whatever. He can only be imagined or, as Piaget prefers to say, arrived at through "reflection".

3. The ego of individual human beings is not Substantial.

4. The Living Intelligence is the Substantial Self. He was alive before history began. He will live during the course of history while He opposes the environment for the purpose of developing Himself. After the environment is assimilated and He is fully developed, He will continue to live forever in a timeless state of rest. The excerpt is Biran's doctrine with which Piaget pretends to disagree. It turns out, however, that he does not disagree with the doctrine at all, but he merely holds

that the individual subject is not conscious of the Substantial Self, while Biran thinks otherwise.

5. Piaget saddles the child with his Dynamism or Substance of living, acting monads. This is the meaning behind the child's supposed "panpsychism" and "hylozoism". Every object is endowed with this Dynamism which is one-of-a-kind.

6. The child agrees with Piaget that every movement in the universe is ultimately caused by the monads - the Special Forces. The natural forces studied by traditional science do not account for any movement.

7. There are two kinds of "permanent" objects - physical and metaphysical. No one has ever mentioned the permanent objects described in this selection. These objects are monads which make up the Substantial Metaphysical Person.

8. General heredity is simply another name for the series of operations by means of which the immanent metaphysical Entity progressively develops from Class to ever more developed Class.

10. *The science of sight has been wrong for centuries; only Piaget truly understands how it happens.* What scientists do not know is that Substantial monads regulate sight by manipulating the brain and optic nerve, while at the same time they communicate with outside monads between the eye and the object. This holds true, for instance, when we look at the stars. It is not light from the stars that enables us to see them, it is the monads between the eye and the stars! Piaget is far in advance of all natural scientists, so much so that they speak entirely different languages.

11. There is only one System for composing dialectic relations, and that is the Substantial Invariant. Piaget reads everything in terms of this metaphysical Being.

12 & 13. "Atomism" is quite obviously defined in terms of Substantial monads.

14. Substance is a Formal Regulator and the Substantial content is the "General Quantum", which means the quanta of monads which make up the Absolute Entity. It might be useful to review some of the synonyms of Substance *which are also said to be regulators.* This will solidify the concept of Substance as the metaphysical Being: **Biology** (Piaget, 1972, pp. 13; 52); **Cognitive Functions** (Piaget, 1971a, pp. 29; 369); **Forms** (Piaget, 1977, pp. 172-3); **Overall Forms** (Piaget, 1973c, p. 36); **Knowledge** (Piaget 1971a, p. 61); **Life** (ibid., p. 27) (Piaget, 1972, p. 61); **Living Being** (Piaget, 1952b, pp. 407-8); **Living Organization** (Piaget, 1971a, p. 145); **Maxwell's Demon** (Piaget, 1978a, p. 227); **Model** (Piaget, 1971a, p.124); **Logical Operations** (ibid., p. 100); **Organism** (Piaget, 1970b, p. 47); (Piaget, 1974b, p. 137); **Structure** (Piaget, 1970b, p. 14); **Logico-Mathematical Structure** (Piaget 1971a, p. 317); (Piaget, 1977, p. 22); **Vast Autoregulatory System** (Piaget, 1971a, pp. 11-12); **The Whole System** (Piaget, 1977, pp. 23; 192); **Totality** (Piaget, 1971a, p. 93).

15. All of the well-known experiments described in this book lead the reader from the physical aspects to the metaphysical realities of Piaget's system.

16. Piaget admits that the Psychological Substance peculiar to true Thought is *not an intrinsic part of of the child.*

17. The External Being accounts for reality. As long as we realize that Sub-Units of the External Being are equally involved in creating reality from within human

beings and other objects, this is an accurate rendition of Piaget's position - as far as it goes.

18. This statement has the same meaning as 16. Personality in 18 means the same as Substance in 16. The child is made to be the mouthpiece for the doctrine that Self-Consciousness or Thought of the Personality does not derive from things such as human beings. Of course the child never becomes aware of this immanent Entity, as Piaget often says, but he must have it both ways according to the particular argument he is making. Sometimes he is said to be aware!

19. The immanent Personality must assimilate its object, which is the ego, before it can accomplish very much. We must add "partially" assimilate, as the complete assimilation of human beings, based on the apparent extremely slow pace in historical time, is far in the future.

20. The lower-level egocentric individual is contrasted with the upper-level Personality.

21. The lower-level individual is considered to be an integral part of physical reality. He is a part of the material universe and physical space, and the small part he represents must be "turned around" by the immanent Personal Body who is aware of the fact that He is gradually displacing "this initial egocentric space". This excerpt is on the very edge of intelligibility; one must know his system well in order to make sense of it.

22. The Formal Structures are in fact the immanent Structures of the Absolute Subject. Thus human beings, as such, can never attain formal thought. In 1977 I attended a two-day workshop that focused on formal thought. The leader of the workshop, like the authors of all the textbooks on child development, did not have a clue regarding Piaget's concept of formal thought. Nevertheless, since 1952 the English-speaking world has been in a position to understand that formal thought is superhuman thought. *Since Piaget insisted early on that "organization, assimilation and accommodation" are "certainly vicarious" we should have realized immediately that none of the stages of intellectual development have to do with people,* and that they could only pertain to the metaphysical Entity (Piaget, 1952b, p. 13). We should have understood this in spite of the fact that he has always muddied the waters of communication in unprecedented ways.

23. The life plan for the adolescent is essentially a plan devised and empowered by the immanent Absolute Himself. Piaget is clearly thinking about his experience as an adolescent. From the time he was "converted" as a teenager he planned, with the assumed guidance of his immanent Subject, to force his view of the Absolute upon the academic world. He certainly failed to achieve this goal, but he did manage to disrupt progress in some areas of academic endeavor, and this disruption will not abate until his system is understood - and discarded.

24. Would Piaget write 50 books about an ego that he detests? This is what all of his followers and all of the textbooks which utilize his theory assume. No, his 50 books are about the metaphysical Ego to whom he devoted himself without stint, not the human ego.

25. Piaget spends an inordinate amount of time and effort trying to explain natural phenomena in terms of the living monads. *He will not admit to any natural phenomena as explained by natural science.* Naturally the child agrees with him.

26. Piaget faults Kant for withdrawing some of the metaphysical notions pertaining to "Our Personal Power" that had been put forth by Descartes and Leibniz. *Kant made a terrible mistake, according to Piaget, because he replaced much of "Our Personal Power" with the detestable psycho-physiological organization known as human beings.*

APPENDIX J TOTALITY - WHOLE - UNIVERSAL

Who composes, imposes and develops the **Totality?** The **Totality** like the **Substance** must perform these functions because the **Totality** is the **Substance** who is the **Self** who is the **Life** who is the **System** who is the **Intelligence** who is the **Structure of Thought** who is the **Schema** who is the **Group** who is the **Form** who is **Space** who is the **Structure** who is the **Subject** who is the **Absolute.**

1. The **Whole Set of Assimilating Processes** are the **Forms of Space** (Piaget, 1977, p. 107).
2. The integrating power of the **Totality** is based on assimilation; **He** is not a deus ex machina, but **He** is the **Deus of Life** (Piaget, 1977, p. 32).
3. The **Whole** is the **Investigator** who forces facts into molds where the facts are carved up and distorted as desired (Piaget, 1974a, p. 31).
4. The **Structured Whole** is a **Psychological Operational Structure** composed of atomic elements. This **Whole** is a **Biological Organization** which is the basis of our investigation of **Mental Life** (Piaget, 1953, pp. 24-5).
5. **Hegel's Structure** is a **Logico-Mathematical Structure** which has an atomistic composition. This **Structure** exists as an **Organized Biological Totality** which is preserved while assimilating the external world (Piaget, 1971a, 327-8).
6. **Space** encompasses the activity in the **Totality** (Piaget, 1954, p. 241).
7. The **Biological** or **Cognitive System** is a **Primordial Whole** which preserves itself. Physical-chemical totalities cannot do this (Piaget, 1977, pp. 22).
8. The **Living Organism** is a **Transformational System** who maintains **Himself** as an **Invariant Totality.** This **Organism** is the **Field** in which multiple interactions take place, but the **Organism** remains unchanged. This is conservation (Piaget, 1971a p. 34).
9. The notion of **Totality** is fascinating but dangerous. The explanation of **Totality** begins when the unfinished **Totality** is placed in relation to the other parts according to the **System of Relations** (Piaget, 1973a, p. 137).
10. The **Structures** that succeed each other are always **Totalities,** which means that they cannot be explained empirically (Piaget, 1952b, p. 377).
11. **Structures** have the characteristics of **Totality,** and if they are real **Structures** they exist independently of theory (Piaget, 1973d, p. 36).
12. **Group Structures** are **Psychological Totalities** (Piaget, 1971b, pp. 114-15).
13. There is a difference between real totalities and **Ideal Totalities** (Piaget, 1952b, p. 247).
14. The final goal of **Action** is the **Ideal Whole** (Piaget, 1952b, p. 10).

15. When the equilibration operations have finished their task the **Form of Equilibrium** will consist of a **Total Structure** (Piaget, 1973a, p. 126).

16. The entire set of operations available to the **Subject** is an **Algebraic Structure** which can operate as a **Totality** or **Structured Whole** (Inhelder & Piaget, 1958, p. 307).

17. The series of whole numbers is a **Structure** and a **Totality** (Piaget, 1970c, pp. 22-3).

18. Assimilation is impossible without the **Totality**. This **Totality** will be the **Ideal Totality** when it is fully realized (Piaget, 1952b, p. 179).

19. The **Logico-Mathematical Universe** is engendered by the **Subject** (Piaget, 1980b, p. 86).

20. The **Subject** organizes the **Structured Whole** (Inhelder & Piaget, 1958, pp. 289-90).

21. Every action is based on a need of the **System as a Whole.** These actions account for the stages of mental development (Piaget, 1973d, p. 38).

22. The operations of the **Group** ensures the equilibrium of the **Whole** (Piaget, 1977, pp. 64-5).

23. **Biological** and **Cognitive** development fuse into **One Whole** which is built up historically (Piaget, 1971a, p. 74).

24. The **Totality** is made up of the actualized parts plus the possible parts. As the possible parts are added to the actualized parts, the **Cognitive Field** is directed more and more toward the actualization of the remaining possible parts of the **Totality** (Inhelder & Piaget, 1958, pp. 330-1).

25. Every organism has a **Permanent Structure** which can never be destroyed as a **Structured Whole** (Piaget, 1971c, p. 8).

26. The **Structured Whole** is the **Combinatorial System** who organizes the individual subject's thought (Inhelder & Piaget, 1958, pp. 288-9).

27. **Intelligence** has always been a **Structured Totality** (Piaget, 1952b, p. 378).

28. **Intelligence** is a self-sufficient **Totality** (Piaget, 1952b, p. 370).

29. The **Causal Totality** is the **Intelligence** (Piaget, 1971a, p. 98).

30. **Structure** is a **System** with the laws and properties of a **Totality**. The **Mind** is the **Complete System** (Piaget, 1967, p. 143).

31. My **System**: a **Totality** exists which imposes an organization on its parts. Reality is necessarily dependent on a **Whole** which pervades it (Evans, 1973, p. 114).

32. The **Encompassing Totality** provides the reasons for whatever is observable but remains unexplained (Piaget, 1980b, p. 108).

33. The **Reflex** is an **Organized Totality** which functions for its own sake (Piaget, 1952b, p. 38).

34. It is only in the past twenty years that the notion of **Structure** or **Relational Totalities** has carried the day (Piaget, 1971a, pp. 98-9).

35. The **Epistemic Subject** is a **Universal Biological Organization** (Beth & Piaget, 1966, p. 285).

Amplifications

1. There is no assimilation apart from the Forms of Space. These Forms are both outside and inside of people. The same could be said regarding all of the synonyms in appendices A through M.
2. The power of the Totality is His capacity to assimilate. He, along with all of His synonyms in appendices A through M, is the assimilating God of Life.
3. The "Whole" and the "Investigator" are identical in this passage, but this identity is not obvious because of the long confusing sentence structure. What we have is an unusual view of assimilation, in which the facts of reality are distorted by the "molds" of monads into which they are forced. On the following page Piaget reverses his statement about distortion, saying that the object is enriched, not distorted. *This is an example of the two answers he always has ready* (Piaget, 1971a, p. 41). The facts about the object are distorted from the point of view of physical reality, but they are enriched from the point of view of the Absolute Subject. So Piaget is correct regarding his dual system, but he does not tell the casual reader enough for him to understand how he is, in a sense, correct. Piaget is happy to leave it as a direct contradiction! He uses "the two answers" hundreds of times in his many books to confuse and bewitch his readers.
4. The Whole is a Bio-Psychological Structure who is composed of monads. "Our" investigation of Mental Life is based on this immaterial Spirit Structure, not people.
5. Hegel's Structure is this immaterial Spirit who is assimilating the real world in order to fully realize his potential as the Deus of Life.
6. This is nonsense unless we place the unstated object within the encompassing activity of the Spatial Totality.
7. The Bio-Cognitive System is the Primordial Whole. That is, this System is the original Continuum of Monads that was eternally in existence before the physical universe was created. *Piaget's ever-present concern with conservation or preservation is apparently an effort to reassure himself that this System is definitely indestructible.*
8. The Living Organism is an Invariant Totality. This means that He could not be a human being as people are not invariant. Furthermore, human beings are not usually considered to be "fields", whereas the Body of Monads make up a very large Field. *Again, Piaget reassures himself that the trillions of interactions per nanosecond will not "damage" the Organism.*
9. Piaget apparently sees himself as engaged in a dangerous relationship with the Totality, who is also dangerous to everyone because of His assimilative ability and baleful intent. He is dangerous because he is "unfinished" and wants very much to be "finished".
10. Structures always succeed each other psychogenetically by metaphysical actions, operations, cooperations, coordinations, equilibrations, regulations, relations, reflexive abstractions or reflective abstractions.
11. Piaget does not speak like a scientist.
12. Group Structures are Psychological Entities which cannot be examined empirically.
13. Ideal Totalities are metaphysical.

14. "Total Structure" means "Ideal Structure".

15. The entire set of operations will supposedly result in the perfectly developed Ideal Structure. Piaget prematurely anticipates what is "available" to the Subject.

17. We deal with number in Chapter 5.

19. The Logico-Mathematical Universe *is* the Subject, so it is Self-engendering.

21. Every action or operation is based on the need of the System to develop Himself fully. *These actions account for the stages of His mental development, not the development of people.*

22. Piaget anticipates that the operations of the Group will eventually produce the final equilibrium.

23. Biological and Cognitive development *never fuse into One Whole* because they have been One Whole from the beginning - see 7.

24. Piaget adds the "possible parts" to the Totality in a premature anticipation of its completion.

25. To call the Mind the complete System is to call the Structure and the Totality the same. Piaget anticipates the final completion.

32. Piaget assures natural scientists that his Body of Monads accounts for everything that they cannot explain!

33. The Reflex is not an intrinsic part of the physical infant. It consists of Ancient Immanent Schemas whose task is to further develop themselves by assimilating a long series of people over their individual life-times.

34. Piaget tells the world that his metaphysical notions had "carried the day" for about 20 years as of 1967 when *Biology and Knowledge* was published in French.

35. Yes, the Epistemic Subject is the Universal Biological Organization, which is the Universal Body of Monads.

APPENDIX K ORGANISM - ORGAN

Who composes, imposes and develops the **Organism?** The **Organism** like the **Totality** must perform these functions because the **Organism** is the **Totality** who is the **Substance** who is the **Self** who is the **Life** who is the **System** who is the **Intelligence** who is the **Structure of Thought** who is the **Schema** who is the **Group** who is the **Form** who is **Space** who is the **Structure** who is the **Subject** who is the **Absolute**.

1. **Consciousness** has a history which connects it with the **Schematism of Action** and by that to the **Organism** (Piaget, 1971c, p. 155).

2. The **Living Organism** is not affected by entropy (Piaget, 1971a, pp. 13; 35) (Piaget, 1973a, p. 169).

3. The **Living Organism as a Whole** has existed from the start (Piaget, 1978b, 158).

4. The **Living Organism** is the **Field for Multiple Interactions** (Piaget, 1971a, p. 34).

5. **Biological Form** is the **Structure** which the **Organism** imposes upon matter (Piaget, 1930, pp. 282-3).

6. The **Individual Organism** is a **Form** imposed on matter by **Causality** (Piaget, 1971a, p. 93).
7. When the baby takes nourishment from the breast it is not nourishment for the **Organism in General** (Piaget, 1952b, p. 35).
8. General heredity of the **Living Organism** accounts for the **Group** (ibid., p. 2).
9. We will examine the connections between the **Organism** as the source of the **Subject**, and **Intelligence** or the **Thinking Subject in General** (Piaget, 1971a, p. 124).
10. The **Intelligent Organism** is **Self**-explanatory (Piaget, 1952b, p. 370).
11. The cognitive behavior of the **Organism** represents **Logico-Mathematical** knowledge (Piaget, 1971a, p. 3).
12. General heredity is connected with the **Living Organism** (Piaget, 1952b, p. 2).
13. The **Organism** is a **Machine Engaged in Transformations of the Environment** and **Transformations of the Forms of Organization** (Piaget & Inhelder, 1973, p. 8).
14. The **Intelligent Organism** is immanent (Piaget, 1952b, p. 370).
15. The **Organism**, the **Thinking Being** and the **Social Group** construct **Structures** (Piaget, 1973d, p. 16).
16. There is only one need regardless of whether one considers the **Psychic** series or the organic series. This need is the **Organism's** development (Piaget, 1952b, pp. 169-70).
17. No **Schema** ever has a clear-cut beginning, and it always includes actions by the **Subject** or **Organism** (Piaget, 1971a, p. 9).
18. The **Organism** consists only of **Spatial Macromolecules** (Piaget, 1974b, p. 42).
19. The **Organism** constructs **Structures** (Piaget, 1973d, p. 16).
20. The **Organism** extends its **Structures** into the universe as a whole; this enables investigators to obtain knowledge within the **Logico-Mathematical Framework** (Piaget, 1971a, pp. 338-9).
21. The **Structures** responsible for all Knowledge are integrated into a **Single Intellectual Organism** (ibid., p. 360).
22. The **Organism** is isomorphic with the **Subject of Knowledge** (ibid., p. 139).
23. **Logico-Mathematical Structures** are not physical; they are within the **Living Organism** (Piaget, 1972, p. 91).
24. The **Organism** as a **Whole** is a **Vast Regulator System** (Piaget, 1971a, p. 13).
25. The **Living Organism** is an **Invariant Totality** (ibid., p. 34).
26. **Organic Life** progressively assimilates the environment (Piaget, 1967, pp. 7-8).
27. The logical coordinations of **Schemata** are the source of **Organic** or **Biological Organization** (Piaget, 1978a, pp. 219-20).
28. **Organic Self**-regulation is not based on bio-physical mechanisms of equilibration: this **Self**-regulation is insured by the differentiated **Organs** of regulation (Piaget, 1970b, p. 47).
29. Experimentation is not possible with **Organic Structures in General** (Beth & Piaget, 1966, p. 203).
30. **Organic Structures** are necessary for **Thought** but physical structures like the nervous system are not necessary (ibid., p. 203).

Amplifications

2. The metaphysical Organism is outside of physical reality so entropy does not affect it.
4. The Organism of Monads is the Field where all dialectical interactions take place.
5. The Form of Monads is alive so it is "Biological". Piaget plays with three synonyms.
6. Piaget uses three synonyms again to make a point when only one is sufficient.
7. *The immanent Organism of Monads within the baby is not nourished by mother's milk.* Those who argue against an immanent entity are presented with a problem!
8. The Body of Monads or Group progressively develops Himself psychogenetically. This series of operations is called "general heredity".
11. Logico-Mathematical Knowledge refers to the progressive development of the metaphysical Entity. Piaget tends to fuse this kind of "Knowledge" with the Entity Himself. Chapter 5 deals more extensively with this notion.
12. General heredity is really the Self-development of the Organism.
13. The Organism is engaged in both the centrifugal and the centripetal transformations produced by operations.
14. Piaget boldly places the two kinds of organism close together.
16. There is only one reason for the existence of the physical universe - the development of the Absolute Organism.
18. The Organism consists of monads. Piaget expresses this variously.
19. The Organism constructs Himself.
20. The Organism or Logico-Mathematical Framework is very large.
23. The Logico-Mathematical Structure or Organism is immanent within the lower-level organism. In this instance the Living Organism is confounded with its synonym, the Logico-Mathematical Structure.
24. The Organism is very large and regulates not only Himself, but also everything else.
28. The Organs of regulation are thus metaphysical. Piaget sometimes inappropriately calls these Organs "operations" (Piaget, 1971a, p. 100)
29. Practitioners of natural science cannot experiment with the Structure of Monads. *Piaget cannot experiment with this metaphysical Structure either, but he must pretend that he can in order to be accepted by the academic community.*

APPENDIX L ORGANIZATION

Who composes, imposes and develops the **Organization**? The **Organization** like the **Organism** must perform these functions because the **Organization** is the **Organism** who is the **Totality** who is the **Substance** who is the **Self** who is the **Life** who is the **System** who is the **Intelligence** who is the **Structure of Thought** who is the **Schema** who is the **Group** who is the **Form** who is **Space** who is the **Structure** who is the **Subject** who is the **Absolute** who composes, imposes and develops Himself.

1. **Action Schemata** make up a **Biological Organization** (Piaget, 1971a, pp. 7-8).

2. The **Biological Organization** is the **Universal** who is responsible for the general coordination of actions. This **Biological Organization** has no experience of an empirically testable biology or psychology (Beth, 1966, p. 285).

3. The **Operational Mechanism** built up with atomic elements is a **Structured Psychological Whole;** it is a **Biological Organization** (Piaget, 1953, pp. 24-5).

4. General heredity is a **Psychological Reality** which comes from the **Biological Organization.** This **Psychological Reality** is the **Functional Nucleus** of the **Intellectual Organization** (Piaget, 1952b, pp. 2-3).

5. **Groups** have existed from the beginning of the **Organizations** of the **Living Being** (Piaget, 1954, p. 112).

6. All movements of every kind caused by the **Living Being** with respect to things are regulated by **His** own **Organization** (Piaget, 1952b, p. 408).

7. **Cognitive Functions** are immaterial **Action Schemata** of the **Living Organization** (Piaget, 1971a, p. 33).

8. The **Most General Forms** of the **Living Organization** are equivalent to **Life** itself (ibid., p. 184).

9. **Life Organization** and **Mental Organization** are one and the same thing (Piaget, 1952b, p. 46).

10. **Logico-Mathematical Structures** are the product of the **Living Organization** (Piaget, 1971a, pp. 211-12).

11. The **Intelligent Organization** is co-extensive with all **Living Structure** (Piaget, 1950, p. 89).

12. Every relation established by the **Schemata** with reality transforms an incoherent datum into an **Organized Environment** (Piaget, 1952b, p. 10).

13. The **Organization** of **Form** is not affected by the genes (Piaget, 1971a, p. 358).

14. The **Organization** integrates into the **Permanent Forms** a continuous stream of objects. The same **Form** is applied to every object and event (ibid., p. 152).

15. **Displacement Groups** make up an **Organized Totality** (Piaget, 1952b, p. 10).

16. We must evaluate all the resources of the immanent **Organization** before having recourse to a **Transcendental Organization** (Piaget, 1971a, p. 362).

17. A **Schema** reflects an **Organization** (Piaget & Inhelder, 1973, p. 7).

18. The **Organization** of **Action Schemata** are not linked together (i.e., integrated) by the subject, but they appear in integrated form (Inhelder & Piaget, 1958, p. 329).

19. The **Scheme** is an **Organization** which accounts for the subject's activities. The laws of the **Scheme** stem from the activities of the **Subject** (Piaget, 1973a, p. 72).

20. Every **Organization** forms a **Self-Enclosed System** (Piaget, 1954, p. 112).

0308

Amplifications

2. The Universal Biological Being does not experience physical biology and psychology because He is composed of immaterial monads.
4. General heredity is based on the operational actions of the Universal Biological Organization. From time to time "general heredity" is also lower-level. Upper-level general heredity has nothing whatever to do with genes and sex.
5. It is interesting that "Organizations" is plural. Piaget, although incorrect regarding his own system, is saying that Groups have existed ever since the Living Being began developing Himself by means of a series of dialectic operations, each operation causing a reorganization of the monads of which He consists. This is incorrect, of course, with regard to the existence of Groups, as they existed before there were such operations. Clarification is easy if we remember that Groups of monads make up the Living Being who is eternal, and that the series of "Organizations" did not begin until the physical universe was created.
8. Piaget defines Life exclusively in terms of the living monads. Human beings do not have a life of their own.
9. Both Life Organization and Mental Organization are defined in terms of the Body of Monads - they are one and the same.
11. The Intelligent Organization is identical to the Living Structure - the Body of Monads.
14. There is only one Form - the Body of Monads.
15. Assimilation requires Displacement Groups which have the function of displacing the physical aspects by adding metaphysical aspects. This occurs during operations.
16. Piaget confounds his own system. The immanent Organization is a subdivision of the Total Transcendental Organization.
18. Sometimes Piaget dares his reader to accept very broad hints such as this one. The human subject does not link together Action Schemata, but they are integrated and thus indeed linked. Who could possibly have linked them!
20. The Self-Enclosed System is based on the very important concept of reversibility, which is covered in Chapter 5.

APPENDIX M STRUCTURE

Metaphysical Structure versus conventional structures

The first list is composed of supposedly "different kinds" of structures which mean exactly the same thing - "Absolute Structure". All 163 different terms refer to the metaphysical Living Structure from which everything is derived and to which everything will eventually return. The shorter list of 23 terms refers to conventional structures. Piaget usually reverts to a conventional structure after making a salient point with an upper-level term. He does this in order to keep his reader confused and off balance. Once one becomes aware of this pattern, however, it is often easy to observe. It is so obvious at times that it appears to be a deliberate attempt by Piaget to provoke specific questions on the part of the reader - questions that Piaget would like to ask, but cannot explicitly broach. The metaphysical terms are synonyms, of course, but that is not the main purpose of the list, which is to demonstrate in a compendius summary how Piaget carried out his early threat to multiply "verbal entities" in order to "create obscurity" and "actually prevent thought from being communicable" (Piaget, 1926, p. 26). As a very young man, Piaget assigned himself a most unique and difficult task: to dress his metaphysical doctrines up in the trappings of empirical science, while at the same time undermining the confidence of his followers in empirical science. The trappings of science were considered necessary in order for him to be accepted by the academic community; at the same time his incompatible metaphysical doctrines were essential components of his agenda because of his early, religiously oriented, commitment to these doctrines. This meant, as he fully realized, that "to the extent to which one would be able to speak of 'Piaget's system' this would be conclusive proof of my failure" (Piaget, 1971c, p. 29). This would be conclusive proof of his failure to prevent a clear formulation of his system by deliberately creating "obscurity". Piaget's success, in his own eyes, depended wholly upon his ability to make his theoretical system so obscure that it could not be clearly formulated and thus communicated to others. This set of incompatibles led to an incredible academic career that could not possibly attain a satisfying closure for Piaget other than chaos. My suspicion is that he was quite proud of the chaos he stealthily created. *The key to understanding Piaget's high motivation, even though he knew in advance that a clear understanding of his system would nullify any possibility of acceptance by the academic community, was his concept that the Absolute Subject does His work of assimilation undercover.* Since the Absolute assimilates surreptitiously, Piaget could well assume that it would be counterproductive, with regard to this vital work of assimilation, to present his theory in a clear manner. Under these circumstances the goal of chaos and confusion probably made good sense to him. The two lists of terms were tabulated from my original notes which contain only a fraction of the "verbal entities" regarding structure that Piaget invented. If a particular term was counted five or more times, the total number is placed in parenthesis.

1.   Abstract Structure (Piaget, 1972, p. 83)
2.   Abstract Model is Structure (Piaget, 1973c, p. 49)
3.   Active Structure (Piagct, 1971a, p. 327)
4.   Actualized Structure (Piaget, 1953, pp. 41-2)
5.   Additive Structure (Piaget, 1973a, pp. 127-8)
6.   Algebraic Structure (Beth & Piaget, 1966, pp. 167-8) (6)
7.   Analytic Structure (Piaget, 1970b, p. 137)
8.   A Priori Structure (Piaget, 1971c, p. 81)
9.   Arithmetic Structure (Beth & Piaget, 1966, p. 255)
10. Authentic Structure (Piaget, 1970b, p. 98)
11. Autonomous Structure (ibid., pp. 69-70)
12. Biological Structure (ibid., pp. 48-9)
13. Bourbaki's Matrix Structure (Beth & Piaget, 1966, pp. 167-8)
14. Causal Structure (ibid., pp. 301-2)

15. Classifying Structure (Piaget, 1970c, p. 38)
16. Cognitive Structure (Piaget, 1970b, p. 69) (16)
17. Coherent Structure (Inhelder & Piaget, 1958, p. 30)
18. Combinatorial Structures (ibid., p. 277)
19. Common Structure (Piaget, 1971c. p. 157)
20. Common General Structure (Piaget, 1973c, p. 32)
21. Common Spatial Structure (Piaget & Inhelder, 1956, p. 153)
22. Concrete Structure (Piaget, 1967, p. 95)
23. Coordinating Structure (Beth & Piaget, 1966, pp. 167-8)
24. Corpuscular Structure (Piaget, 1974b, p. 29)
25. Cosmos as the Structure of All Structures (Piaget, 1970b, p. 142)
26. Cyclic Structures (Piaget, 1971a, p. 166)
27. Deducible Structures (Piaget, 1973d, p. 51)
28. Deductive Structure Piaget, 1971a, p. 211)
29. Deep Structure (Piaget, 1970b, p. 98)
30. Dynamic Structure (Piaget, 1971a, p. 33)
31. Elementary Structures (Inhelder, Sinclair, & Bovet, 1974, p. 270)
32. Endogenous Structure (Piaget, 1980b, p. 80)
33. Equilibrated Structure (Piaget, 1967, p. 157)
34. Equilibrium Structure (Piaget, 1953, p. 40)
35. Extended Hierarchical Nesting Structure (Inhelder & Piaget, 1964, p. 104)
36. Extratemporal Structure (Piaget, 1967, p. 157)
37. Formal Structure (Piaget & Inhelder, 1974, p. 274)
38. Formal Operational Structure (Inhelder, Sinclair & Bovet, 1974, pp. 246-7)
39. General Structure (Piaget, 1971a, p. 327)
40. General Hereditary Structure (Piaget, 1952b, pp. 13-14)
41. General Mental Structure (Piaget, 1973c, p. 32)
42. General Operatory Structure (Piaget & Inhelder, 1969, p. 154)
43. General Social Structure (Piaget, 1973c, p. 32)
44. Group Structure (Piaget, 1971b, pp. 114-15) (5)
45. Grouping Structure (Piaget et al., 1977, p. 150)
46. Hegel's Structure (Piaget, 1971a, p. 327)
47. Human Structure (Piaget, 1970b, pp. 62-3)
48. Implicative Structure (Piaget, 1978a, p. 222)
49. Inclusion Structure (Piaget, 1971a, p. 330)
50. Initial Structure (Inhelder & Piaget, 1964, p. 1) (6)
51. INCR Structure (Piaget, 1967, pp. 147-8)
52. Integrated Structure (Inhelder & Piaget, 1958, p. 330) (6)
53. Integrated Structure as a Lattice (ibid., p. 329)
54. Intellectual Structure (Bringuier, 1980, p. 62)
55. Internal Structure (ibid., p. 42)
56. Internal Structure of Actions (Piaget, 1972, p. 26)
57. InterpropositionalStructure (Piaget & Inhelder, 1969, p. 141)
58. Lattice Structure (Piaget, 1980b, p. 80)
59. Life as the Structure of All Structures (Piaget, 1970b, p. 142)
60. Living Structure (Piaget, 1950, p. 89)
61. Logical Structure (Piaget, 1967, p. 127) (22)

62. Logicizable Structure (Piaget, 1972, p. 66)
63. Logico- Algebraic Structure (Piaget et al., 1977, p. 169)
64. Logico-Mathematical Operational Structure (Piaget, 1967, p. 81)
65. Logico-Mathematical Structure (Piaget, 1971a, pp. 211-12) (33)
66. Mankind as the Structure of All Structures (1970b, p. 142)
67. Mathematical Structure (Piaget, 1973c, p. 55) (7)
68. Mathematical Structure of Group Transformation (Piaget, 1971a, p. 324)
69. Mental Structure (Beth & Piaget, 1966, pp. 167-8)
70. Metrical Structure of Space (Piaget, 1974b, pp. 166-7)
71. Model as Hierarchy of Structures (Piaget, 1973c, p. 52)
72. Model as Special Mathematical Structure (Piaget, 1972, p. 80)
73. Model as Structure (Piaget, 1973d, p. 25)
74. Multiplicative Structure (Inhelder & Piaget, 1964, p. 195)
75. Natural Logico-Mathematical Structure (Piaget, 1971c, p. 27)
76. Natural Operational Structure (Piaget, 1972, p. 67)
77. Natural Structure (Beth & Piaget, 1966, pp. 168-9)
78. Necessary Structure (Piaget, 1967, p. 112)
79. Normative Structure (Piaget, 1973d, pp. 60-1)
80. Operational Forms as Structure (Piaget, 1974b, p. 130)
81. Operational Structure (Piaget, 1980b, p. 85) (23)
82. Operational Structure as an Organ (Piaget, 1967, p. 114)
83. Operational Structures of Intelligence (Piaget, 1971b, p. 151)
84. Operational Structures of Reversibility (Piaget, 1974b, p. 23)
85. Operational Structures of the Set of All Sub-Sets (Piaget, 1972, p. 49)
86. Operational Structures of the Subject (Piaget, 1974b, p. 126)
87. Operative Structure (Piaget, 1973c, p. 54)
88. Operatory Structure (Piaget et al., 1977, p. 184) (8)
89. Order Structures (Beth & Piaget, 1966, pp. 167-8) (5)
90. Organic Structure (ibid., p. 203)
91. Organizing Structure (Piaget, 1971a, p. 358)
92. Original Structure (Piaget, 1928, p. 200)
93. Overall Explanatory Structure (Piaget et al., 1977, p. 179)
94. Overall Operatory Structure (Piaget, 1980a, p. 302)
95. Overall Structure (Piaget & Inhelder, 1969, p. 153)
96. Overall Structure of Euclidean Space (Piaget, 1969b, p. 334)
97. Overall Structure of the Combinatorial Operations (Inhelder & Piaget, 1958, p. 122)
98. Parent Structure of the Bourbaki (Piaget, 1970b, p. 26)
99. Permanent Structure (Piaget, 1971c, p. 8)
100. Possible Structures (Beth & Piaget, 1966, pp. 301-2)
101. Propositional Operatory Structure (Piaget, 1973a, p. 120)
102. Psychological Structure (Piaget, 1953, p. XVII)
103. Real Structure (Beth & Piaget, 1966, p. 301)
104. Regulating Structure (Piaget, 1977, p. 173)
105. Relational Structure (Piaget, 1971a, pp. 93-4)
106. Reversible Operatory Structure (Piaget, 1971b, pp. 20-1)
107. Reversible Structure (Piaget, 1973a, p. 131)

108. Reversible Structures of Intelligence (ibid., p. 132)
109. Self-Regulating Structure (Piaget, 1970b, pp. 13-14)
110. Semireversible Structure (Piaget, 1967, p. 106)
111. Sensorimotor Structure (Piaget, 1973c, pp. 22-3)
112. Social Structure (Piaget, 1970b, p. 98)
113. Society as the Structure of All Structures (ibid., p. 142)
114. Spatial Structure (Piaget, 1974b, p. 42)
115. Structure as a Living System (Piaget, 1970b, p. 142)
116. Structure as a Network (ibid., p. 138)
117. Structure as a Relational Totality (Piaget, 1971a, pp. 98-9)
118. Structure as a Semi-Group (Piaget, 1970b, p. 138)
119. Structure as a Single Intellectual Organism (Piaget, 1971a, p. 360)
120. Structure as a System of Transformations (Piaget, 1973d, p. 15)
121. Structure as a Totality (Piaget, 1967, p. 143)
122. Structure as a Psychic Organ (ibid., p. 8)
123. Structured Being (Piaget, 1971c, p. 109)
124. Structured Representational Space (Piaget & Inhelder, 1956, p. 42)
125. Structured Set of Possible Transformations (Inhelder & Piaget, 1958, p. 255)
126. Structured Spatial Container (Piaget, Inhelder & Szeminska, 1960, p. 405)
127. Structured Totality (Piaget, 1952b, p. 379)
128. Structured Whole (Piaget, 1970b, p. 5) (11)
129. Structure of All Structures (ibid., p. 142)
130. Structure of Intelligence (Piaget, 1973d, pp. 60-1) (9)
131. Structure of Reasoning (Piaget, 1926, p. 180)
132. Structure of Synthetic Power (Piaget & Inhelder, 1973, p. 26)
133. Structure of the Body (Piaget, 1974b, p. 66)
134. Structure of the Child's Mind (Piaget, 1930, p. 281)
135. Structure of the Group (Piaget, 1973a, pp. 34-5)
136. Structure of the Mind (Piaget, 1973b, p. 29)
137. Structure of the Organism (Piaget, 1930, p. 286)
138. Structure of Transformation (Piaget, 1970d, p. 29)
139. Structures of Co-operation (Piaget, 1973a, p. 149)
140. Structures of General Knowledge (Beth & Piaget, 1966, p. 308)
141. Structures of Intelligence in General (Piaget, 1973d, pp. 62-3)
142. Structures of Knowledge (Piaget, 1973c, p. 22)
143. Structures of Logical Groupings (Inhelder, Sinclair & Bovet, 1960, pp. 31-2)
144. Structures of the Whole (Evans, 1973, p. 141)
145. Structures Used by the Subject (Piaget, 1974a, p. 66)
146. Structures which the Organism Imposes on Matter & Energy (Piaget, 1930, pp. 282-3)
147. Subject as Living Structure (Piaget, 1970b, p. 142)
148. Subject as the Structure of Structures (ibid., p. 142
149. Subject's Operational Structures (Piaget, 1977, p. 60)
150. Subject's Structures (Piaget & Inhelder, 1971, p. XIII)
151. Superior Structures (Piaget, 1969b, p. 304)

152. The Continuum as a Structured Whole (Beth & Piaget, 1966, p. 255)
153. The Fundamental Biological Structure (Piaget, 1971a, p. 158)
154. The Fundamental Structure (Piaget et al., 1977, p. 192-3)
155. The One Vast Explanatory Structure (Piaget, 1970b, p. 42)
156. Thought Structure (Piaget, 1973a, p. 159)
157. Topological Structure (Beth & Piaget, 1966, pp. 167-8)
158. Total Structure (Piaget, 1970c, pp. 22-3)
159. Underlying Overall Structure (Piaget, 1974a, p. 23
160. Underlying Structure (Piaget, 1976a, p. 352)
161. Universality of Operational Structures (Piaget & Inhelder, 1969, p. 95)
162. Valid Biological Structures (Piaget, 1971c, pp. 184-5)
163. Whole Structure (Piaget, 1973a, p. 113)

Different Terms for Lower-Level Structures

1. abstract structure (Piaget, 1971a, p. 344)
2. ahistorical structure (ibid., p. 248)
3. atomistic structure (Piaget, 1973c, p. 36
4. causal structure (Piaget et al., 1977, p. 167)
5. contingent structure (Piaget, 1973d, p. 51)
6. conventional structure (Piaget, 1970b, p. 79)
7. global structures (ibid., p. 98)
8. inferior structure (Piaget, 1971a, pp. 38-9)
9. innate structure (Piaget, 1977, p. 191)
10. irreversible structure (Piaget, 1973a, p. 133
11. linguistic structure (Piaget, 1973d, p. 28)
12. living structure (Piaget, 1971a, p. 333)
13. material structure (ibid., p. 33)
14. nerve structure (Piaget, 1973c, p. 47)
15. neurological structure (Inhelder & Piaget, p. 337)
16. objective structure (Piaget, 1972, p. 91)
17. organic structure (Piaget, 1973a, p. 172)
18. perceptual structure (Piaget & Inhelder, 1974, p. 271)
19. physical structure (Beth & Piaget, 1966, p. 203)
20. real structure (Piaget, 1970b, p. 38)
21. RNA structure (Piaget & Inhelder, 1973, p. XI)
22. spatio-temporal structure (Piaget, 1952b, p. 12)
23. structured perceptual space (Piaget & Inhelder, 1956, p. 42)

BIBLIOGRAPHY

Battro, A. M. *Piaget: Dictionary of terms.* New York: Pergamon, 1973.

Beardsley, M. C. (Ed.) *The European philosophers from Descartes to Nietzsche.* New York: Random House, 1960.

Berger, K. S. *The developing person through the life span.* (3rd ed.) New York: Worth, 1994.

Berko, J., & Brown, R. *Psycholinguistic research methods.* In P. H. Mussen (Ed.), *Handbook of research methods in child development.* New York: Wiley, 1960. pp. 517-557.

Beth, E. W. & Piaget, J. *Mathematical epistemology and psychology.* Dordrecht-Holland: Reidel, 1966.

Bringuier, J. *Conversations with Piaget.* Chicago: University of Chicago Press, 1980.

Copleston, F. *A history of philosophy* (Vols 1-8). Image Books Edition, 1965. Garden City, New York: Doubleday, 1963.

Edwards, P. (Ed.) *The encyclopedia of philosophy* (Vols 1-8). New York: Macmillian, 1967.

Elkind, D. & Flavell, J. H. (Eds.) *Studies in cognitive development.* New York: Oxford University Press, 1969.

Evans, R. I. *Jean Piaget: the man and his ideas.* New York: Dutton, 1973.

Flavell, J. H. *The developmental psychology of Jean Piaget.* New York: Van Nostrand, 1963.

Foster, H. (Ed.) *An outline of European intellectual history: Locke to Hegel.* Toronto: Forum House, 1969.

Furth, H. *Piaget and Knowledge.* Englewood Cliffs, New Jersey: Prentice-Hall, 1969.

Hegel, G. W. *The philosophy of the right and the philosophy of history* (Vol. 46). In R. M. Hutchins (Ed.), Great Books of the Western World. Chicago: Encyclopedia Britannica, 1952.

Inhelder, B. & Chipman, H. H. *Piaget and his school.* New York: Springer-Verlag, 1976.

Inhelder, B. & Piaget, J. *The growth of logical thinking from childhood to adolescence.* New York: Basic Books, 1958.

Inhelder, B. & Piaget, J. *The early growth of logic in the child.* London: Routledge & Kegan Paul, 1964.

Inhelder, B., Sinclair, H. & Bovet, M. *Learning and the development of cognition.* Cambridge, Massachusetts: Harvard University Press, 1974.

Jones, W. T. *Kant and the Nineteenth Century.* (2nd ed.) New York: Harcourt Brace Javanovich, 1975.

Karczmar, A. G. & Eccles, J. C. (Eds.) *Brain and human behavior.* New York: Springer-Verlag, 1972.

Kohnstamm, G. A. *Piaget"s analysis of class inclusion: right or wrong?* The Hague: Mouton, 1967.

McDermott, J. J. *The writings of William James.* New York: Random House, 1968.

Papert, S. "Jean Piaget, child psychologist", *Time*, Vol. 153, No. 12 (March 29, 1999), pp. 104-107.

Piaget, J. *The language and thought of the child.* (2nd ed.) New York: Meridian Books, 1955. First published in English by Harcourt, Brace, 1926.

Piaget, J. *Judgment and reasoning in the child.* New York: Harcourt, Brace, 1928

Piaget, J. *The child's conception of the world.* New York: Harcourt, Brace, 1929.

Piaget, J. *The child's conception of physical causality.* London: Routledge and Kegan Paul, 1930.

Piaget, J. *The moral judgment of the child.* London: Kegan Paul, 1932.

Piaget, J. *The psychology of intelligence.* New York: Harcourt, Brace, 1950.

Piaget, J. *The child's conception of number.* New York: Humanities, 1952. (a)

Piaget, J. *The origins of intelligence in children.* New York: Norton, 1963. First published in English by International Universities Press, 1952. (b)

Piaget, J. *Logic and psychology.* Manchester: Manchester University Press, 1953.

Piaget, J. *The construction of reality in the child.* New York: Basic Books, 1954.

Piaget, J. *The significance of John Amos Comenius at the present time.* Introduction to *John Amos Comenius on education,* Classics in Education series No. 33, New York: Teachers College Press, Columbia University, 1957.

Piaget, J. *Play, dreams and imitation in childhood.* London: Routledge and Kegan Paul, 1962.

Piaget, J. *Six psychological studies.* (D. Elkind Ed.) New York: Vintage Books, 1968. First published in English by Random House, 1967.

Piaget, J. *The child's conception of time.* London: Routledge & Kegan Paul, 1969. (a)

Piaget, J. *The mechanisms of perception.* London: Routledge & Kegan Paul, 1969. (b)

Piaget, J. *The child's conception of movement and speed.* London: Routledge & Kegan, 1970. (a)

Piaget, J. *Structuralism.* New York: Harper Torchbook, 1971. First published in English by Basic Books, 1970. (b)

Piaget, J. *Genetic epistemology.* New York: Columbia University Press, 1970. (c)

Piaget, J. *Science of education and the psychology of the child.* Viking, 1970. (d)

Piaget, J. *Biology and knowledge.* Chicago: University of Chicago Press, 1971. (a)

Piaget, J. *Psychology and epistemology.* New York: Viking, 1971. (b)

Piaget, J. *Insights and illusions of philosophy.* New York: World, 1971. (c)

Piaget, J. *The principles of genetic epistemology.* London: Routledge and Kegan Paul, 1972.

Piaget, J. *The child and reality.* New York: Viking, 1973. (a)

Piaget, J. *To understand is to invent.* New York: Grossman, 1973. (b)

Piaget, J. *Main trends in psychology.* New York: Harper Torchbooks, 1973. (c)

Piaget, J. *Main trends in inter-disciplinary research.* New York: Harper Torchbooks, 1973. (d)

Piaget, J. *The place of the sciences of man in the system of sciences.* New York: Harper & Row, 1974. (a)

Piaget, J. *Understanding causality.* New York: Norton, 1974. (b)

Piaget, J. *The grasp of consciousness.* Cambridge, Massachusetts: Harvard University Press, 1976. (a)

Piaget, J. *Piaget sampler: an introduction to Jean Piaget through his own words.* (S. F. Campbell Ed.) New York: John Wiley & Sons, 1976. (b)

Piaget, J. *The development of thought.* New York: Viking, 1977.

Piaget, J. *Success and understanding.* Cambridge, Massachusetts: Harvard University Press, 1978. (a)

Piaget, J. *Behavior and evolution.* New York: Random House, 1978. (b)

Piaget, J. *Experiments in contradiction.* Chicago: University of Chicago Press, 1980. (a)

Piaget, J. *Adaptation and intelligence.* Chicago: University of Chicago Press, 1980. (b)

Piaget, J. *Intelligence and affectivity.* (T. A. Brown & C. E. Kaegi Eds.) Palo Alto, California: Annual Reviews, 1981.

Piaget, J. *The equilibration of cognitive structures.* Chicago: University of Chicago Press, 1985.

Piaget, J. *Morphisms and categories: comparing and transforming.* (T. A. Brown Ed.) Hillsdale, New Jersey: Lawrence Erlbaum, 1992.

Piaget, J. *Sociological studies.* (L. Smith Ed.) London: Routledge, 1995.

Piaget, J. & Garcia, R. *Toward a logic of meanings.* (P. M. Davidson & J. Easley Eds.) Hillsdale, New Jersey: Lawrence Erlbaum, 1991.

Piaget, J. & Inhelder, B. *The child's conception of space.* London: Routledge and Kegan Paul, 1956.

Piaget, J. & Inhelder, B. *The psychology of the child.* New York: Basic Books, 1969.

Piaget, J. & Inhelder, B. *Mental imagery in the child.* London: Routledge & Kegan Paul, 1971.

Piaget, J. & Inhelder, B. *Memory and intelligence.* London: Basic Books and Routledge & Kegan Paul, 1973.

Piaget, J. & Inhelder, B. *The child's construction of quantities.* New York: Basic Books, 1974.

Piaget, J., & Inhelder, B. *The origin of the idea of chance in children.* New York: Norton, 1975.

Piaget, J., Inhelder, B., & Szeminska, A. *The child's conception of geometry.* New York: Basic Books, 1960.

Inhelder, B., Sinclair, H., Bovet, M. *Learning and the development of cognition.* Cambridge, Massachusetts: Harvard University Press, 1974.

Piaget, J. et al. *Epistemology and psychology of functions.* Dordrecht-Holland: Reidel, 1977.

Popper, K. R., *The open society and its enemies.* Vol. 2. (5th ed.) Princeton: Princeton University Press, 1966.

Sullivan, E. V. *Piaget and the school curriculum - a critical appraisal.* The Ontario Institute for Studies in Education. Bulletin No. 2, 1967.

Teachers' Handbook, *Science teaching and the development of reasoning.* University of California, Berkeley, 1977.

INDEX

This unusual index is necessary because of Piaget's unprecedented misuse of language.

will be dissolved in the current of
development 69

civilization
   two kinds 85-86
   METAPHYSICAL
   Civilization assimilates civilization 85-
      86
   Civilization is Normative and
      assimilative 85-86
   Civilization is the Subject composed of
      monads 85
   PHYSICAL
   underlying civilizations there is
      Civilization 85

class, classes
   METAPHYSICAL 233
   Class and number have a common
      Mechanism (producer of operations
      252
   Classes of monads improve as classes
      of matter are assimilated 219
   each dialectic synthesis produces a
      more developed 93, 212
   each equilibration produces a more
      developed 213
   each operation produces a more
      developed 93-94, 212
   each relation produces a more
      developed 93-94, 212, 252
   each Self-regulation produces a more
      developed 213
   new Classes must be integrated into the
      Body of Monads 212
   Science produces a progressive series of
      236-237
   Space (personal) is able to measure for
      the proper engagement of 179
   PHYSICAL 18, 213

cognition 1, 3
   two kinds 79
   METAPHYSICAL
   based on vicarious behavior of the
      Epistemological Subject 83

cognitive development is the
   development of the Body of Monads
   163
cognitive development of Form 242
cognitive development of the Absolute
   Subject 242
cognitive regulation is internal to
   Cognitive Structure 163
infants of two years or less told Piaget
   the secrets of cognitive development
   30
Knowing Self cognizes (assimilates)
   known self 129-130
the Cognitive Field is the Logico-
   Mathematical Structure 211
PHYSICAL
actions (cognitive) of human objects 77
Cognitive Structure(s) are Self-
   developing 235
a System of Connections 161
Body of Monads 82-83
can only be constructed by operations
   (Self-constructed) 82
Cognitive Nucleus 58
cognitive regulation is internal to 163
determines what the individual subject
   can and must do 127, 161-162
developed by Epistemic Subject (Self-
   development) 83, 137
imposes Forms on individual subject
   127, 161-162
is a "He" 127, 161
is alive 83
is derived from the General Mechanism
   228-229 *(contradiction 229)*
is the Epistemic Subject 83
is the Subject 227
of Epistemic Subject are eternal 229
only uses the subject as an object to
   assimilate 227
Self-regulations of the Epistemic
   Subject produce (Self-produce) 163
the "lived" have only a minor role in the
   development of 83, 162-163, 227
   (contradictions 58, 149, 162)

the Biological Organization opposes
empirical entities (people) 221
the Mind feels no need for empirical
verification 240
there is no internal construction in 69
the System of Operations subordinates
empirical reality 244

encounters (see coupling)

endogenous 70
activity imposes on the physical by
progressive equilibrations 90
activity is engendered by coordinations
of the Individual (not the individual)
149
activity is engendered by the
Assimilatory Framework 149
construction is not anchored in the
genome 232
developed by internal Logico-
Mathematical activity 149
developed by regulations 149, 232
development depends entirely on
operations 8, 19-20, 149, 215, 232
immanent Absolute Subject
endogenously develops Himself 211
Knowledge (synonym of Absolute) is
based on equilibrations 19-20, 232
Knowledge is based on reflexive
abstractions 19-20
Knowledge is based on Self-regulations
19-20
Knowledge is not based on learning 232
Logic (synonym of Absolute) is an
endogenous construction 189
number construction is 42, 253-254
number construction is not a human
activity 253-254
only Schemata of monads enjoy this
kind of Knowledge 5
Piaget's new form of Knowledge is
229-230
processes produce Normative
Knowledge 149
science (exogenous) is incorporated
within the Overall System
(endogenous) 20

stages are regulated by Endogenous
Regulating Mechanisms 8, 211
Structures are Normative and belong to
the Subject 214-215
Structures can only develop by Self-
regulation 215

endomorph 26, 58-59
a part that can know everything the
Whole knows 54
the immanent Body of Monads 55

environment
METAPHYSICAL
Homogeneous Environment (of
monads) 31, 204-205
Homogeneous Environment is the
Absolute Subject 204-205
Homogeneous Environment is the
Spatial Field 204-205
operational displacements take place in
the Homogeneous 204-205
Organized Environment is transforming
homo faber into Homo Sapiens 170
source of all operations is the
Homogeneous 170
PHYSICAL 77, 205
basis of all physical, exogenetic and
socially acquired knowledge 152
basis of all thought processes based on
the brain 152
domain that must be eliminated 37
genetic inheritance is based on the
environment of genes 152
homo faber is part of 170
if knowledge is environmentally
derived it is not true Knowledge 49
matter is exercised on the Organism
151-152
only know about because Structures
extend into whole universe 65

Epistemological Domain
contrasted with physical-organic
domain 140
is off-limits to people 140
occupied by Biology 33

specific heredity 73-75
specific heredity is studied by natural
    science 73

Hinduism (see philosophy and theology)

history
    two kinds 228
    METAPHYSICAL
    all Human Knowledge (Eidetic or
        endogenous) is integrated into a
        Single Organism 223
    historico-critical (synonym of
        psychogenetic) 185
    of Science is based on equilibrations or
        operations 242
    of Science is historical development of
        of the Absolute Subject 242
    of Science is psychogenesis of the
        Absolute Subject 242
    of Underlying Dynamism (invisible
        activity of monads) 228
    Piaget's father was a historian but he
        did not believe in History 228
    PHYSICAL
    of visible partially contingent events
        228

human being(s)
    METAPHYSICAL
    concerned only with development of a
        non-human Entity 58
    Homo Sapiens 217, 241
    Homo Sapiens must be liberated from
        homo faber 169
    Human action progresses toward
        equilibrium 217
    Human Knowledge (Eidetic) is
        integrated into a Single Organism 92,
        223
    Human Spirit goes through a number of
        stages 194
    Human Subjects in General 78
    "I" bound up with universe is the source
        of Operational Structures 137
    Individual who is a Population (of
        monads) in itself 194

Knowing Subject directs operations at
    those He indwells 130
person (ego) contrasted with the Ego or
    Epistemic Subject 139-140
Person is the Ego not the ego (person)
    83
Person must assimilate the ego (person)
    211
Piagetians ignore superhuman
    statements 32
the Intimate Mechanism who directs
    thought in every human being 237
the Natural Inclination of the Human
    Mind is reflection 227-228
the true Individual is the Medium (of
    Monads) 16
PHYSICAL
Absolute's posture toward humans
    characterized as gross duplicity 127
abstractions from objects (by people)
    are non-necessitous 9, 133, 139, 170,
    195
action-derived Knowledge is impossible
    for 49
are alive by proxy 83, 96, 198
are constructed by scientific objects
    (monads) 68
are descended from the Living Being
    132
are descended from the Logico-
    Mathematical Construction
    (Absolute) 132
are descended from the monads 96
are detestable 164
are hateful 164
are not autonomous 133, 194
are not aware of the organized Spatial
    Surround 172
are not capable of autoregulation 142,
    144
as objects 9, 37, 47, 194
assimilation of spatio-temporal powers
    (people) is certain 164
as things 9, 37, 164, 194
cannot acquire Eidetic Knowledge 69
cannot acquire genuine Knowledge 38,
    44, 195

the Psychological Subject is
    investigating the human subject 77,
    177
the Subject-Psychologist is not a human
    being 67
"They" (monads) decenter scientists
    from their own research 181-182
"They" decenter the physical selves of
    scientists 181-182
"They" refers to immanent Entity in
    scientists 181-182
"They" refers to "Spatial Metrics" or
    the monads inside scientists 181-182
will "pass over" into the Subject 135

Hume, David 146

"I"

METAPHYSICAL
air becomes the "I" within the child
    116-117
composed of monads 58
consists of Operational Structures 137
every cause is based on the "I" or Ego
    65
is a Medium 116-117
is bound up with whole universe 137,
    173
is immanent in the "lived me" 137
reference to Body of Monads 11-12
source of Operational Structures (by
    Self-development) 149
source of operations 18, 58
source of praxic Intelligence 18
the immanent Subject 18
the "I" versus the "lived me" 18, 58
what remains after "lived me" is
    precipitated out 58, 149-150
wishes to be liberated from ego 11, 169-
    170
PHYSICAL
Collective Cause wishes to be liberated
    from this lower-level "I" 169-170
"I" that must be decentered 170
very tricky lower-level "I" 170

idea
METAPHYSICAL 123
developed by operations 147-148
developed by regulations 147-148
eternal 106
Logical Mathematical Body elaborates
    (Self-development) 138, 178
synonym for Absolute Subject 106
the implicatory function of the Mind
    develops the Idea 147-148
PHYSICAL 18, 160, 199, 209, 219

ideal
METAPHYSICAL
Ideal movements do not take time 80
Ideal Society (of monads) 85
Ideal Totality 186-187
synonym for Absolute Subject 106
PHYSICAL
German Idealism 40, 229
idealistic interpretation of epistemology
    140-141
ideal of a suprascientific Knowledge 40
Transcendental Subject of idealism 143

immanent Space
assimilates the child 69-70
distorts the child 69-70
measures in order to assimilate the child
    35-36

immanent Subject 4, 5-6, 14, 41-42, 59, 73,
    77-78, 143, 202-203
Absolute endogenously develops
    Himself 211
Absolute exists inside things 129-130
Absolute Mind 45
Absolute Subject 45, 76, 197
accounts for memory 207-209
Action (Subject) regulates physiology
    108
alone is capable of Logico-
    Mathematical Knowledge 79
alone is capable of reflective
    abstractions 78
baby of 4 months or less assumes that
    He could create the world 202

there is a passage from exogenous to
endogenous 232-233 *(contradictions)*
54-55, 120-121)
ultimately depends upon the Epistemic
Subject 138
university sponsored knowledge is only
matter 152
what we acquire at all levels of the
educational process 160-161

Kohnstamm, Geldolph
Criticizes "inclusion" at physical level
48

Lake Annecy 2, 108, 239

language
two kinds 188
METAPHYSICAL
of operations 188-189
PHYSICAL 192
corruption of 220-221
cryptic 1
operations do not arise out of 188
Piaget claims that science sees reality as
phenomena plus a language 24

Lattice 10-11, 35, 154-156
Action (synonym) 156
Combinatory System 176
Field of Monads 35
Flavell claimed that He (Lattice) is
nonpsychological 35, 174
Fundamental Psychological Reality 35,
178
Horizontal and Vertical References 10-
11, 35, 155
immanent existence and work of
monads is called "Spatial Metrics"
181-182
Living Being with eight Psychological
characteristics 175
Logico-Mathematical Structure 178
measures child for purpose of
assimilation 10-11, 35-36
Operationally Organized Psychological
Space 35
Set of All Sub-Sets 178

Space endows the Lattice to all objects
and people 181
source of operations 176
Structure 154-155
the Lattice-Group develops operational
Schemata (Self-development) 138
true Psychological Being 11

law(s)
METAPHYSICAL
Alpine embryology obeys the same
laws of development as people 209
both causality and operations adhere to
laws of Reality 245
development of Knowledge is based on
process law (law of assimilation) 185
Field of Force is governed by
(assimilatory) laws of equilibrium
154-155
immanent Forms are transformed
according to Structural laws 179-180
individuals must submit to
(assimilatory) laws of logic 127, 132
Logico-Mathematical Construction
imposes its (assimilatory) laws on
every subject 132
Mathematical operators (monads) make
own laws independent of people 243
must go behind physical law to explain
movement (based on monads) 174
number is engendered by law of
formation 41, 252
of Biology provide a teleonomy 36
of Logic are based on the System of
Operations 127, 132
of Logic are Normative 132
of Logic are the functions of the
Organization 132
of Logic are the general coordinations
of actions 132
of the Structure are not subject to error
156
of the Whole Operational Field 154-155
operational behavior is based on own
laws of equilibrium 166
the Field of Force is governed by the
laws of equilibrium 154-155

a metaphysical Observer is inside of all 107

assimilation of 60

assimilation of the object is a concomitant of Subject's development 219

cannot be the source of Intelligence 78

child is an egocentric 20-21, 203

child of 8 to 12 months sees people as practical 202

complete Knowledge of an object involves its elimination 230

development is based on the dialectic of Subject and 216

Homogeneous Medium is common to all 100

human 9, 19, 38, 47, 58, 194-195

human objects are expendable 128

human objects are hateful 63

human objects are manipulated by the Medium (of monads) 16

human objects are not-selves 37-38, 195

(human) objects can only make non-necessitus statements 133, 139, 170, 190

human objects must be assimilated 16, 63

human objects resist assimilation 20-21

Knowledge is assimilation of an object into a Schema 230

living acting subject 15

no objects are in the experience of the young baby 56, 201-202

objective structures 143-144

"objectivity" means assimilation of the 74-75

object-person is of no importance 37-38

people are the primary objects to be assimilated 203

physical things (people) are objects not Subjects 132

relations are not possible between people and 168-169

relations are only possible between the Subject and 168-169

"restructuration" of objects is the centrifugal function of operations 216

"Scientific Objects" refers to Absolute's composition (of monads) 203-204

shared common roots with the Subject 131

source of exogenous knowledge 19-20

subjects are 179-180

the object to be assimilated by the Formal Structure is the ego 211

the object will "pass over" into the Absolute Subject 131, 135

time is created when monads move celestial 100

universe as a whole is the 204

why practical objects were created 68

will become a part of the Absolute 131, 209

will be dissolved in the current of development 39, 69

will be transformed into the Subject 131, 237, 246-247

ontogenetic development
two kinds 82
METAPHYSICAL 45
controlled by a series of regulations 82-83
Epigenotype (immanent Absolute) controls the order of stages 82-83
is not a physical process 82
is Self-development 82-83
Ontogeny recapitulates Phylogeny 45
PHYSICAL
ontogenetic development of humans is physical 82

operation(s), (assimilative)
METAPHYSICAL 3, 9, 15-16, 22-23, 37-38, 93, 146-148, 185, 224, 254-255
accounts for stages 38, 195-196
action (synonym) 18
actions or operations are always informed by teleonomies 17, 68
a dialectic synthesis 93
all constructions based on operations are predetermined 212-213
all possible operations occur within the Single Body of Monads 254

forced willy nilly to submit to laws of
logic 132
has a minor role in constructing
Cognitive Structures 83, 162, 227
(contradictions 18, 58, 149-150)
has no role in constructing Cognitive
Structures 18, 58, 149-150
(contradictions 83, 162, 227)
individual 18, 58
intelligent acts are based on a
Mechanism of which he is
unconscious 149-150 *(contradictions
120-122, 165-166, 172-173, 198,
204-205)*
is detestable and faces danger 63
limited 189
lived subjects are disliked by Piaget 63,
83, 195, 227
living and acting 135
must be decentered 21
must obey the Subject 34
must submit to Logico-Mathematical
Structures 127, 161-162
not aware of Framework added by the
Subject 162 *(contradictions 120-122,
165-166, 172-173, 204-205)*
not the origin of any Structure of
General Knowledge 141, 228-229
operations are not possible for him 69
part of physical universe 20-21
part of spatio-temporal world 57
Piaget despises 136
produces only exogenous knowledge 79
studied to follow formative process of
Subject in subjects 213
subject number one 77-78
subject "passes over" into the Subject
131, 139
Subject wishes to be rid of the subject
11-12
the individual subject is external to the
Psychological Subject 58
the "me" which is precipitated out
leaving only the "I" 18, 58, 149-150
the stage where the immanent Subject
performs His operations 215
the System of Connections imposes
Himself on 161-162

vulnerable to assimilation as he is well
on the way to being transformed 63

substance, substantial
METAPHYSICAL
Absolute Subject 119
air becomes an All-Pervading
Substance (monads) 29, 113-114,
198
a Substantial Reality (monads) projects
from the eye to the object 110-111
composed of an invariable permanent
quanta of monads 211
corpuscles (monads) 54, 224-225
Ego composed of monads 27
Field of Monads 122
force underlying all phenomena 5
Form 122
God 122
Integrated Structure consists of 211
of General Quantum is invariable 120
of General Quantum is the Formal
Regulator 120
on which operations are based 54
outside and inside atomic forces are 116
powder metaphysics 120, 224-225
Powerful Object 116
Psychological Substance assimilates
educational influences 158
Psychological Substance is peculiar to
Thought of child 158
Spiritual Entity 119
synthetic activity of Substance is
primitive atomism 122
young child sees people as practical
objects not Substantial Beings 202
PHYSICAL 201

Sullivan, Edmund
equilibration model precludes higher
stages through education 48
thought structures cannot be facilitated
by teaching 48

Sunier, A. 53, 68

superhuman, supernatural
action 18